MW01620939

GRANT WOOD'S
SECRETS

FROM GRANT WOOD • NO. FIVE TURNER ALLEY • CEDAR RAPIDS • IOWA

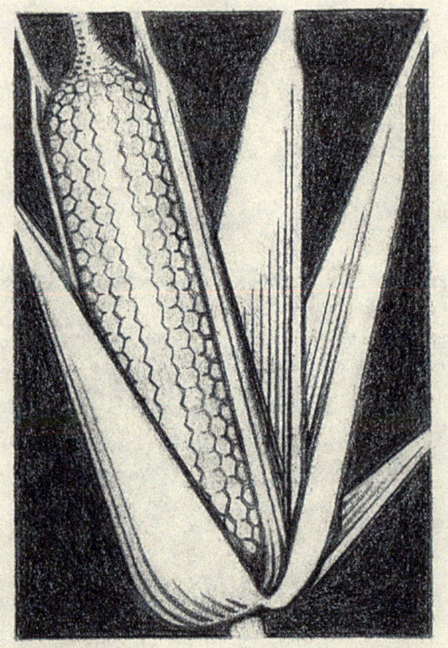

RETURN FROM BOHEMIA

GRANT WOOD'S **SECRETS**

Sue Taylor

UNIVERSITY OF DELAWARE PRESS · NEWARK, DELAWARE

DISTRIBUTED BY THE UNIVERSITY OF VIRGINIA PRESS

University of Delaware Press

Publication of this book has been aided by grants from

The American Psychoanalytic Foundation
through the American Psychoanalytic Association

Society for the Preservation of American Modernists

The Wyeth Foundation for American Art Publication Fund of CAA

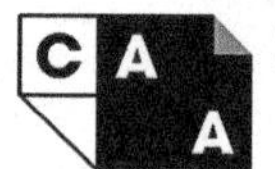

Printed in the United States of America on acid-free paper

First published 2020

ISBN 978-1-64453-165-5 (casebound)
ISBN 978-1-64453-167-9 (e-book)

1 2 3 4 5 6 7 8 9 0

Library of Congress Cataloging-in-Publication Data
is available for this title.

Book design by Robert L. Wiser, Silver Spring, Maryland

Frontispiece. Grant Wood, *Corn*, 1935–36.

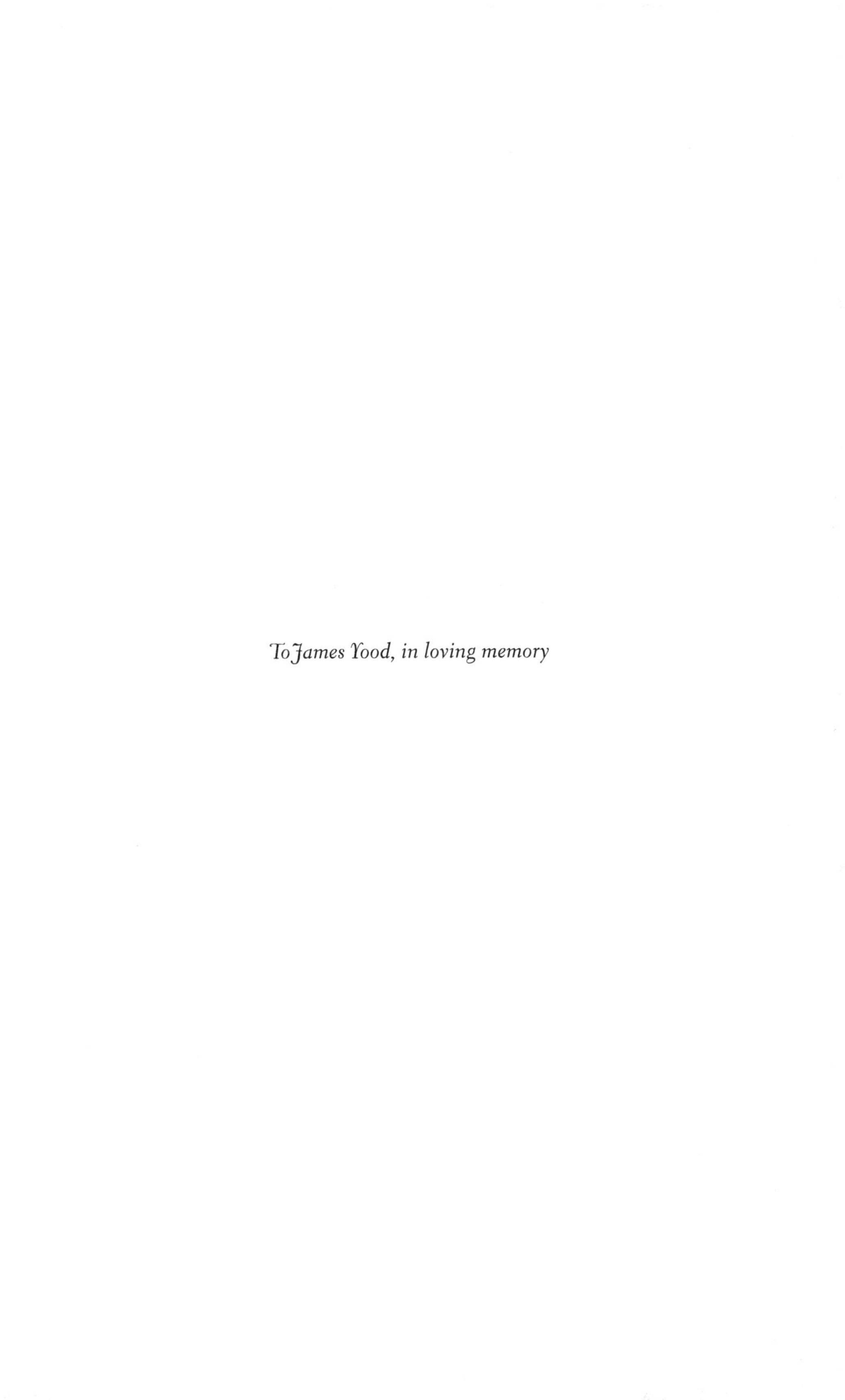

To James Yood, in loving memory

❖ CONTENTS ❖

❖ LIST OF ILLUSTRATIONS ❖

❖ ACKNOWLEDGMENTS ❖

CERTAIN INKLINGS about Grant Wood's *American Gothic* (1930) first came to me years ago, when as a graduate student I had the opportunity to see the painting alongside the artist's other works in a retrospective organized by Wanda Corn, and to hear her speak at the Art Institute of Chicago. For all of us who puzzle over Wood's art, Corn's research remains foundational. My now dog-eared copy of her catalogue, *Grant Wood: The Regionalist Vision* (1983), still bristles with sticky notes and is held together with tape along its spine. I carried it with me to New York where, on my first sabbatical from teaching at Portland State University, I worked out my intuitions about *American Gothic* in an essay for *American Art*—and discovered there was much more to say.

With an American Scholarship at the Georgia O'Keeffe Museum Research Center in Santa Fe in 2005, I began research for this book, welcomed there by Barbara Buhler Lynes, Heather Hole, and Eumie Imm-Stroukoff. That year, too, a grant from the American Psychoanalytic Association meant that I could importune a psychoanalyst consultant, Gerald Fogel, to assess my ideas about Wood's inner life and later to read and comment on individual chapters. Those conversations with Jerry were for me among the most intellectually exhilarating aspects of this project. So too were those with other friends and colleagues who have taken an interest in this work over the years—Jeffrey Abt, Catherine Bock-Weiss, Suzaan Boettger, Norma Broude, Mary Mathews Gedo and the late John Gedo, Judith and Jules Kirshner, Donald Kuspit, John Neff, Sherwin Simmons, and Jeff Taylor and Yunxia Ma. Janice Coco, so well versed in art history, psychology, and psychoanalysis, reviewed the manuscript with equal measures of criticism and kindness, and Richard Vine added editorial refinements as I brought the work to its conclusion.

On repeated visits to Iowa, I discovered Wood's own terrain and a treasure trove of research materials and experts. I became indebted to Joan Liffring-Zug Bourret, Penfield Press, Iowa City; John Beldon Scott and his successor, Mara Pilcher, at the Grant Wood Art Colony, University of Iowa, and James P. Hayes, the Colony's magnanimous leading light; inspired Wood collector and scholar Randy Lengeling, Dubuque; Lynette Pohlman,

University Museums, Iowa State University, Ames; and Kristy Raine, Mt. Mercy College, Cedar Rapids. For providing me access to documents, works of art, or provenance information, in Iowa and elsewhere, I thank Mary Bennett, State Historical Society of Iowa, Iowa City; Virginia Cooper, Muscatine Art Center, Iowa; Kristina Dvorak, Cedar Rapids Community School District; John Faubion, Lawrence Tenney Stevens Trust; James L. Jackson, Jackson's International Auctioneers and Appraisers, Cedar Falls, Iowa; Dennis Michael Jon, Minneapolis Institute of Art; Danielle M. Knapp, Jordan Schnitzer Museum of Art, University of Oregon, Eugene; James Maroney, James Maroney, Inc., Leicester, Vermont; Virginia Mecklenburg, Joann Moser, and the late Cynthia Mills at the Smithsonian Institution, Washington, D.C.; Donald Myers, Hillstrom Museum of Art, Gustavus Adolphus College, St. Peter, Minnesota; Mark Pascale, the Art Institute of Chicago; Stacy Peterson, Dubuque Museum of Art; Shirley Reece-Hughes, Amon Carter Museum of American Art, Fort Worth, Texas; Nancy Richard, Herbert Hoover National Historic Site, West Branch, Iowa; Maria Saffiotti-Dale and Andrea Selbig, Chazen Museum of Art, University of Wisconsin-Madison; Linda Speight, Indianapolis Museum of Art; Mary Suzor, Cleveland Museum of Art; Sean Ulmer and Jacqueline Falco-Smith at the Cedar Rapids Museum of Art; Teri Van Dorston, Veterans Memorial, Cedar Rapids; Rebecca Vernon, Anamosa Library and Learning Center, Anamosa, Iowa; and Andrew Wallace, Figge Art Museum, Davenport, Iowa. Andrew's creation of his museum's Grant Wood Digital Collection, hosted by the University of Iowa Digital Collection, is a boon to all present and future Wood scholars. I am grateful to William R. Crawford, Grand Lodge of Iowa, Cedar Rapids, who guided me through the Lodge's collection, showing me Wood's *First Three Degrees of Free Masonry* (1921–22). In keeping with requests from all those individuals and institutions that permitted me to reproduce works from their collections, I have included the pertinent dates, dimensions, donor information, and photo credits in the list of illustrations in this volume.

Individuals with personal or family connections to Wood shared their memories of him or documents or works of art they inherited and have long treasured. It was an honor to interview the late Willis Guthrie, a one-time student of Wood's at the University of Iowa, at his home in Waukesha, Wisconsin. In Madison, where Nancy Rose Marshall showed me the kindest hospitality, Mary and John Varda, the late Martha Nesbit Frankwicz, and Nancy Frankwicz Turner offered information about Wood's friendship with the Wellwood Nesbit family and the works of art the family had acquired directly from the artist. Wendy Guida of Monkey Island, Oklahoma, discovered and permitted me to publish the photograph of her late grandmother's friend Bette Sandbourne, model for the country woman in Wood's *Appraisal* (1931). Phyllis Rinard received me at her then home in Falls Church, Virginia, and granted me permission to publish the manuscript for "Return from Bohemia" in which her late husband had had a hand; I am also grateful to Judith Rinard for clarifying the nature of her father's role in that endeavor. Sally Maxon Harris of Walla Walla, Washington, who had lived as a child in Wood's Iowa City home while he was married to her grandmother, Sara Sherman, recalled him lovingly to me in our phone conversations. Sherman's papers were rescued and carefully preserved by Donna Clausen of Marysville, Washington. Daughter of the late Ed Bartholomew, a kind landlord to Sherman in her final years, Donna shared those precious papers with me, as well as her teenage recollections of Sherman in retirement on Orcas Island.

For their contributions to Grant Wood scholarship and their collegiality, I am most indebted to Henry Adams, Lea Rosson DeLong, Jane Milosch, and Alan Wallach. All of them make appearances in this book as I build on their respective discoveries and scholarly insights. To Jane, I also owe the opportunity of a productive short-term visitor's appointment at the Smithsonian American Art Museum in Washington, D.C. in 2006; I can never thank her enough for all she has done for Wood studies and for me personally. Paul Juhl's detailed archival research is a tremendous gift to the field, and the times we spent together on Wood's trail in Cedar Rapids and Iowa City are etched as much in my heart as in my mind. I found another kindred spirit in R. Tripp Evans. In his company, I visited the Eldon house for the first time and paid my respects at the artist's grave in Riverside Cemetery in Anamosa. In the wake of his indispensable Wood biography, repeatedly cited in *Grant Wood's Secrets*, Tripp has become an unstintingly generous intellectual support and cherished friend.

At the University of Delaware Press, Director Julia Oestreich saw something valuable in my proposal for this book and then carefully stewarded the work toward publication. Robert Wiser merits grateful acknowledgment for its exquisite design. In the last stages of production, publication grants from the American Psychoanalytic Foundation through the American Psychoanalytic Association, the Society for the Preservation of American Modernists, and the Wyeth Foundation for American Art helped to make what had at times seemed a pipe dream into a tangible reality.

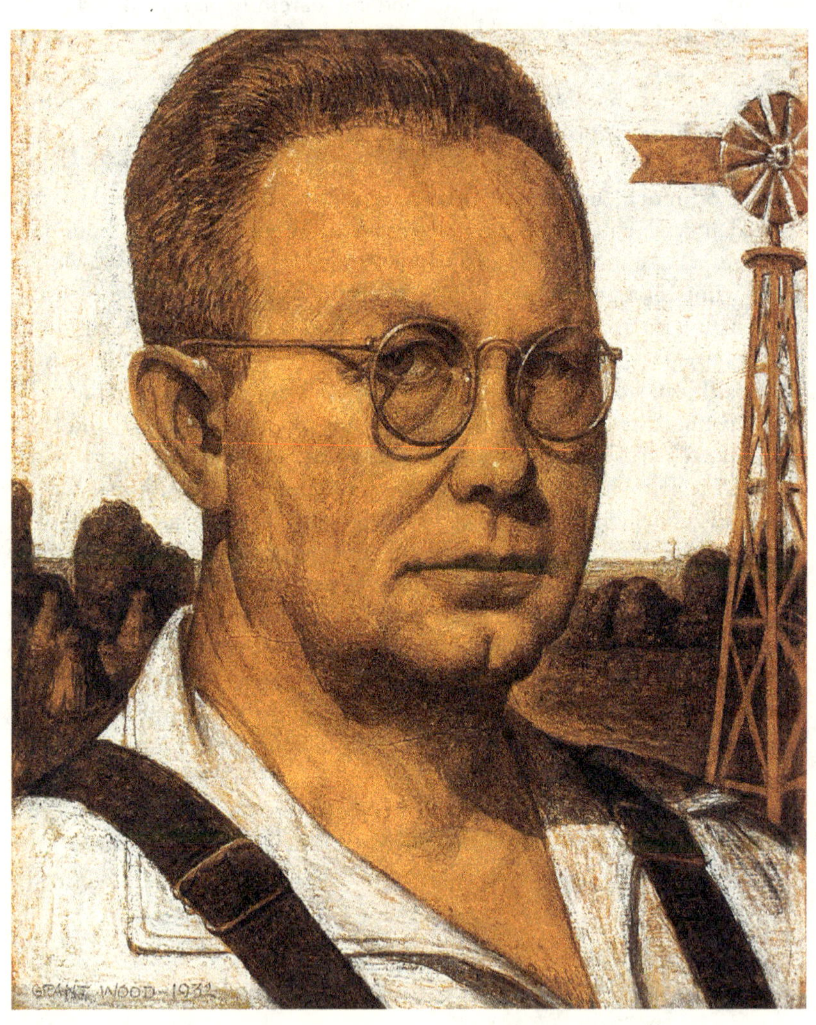

Grant Wood, *Study for Self-Portrait*, 1932.

Introduction

"PSYCHOLOGISTS TELL US that we're conditioned in the first twelve years of our lives and that everything we experience later is tied up with those first twelve years."[1] So stated Grant Wood to a Los Angeles reporter in 1940, during one of his many national lecture tours promoting his Regionalist art. Convinced of the childhood sources of his own creativity and character, he remained in art and life preoccupied with his origins. He was fascinated with his past as with his nation's past, distorting and idealizing both as golden eras of happy innocence. Born in humble circumstances on a farm in Anamosa, Iowa, in 1891, Wood forged an unlikely artistic career, punctuated by the remarkable impact of his 1930 masterpiece, *American Gothic* (Fig. 1.2). From there he went on to a prestigious university appointment and just over a decade of fame before his death in an Iowa City hospital in 1942. "Sudden success also brought almost instant sadness/darkness to Grant," his writer friend Paul Engle remembered. "That is another story. He was a gifted, fine, complicated person. As with Robert Frost, his outward, cheerful, plain-person image concealed a troubled life."[2] The engrossing other story that Engle quickly passed over, and the sometimes anxious emotional world obscured by the artist's self-created myth, provides the major rationale for this book.

Wood's 1942 memorial exhibition at the Art Institute of Chicago brought mixed reviews. Despite the unflagging renown of *American Gothic*, his art sank into critical neglect for several decades thereafter. His sister, Nan Wood Graham (1899–1990), strongly objected to biographies by Darrell Garwood (1944) and Hazel Brown (1972) and hoped to no avail that the artist's erstwhile secretary, Park Rinard, would produce the corrective account of Wood's life and greatness.[3] In 1971, she agreed, with some hesitation, to cooperate with art historian James Dennis on *Grant Wood: A Study in American Art and Culture* (1975).[4] With an eye to controlling the artist's legacy, Graham was, impossibly, both a primary source and formidable impediment to Wood studies.[5] Wanda Corn's historic exhibition and catalogue *Grant Wood: The Regionalist Vision* (1983) had thus to be politic as well as scholarly.[6] In reintroducing Wood to a national audience—the exhibition traveled from New York to Chicago, Minneapolis, and San Francisco—her project provided a stimulus for subsequent research.

In Iowa, museums have proved excellent stewards of Wood's art and archives.[7] Graham transferred a number of her brother's possessions along with her lovingly assembled scrapbooks to the Davenport Municipal Art Gallery, now the Figge Art Museum, in 1984. She did not live to see her personal reminiscences published in *My Brother, Grant Wood* (1993) by John Zug and Julie Jensen McDonald, with the cooperation of the State Historical Society and Joan Liffring-Zug Bourret, editor of the earlier compilation *This Is Grant Wood Country* (1977).[8] The passionate devotion to Wood in his home state has ensured the preservation in such volumes of all manner of colorful anecdotes and commentary, a goldmine for scholars. At the same time, concern that his reputation not be "tarnished" perpetuated the denial of his homosexuality—and thus of his valiant struggles—among many of his most ardent admirers. This is the persistent and pervasive "heterosexual will to not-know" discussed by Christopher Hommerding (2015) in his essay on reactions to Wood and his Stone City Art Colony in the early 1930s.[9] Disavowal of this aspect of the artist's humanity and experience began with his sister, diminishing after her death and in response to broadly liberating societal change.

Thanks to the bold scholarly insights of Alan Wallach (1990), Henry Adams (2000), and John Seery (2002), art historians began to recognize how Wood's sexual orientation positioned him as an outsider in his own community, giving his art its caustic edge.[10] Adding to an increasingly complex understanding of his character, Lea Rosson DeLong (2004, 2006) presented Wood convincingly as no rube but as a literary and artistic intellectual, as evinced by his illustrations for Sinclair Lewis's novel *Main Street* and by the Works Progress Administration murals he supervised at Iowa State University in Ames.[11] From Jane Milosch, curator of *Grant Wood's Studio: Birthplace of American Gothic* (2005), we learned the impressive range of his talents as an interior designer and the breadth of his decorative work in wood, wrought iron, stucco, and glass.[12] Detailed documentary research by Joni Kinsey (2005) and Paul Juhl (2011, 2012) shed light on Wood's vexed tenure at the University of Iowa and his late and abandoned projects, respectively.[13] This recent enrichment of Wood studies includes research by Italian scholar Luciano Cheles (2012) that deepens our understanding of the artist's sensitivity to past European masterpieces, especially by Piero della Francesca, and Travis Nygard's thoroughly original *Seeds of Agribusiness* (2009), which relates many of Wood's images to socioeconomic issues of labor, cash crops, farm equipment, corn breeding, and flour milling in the late nineteenth and early twentieth centuries.[14]

None of this literature takes up Wood's emotional world. The exception is R. Tripp Evans's *Grant Wood: A Life* (2010).[15] Describing widespread efforts to impress notions of a rugged American masculinity on boys of Wood's generation, Evans understands the child in conflict at a young age as he aligned within his family with his mother and sister rather than with his stern father and two brothers. Evans is the first scholar to discuss the artist's homosexuality candidly and in depth, identifying in a series of likely one-sided crushes the artist developed on younger men a certain dark-haired, slender Wood "type," from Amana artist Carl Flick, whom Wood befriended in the late 1920s, to his studio assistants Arnold Pyle and Edgar Britton, and his secretary Park Rinard. From this newly empathic perspective, the biographer penetrates the ruses that Wood of necessity devised to conceal the nature of his desire. Evans also explores the lifelong impact on Wood of a major life tragedy: the death of his father when Grant was only ten years old. A haunting oedipal guilt remained with Wood ever after; from his irrational, unconscious but no less powerfully influential point of view, his paternal rival, who disapproved strongly of art, had been sacrificed not just for his mother but for the pursuit of a creative life. Understanding this overarching component of the artist's psychic experience enables Evans to develop unexpected and compelling interpretations of paintings including *American Gothic*, *Dinner for Threshers* (1934, Fig. 3.33), and *Parson Weems' Fable* (1939, Fig. 3.25).

This book shares Evans's fundamental premises while investigating four particular themes: family relations, sexual orientation and desire, irony and deception, and the outer world as a projection of the artist's inner life. Chapter 1 examines how Wood's ambivalence toward his parents—his intense love as well as, from a Freudian perspective, his unconscious jealousy, guilt, and fear—informs several of his most famous paintings, starting with *American Gothic*, a disguised parental portrait. Indeed, the notoriety of this painting and its endless parodies may ensue at least in part from viewers' subliminal recollection of their own conflicted filial feelings, a recognition that is then defended against by a humorous response. Significantly, in the emblematic cover image Wood conceived for "Return from Bohemia" (1935, Fig. 1.15), the autobiography he failed to finish, the country folk encircling the self-portrayed Regionalist artist correspond precisely to members of his immediate family. Though his father was long dead by this time and his brothers estranged, Wood here imagines them as worshipful, along with his mother and sister, toward his triumphant artist self. Their eyes are reverently lowered. Or, perhaps, they are blind—to what they and others refused to acknowledge about him, his homosexuality.

That subject comes to the fore in Chapter 2 relative to a recurring theme in his oeuvre, the male nude. Wood's tender artistic treatment of the male body contrasts markedly with his diffident or satirical approach to rendering the bodies of women. His homoeroticism culminates in the sensitive frontal nude in the lithograph *Sultry Night* (Fig. 2.24), published by Associated American Artists and famously banned as obscene from the U.S. Mail in

1939. With this image, Wood had seriously misjudged his audience; his reaction to mutilate the print's painted counterpart seems to have been at once a defensive move and a form of masochistic self-punishment. A landscape portion of the painting survives, showing a water trough and tree. Missing its main motif, the fragment bears tragic witness to the historical erasure of homosexual experience and desire.

Chapter 3 details the hostile conditions that forced upon Wood an urgent need to pass for straight. His duplicitous schemes were inventive survival tactics, bolstering an image of conventional masculinity in a homophobic environment. Resilient in the face of such adversity, Wood relied handily on his ingenious artifice, which emerges in some of his projects as a kind of homosexual camp, exhibiting enmity toward an unsuspecting audience and gleeful amusement at their expense. His imposture functioned on levels both conscious and unconscious, exemplified in the signature overalls he wore, as he masqueraded as the farmer he never actually became. The overalls were a calculated sign of his Regionalism to be sure, a bid for approval from his community, while also a means of dressing up like the farmer-father he had triumphed over and displaced in his mother's affections. His ironic relationship to truth culminates in this chapter with a discussion of *Parson Weems' Fable*, which rehearses the threat of paternal punishment while satirizing the guilty little George Washington's inability to tell a lie.

The final chapter explores Wood's ecstatic depictions of Iowa farmland. Unlike pictures of environmentally devastated terrain that were common during the Depression, Wood's anachronistic visions of a Midwestern Eden belong to a pastoral tradition and to his nostalgia for the idyllic farm-world of his boyhood. These Housmanesque landscapes echo corporeal yearnings and blissful reminiscences of the maternal body. In his celebrations of an agrarian nature, Wood also searches for solace in the face of loss: by the mid-1930s, three family members had predeceased him. Finally able to mourn in a way that had been impossible for him as a child in shock and denial over his father's death, he created elegiac images of his native soil that hold out the possibility of peace and forgiveness.

The abiding love Wood felt for Iowa is similarly conveyed in the engaging story he offers in "Return from Bohemia," the full text of which appears as an appendix in this book. Despite disagreements about the respective roles he and Rinard played in writing this memoir of life on the Anamosa farm, the work is here accepted as Wood's own, for reasons put forth in the background note that introduces the document itself. With its charmingly rendered vignettes and tales of humorous adventure, "Return from Bohemia" seems of a piece with Wood's visual art and invites a similar kind of close reading. The text's exclusive focus on Wood's boyhood, up to and including the death of his father, underscores his conscious conviction that "everything is tied up with" one's earliest years. This is the developmental perspective of psychoanalysis, which holds that experiences in childhood and even infancy inform much if not all of an individual's subsequent behavior and emotional vicissitudes. Psychoanalysis offers a theory of mind, postulating a dynamic unconscious engendered by the repression of certain inadmissible wishes and affects, and also a method by which meaning is inferred from seemingly insignificant details, deflections, or repetitions. With knowledge of the salient facts of Wood's life, and by applying classical psychoanalytic concepts to an understanding of his oeuvre as a whole, one may conceivably deduce certain of his particular unconscious struggles. Of interest in this regard and worthy of our compassion are his intense attachment to his mother and repressed hostility toward his father, an inability to mourn the traumatic loss of that father at a most vulnerable age, unrelenting guilt over his father's death and a fear of retribution, imposture related to having supplanted his father and surpassed him in achievement and fame, remorse over fantasized aggression toward both parents, and finally a desire to repair and make amends to those damaged inner objects.

External circumstances fail to explain to any satisfactory degree why Wood abandoned his autobiography *in res medias* in 1935 and never returned to it. The most crystalline recollections contained therein resemble what psychoanalysts understand as screen memories, dreamlike scenes that, whether historically accurate or completely fantastic, cover over some form of latent (often sexual) content. These memories are always convincingly real, even hyperreal, and date invariably to early childhood; it is possible then that Wood's later memories seemed to him in comparison insufficiently riveting to warrant recording. In their gemlike effects, the pertinent passages in "Return from Bohemia" parallel the crisp, lapidary style the artist adopted in his mature paintings. In Chapters 1 and 3, several of these uncanny screen memories, encoded in Wood's images as well as in his text, are plumbed for their potential relevance to the primal scene—the remembered or imagined scene of parental lovemaking that, according to Freud, provides for every child a troubling key to the mystery of his or her very origin.

Something of that disconcerting fact of life may undergird the peculiar manifest content of *American Gothic* and imbue it with an otherwise inexplicable universality. It is a truism in art history that the most enduring works of art open to multiple, complementary interpretations. Psychoanalysis may contribute a few of the panoply of possible readings, frequently of a provocative nature and subject to resistance. The speculative study of Wood's art and inner life in the pages that follow joins the diverse interpretive efforts already applied to his oeuvre, with the aim of producing a more expansive construction of his identity and complex humanity. Poseur that he could and too often had to be, he was earnest about the inner sources of his pictures. "Great art," he wrote, "works from the inside out—individual, regional, national, universal—not vice versa. We shall never produce a great national art or a lasting universal art by starting out consciously to do so. We have to start by looking inside ourselves, selecting our most genuine emotions."[16]

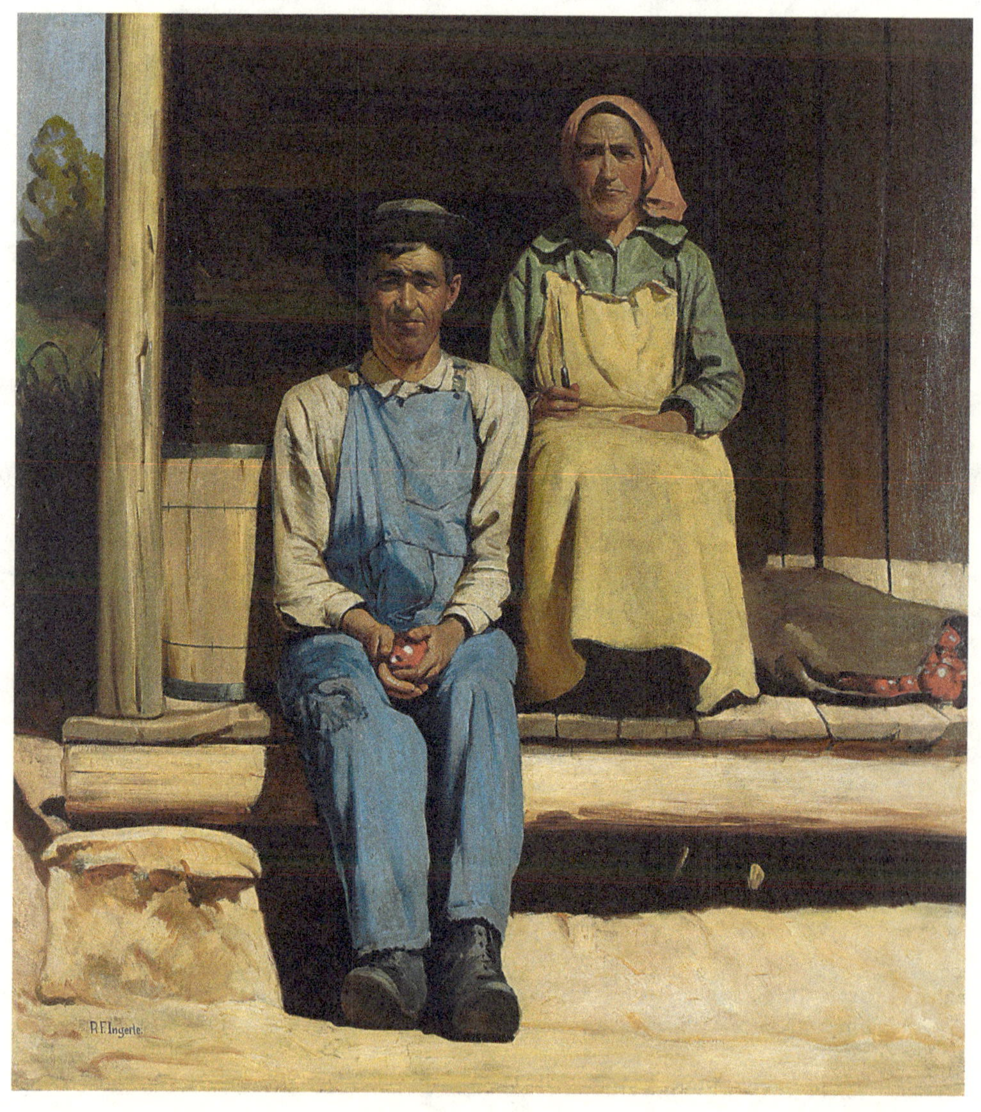

Fig. 1.1. Rudolph Ingerle, *Salt of the Earth*, 1930.

❖ CHAPTER 1 ❖

A Family Affair

WHEN REGIONALIST PAINTER Rudolph Ingerle (1879–1950) set out in search of authentic American subjects in the late 1920s, he traveled from his home in Illinois to Indiana and Missouri, and was excited to encounter folks he declared "the salt of the earth" in the Smoky Mountains of Tennessee. His eponymous picture of a rustic couple posed in front of their house (Fig. 1.1), the man wearing overalls and the woman in kerchief and apron, proved a popular success throughout the 1930s. At the Art Institute of Chicago, when it shared the limelight with Grant Wood's contemporaneous masterpiece, *American Gothic* (1930, Fig. 1.2), the paintings' many similarities were not lost on appreciative critics. With their somewhat tattered clothes and furrowed brows, Ingerle's couple bear signs of a hard life, yet the large sack of apples that spills open on the porch of their log cabin implies a bountiful harvest and the Edenic locale the artist indeed called paradise. The shiny red apples—one cradled emblematically in the man's hands—also account for the knife held sharply erect by the woman, who will set about peeling them once her posing is done. Ingerle thus added a bit of narrative to his study of a type he exalted unequivocally as "the grandest people in the world, the finest Americans in the country."[1] He conveyed their upright character by means of their postures, echoed in the emphatic verticals of the planks and post that frame them, and in their facial expressions: the man appears affable, open and direct, while the woman, with her firmly set jaw and unflinching gaze, exudes capability, strength, and determination.

Wood, too, strove in his signature painting to assert a kind of regional character, presenting an anonymous couple, their homestead, a glimpse of their natural surroundings, and objects suggesting their industrious nature—pitchfork and well tended house plants. Yet how to account for the wildly incommensurate cultural fates of these two images, which share so much and which emerged, albeit independently, at the exact same historical moment? *American Gothic* quickly outstripped *Salt of the Earth* in popularity, achieving iconic status and bringing its artist immediate national renown while Ingerle continued to labor in relative obscurity. Why? Though formal differences between the paintings may offer only a partial answer, they do provide a starting point for analysis. Stylistically, Wood departed in *American Gothic* from the agreeable naturalism Ingerle practiced in favor of a fussier, almost hallucinatory verism, all forms crisply delineated, even down to the distant treetops. Wood, moreover, presented his figures quite confrontationally in the very foreground of the painting, giving them a looming presence and a corporeal breadth that exceeds the limits of his panel; Ingerle's couple seems positively retiring in comparison with their aggressively positioned Iowa counterparts.

Further, while Ingerle offered viewers a toehold into a three-dimensional space by means of a strip of dry earth at the bottom of his picture, Wood erected a fourth wall so to speak, and, as James Dennis observed, handled pictorial space "like the successive layers of scenery on the stage."[2] Thus, in *American Gothic*, three painted flats, each parallel to the picture plane, construct a theatrical space: figures define a foreground, house and barn the middleground, and foliage and church steeple the background. In this way, Wood established an engaging dialectic between surface and depth, an effect enhanced by the repeating verticals of tines, seams, stripes, posts, and battens, which mark off degrees of recession in space while also, as a pattern, collapsing it. Despite his believably three-dimensional treatment of the heads and hand of the man and woman, the figures themselves are curiously flat, unlike Ingerle's seated couple, whose knees jut forward, and whose bodies cast shadows and make physical contact with each other. Wood's figures merely overlap, like cutouts placed one before the other.

The formal tension Wood set up between two and three dimensions constitutes just one of the many ambivalences informing *American Gothic*. On the level of subject matter, confusion has always reigned over the identity of the figures and their relationship to each other. Ingerle's mountain folk seem completely believable as husband and wife, but not so Wood's peculiar characters, with their troubling May–December age disparity. For decades after his demise, Wood's sister, Nan Wood Graham, objected far and wide to the interpretation of these figures as a married couple, insisting that they were meant to represent small-town folk rather than farmers and that the woman "is supposed to be the man's daughter, not his wife."[3] Although Graham modeled for the female figure in the painting and felt she had a direct line to the artist's intentions, her claim resolves nothing and only thickens the plot, leaving us to puzzle over the whereabouts of the intimidating pitchfork man's absent spouse and the nature of this strange household. "What kind of family is this?" demanded John Seery in his unsparing interrogation of everything gothic in *American Gothic*, indecorously inquiring "whether the spinster

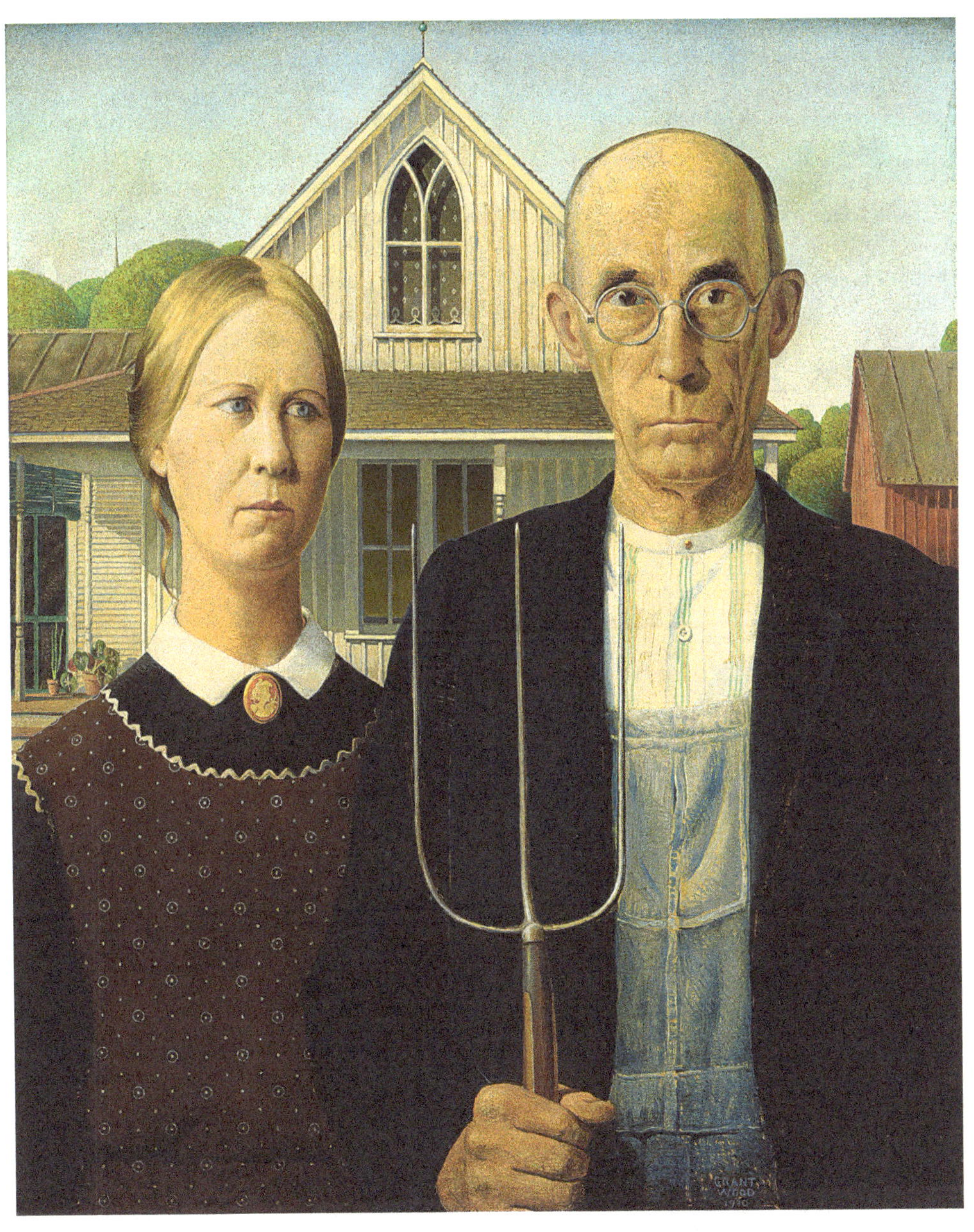

Fig. 1.2. Grant Wood, *American Gothic*, 1930.

daughter acts as a wifely substitute, out there on the isolated plains, in more than merely housekeeping ways?"[4]

In such speculations, the disturbing mysteries of the nineteenth-century gothic novel begin to come to the fore, along with "the hideous darkness of existence on the farms and in the hamlets" explored by Ruth Suckow, Wood's contemporary in Regionalist literature.[5] Unlike the Vienna-born, Chicago-based Ingerle who approached his regional types in *Salt of the Earth* with the detachment of an outside observer, Wood painted as Suckow wrote, from the perspective of a native Iowan. He was an uneasy insider, however, and his relationship to the puritanical, buttoned-up Midwesterners he presented in *American Gothic* was as much problematic as it was intimate and profound. Issuing from deeply mixed feelings, the painting is riddled with irreducible ambiguities, its ostensibly realist style at odds with its fundamentally obscure content. Is it, after all, paean or parody? Either way, the image possesses an affective power, subliminally registered by viewers but perhaps nervously covered over in the spirited humor of the picture's endless, mocking iterations. Something about Wood's curious characters may hit close to home.

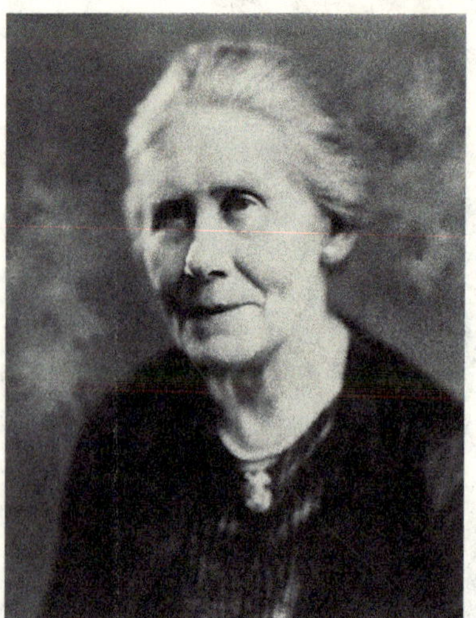

Fig. 1.3. Hattie Weaver Wood , c. 1930.

PORTRAIT OF MOTHER

As model for the daughter/wife, Graham was a convenient surrogate for the woman I believe Wood truly wished to depict in *American Gothic*—his mother, Hattie Weaver Wood (Fig. 1.3), modest helpmeet to Francis Maryville Wood, the artist's farmer-father who had died of a heart attack in 1901. Grant, the couple's middle son, was ten years old at the time of this sudden loss, and he felt it painfully ever after. Late in life, when asked about the stalwart couple in his famous painting, Wood declared them "tintypes from my own family album."[6] Among the various assertions he made about *American Gothic*, this one seems to me the most pointedly personal, the closest he ever came to admitting the picture's private meaning or at least to bringing that meaning to consciousness: while not portrait likenesses, his figures suggest parental imagoes. Even in 1930, they appeared anachronistic, shades from long ago, as Wood dressed them up in clothing his parents would have worn when he was a child. In preparation for the painting, he asked Graham to make an apron edged with rickrack, an old-fashioned embellishment no longer readily available in local stores. She resorted to ripping some trim off of mother Hattie's old dresses.[7] Similarly, the man's shirt in the painting, missing its detachable collar, was

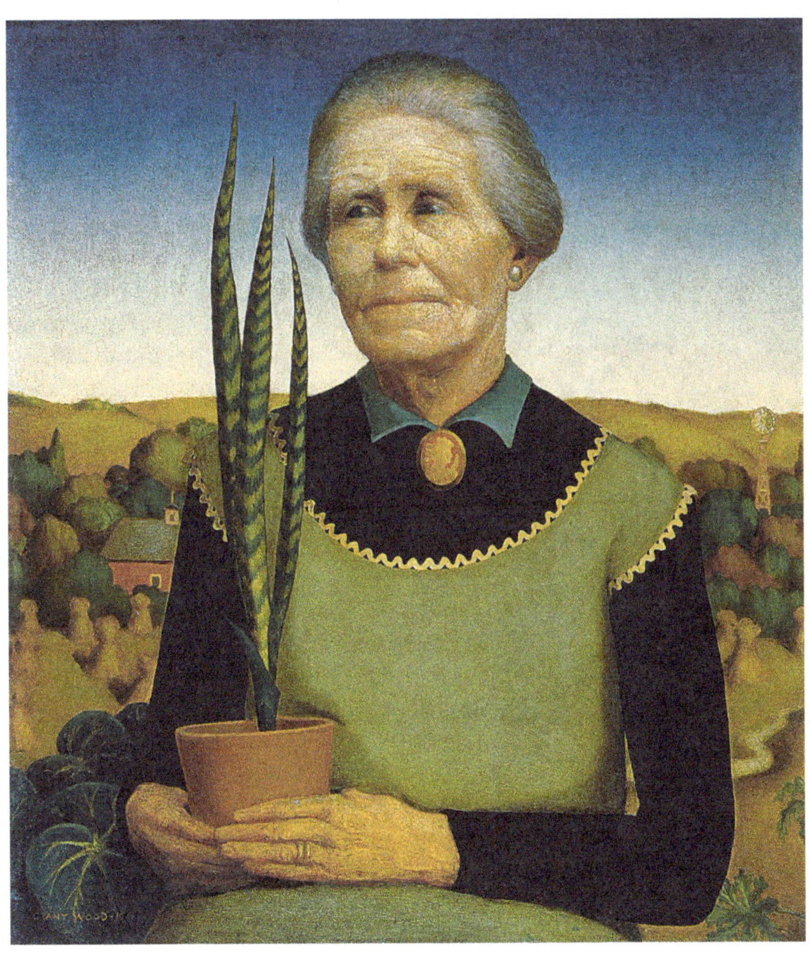

Fig. 1.4. Grant Wood, *Woman with Plants*, 1929.

of a kind that had disappeared by the 1920s; Wood salvaged this example from the rag bin.

If, in the spirit of authenticity, Ingerle based his picture on direct observation, Wood staged everything in *American Gothic*, creating a peculiar pastiche. His sitters posed in Cedar Rapids, but the house depicted was in Eldon. All details were carefully orchestrated and pieced together, the whole made seamless by Wood's meticulously tidy brushwork, as in the secondary revision of a dream. Indeed, Wood's entire process in creating this image could be described along an oneiric model, in which the secondary revision renders the dream coherent and credible by adding otherwise non-essential elements to fill in narrative gaps or leaps in logic in the dream's often bizarre manifest content.[8] Along with other psychic mechanisms that operate on the raw material of the dream (condensation, displacement, symbolization), secondary revision helps disguise the latent content of which the dreamer remains unaware. Wood combined the raw material of memories and of what was immediately at hand, just as dreams mix past experience with the fresh "day residue" of everyday life.[9]

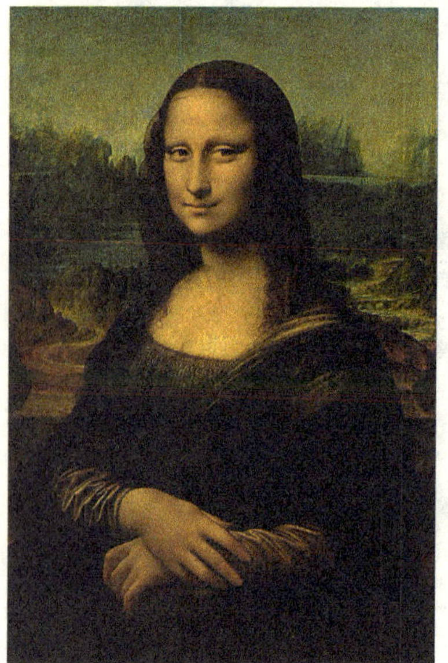

Fig. 1.5. Leonardo da Vinci, *Mona Lisa*, c. 1503.

Woman with Plants (1929, Fig. 1.4), the artist's tender portrait of his mother at age seventy-one, provided the direct prototype for the female figure in *American Gothic*. Among his earliest mature paintings, in which he incorporated stylistic lessons learned during a three-month trip to Germany in 1928,[10] Wood depicted Hattie in front of an Iowa landscape at harvest time, complete with corn shocks, red barn, and windmill. Pressing his sitter up close to the picture plane, he provided her with a symbolic attribute, a potted sansevieria, in the manner of portraits by Northern Renaissance masters he had studied in Munich's Alte Pinakothek. The tall plant suggests the authority within the family that passed to Hattie on the death of her husband; she holds it delicately, and its leaves number four, like her children, three boys and a girl. Wood's placement of his seated half-figure against a faraway vista, omitting a middleground, brings Leonardo's *Mona Lisa* (c. 1503, Fig. 1.5) inevitably to mind, and the addition of a little winding creek at the lower right of the composition strengthens this association. Through the generic titling of her portrait, Hattie achieves the archetypal status of a humble and hardy Midwestern pioneer, which seems to have been Wood's primary conscious aim. At the same time, personal references inserted in the painting identify her as none other than the artist's own mother, whom he idealized extravagantly as "the most beautiful lady in all the world."[11] In addition to the sansevieria, Hattie's houseplants include begonias at the lower left of the picture, where Wood signed his name, identifying himself with the objects of her nurturing care. The windmill in the background also telegraphs his presence: "The Old Masters all had their trademarks," he explained to Graham, "and mine will be the windmill";[12] the device appears behind him in an imposing self-portrait of 1932/41 (Figge Art Museum, Davenport, Iowa) and in its charcoal and pastel study (Introduction, opposite p. 1). Most tellingly, the cameo brooch Hattie wears at her throat testifies to her son's heartfelt devotion: Wood had purchased it for her as a souvenir of his sojourn in Sorrento, Italy, in the winter of 1923–24.[13]

The cherished brooch reappears on the woman in *American Gothic*, as does Hattie's simple black dress, worn beneath the rickrack-trimmed apron. Sansevieria and begonias are there too, though moved to the background, behind the woman's shoulder, at the entrance to her house. Wood reprised in this younger female figure Hattie's plain hairdo in *Woman with Plants* and her averted gaze. In both paintings, the women are rendered sexless, with flat chests; the "miniature breast–hieroglyph" Wanda Corn has identified in the dot-and-circle pattern of the apron in *American Gothic* suggests what Wood otherwise chose not to acknowledge.[14] Curiously, the right breast of this figure seems to have dropped down to just above waist level. Wood also had some difficulty in "handling" his mother's body in *Woman with Plants*, where her lap is rather clumsily delineated in visibly horizontal brushstrokes without convincing foreshortening. The ineptitude of this passage reminds us how maternal portraits are sometimes riddled with parapractic evidence of the artist's emotional struggles, involving opposing desires for intimacy with and separation from the mother. Representing one's mother can be a terribly "ticklish situation," as critic Donald Kuspit observes, "fraught with the dangers of infantile response, with the threat of a regressive bonding with the mother" even as the artist strives to retain his autonomy as a mature adult.[15] Wood idealized and clung to his mother, yet conflicts he was probably unaware of emerge in this portrait. It is worth noting, for example, how the indestructible sansevieria, typically understood to symbolize Hattie's steadfast endurance, also goes by other names—snake plant, mother-in-law's tongue, snake tongue, Saint George's sword—all countering the benign aspect of Wood's subject with dangerous, barbed, aggressively phallic associations. The serpentlike motif may point to the artist's masturbatory ideation and religious fears to be discussed below, at the very least distilling a memory of "tongue lashings" his mother had meted out to him as a naughty child.

The story he offered in 1937 about the genesis of *Woman with Plants* has a halting redundancy to it. Recollecting what must have been his homecoming after the Munich trip and his decision "to paint life as it is," Wood stated that the sight of his mother in the kitchen, cooking, had provoked an artistic epiphany: "In her apron I saw just as paintable decorative material as the old painters had. When I painted the picture of mother something went into it. I painted from personal experience. It has an emotional quality strong enough to get across in the painting."[16] Wood's point about how his picture was based on personal experience seems gratuitous, for how could a portrait of one's mother be otherwise? As Wood biographer R. Tripp Evans notes, the artist felt "a deep attachment to Hattie's aprons (the strings of which, it must be said, were never cut)" and "to the tablecloths, hooked rugs, and quilts she made; the wedding dress and mourning veil that marked her marriage to Maryville; and even her pink flannel nightgown, an article Wood himself wore to a costume party in the late 1920s."[17] His exaltation of these artifacts suggests that his individuation from his mother was incomplete, his longing for nurture and love never fulfilled. The strong emotional quality he claimed was in *Woman with Plants*, moreover, is hardly borne out by the picture.

Hattie in her portrait remains reserved, somehow withholding, refusing eye contact. Here, the analogy to Mona Lisa breaks down, despite the compositional trappings Wood provided. If Freud traced the beguiling smile of the Giaconda—whose eyes, unlike Hattie's, follow you everywhere—to Leonardo's unconscious neonatal memory of gazing into the loving face of his birth mother,[18] then Wood literally turned that famous smile upside down in *Woman with Plants*. Mona Lisa engages the viewer seductively, but Hattie, tense and melancholy in her severe black dress and pained, tight-lipped expression, appears preoccupied, absorbed in her widowhood like the aloof and similarly solitary mother in James Whistler's *Arrangement in Grey and Black* (1871), that other great image of filial ambivalence and devotion. Painting Hattie's joyless image, Wood participated in her mourning.

In the year after he completed *Woman with Plants*, Wood projected a dolorous mien onto the black-clad couple in *American Gothic*. Their blank stares recall a passage about his ancestors' kinship with the Iowa prairie in "Return from Bohemia, A Painter's Story," the autobiography Wood began in 1935 with the help of his secretary and confidant, Park Rinard. Those pioneering folk, Wood reminisced, "developed a character . . . akin to that of the land itself. One could see it reflected in their eyes. I saw it in the eyes of my father and mother—a quality bleak, far-away, timeless" (Appendix, p. 194). The chilly stupor Wood projected onto his parents in this text echoes the emotional tenor of the figures in his picture. Their psychological remoteness contrasts dramatically with their physical closeness in the foreground of the composition but parallels the temporal distance of this familial vision for Wood in 1930—a dream of his mother still young and his father still alive.

THE PATERNAL IMAGE

Wood lost his father at a particularly vulnerable age for any boy. In such cases, idealizations are frozen and exaggerated for all time, and the child is bereft of the modulation of and protection from the mother provided by the father-son relationship.[19] He is thrown back entirely on the mother-son relationship just as puberty's fires begin to rage. These poignant circumstances were significantly shaped in Wood's case by his homosexuality, for he was not like his father or brothers. All his life, he suffered the absence of the tender, flesh-and-blood father he never had, even while Maryville was living. That unusual given name adds to the enigma of his father's persona: why he went by this appellation rather than by his first name, Francis, is unknown; the ambivalently gendered "Francis/Frances" was hardly masculinized by the substitution. So Maryville was pronounced "Mur-vil"[20] by all who knew him, eliding the name's feminine associations. He was not warm and approachable to his middle son, for among the vivid impressions the artist recorded in "Return from Bohemia" of his childhood in Anamosa, Iowa, we find Maryville a formidable paterfamilias:

> There was a certain mystery and loneliness about father that I sensed even as a child—a strange quality of detachment which no-one would ever be able to understand. Perhaps it revealed itself in the furrows of his long, severe forehead; perhaps in his austere eyes, or in the attitudes to which his lean frame lent itself. . . . One sensed that he understood the soil and was subtly related to it. Yet, there was in him always that stern, haunting loneliness that would never surrender—even to the earth.
>
> This quality stood between Maryville Wood and his family. We loved him and revered him; yet knew that he was not of us.
>
> To me, he was the most dignified and majestic of persons. His low, carefully spoken words were law. I never questioned the infallibility of his judgments or even resented being punished by him. But he was more a god than a father to me [App., 199–200].

The character in this passage resembles the forbidding figure in *American Gothic*, although the actual sitter for the painting was, famously, Wood's dentist (Fig. 1.6). The kindly Dr. Byron McKeeby (1867–1950) had known Wood for years, was a patron of the arts and sponsor of local talent, and had encouraged Wood in his European travels, lent him financial support, and urged him to submit his work for exhibition at regional fairs.[21] Wood selected McKeeby as a model because he admired the man's face—"It's all long straight lines," the artist stated—and powerful hands.[22] At the same time, given the menacing demeanor of the figure in the painting, it is hard to avoid the association of the dentist with a powerful, punitive father. We know that McKeeby inflicted pain on Wood, pulling several teeth and replacing them with a bridge,[23] duplicating with his ministrations Maryville's concerned but disciplining attentions to his son. "Later, he had whipped me," Wood recalled in "Return from Bohemia" with a certain sangfroid, when the father snatched his child from the pasture of a grazing bull and saved him from harm, but then punished him severely for trespassing in the first place (App., 200).

According to Wood's early biographer Darrell Garwood, when the reluctant McKeeby finally agreed to pose, the artist "had him wear a dress shirt, overalls, and a dressy coat, to represent a farmer 'who might be a preacher on Sundays.'"[24] Maryville is introduced in "Return from Bohemia" as "the superintendent of the Sunday School . . . a tall, bony young farmer with solemn blue eyes and a stern, angular face" (App., 204). Except for his eye color, this father-farmer and part-time preacher corresponds precisely to the older man in *American Gothic*, who wears a style of round wire rim glasses that Maryville had also worn.[25] The farmer in the picture wields a three-tined fork—the type used for pitching hay, not, *pace* Wood's claims about townsfolk, for turning garden soil. In a tiny pencil sketch for the composition, drawn on the back of an envelope, Wood had originally depicted the man holding a rake, but given the overall emphasis on verticals, the pitchfork proved more appropriate formally. In terms of content, the fork could be a makeshift weapon, or the devil's attribute. Indeed, Evans associates the figure with Hades alongside his captive Persephone, and Matthew Baigell has speculated that the man with his pitchfork might represent the very Devil himself, or at least "a symbol of the Devil's presence in Iowa."[26]

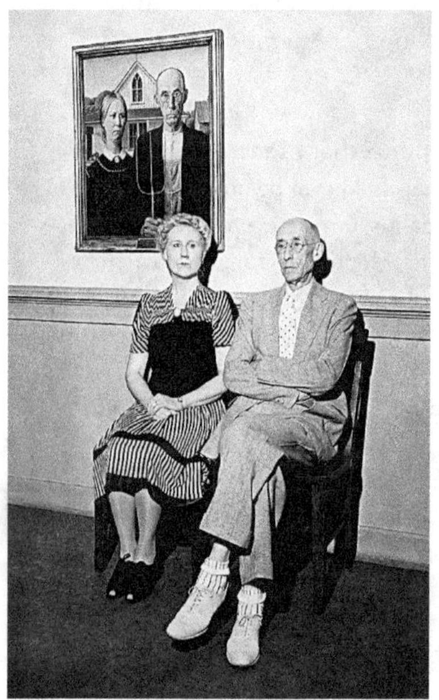

Fig. 1.6. Nan Wood Graham and Dr. Byron McKeeby, at the Grant Wood Memorial Exhibition, Cedar Rapids Art Association, September 1942.

If Wood characterized the emotionally distant Maryville as a majestic, infallible, judging deity whose words were law, then the pitchfork-wielding figure constitutes his avenging the flip side. Freud postulated that concepts of God and the Devil stem from the individual's ambivalence toward his personal father, benevolent and righteous on the one hand, inspiring hostility and hatred on the other.[27] Maryville fully expected his son to become a farmer, developing in his own image; his oft-cited and probably overstated opposition to "graven and pictorial representation" has the ring of a biblical injunction (App., 200), so that his son's pursuit of a career in art seemed to defy not just a paternal but an even higher authority. Though Wood's ambivalence toward this authority was pervasive, he worked to cover over his antagonism, probably even to himself. His heroic idealization of the father was a defensive denial of all negative feelings. Repeatedly in his autobiography, he insisted on his love for Maryville, dubiously professing, for instance, not to have minded his whippings. In *American Gothic*, however, endowing his father-surrogate with a devilish pitchfork, Wood revealed his otherwise unacknowledged hostility.

Uncannily, I believe, viewers may experience this figure as deeply *familiar*, that is, in an intimate, familial sense: "Yes," one commentator blithely wrote, "every school child knows these features almost as well as he knows those of his own father."[28] Moreover, responses to the figure invariably ascribe to him a power disproportionate to that of a simple farmer or townsman. To Robert Hughes, the man's pitchfork resembles "a scepter" of paternal rule; for Norman Mailer, "the hollows in his cheeks give a hint of the hanging judge."[29] To a child, of course, the father often seems omnipotent no matter how benign or ordinary he might be in reality. Viewers of *American Gothic* who sense the threatening aspect of Wood's farmer reflect the artist's own conflicted position, the intensity of which he strove to vitiate in the painting by means of humor. Despite the work's satirical edge, astute critics have intuited the anxious nature of the artist's relationship to the parental couple he had created. When *American Gothic* was first exhibited at the Art Institute of Chicago, Walter Prichard Eaton described in the *Boston Herald* how "the farmer, spectacled and bald, and looking like a revival preacher, as perhaps he is on Sundays, grasps a pitchfork with erect prongs. . . . His eyes pierce you with a fanatical stare, and his grim mouth is a straight slit."[30] In the same review, Eaton deemed the prize-winning painting "realistic, hard, almost shellac-like in texture, caricatured so slightly that it is doubly cruel, and though we know nothing of the artist and his history, we cannot help believing that as a youth he suffered tortures from these people, who could not understand the joy of art within him and tried to crush his soul with their sheet iron brand of salvation."

DIVINE PUNISHMENT

Not surprisingly, we learn from Wood in "Return from Bohemia" that Maryville was not one to spare the rod. When the child disobeyed, Maryville would give him a tanning with a razor strop or banish him to the dark cellar to repent his ways. Such measures were probably not unusual child-rearing practices of the period; what matters is that Wood remembered them, even as an adult, while suppressing any anger he might have felt toward the father who implemented them. Maryville's vengeful parenting seemed divinely ordained, part of the larger order of existence. In his autobiography, Wood presented natural disasters, too, as a function of paternal-like wrath: when cholera kills the family's herd of pigs in the narrative and grass fires threaten the homestead, the chapter is titled "Whom the Lord Loveth He Chasteneth."

Though the artist poked fun throughout the autobiography at his youthful self with his exaggerated childish fears, the overall moral of this chapter is ominous and oppressive. In it, a petrified boy Wood is subjected to the soul-crushing treatment that Eaton inferred from *American Gothic*, as the local minister intones warnings of eternal damnation in a "thunder-voice" as

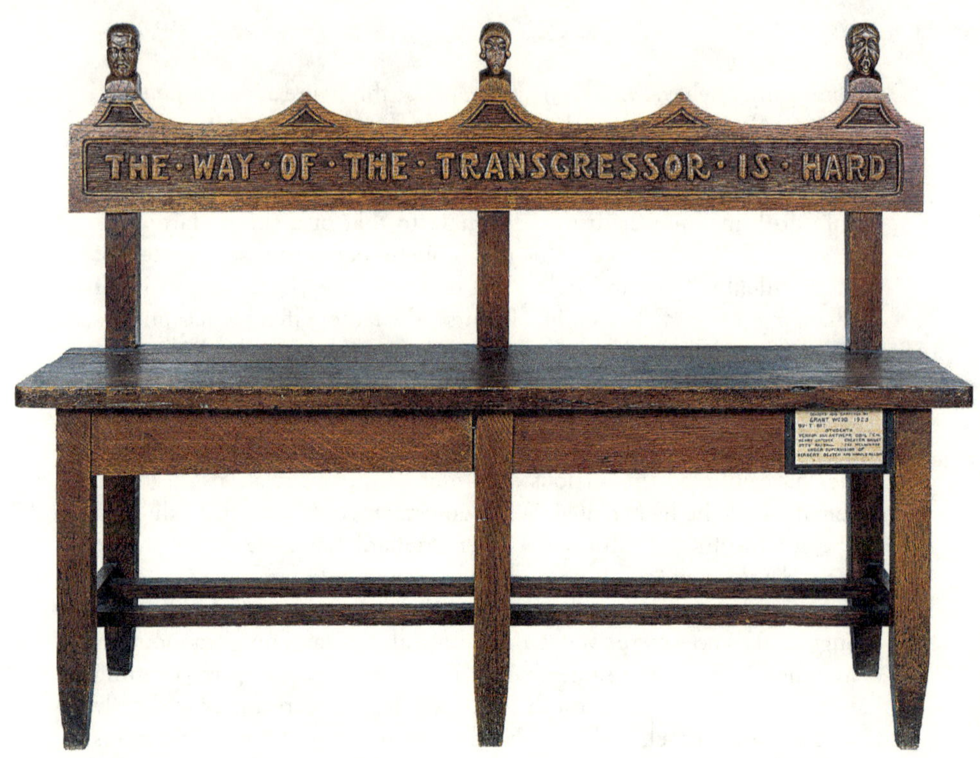

he sermonizes on the fate of Sodom and Gomorrah to frighten his flock (App., 232). Walled in on either side by his parents in the hard pew, little Wood withers in the "grim Calvanistic twilight" of the Presbyterian church of which his paternal grandfather had been a founding member and trustee. Indeed, the alignment here of family and church as institutions of oppression and control could hardly be stronger: Wood's parents had met in this very church when Hattie was the organist and Maryville, as mentioned above, the Sunday school superintendent.[31] Though this churchy scene of Wood's intimidation unfolds in Strawberry Hill, Iowa, it has all the fire and brimstone of Stephen Dedalus's Catholic indoctrination in Joycean Dublin.

In a literary portrait of himself as a young congregant, Wood spins a remarkable allegory of childhood sexuality and masturbatory guilt, where he cowers under the accusatory glare of the preacher. His sin: allowing his mind to wander instead of paying attention to the sermon, daydreaming about his recent obsession—joint snakes—and his future as a snake charmer in the circus. The legendary joint snake can break up into pieces to evade capture, and then magically reconstitute itself when danger is passed.[32] The sexual symbolism of this account is almost comical, as Wood projected onto the clergyman's very speech the serpentine aspect of his own mesmerizing onanistic fantasy. "The minister's voice was coiling and uncoiling in a monotonous flow," he reported, as, seeking relief from the spell of this "nasal"

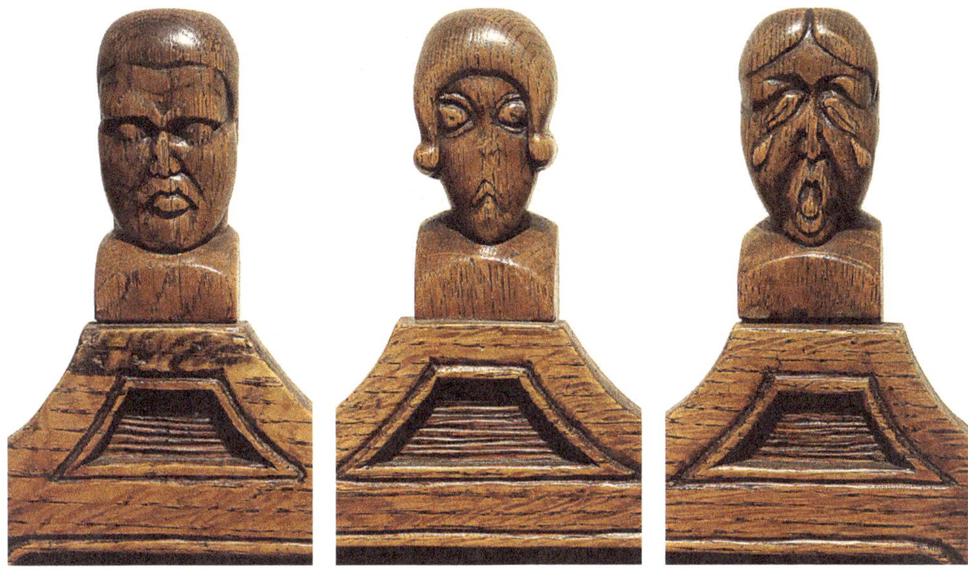

Figs. 1.7 (opposite) and 1.7A–C (details, above). Grant Wood, *Mourner's Bench*, 1921–23.

drone, the hapless boy rubs his nose, which "had been itching for what seemed like hours." Forbidden sexuality and aesthetic experience come together in this tableau; the child's nose-rubbing, a barely disguised masturbatory wish, is accompanied by the sudden appearance of sunlight, which floods through the stained-glass windows, creating a "a gorgeous rainbow" of green and lavender. In the meantime, "the minister's voice writhed on," tension building, until finally "his voice was coiling now, ready to strike out in the climax of his sermon." Maryville's intervention rouses the errant son from his snaky reverie: "Father's hand came down firmly on my arm. . . . No wriggling allowed here." Boy Wood easily translates paternal interdiction—the father's prohibition of his sexual activity—into divine judgment, confessing, "I no longer needed father's hand to keep me still. I was scared stiff. Surely the Lord's punishment was aimed at me." Total submission to this awesome authority was the only course available.

Wood memorialized the boyish distress he had suffered in church in the celebrated oak *Mourner's Bench* (1921–23, Fig. 1.7) he fashioned while teaching at McKinley Junior High School in Cedar Rapids. Among certain evangelical Presbyterians, Quakers, and Baptists, the mourner's bench was introduced in the nineteenth century as part of a humiliating ritual in which individual members of a congregation were called out by name to come forward and repent their wrongdoing. Taking a seat on the bench near the pulpit, or sometimes kneeling before it, the shamed person might experience a terrified conversion and merciful absolution. Wood's bench, installed outside the principal's office for pupils awaiting reprimand, bears an inscription across its back rail: "The Way of the Transgressor Is Hard." The three finials Wood carved for the bench (Figs. 1.7A–C) take the form of two scowling adult heads, one male and one female, and a wailing boy. Depicting disapproving teachers and a tearful student at school, the finials also figure a primal core, the parental pair—father's eyes now closed in death—and their wayward child, just as the bench itself literally reproduces the hard pew once occupied by the fearful miscreant in "Return from Bohemia." Admonishing and mocking the little troublemakers who would take their seats in the worrisome antechamber at school, Wood also empathized with them. The title he gave this object points to an American religious tradition and also seems self-referential, as if Wood were mourning the loss of his own guileless innocence, extinguished by the effectively internalized, disciplining recriminations of parents and preacher and society at large.

Following the church episode in "Return from Bohemia," the Wood farm is imperiled by a prairie fire and narrowly escapes destruction. The drama of the event is intense, with the whole family and a hired man working frantically to avert disaster, digging firebreaks and smothering the edges of the burn with wet sacks. "The grass fire was a billowing irregular wall of smoke," Wood wrote, "orange flames reached out like snake-tongues as it moved forward . . . , hurling sparks into the air" (App., 236). Reading between these suggestive lines reveals a connection between the incendiary scourge and a child's guilty conscience, as little Wood's hand (the instrument of his self-pleasuring) is burned in the fire. That night, primed by preacherly warnings and haunted by that universal feature of an immature imagination, magical thinking, he asks Hattie as he and brother Jack are put to bed, "Did God punish us with that fire like the minister said in church?" Hattie is non-committal. Jack, too, apparently feels he has roused heaven's wrath, for "he lay there in the darkness for a long time," murmuring remorsefully, "God punched us" (App., 237). Instead of administering a simple tanning to sons who wander from the straight and narrow, this Father had effected a conflagration.

GUILT AND DEVOTION

In the face of such retaliatory power, whatever resentment Wood may have felt toward paternal authority had to be repressed: it is wrong to hate one's father, divine or human. Hostile feelings of this sort inspire guilt. This phenomenon has roots in infancy and is central to the theories of British psychoanalyst Melanie Klein, who postulated alternating sadistic and reparative fantasies relative to the child's loved objects in the course of normal development. According to Klein, the baby experiences its caretakers, especially the mother, as a split source of satisfaction as well as fear. The child harbors angry, hostile feelings, often repressed, and their violence is "in line with the extreme frightfulness of his persecutors."[33] In the wake of his destructive wishes, however, and remembering his blissful experience of the good parent, the infant is overwhelmed by feelings of loss and guilt, and desires imaginatively to restore and recreate the loved object.

This reparative impulse, moreover, forms the basis in Kleinian theory for all artistic creativity. In her study of the emotional vicissitudes of the creative process, Kleinian analyst Marion Milner confronted the inevitable effects of "lived-through experiences of the frightening father, in league with the mother, as a commanding and punishing authority."[34] Milner explored the psychic resonances of art-making itself, focusing on the way primal relationships and the emotions they arouse can inform artistic products: "One feels guilty," she wrote, "not only because one has been made to, but also because one knows only too well that there are real grounds for it; in the psychic reality of feeling and wish, one has failed, one has certainly, some time or other, been callous and greedy and resentful and destructive. So in one's inner world, perhaps locked up and hidden far away beyond one's knowing, there do exist loved people who have been hurt or even made into dead skeletons by one's angry wishes."[35]

Never completed, "Return from Bohemia" ends with Maryville's death and the family's move from the farm in Anamosa to Cedar Rapids, Wood's familiar childhood world shattered. If angry wishes could kill, then the boy was surely culpable on some irrational, psychic level for his father's demise. We are given a hint of Wood's felt patricidal guilt in the final, dramatic paragraphs of the truncated autobiography, when an agitated stranger on a (symbolic) white horse accosts the widowed Hattie and her children when they're departing their farm in a buckwagon: "The big horse wheeled on its hind legs with a storm of hooves, splattering mud in all directions. The rider turned in his saddle and shouted: 'President McKinley has been assassinated!'" (App., 280). This association of Maryville's death and a presidential murder compares the Wood family's loss to a national catastrophe, an unfortunate act of nature to the willful, criminal deed of a treasonous subject. And another president—Wood, significantly, had been named for Ulysses S. Grant—would now take his place in the line of succession.

For the rest of her life, and almost all of his own, Wood lived with his mother, while his siblings married and went their own ways. His older brother, Frank, at age fifteen, went into the automobile sales and repair business as a full partner with their grandfather Weaver in Cedar Rapids. When he became president of the Standard Battery and Electric Company, Frank ran the business alone, moving to Waterloo, Iowa, with his wife in 1912. Graham later complained of his neglect of Hattie. John Clifford Wood, "Jack," two years Grant's junior, worked as a mechanic. Jack married and moved out of his mother's home before he came of age and, though residing in the same town, had no contact with his family for fifteen years. At some point, he sued Hattie (unsuccessfully) for what he believed was his rightful portion of the proceeds from the sale of the farm. Nan, the youngest child, relocated with her husband, Emmett Edward Graham, to New Mexico and eventually to California.[36] Grant remained in close touch with her; not so with his brothers. His devotion was to the women in his family, whom he honored with affectionate portraits.

In addition to *Woman with Plants*, he created *Portrait of Nan* (1931, Fig. 1.8), where the sitter appears as a modern young woman, far removed from her dowdy persona in *American Gothic*. The sweet symbolic attributes she holds in her lap were, according to Graham, immediately at hand; Wood selected them with an eye to their colors, the plum to coordinate with the rosy background, the baby chick to echo the yellow of her hair.[37] With its oval format, heavy green drape casting a dramatic shadow, and Graham's serious, unsmiling demeanor, the painting aspires to an almost regal formality. Couching his subject in portraiture's ennobling conventions, Wood also desired to flatter her, to present her as feminine and alluring in compensation for the primly plain role he had previously imposed upon her. Thus Graham appears in makeup, with waved blonde hair falling around her shoulders, in a sleeveless blouse whose giant black-on-white polka-dot pattern the ever inventive Wood had designed himself with a potato stamp. The big dots exaggerate the breast hieroglyph of Graham's *American Gothic* apron. It is as if the artist offered an abstract sign for a kind of sexiness that was alien to him. Wood cherished this strange portrait always. It hung over the mantel in his living room in Iowa City when he died, the only picture in his mature style that he had retained for himself.[38]

In 1916, when Hattie lost the house she had purchased in Cedar Rapids after Maryville's death, she and Grant, then in his twenties, lived together in a tiny, ten-by-sixteen-foot cottage Wood erected on the property of his friend Paul Hanson near Indian Creek. The following year, mother and son moved into a bungalow Wood built with Hanson in the Kenwood Park neighborhood of Cedar Rapids. For ten years beginning in 1924, they occupied a 975-square-foot converted hayloft over the carriage house behind the town's Turner Mortuary (Fig. 1.9), sometimes joined by Graham. Wood's patron, David Turner, provided the space rent free; the artist ingeniously created efficient living quarters and a studio in what became known as 5 Turner Alley. It was here that Wood painted *American Gothic* and achieved his fame, leading to his position as the Iowa director of the Public Works of Art Project. In 1935, newly appointed to the faculty at the state university (now the University of Iowa), Wood relocated to Iowa City, and took Hattie with him. While her quarters were being readied in the new house, she stayed behind in Cedar Rapids at the home of Wood's friends Marvin and Winnifred Cone. It was only a brief separation, but the reunion, according to Wood biographer Hazel Brown, was most joyous. When the artist came to

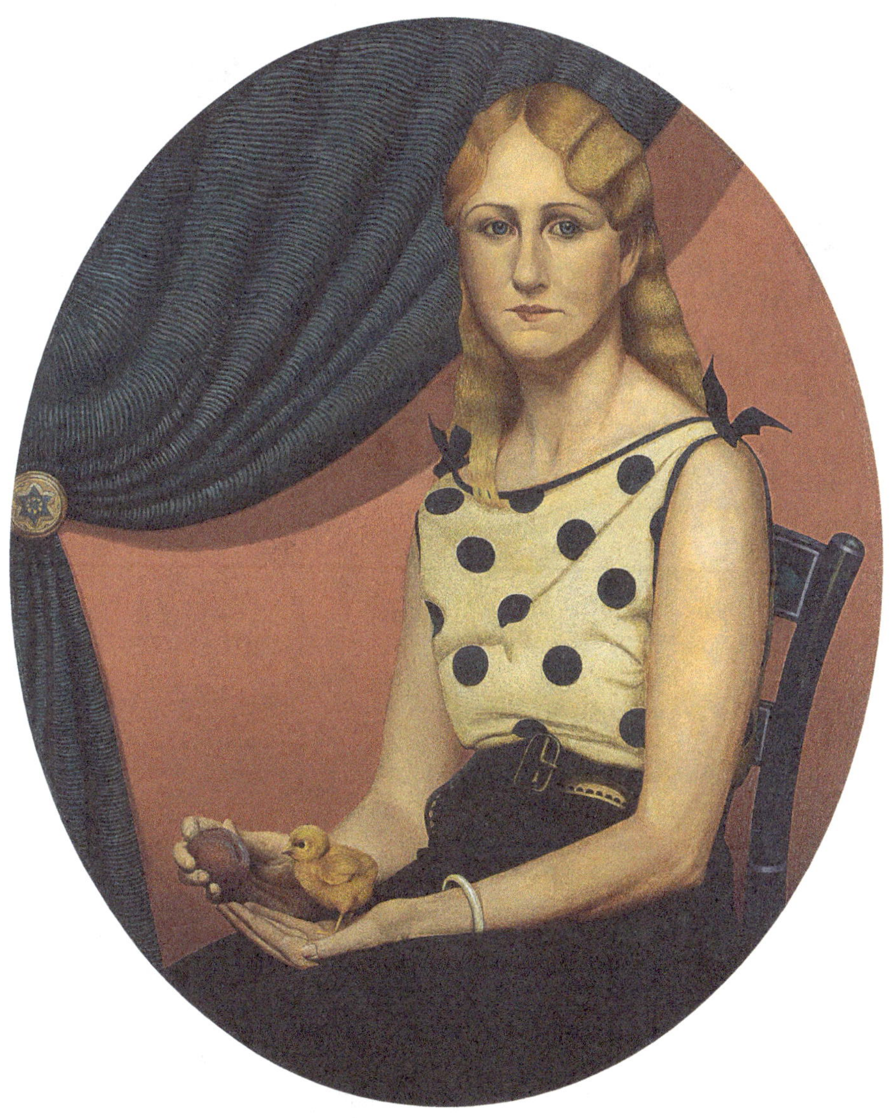

Fig. 1.8. Grant Wood, *Portrait of Nan*, 1931.

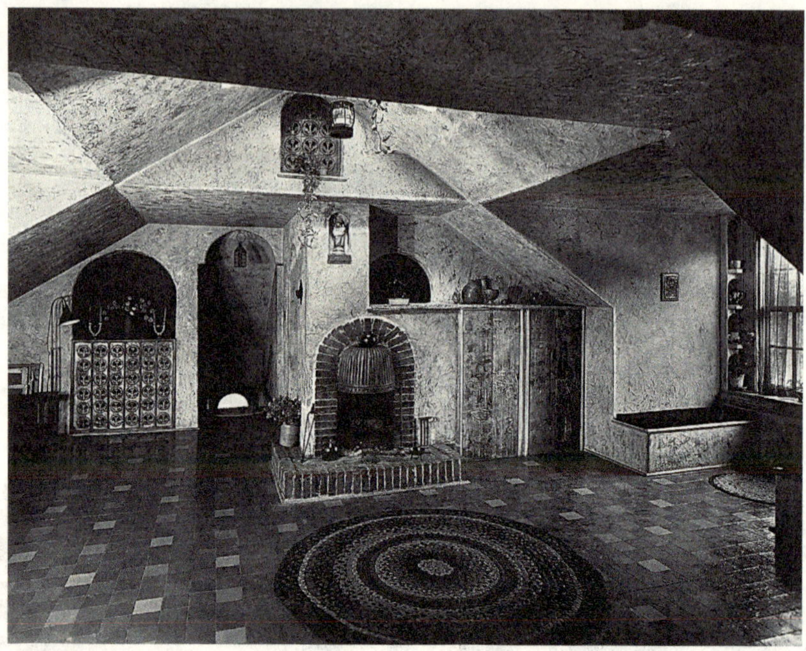

Fig. 1.9. Interior of 5 Turner Alley, Cedar Rapids, Iowa, c. 1925.

collect Hattie, the pair greeted each other like long-lost lovers, exclaiming "Grant!" and "Mother!" "And Winnifred [would] never forget the emotion and love conveyed between the two, in those two words."[39]

THE PARENTS REUNITED

Keeping always close to his mother, the artist had reason to feel that he had usurped Maryville's rightful place in her life. In *American Gothic*, we find her restored to her husband's side, as if the adult Wood were trying in this image to undo the fatal damage brought about by his angry childhood self. Here, the farmer-preacher stands before his wife, clearly possessive, barring access to her and their conjugal world. Their solidarity is enduring and monumental. The rigid poses, rectilinear forms, and crisp edges freeze the image, while the shellac-like finish that so amazed the Boston critic seals the pictorial space, preserving it forever from time and from change. And this eternal remove of the parental couple is unnerving. "The childhood spectacle of the parents together and oneself shut out," Milner reminds us, inspires "certain painful and intense emotions connected with the earliest experiences of difference," the difference, that is, between what one wants and what is, between dream and reality.[40] This inevitable disaffection of desire informs *American Gothic* and our reception of it, and it distressed Wood even as he struggled with the oedipal guilt that motivated him symbolically to reunite his parents in the painting. He had to mock their union, render it ridiculous by stripping it and them of warmth and human emotion. Making them sullen, even forlorn, he projected onto them the alienation he himself knew only too well in the face of their togetherness. He laughed at them, and, to conquer our own infantile experiences of jealousy and loss, we laugh with him.

Acknowledging this buried level of psychological meaning helps explain the painting's baffling fame as well as its perceived hilarity. "Why," wonders Baigell, marveling at *American Gothic*'s continuing hold on the popular imagination, "do people invariably laugh when they either stand before it or see it in reproduction? Is it a laugh offered in nervous recognition of what they know is true about themselves but try so hard to repress?"[41] Although he does not broach the precise nature of the troubled truth he suspects, I believe that Baigell here begins to penetrate the essential mystery of *American Gothic* and its ascension, over even very similar works like Ingerle's *Salt of the Earth*, to such astounding notoriety. Formal analysis takes us only so far, and citing "aesthetic richness" as a source for the picture's myriad interpretive possibilities, as Steven Biel does in his excellent social history of "America's Most Famous Painting," similarly begs the question.[42] An accessible style and subject matter have no doubt to be taken into account, but it seems to me that it is the latent content above all else that exerts such a powerful effect on viewers.

In this light, it is striking how other contenders for the winning title Biel confers on *American Gothic*—Jonathan Weinberg nominates Whistler's *Arrangement in Grey and Black* along with Gilbert Stuart's *George Washington* (1796) and Emanuel Leutze's *Washington Crossing the Delaware* (1851)[43]—all portray *parents*, whether the mother of the artist or the father of his country. Wood's picture ups the emotional ante by presenting both parents at once, stirring up, in addition to already intense feelings aroused by mother or father, all kinds of confused reactions to the relationship between the two. Hence the widespread obsession among viewers and critics with verifying the nature of that relationship once and for all, father/daughter versus husband/wife, as well as the vague sense of something awkward or embarrassing about the scene, involving family secrets concealed behind that dainty lace curtain drawn across the gothic window. The repressed (sexual) truth of *American Gothic* has to do with that universal enigma of human origins, the question every child asks: "Where do I come from?"

It may well be then that nervous laughter offsets the discomfiting fact of parental relations implied by the picture. In a brilliant insight, Seery suggests how the painting, "exceeding its representational limits, . . . reproduces the experience of, and the difficulties in, talking about our family secrets out in public."[44] Viewers may intuit the kinship problem underlying *American Gothic* even if they stop short of bringing it to consciousness. Brady Roberts's

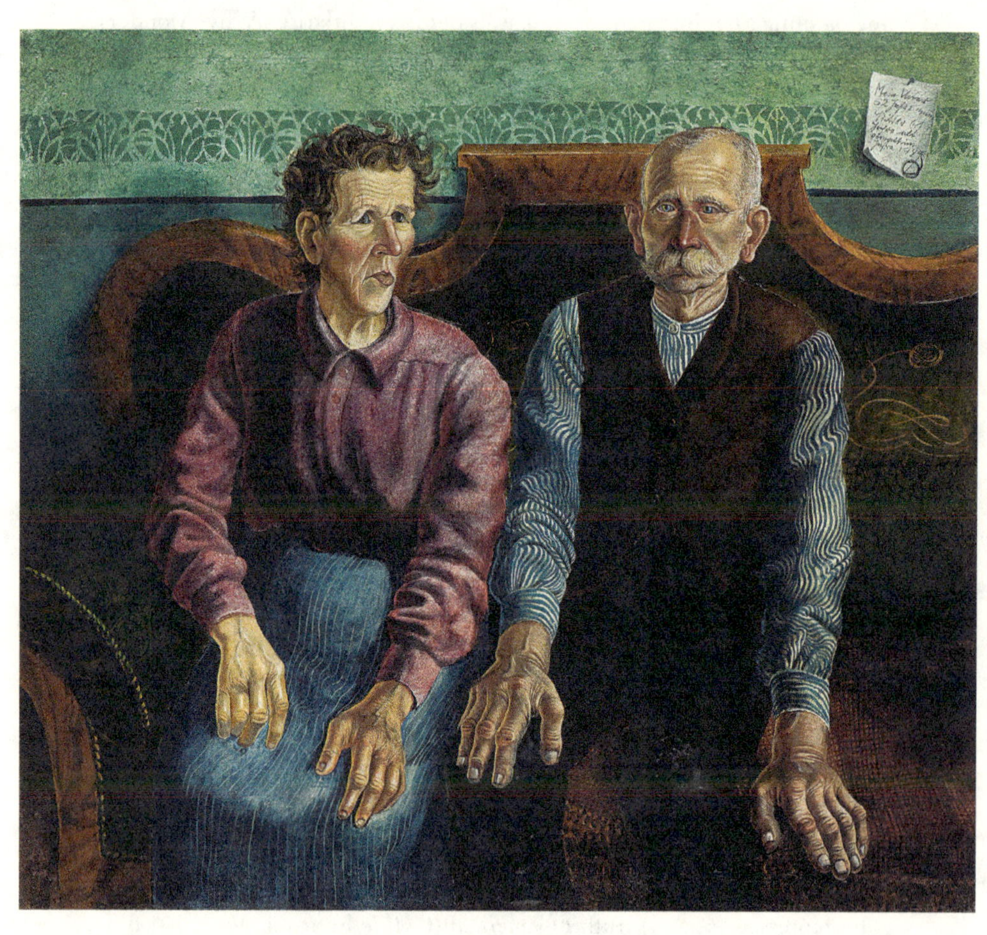

Fig. 1.10. Otto Dix, *Die Eltern des Künstlers II* (The Artist's Parents II), 1924.

scholarly treatment of the painting evinces this tendency beautifully. Linking *American Gothic* with the type of New Objectivity painting Wood encountered in 1928 in Munich, Roberts finds an affinity in outlook and style with a work by Otto Dix, *Die Eltern des Künstlers II* (1924, Fig. 1.10), that is, a portrait of the German artist's parents.[45] And although Roberts identifies Wood's figures merely as rural Midwesterners, his description of them suits Hattie and Maryville perfectly: they are "the people [Wood] knew best and with whom he maintained an affectionate yet ambivalent relationship."[46] Intimacy, love, greed, jealousy, fear, contempt, and guilt, all are mixed up in that ambivalence.

THE OEDIPAL SON

Such was Wood's own psychological dilemma that *American Gothic*, his act of filial contrition, is charged with equivocation. By dubbing the woman in the image "daughter," he disavowed the couple's sexual connection, rendering it taboo. The placement of his signature on the painting, the point at which he chose to insinuate his own presence, marks his position in the oedipal triangle. He signed on the farmer's overalls, below the waist, acknowledging that he was his father's progeny but also suggesting that by his art-making he would assume or surpass his father's creative role, just as he replaced him as the center of Hattie's emotional world. Wood's conflict surfaced as well in the various stories he told about the picture as he strove to placate irate Midwesterners who felt themselves misrepresented by the dour, old-fashioned couple. In these statements, the artist often contradicted himself, professing, for instance, to have "induced [his] own maiden sister to pose" (Graham had not been a "maiden" since 1924), and then searched for an appropriate man "to represent the husband."[47] Wood played with the facts in interesting and revealing ways. "I posed them side by side," he claimed of the patient models who were his parental surrogates in the painting, but Graham had a different account: "Dr. McKeeby and I never posed together," she remembered, "Grant worked on Dr. McKeeby in the dental office in the evening, and I posed at home—No. 5 Turner Alley."[48]

Wood's difficulty in bringing Hattie and Maryville back together even imaginatively in 1930 predicted his behavior five years later, as he mourned his mother's death. Bedridden for six months following a heart attack, Hattie died on October 11, 1935, at age seventy-seven.[49] A burial plot was waiting for her next to her husband's in Riverside Cemetery southwest of Anamosa, on a lovely hill overlooking the Wapsipinicon River. Wood, however, would not have it. Garwood recounted how the artist detested the monument that marks two generations of Wood family gravesites, a large granite block surmounted by a sleeping stone lion (Fig. 1.11): "Grant's hatred of the lion was a family joke, and even he smiled wryly about it. But as an artistic matter, it was also serious with him. When Mrs. Wood died, he showed how

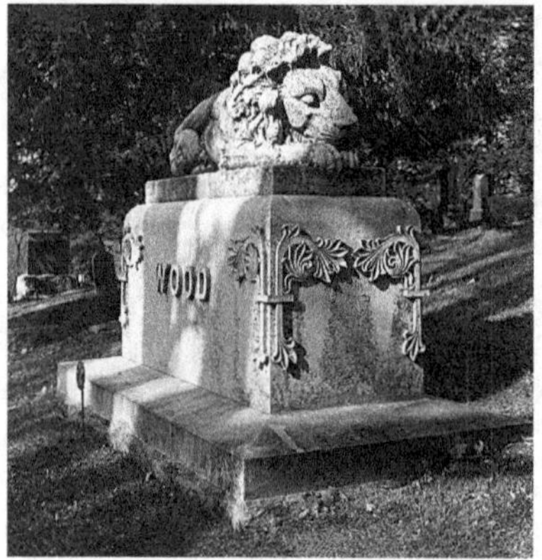

Fig. 1.11. Wood family monument in Riverside Cemetery, Anamosa, Iowa.

serious it was. In his grief over her loss it became fixed in his mind that there was still one thing he could do: he wouldn't let his mother be buried in the Wood family cemetery lot, not while that lion was there."[50] Wood's contempt for the monument, which had been proudly installed by his paternal uncle Clarence, seems bizarre. To the disinterested viewer, the recumbent lion appears quite benign, and one suspects that Wood associated this dormant king of beasts with his father, whose remains repose nearby. In "Return from Bohemia," Wood remembered how fascinated he was as a child by the "strange spectacle" of a lion, paired with a unicorn, on the verso of the family's dinner plates (App., 196). The venerable Royal Arms mark, used on both English Victoria and Early American ironstone, depicts the rampant lion and unicorn flanking a central shield topped by a crown. Little Wood observed this heraldic device daily, peeking at it during grace, and interpreted it inventively as a battle, pitting the ferociously sovereign animal against the fabulous creature of legend, famously timid but super-endowed with his phallic horn.

Transparently oedipal, the imaginary contest is a dangerous one, as child Wood is reminded in his story by big brother Frank (Francis Maryville Wood, Jr.), who steps in as their father's surrogate and predicts how the hungry lion "would make short work of that unicorn" (App., 196). Thus threatened, the shy boy/beast nonetheless continued to struggle for the crown, finally defeating the father in death. And the artistic problems Wood later claimed to have with the stone lion in the cemetery served as a convenient pretext for preventing his mother from being interred next to Maryville. He chose for Hattie a spot in the adjacent, maternal Weaver family section of the cemetery, to which no monument calls attention. Others in the family wanted her placed alongside her husband—"it seemed to them both customary and right"[51]—and the dispute escalated. Uncle Clarence went to the cemetery to intervene, Graham later recalled, demanding the gravedigger stop his work and prepare instead the Wood lot for Hattie, "and the gravedigger didn't know what to do."[52] Wood's feelings on the subject were so passionate that he was ultimately able to prevail. When he himself died on February 12, 1942, he was laid to rest by his mother's side (Fig. 1.12).[53]

In this arrangement, Wood maintained forever the proximity to Hattie he enjoyed throughout most of his life. He was never able to detach himself from her, to transfer his feelings to an appropriate love object, despite the pressures from his community. A column in the *Des Moines Sunday Register* on June 23, 1929, during a month of weddings, exemplifies the gentle social coercion applied to Wood from the time he came of age. Under the headline "There Have Been Brides and Brides but Bachelors Still Elude the Fair Sex," we find that "a topic of conversation at many tea tables and boudoir babbles is Grant Wood, Cedar Rapids artist. But he paints on and on and maintains a discreet silence about marriage." In his early twenties, according to Garwood, Wood "had no friends among girls and seldom spoke of women," and although "there were times when people thought he might marry, . . . there were no sound reasons for these expectations."[54] With such observations, Garwood coyly intimated what many knew about the artist's sexual orientation. More recently and candidly, Evans points out how living with and caring for Hattie provided a "sexual shield" for her son and excused his otherwise problematic bachelorhood in the eyes of his neighbors.[55] He was protected by his filial obligations. When Frances Prescott, the principal who hired Wood to teach at Jackson Junior High School following his military service in 1919, inquired if he would ever marry, he replied, "I don't think so, not while my mother is living."[56]

He was almost true to his word. At age forty-four, Wood suddenly wed Sara Sherman Maxon (Fig. 1.13), an actress and opera singer originally from Monticello, Iowa, with family in Cedar Rapids. On March 3, 1935, a small notice ran in the *New York Times* reporting the marriage of the well known artist on the prior evening in Minneapolis. Such matches made by

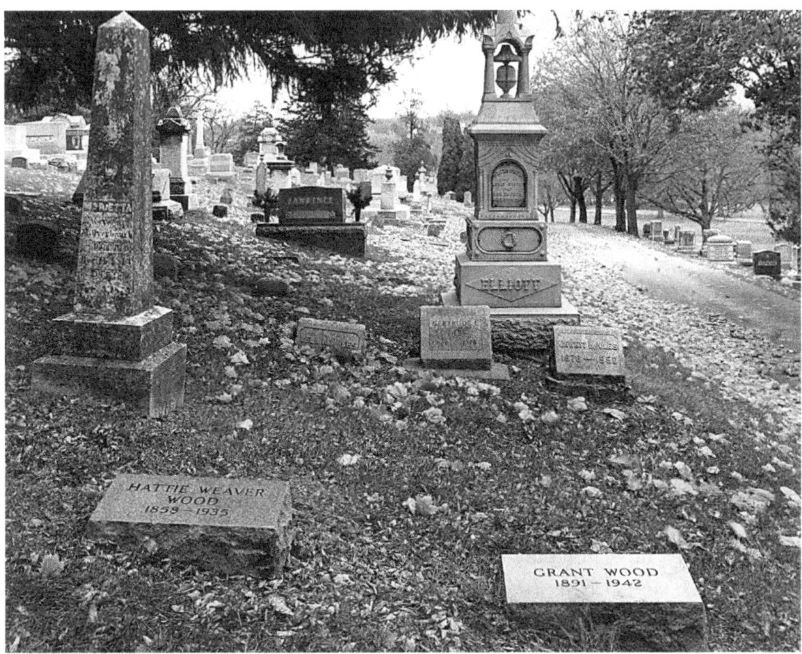

Fig. 1.12. Graves of Hattie Weaver Wood and Grant Wood, Riverside Cemetery, Anamosa, Iowa.

gay men were hardly unheard of during that period—the marriages of Jared French, Lincoln Kirstein, Cole Porter, and Carl van Vechten come to mind—and thanks to Evans's discovery of Sherman's unpublished memoir (she later dropped "Maxon," the name of her first husband), we can be certain that she was a sophisticated woman and fully aware of what she was undertaking. As a talented choral director, moreover, Sherman may have reminded Wood on some level of his own Aunt Sarah, whose name she shared. In "Return from Bohemia," he recalled his paternal aunt, "a determinedly literary woman" who read him Kipling and "even tried her own hand at writing" (App., 246), organizing delightful church socials, complete with floral decorations, Japanese lanterns, and musical performances. Aunt Sarah took Grant to his very first play, which even as an adult he thrilled to remember, at the opera house in Anamosa. Perhaps, too, there existed between Sherman and Wood an affinity of the sort that often informed relationships between actresses and gay men, indeed that drew them together—as performers, in art and in life, respectively, both types were necessarily skilled in artifice, concealment, and judicious disclosure. But for those in Cedar Rapids who were well acquainted with Wood, the partnership was an odd and truly unexpected development; his friends (and hers) cautioned against it. Breaking the news to his mother and sister, Wood listed Sherman's qualifications in ascending order: she was an artist, would be a gracious hostess, and "fits in with you two."[57]

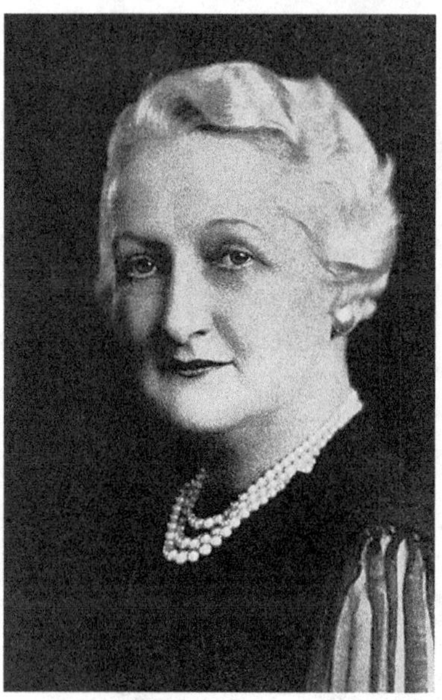

Fig. 1.13. Sara Sherman Wood, 1939.

COPING WITH DISASTER

It seems to me that Wood was propelled into this relationship at least in part by panic over his mother's failing health. Hattie was still seriously ill when Wood decided to marry Sherman, who nursed his mother for several months until the end. Fearing Hattie's imminent demise, Wood sought someone to take her place in his life. The maternal Sherman was more than seven years his senior,[58] taller than he, white-haired, with a grown son by a previous marriage and a grandchild. But there was more at stake for Wood than duplicating with Sherman, as he certainly hoped to do, the idealized and sexless bond he had with his mother. In advance of the inevitably traumatic and final separation from Hattie, he made an attempt through his marriage to individuate from her. He was already in mourning, a complex psychic process in which, according to Klein, "the greatest danger for the mourner comes from the turning of his hatred against the lost loved person himself." This unconscious hatred arises from the grieving person's fear that the loved one has retaliated against him for his secret resentments, dying in order "to inflict punishment and deprivation upon him."[59] There may then have been an element of acting out against Hattie in Wood's move to marry, and she was indeed injured: "Wiping away a tear," Graham recalled of her long-suffering mother, "she told me, 'Grant has been so wonderful to us—his happiness comes first. . . . We mustn't stand in the way, and we will pray that the marriage works out.'"[60] The ill-starred union, though, lasted less than three years; Wood and Sherman separated in 1938 and divorced in 1939.

Wood created only one painting in 1935, the year Hattie died, the unusually dark *Death on the Ridge Road* (Fig. 1.14), a work always interpreted as a Regionalist critique of modern technological incursions on rural life, but surely, in addition to this, a premonition of the artist's own personal disaster in the impending loss of his mother. Wood's Regionalist manifesto, *Revolt against the City*, appeared that year, penned with his colleague Frank Luther Mott, a professor in the English department at the University of Iowa. Acknowledged in the pamphlet are changes wrought to the farmer's experience by the introduction of the automobile, radio, paved roads, and railroads, but there is no hint in the essay of the sense of doom that pervades *Death on the Ridge Road*.[61] With its dark green palette and brooding shadows, the picture is probably the eeriest image Wood created, its formal elements brilliantly supporting its calamitous content. The red hue of the speeding truck, the only warm color in the composition, signals danger while attracting the viewer's eye. Framed by storm clouds and silhouetted against the treeless horizon at the apex of the hill, the truck bears down on a hearse-like blue-black town car, as angled utility poles appear to recoil in horror from the looming collision. Stark contrasts of light and dark heighten the dramatic intensity of the rural scene, a modern American reprise of that chilling, age-old admonition about human mortality, *Et in Arcadia Ego* (meaning that death lurks even in the idyllic countryside).

Scholars have effectively elucidated Wood's painting and called attention to its unique position within his oeuvre: it is his only overtly tragic image. In discussions of *Death on the Ridge Road* as a social metaphor, Corn points out the significance of the ridge road, created by pioneers in wagons who chose the high ground to avoid mud and slush, but precarious to travel once it was paved over for high-speed motor traffic in the twentieth century. Anedith Nash cites a national concern in the 1930s over increasingly frequent highway accidents.[62] Indeed, a cluster of actual crashes fueled Wood's personal interest in the theme. The first and most serious occurred in August 1933 on Ridge Road north of Stone City, involving the artist's poet

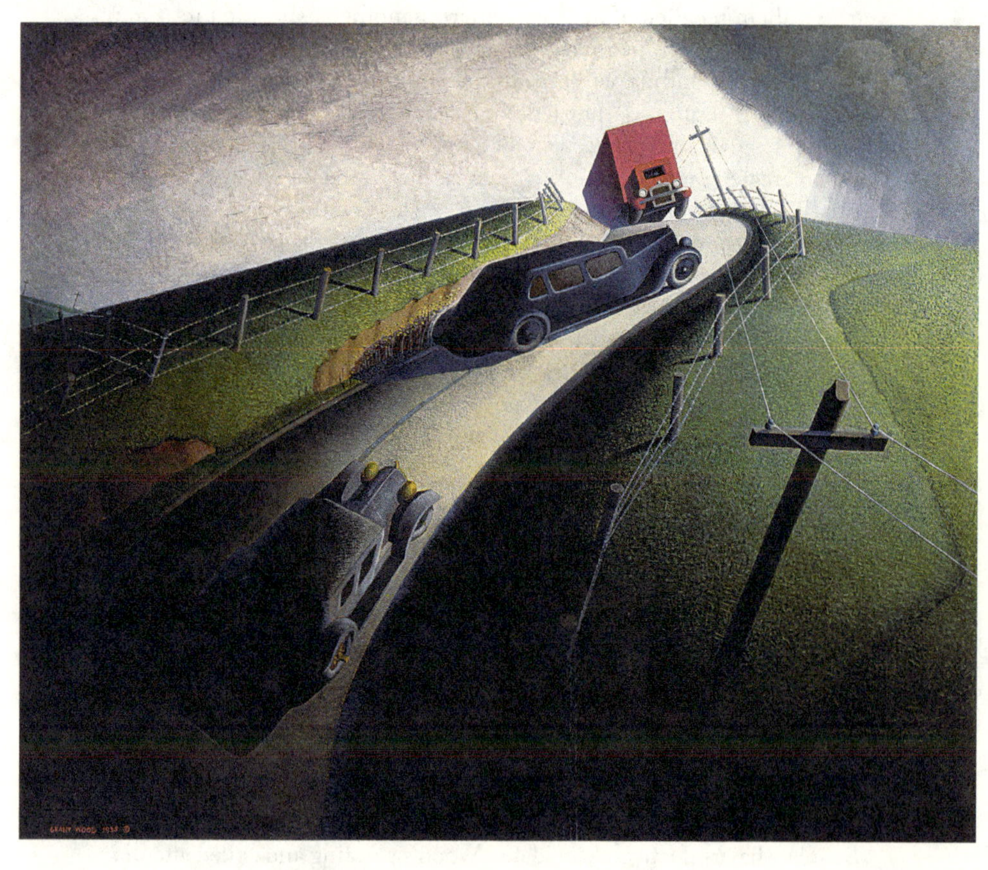

Fig. 1.14. Grant Wood, *Death on the Ridge Road*, 1935.

friend Jay Sigmund and his family. The Sigmunds were en route from their home in Waubeek to visit Wood at the Stone City summer art colony he had founded the previous year. In one account, "a car tried to pass them just as a truck came over a hill. Jim Sigmund [the poet's son] was driving, and swerved to miss but got sideswiped, rolling the car over."[63] Although Jim and his two sisters escaped injury, their parents were hospitalized, Louise with several broken ribs and Jay with his right hand so badly mauled that his index finger had to be amputated.[64] Wood rushed to the scene, likely arriving after the victims had been removed, but "the vivid images of the accident remained with him."[65] The following summer, Wood himself acquired a car, and within weeks both he and his young friend Arnold Pyle had "banged it up," according to Garwood, with Pyle at one point crashing into a milk truck in downtown Cedar Rapids.[66]

So it was in 1934 that the artist created the large pencil-and-chalk drawing *Death on the Ridge Road* (private collection), sometime in late fall or winter, I suspect, inspired by the publication of Sigmund's grim verse in the October issue of *American Poetry Magazine*, "Death Rides a Rubber-Shod Horse":

A pale grey ribbon of cement
Rippled along the jutting hill,
And down its silken course there went
The horse Death rode when out to kill.

A rubber-footed silvered steed,
Needing no impact from a lash;
An eagle's grace; a greyhound's speed—
Two glassy eyes to burn and flash.

Love in the saddle; Death to guide
This devil-horse of steel and brass:
Death riding down the countryside
Supplied with lances made of glass.

Death used to ride a white-maned horse
Before these grey roads lined the sod,
But now he travels on his course
Astride a sleek thing, rubber-shod.[67]

Clearly Sigmund brooded over his experience, constantly reminded of the accident by his mutilated hand, and though no one had died, the event shocked him with a fatal threat to himself and those he loved. His transmutation of mortal fear into a work of art provided a model for Wood, whose finished painting went on view at the Ferargil Galleries in New York on April 15, 1935. Corn notices the resemblance of the utility poles in the painting to funereal crosses, as does Evans, who associates the content of this image with Wood's "oldest trauma—the sudden death of his father—as well as the escalating, and equally unresolved, anxieties of his adult life."[68] Among those anxieties must have been the realization that Hattie would not live much longer. Her ill health could never have been far from Wood's consciousness at this time, as he worried for her, and for himself.

The second car in *Death on the Ridge Road* will be a witness to the destruction of the first, and will certainly not escape collateral damage from the crash. In this regard, it seems to me significant that although he had seen the aftermath of the Sigmunds' accident, with its two cars and a truck, Wood selected a moment *before* the crash for his picture. At the same time, in assigning its title he was unambiguous about the imagined outcome of his suspenseful scene. The quality of frightened anticipation that haunts the painting echoes the artist's own emotional condition during his mother's final illness. Complicating matters further, automobiles were the preoccupation of both of his brothers (Frank the battery salesman, Jack the mechanic). As Wood worked on his picture, Jack was also dying; he attended his mother's funeral in mid-October, then succumbed to tuberculosis on December 20, 1935.

THE ARTIST TRIUMPHANT

Return from Bohemia (Fig. 1.15), Wood's handsome illustration in crayon, gouache, and pencil for the cover of the autobiography on which he and Rinard were still working, also dates to that fateful year. Compositionally, the image recalls *American Gothic*, with foreground figures pressed close to the picture plane and an architectural backdrop indicating a farm, in this case a red barn. Here, instead of the pitchfork, or the phallic sansevieria in *Woman with Plants*, palette and brush become the distinctive attributes, with Wood himself seated before his canvas as the center of attention and a group of country folk gathered quietly around him, their heads solemnly bowed. Corn has characterized the drawing as "a conundrum not unlocked by the one statement we have by the artist about a work of this subject," his announcement to the *Cedar Rapids Gazette* in 1931 of plans for a self-portrait with "the usual loafing bystanders who find time to watch an artist sketching faces with contempt, scorn and an I-know-I-could-do-it-better look."[69] For his cover illustration, Wood transformed the "loafing bystanders" into reverent onlookers. But curiously, with their downcast eyes, these witnesses seem blind; Corn reasonably proposes that the image is "a general treatise about the artist and his public, a relationship fraught with misunderstanding and tension."[70] His public in Iowa included dedicated patrons whose proud support was crucial to his career and his legacy, as well as cantankerous critics, often ignorant of art, who kept him explaining and backpedaling at every turn.

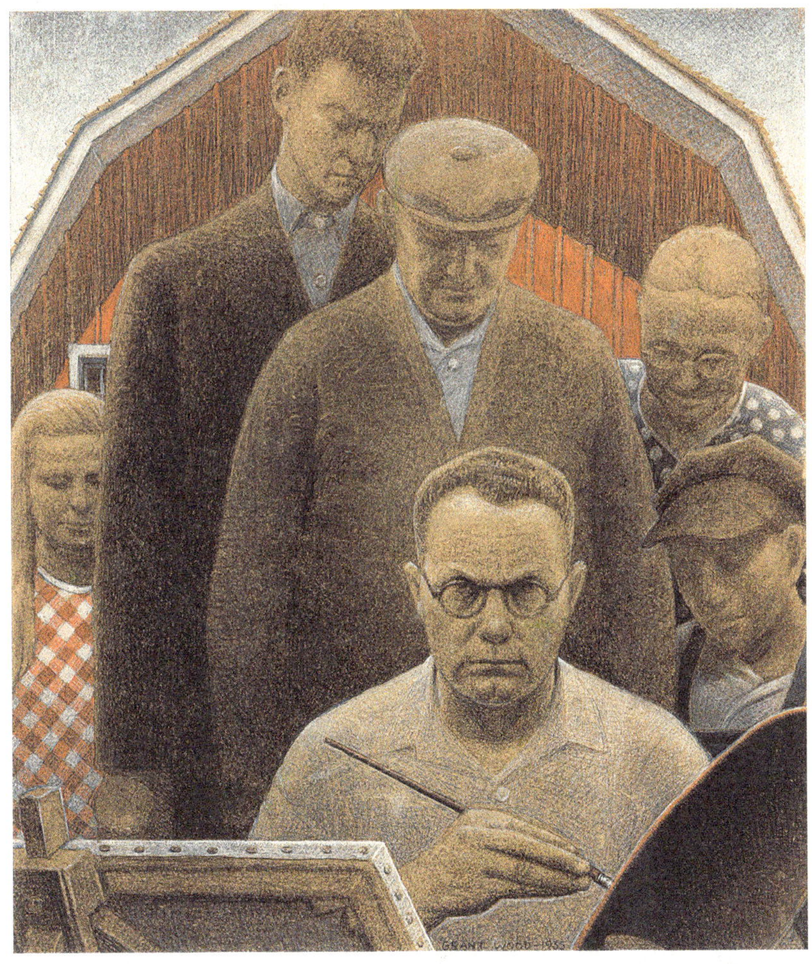

Fig. 1.15. Grant Wood, *Return from Bohemia*, 1935.

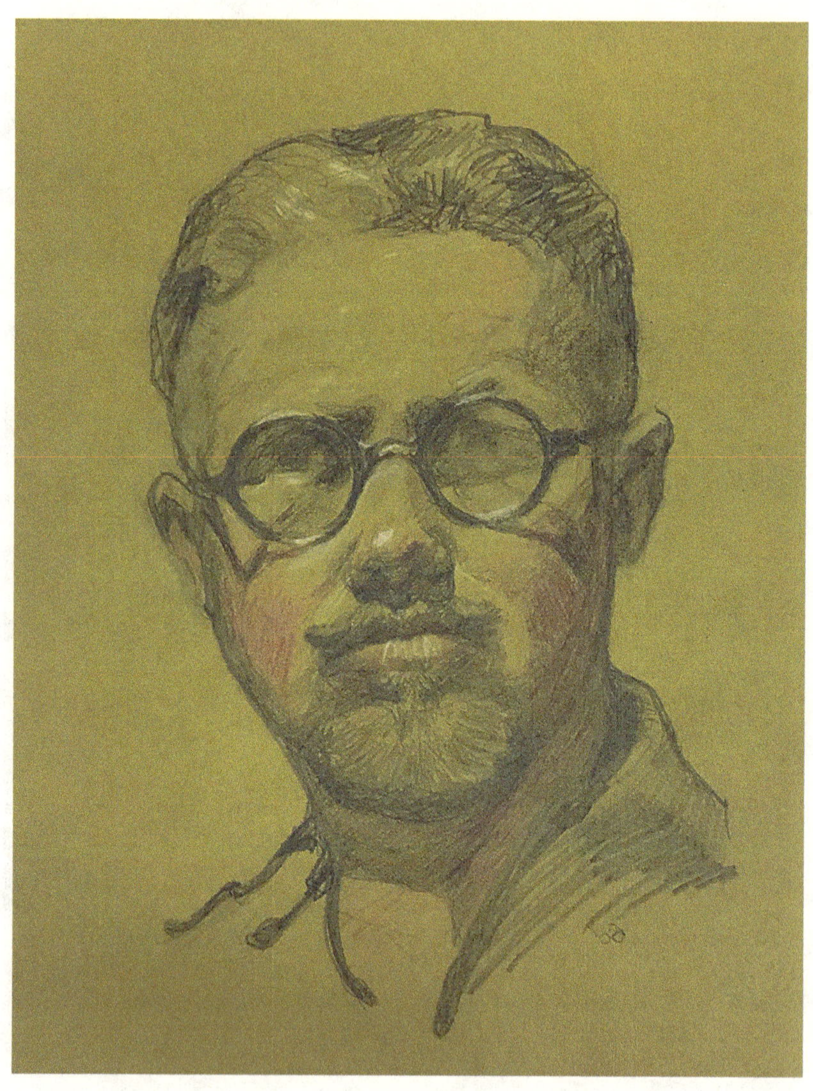

Fig. 1.16. Grant Wood, *Self-Portrait Sketch*, 1920.

The legend Wood promoted about himself hinged on his conversion to Regionalism, his "return from Bohemia," from European decadence and arcane aesthetics in favor of his true Midwestern culture. He had traveled to Paris in 1920, 1923, and 1926, practicing an Impressionist painting style and adopting a libertine lifestyle, but, like the biblical Prodigal Son, was soon to realize the error of his ways. The later Munich trip, during which he paid his formative visits to the Alte Pinakothek, represented a defining moment for him: in Weimar Germany, as Evans suggests, he was confronted with a very visible and vibrant homosexual society—from which he seems to have recoiled.[71] *Return from Bohemia* situates him squarely back in his original milieu. It is a pictorial manifesto of his determined commitment to his art and to his Iowa roots. When the *New York Herald Tribune* reproduced the drawing in January 1936 to announce the forthcoming autobiography, Wood colored his conversion myth with typical beguiling humor:

> I lived in Paris a couple of years myself and grew a very spectacular beard that didn't match my face or my hair, and read Mencken and was convinced that the Middle West was inhibited and barren. But I came back because I learned that French painting is very fine for French people and not necessarily for us, and because I started out to analyze what it was that I really knew. . . . I realized that all the really good ideas I'd ever had came to me while I was milking a cow. So I went back to Iowa.[72]

Corn perceptively observes that in the drawing Wood sports the tortoise-shell glasses he had affected in his Paris period (Fig. 1.16, where he also uses the glasses as a tiny signature device) rather than the wire rim glasses he adopted by 1932 (see Introduction, opposite p. 1). From this anomalous detail, she proposes that *Return from Bohemia* may represent "a compression of time," and Evans too notes how the group of onlookers seems "chronologically misaligned," with, in his view, its two female figures representing Nan as a child and Hattie as septuagenarian, and the men behind the artist representing Wood's contemporaries, the directors of, respectively, the Little Gallery and Turner Mortuary in Cedar Rapids, Ed Rowan and David Turner.[73] It does appear that Wood conflates childhood and adulthood in this picture, for it seems to me striking that the figures surrounding Wood at his easel correspond precisely to the members of his immediate family, three of whom were, or were about to be, ghosts in 1935. From left to right in this interpretation stand little girl Nan, in the favorite red gingham pattern she wore throughout her life; brother Frank, five years older than Grant; a father figure; an aging mother in a polka-dotted, rickrack-trimmed dress, wearing glasses like Wood; and boy Jack. As in *American Gothic*, these are not so much portraits in the sense of physical resemblance as they are images that arise out of psychological conflict and lend the picture the very puzzling quality that impressed Corn.

The sense of exclusion so pronounced in *American Gothic* is overturned in *Return from Bohemia* as Wood inserts himself—signature emblazoned just below his chest—at the center, displacing the parents to the background and commanding homage from the entire family. The scene is reminiscent of Joseph's narcissistic premonition in Genesis, when he dreamed his brothers would bow down to him, and later realized his princely ambition in Egypt. Through his success as an artist, Wood is similarly vindicated, the family penitent. Grasping his paintbrush, *he* has power, the phallus. He sits while they stand, his expression, brows knit from glancing up at himself in the mirror, seems stern while they are humbled. The principals in this rectification of power relations are the rival males; father and brothers are closest to the artist and to the picture plane, with mother and sister relegated to the sides and background. However, with their downcast eyes, there is something about Wood *all* of them refuse to see (his homosexuality). When Wood spoke of plans to depict bystanders who "watch an artist sketching faces with contempt," he assigned that contempt ambiguously—it could be theirs or his, or both theirs and his. In the drawing, contempt is repressed, disguised as artistic gravitas as Wood turns his back on the family group to focus on his painting.

Negative feelings for his father and brothers had to remain unconscious, as they appear also to have been in the autobiography itself, where Wood, though recounting the births of Frank and himself in Chapter 1 and of Nan in Chapter 3, forgets even to mention the arrival of Jack, who shows up out of nowhere in Chapter 2 as a talking toddler in his high chair. Grant is given the responsibility of looking after him, and Wood masked fratricidal fantasies in relating several mishaps involving this younger sibling (App., 220). Jack "had a habit," we are told, of disappearing, "of wandering into some out of the way place and falling sound asleep"—dying? Indeed, Grant's little charge often went missing: "After a frantic search, we were sure to find him asleep in an old, abandoned buggy; out along the fence-row; or even in the outhouse"—where he belonged? Later, old enough to accompany Grant to school, Jack eats poison sumac berries along the route. "I turned just in time," Wood reported with irritation and apparent relief, ignoring his own lack of vigilance for his brother's welfare (App., 255). If Grant had resented being his brother's keeper, one wonders whether he somehow helped precipitate Jack's flight from the home as a teenager. He penned the vignettes of baby Jack sleeping/expiring or in danger in "Return from Bohemia" at the very time that the adult Jack was dying of tuberculosis. In this tragic scenario, we are reminded of how, according to Klein, infantile death wishes against parents, brothers, or sisters, though long repressed, are actually fulfilled when one of them dies, so that the death, "however shattering for other reasons, is to some extent also felt as a victory, and gives rise to triumph, and therefore all the more to guilt."[74]

A sense of triumph pervades the drawing *Return from Bohemia*, where the artist humbles and upstages everyone, all of them representatives of his earliest important figures. Reuniting them—the living, the dead, and the dying—in this image, Wood affirmed their profound psychological significance to him, including even Frank and Jack from whom he was so distant in reality. The brothers' estrangement in adulthood suggests then, more than simple indifference, lingering hostility rooted in a competitive and strained sibling dynamic, an unbreachable split between hetero- and homosexual masculinities, and, perhaps above all, a fragmented nuclear family torn apart by the death of the father.

RETURN TO CHILDHOOD

"Return from Bohemia" was to comprise three parts, describing Wood's childhood in Anamosa, his travels to Europe and early Impressionist-inspired artistic activities, and his enlightened maturity as a Regionalist.[75] The overall tripartite plan as well as a number of episodic similarities suggest to me that Wood may have had in mind Regionalist writer Hamlin Garland's autobiography, *A Son of the Middle Border* (1917), as a model. A generation older than Wood, Garland grew up on farms in Wisconsin, Minnesota, and Iowa; his personal bildungsroman recounts, over the course of thirty-five chapters, his boyhood life on the farm, his wanderings and education, and finally his self-discovery as a writer and poet. But in Wood's case, with part one of his autobiography finished, the project stalled. Despite the indispensable assistance of Rinard, the contract Wood had signed with Doubleday Doran to publish the book was never fulfilled.[76]

There were certainly practical reasons for this. Wood's teaching responsibilities at the university may have left insufficient time for writing, and he was much in demand on the lecture circuit. Garwood cynically believed that "the book dragged on for years" because the factual details of an autobiography conflicted with the myth Wood had already created: "Such a dramatized version of his life is often part of an artist-lecturer's stock in trade. It didn't seem a good idea to debunk himself, especially since the commonly accepted story was the peg on which the book was hung."[77] My own suspicion is that Wood's interest in the project waned once the narrative foundation of his childhood had been laid, and Rinard could not proceed without the artist's full engagement. At a certain juncture, Wood and Rinard had shortened the title of the book-in-progress to "Return," I think to de-emphasize *whence* the artist was returning and implicitly to stress instead the goal of his return—his origins. His return trajectory was, funnel-like, to America, the Midwest, Iowa, his family, his parents. "When Wood was trying to recall exactly how it was that he changed," Garwood writes, "he told of returning from Paris, fed up with all the fine talk and useless gesturing connected with his one-man show [at the Galerie Carmine in 1926], and of seeing his mother in the doorway. And the thought that then crossed his mind was: 'This is the thing.'"[78] Wood did not return to his roots in his art simply "out of a nostalgic desire to record the fading [American] past, but," as Kuspit has suggested, "out of a personal desire to recapture his own childhood, which in fact he never escaped."[79] The failure of Wood's autobiography parallels his failure to resolve and integrate his ambivalent, compartmentalized relationships and the innocent illusions of his youth.

Reviewing the major retrospective exhibition organized by Corn in 1983, Kuspit concluded that Wood "never fully achieved personal autonomy, remaining throughout his life thoroughly influenced by his mother and father."[80] In painting Hattie's portrait in 1929, Wood consciously publicized his filial devotion; in this work, as well as in *American Gothic* and *Return from Bohemia*, his complex emotions obscured, arguably even to himself, the fundamental content of his work. That he was only dimly aware of these pictures as family documents is evinced in his dying wish to create a portrait of Maryville. Hospitalized for several months before his demise from pancreatic cancer in 1942, the ailing Wood, as Corn notes, "wrestled with his father's psychological presence":

> In his final illness, the artist talked to several bedside callers about wanting to paint his father's portrait as a companion piece to *Woman with Plants*. . . . He had never before talked about painting his father; only when he sensed that his illness was fatal could he approach this painful topic. He would use, he said, his memories and family photographs to make his portrait. Though Wood died before he could execute the work, his final thoughts were to capture the archetypal Midwesterner one more time and to put a difficult personal matter to rest.[81]

If for Wood, as for Milner, "one of the functions of painting was surely the restoring and re-creating externally what one had loved and internally hurt or destroyed,"[82] then his last creative desire was to make amends to his father, perhaps ultimately to repay him for the gift of life by immortalizing him in art. He had done this for Hattie in *Woman with Plants*, the painting he considered his most enduring work. Although it proved too late for him in his last days to render the same homage to Maryville, Wood had in a sense already realized his dying wish, years earlier, in *American Gothic*, albeit in disguised or distorted form. Ironically, the disgruntled Iowa viewer who in 1930 had dubbed the glum painting "Return from the Funeral" grasped something of its unconscious meaning for Wood.[83] He had been unable fully to accept his father's death, which still haunted him even as he faced his own.

Picturing Maryville's funeral in "Return from Bohemia," Wood remembered how numbed and disbelieving he had been as a boy who was supposed to grieve.

> At last the minister arose to give the funeral sermon. . . .
>
> I listened but could not realize he was talking about my father in that hollow voice. He was talking about someone far away whom I had never known, someone

who had died. . . . Presently I was crying, but it was because I was tired and frightened, not because I realized my father was dead and that I should mourn. They had told me what had happened all right; that father had been called to heaven and would not come back in this life. I had heard the words and repeated them. I was very brave about it, they said. But inwardly I had not understood. Nor did I know [App., 269].[84]

More than twenty years would pass before Wood resurrected his father as the dolorous farmer-preacher in the celebrated masterpiece of his artistic career. Psychologically, *American Gothic* may be interpreted as an example of what Freud called *Nachträglichkeit*, or belated response, to *the* traumatic event of the artist's youth. The success of the painting has at least something to do with its lengthy gestation in his mind and the depth and intricacy of emotion that called it into being. In a compelling, unsettling vision of the Midwestern couple he consciously considered "the salt of the earth," Wood grappled with unresolved primal conflicts at odds with his idealized fairytale version of his upbringing and its cultural context. That myth was the massive defense he erected against his own buried feelings of emotional deprivation, even of victimization, hostility, guilt, and grief. Yet in the brilliance of his art, he revealed a glimmer of truth: how his professed and very real fondness for his regional subjects could never be straightforward in the manner of someone like Ingerle, whose disinterested celebration of plain folk exudes affection pure and simple. Infused with ambivalence, both love and dread, *American Gothic* fulfilled a psychic need for Wood and embodied a personal philosophy of art. "He spoke with contempt," Garwood asserted, "of self-conscious technical exercises, peeled off the top layer of experience. He didn't think you could paint a picture unless it was based on something you had felt for a long time, something rooted in earlier years. It took that long for feeling to develop in him."[85]

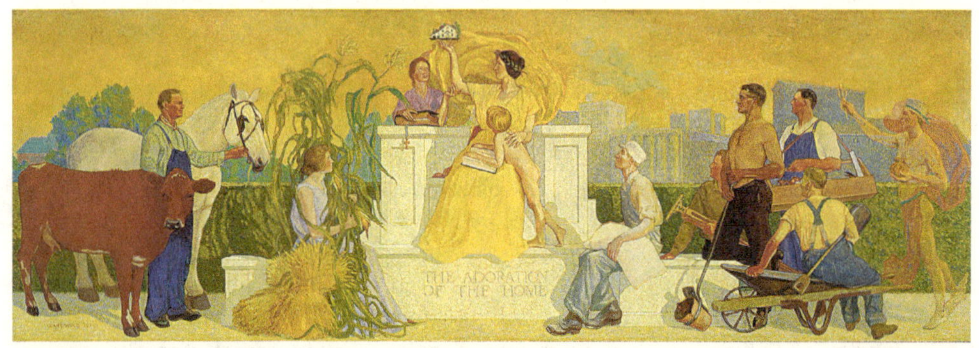

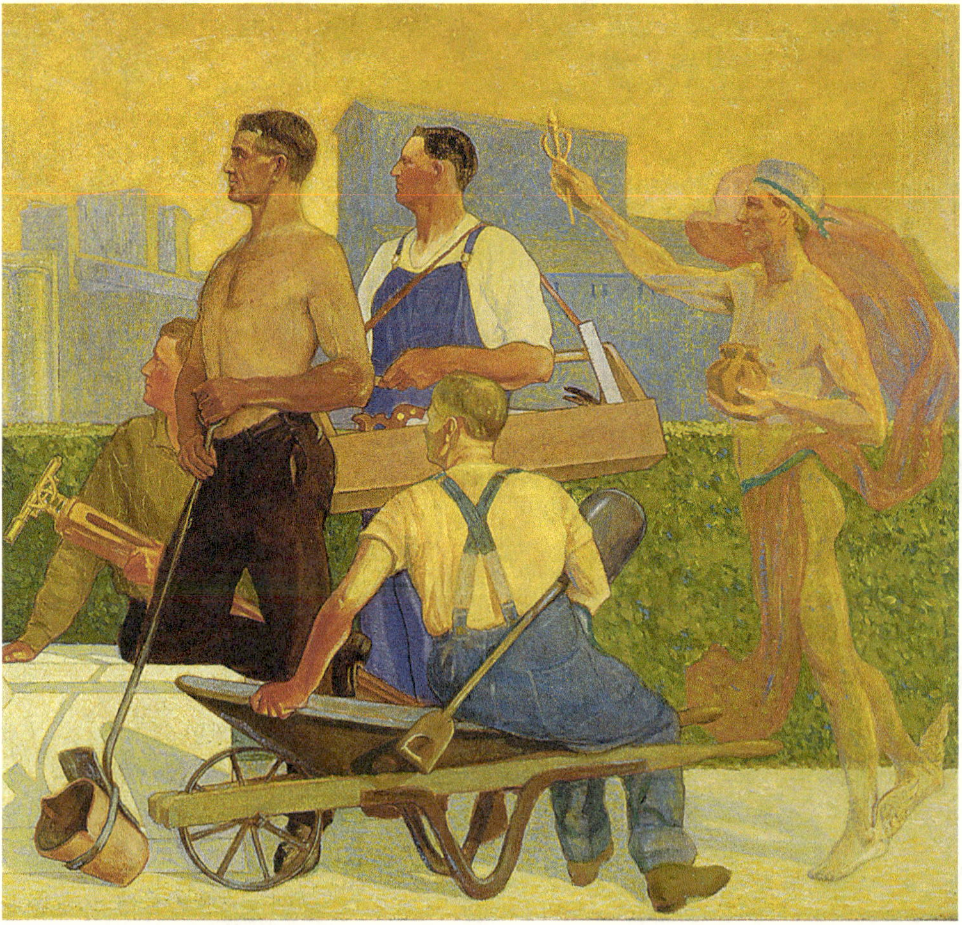

Figs. 2.1 (top) and 2.1A (detail, above). Grant Wood, *Adoration of the Home*, 1921–22.

❖ CHAPTER 2 ❖

Fear and Desire

FOR HALF A CENTURY after Grant Wood's death in 1942, his sexuality remained off-limits in formal discussions of his art and life, due in no small measure to his sister's energetic efforts to manage his myth. The silence also signaled scholars' reluctance to address a topic that many considered irrelevant and that most realized was fundamentally unknowable. As art history itself opened as a discipline to new and ever richer forms of inquiry, however, Wood scholarship also took on a more interesting cast. In 1990, observing that "historians of American art often said (but never wrote) that Grant Wood had been a homosexual," Alan Wallach explored how such a possibility "might account for qualities in his art that set it apart from the work of other Regionalist painters."[1] Wallach suggested that homophobic attitudes in the 1930s had rendered Wood an outsider amidst the hypermasculine posturing of his artist contemporaries, imbuing his work with a double-edged vision—both boosterish *and* satirical—of Midwestern life. Less sympathetically, in a survey of American art published in 1997, critic Robert Hughes pronounced Wood "a timid and deeply closeted homosexual" whose work seemed "an exercise in sly camp."[2] Close on the heels of this assertion, John Seery offered a nuanced and penetrating assessment of Wood as "a self-betraying ironist," concluding, like Wallach, that the artist's sexual orientation and gender nonconformity might be linked to unresolved ambivalences apparent in many of his paintings, including *American Gothic*.[3]

In 2000, Henry Adams provided documentary evidence for what these and other scholars had intuited from Wood's work, discovering in his personnel file at the University of Iowa how fellow faculty trying to undermine him in the art department had stated baldly in 1941 that "Grant Wood was a homosexual" who maintained a "strange relationship with his publicity agent," namely, Park Rinard.[4] Relying as well on oral histories passed down by individuals who knew the artist, Adams went on to examine themes of social disapproval and possible homoerotic meanings in Wood's pictures. This fresh line of investigation culminated in R. Tripp Evans's truly transformational biography *Grant Wood: A Life* (2010), in which the artist's sexual orientation is candidly acknowledged and thoroughly considered for its ramifications in his personal relationships and in his oeuvre. In light of Evans's revelations, which include the sensitive, firsthand insights of the artist's wife, it is hardly possible any longer to disregard this aspect of Wood's experience in his particular social milieu and at his particular historical moment—in Iowa during the first half of the twentieth century. Looking back in her unpublished memoir on Wood's career nearly two decades after his death, Sara Sherman drew a parallel between her erstwhile husband and Oscar Wilde, whose genius, she asserted, the world still recognized despite "the reason . . . behind his final degradation."[5] Although many in Wood's community had been happy to accommodate the artist's "eccentricities," the campaign waged against him at the university during the last few years of his life, which took a heavy toll on his emotional well-being, evinces the kind of difficulty he must have encountered frequently during his career, compounded by the psychological effects of his severe upbringing. Turning a blind eye to these issues risks reducing Wood's art, as Adams cautioned, "to a kind of blandness that is not very interesting"[6] and, even more problematically, performs a kind of erasure in which homosexual experience and desire are deemed without significance or meaning.[7]

What then, we may ask, was the nature of Wood's desire? Given his apparently incomplete individuation/separation from his mother posited in Chapter 1, it is conceivable that he was never entirely comfortable with sexual intimacy, that his famous self-described "return" was a flight not just from Bohemia but also from a homosexuality he could not fulfill. His journalist friend MacKinlay Kantor, a neighbor in Cedar Rapids when Wood lived with Hattie at 5 Turner Alley, was perhaps quite earnest in his allusion to the artist's withdrawal from the sexual realm, in a colorful prose portrait of the "stubby man with high bald forehead and scrubby pink hair receding from the crown":

> He wore the thick glasses of the forever myopic, and behind them his eyes leaped like bright caged birds. His forearms were covered with hair of the same tint that shone on his head, and they were thick and muscular, suggestive of calm power and virility. . . . Virility in the sexual sense he did not admit or practice. He told me in after years how the whole sexual problem was a closed book to him, and why. It was a secret which I retain. People who did not know him well, and read about him or met him casually during the term of his greatest achievement, whispered that he was a homosexual. He was nothing of the kind. He was simply asexual—withdrawn by inclination, habit and choice from such emolument.[8]

This seems a rare and intimate account indeed. However, Kantor, in offering this denial, may have been colluding with his friend to cover up the actual state of affairs, or serving as an unwitting pawn in Wood's defensive manipulations. It is impossible to know, an irreducible conundrum. Whether secretly active or frustrated and unrealized, though, the artist's homosexuality has interpretive consequences. Most importantly, societal reactions to it put him in a hard place, making him vulnerable to homosexual blackmail as Evans has posited,[9] and, on a profound level, producing the double consciousness Wallach perceived, while necessitating all manner of pretense and masquerade.

MALE BODIES, FEMALE ABSTRACTIONS

Additionally, on the level of subject matter, there is a conspicuous asymmetry in Wood's respective treatments of female and male bodies, suggesting a certain anxiety and phobic avoidance of the one and a loving appreciation of the other. In two ambitious commissions he undertook in Cedar Rapids in the 1920s, for instance, where the sexes are brought together to support an allegorical program, he arrayed the female figures in decorous robes and presented the more numerous male figures both clothed as representative types and, as Evans notes, "in rather arresting states of undress."[10] In the eleven-foot-long advertising panel *Adoration of the Home* (1921–22, Fig. 2.1), painted for the local real estate developer Henry Ely, the boy nude, the burly, bare-chested foundry man, and the balletic Mercury, naked except for his long flowing loincloth, are notable examples. Mercury, less fey and animated than his prototype in Giambologna's sixteenth-century statuette,[11] is here given a money purse and stands for Commerce. The women, too, are allegorical abstractions: Agriculture with her stalks of corn and sheaves of wheat, Cedar Rapids holding the emblematic house aloft, and Religion with her Bible, figures modeled respectively by Wood's sister, a cousin, and the wife of a friend. In their timeless pastel-colored gowns, the three feminine personifications are of a different temporal order than their manly fellows in the picture. The laboring men *do* what they represent, whether milling, carpentry, animal husbandry, or civil engineering,[12] whereas the women have no existence apart from their merely symbolic roles.

Again in the monumental Veterans *Memorial Window* (1928, Fig. 2.2), Wood applied the formula of woman as ethereal abstraction with men as corporeal presences. The iconography of this civic memorial—a testament to Wood's capacious talent, for he had never before worked in stained glass or at such a large scale[13]—is altogether in keeping with its brief to honor soldiers of past U.S. conflicts. At the base of the window, from left to right, are representatives of the American War of Independence; the War of 1812; the Mexican-American, Civil, and Spanish-American Wars; and World War I or, at that time, the Great War. The giant figure of Peace, floating above them amidst the clouds, displays the symbolic palm of martyrdom in her right hand and the wreath of victory in her left. Nan Wood Graham posed for this celestial apparition, and she recorded the names of the young men who

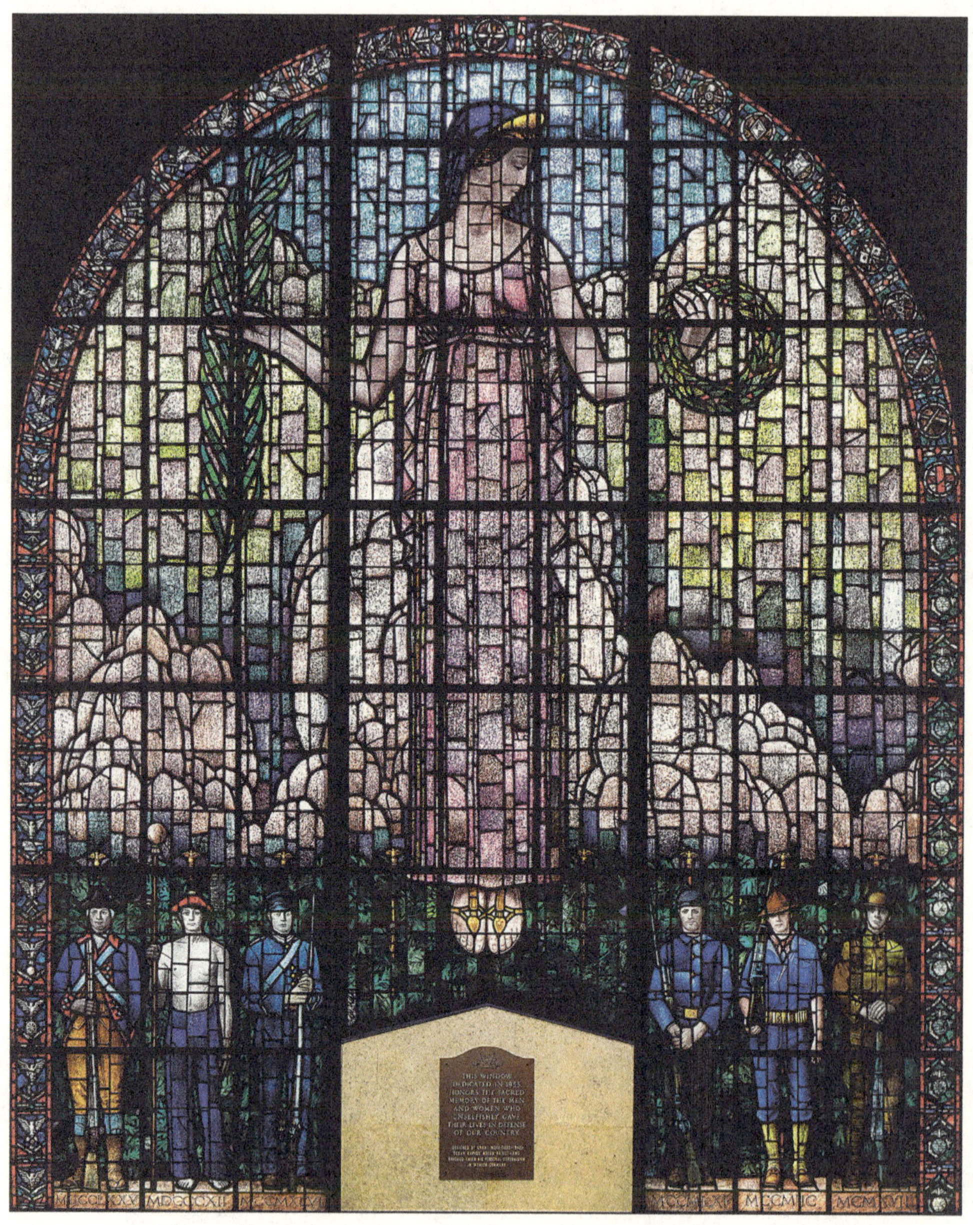

Fig. 2.2. Grant Wood (designer), *Memorial Window*, 1928–29.

modeled for the mortal soldiers—Thomas, Sam, David, Butch, Johnny, Jacob, and also one Harry Robinson, all former students of the artist.[14] Although it is difficult to discern Graham's features in the generalized classical profile of Peace, the men are individualized, both in the window itself and more so in the full-scale drawings Wood made in preparation for it. Anomalous among this rank of uniformed comrades, from revolutionary to doughboy, is the 1812 cannoneer, second from the left on the window. He is barefoot and shirtless, and in the preparatory cartoon for the window (Fig. 2.3) even provocative, with a smooth-muscled body and pliant, clinging, bell-bottomed pants with a suggestively bulging fly. He is a sailor whose distant ancestor in art Evans recognized as the noble Doryphoros, or Spear Bearer, by Polykleitos from the fifth century BCE.[15]

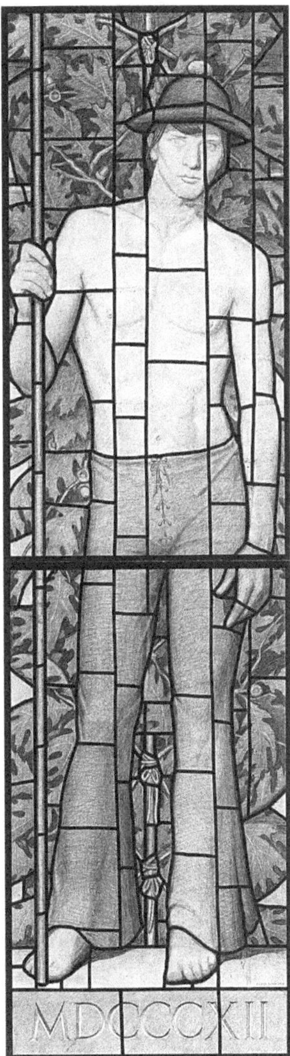

Fig. 2.3. Grant Wood, *Soldier in the War of 1812*, 1927.

But Wood's cannoneer does not hold a spear—nor a musket, bayonet, or rifle like the other figures with him on the window. His attribute is not even a weapon at all but an implement used to clean the cannon bore, comprised of a sponge wrapped in lambskin and tied at one end of a long staff. In a line of military men with firearms, the cannoneer instead wields a benign probe. A veritable emblem of the figure's alterity, the tall sponge protrudes over the top of the screen of oak leaves behind the soldiers, and he holds it like a scepter. Wood oversaw the manufacture of the window in Munich at Emil Frei Art Glass, working closely for three months with the craftsmen there;[16] they may have helped him with color choices that worked best in stained glass while supporting the content of his image. The cannoneer's hat seems an inversion of the traditional French sailor's white beret with red pom-pom, and his pants are royal blue. These hues link him nicely to the brightly dressed revolutionary to his right, and the more one considers the two figures together, the more they form a colorful pair apart from the lighter blue- and brown-uniformed rank. They may have a further distinction, moreover, as secret avatars: Jane Milosch has noticed in the cannoneer "a curious resemblance to Arnold Pyle, Wood's Cedar Rapids assistant for the project," with "the Revolutionary War soldier [looking] suspiciously like Wood himself."[17]

A presentist reading evoking the perpetual if unacknowledged and tenuous presence of gays in the military might seem pure projection, but Wood's own

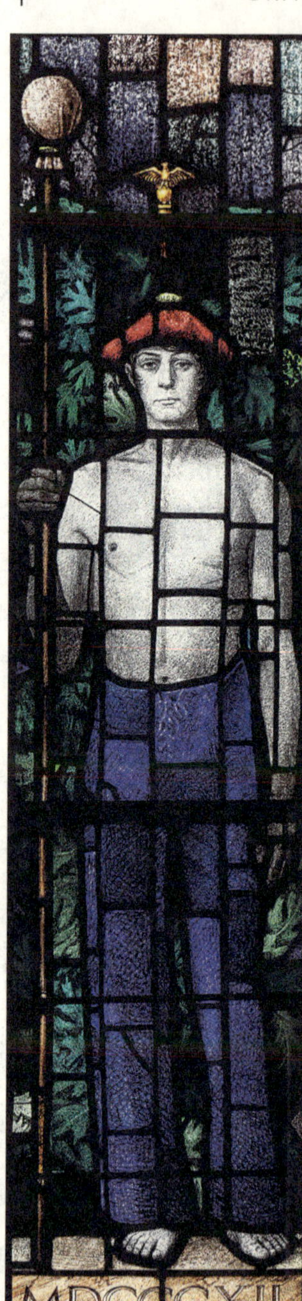

Fig. 2.4 (left). A mahlstick.

Fig. 2.5 (right). Grant Wood (designer), *Memorial Window* (detail).

personal experience suggests otherwise. He had enlisted in the Army in 1918 toward the end of the Great War, and was stationed first outside Des Moines, then at Camp Leach near Washington, D.C., where his assignment was painting artillery camouflage.[18] His particular responsibility, according to his sister, "was to make dummy *cannons* and to camouflage the real ones" (my emphasis).[19] When not on duty, he made drawings of fellow soldiers, continuing to practice his art and to identify as an artist despite the real risk at that time of being perceived as less than manly in his all-male environment. Ten years later, Wood, who had not seen action but had nevertheless served his country in his own way, could insinuate himself, or perhaps an avatar of himself, accompanied by his artist-assistant, among the veteran honorees on the *Memorial Window*. It is a brilliant conceit, for the cannoneer's sponge that stands between the two of them doubles as an artist's tool, the mahlstick (Fig. 2.4), a long pole with a pad wrapped in leather or suede tied at one end, used to steady the painting arm and to keep the hand from brushing against the painting's wet surface. For centuries, along with the easel and palette, the mahlstick has been a prop of the painter's profession.

The mahlstick/sponge brandished by the cannoneer (Fig. 2.5) serves as a kind of signage within the *Memorial Window* for an alternative type of masculinity to the one promoted in other contemporaneous postwar commemorations, bronze sculptures that proliferated across the country depicting the heroic doughboy aggressively charging, often with bayonet pointed at an unseen enemy.[20] Wood's men, standing at ease, are passive in comparison, and he gathers them beneath an overarching, feminine spirit. That hieratic figure, a chaste fusion and idealization of sister/mother, towers over her little male subjects in the manner of a Renaissance Madonna Misericordia,[21] aloof and powerful, doling out punishment (death, martyrdom) or reward (victory, glory). Like Hattie in her portrait, also holding her symbolic plant attributes, this figure turns her majestic regard away from the son who represents a different kind of man among men and who fought his own war of independence—from her—but never did manage to break free. The would-be revolutionary stands here defiantly and resolutely, aligned with his semi-nude comrade-in-arms under the sign of art.

TWO KINDS OF PORTRAITS

The cannoneer began, according to Graham, as a drawing of a young man named Jacob. Significantly, Wood retained this sensitive study of male beauty for himself while turning the other working drawings for the window over to the Veterans Memorial Coliseum Commission. Those studies deteriorated somewhat over time, but Wood preserved his precious cannoneer carefully.[22] When he translated the drawing into stained glass, he thought of his assistant on the project, to whom he was emotionally attached as doting friend and mentor. If Jacob was a one-time hired model, Pyle had a longer history in the artist's life. Wood had been his eighth-grade art teacher at McKinley Junior High in Cedar Rapids and employed him as a helper after he graduated from high school in 1927. In 1930, Wood painted a tender portrait of Pyle, *Arnold Comes of Age* (Fig. 2.6), when the youth reached twenty-one. With springtime trees blossoming pink on the right and autumn-red foliage and corn shocks casting long shadows on the left, Wood alludes in the portrait to the passage of time, and perhaps to the age difference between himself and his friend—Wood was then forty years old. The insect that appears at the youth's right elbow (Fig. 2.6A), often mistaken for a butterfly but with a moth's fat furry body and short antennae, brings to mind that old simile for a dangerous kind of attraction, "like a moth to a flame." It is a telling motif, too, in terms of the camouflaged appearance and behavior of moths, whose colors, patterns, and habitat choices allow them to achieve a protective invisibility in a way that Wood and Pyle may have sought, concealing their difference, to blend into their sometimes inhospitable environment. In the middleground of the painting, two nude bathers in the sylvan river have left pants and socks on the bank; the Whitmanesque vignette pays tribute to a prelapsarian moment of carefree male camaraderie in nature. The sitter's blue-black sweater, nocturnal moth, and crepuscular shadows contribute an elegiac quality to this picture that acknowledges the inevitability of growth, change, and eventual loss.

Shortly after painting this image, Wood made his young friend the touching gift of a self-portrait drawing (Introduction, opposite page 1).[23] The unique monogrammed belt buckle Pyle wears in *Arnold Comes of Age*, with the entwined initials "ARP," must likewise have been a present from the

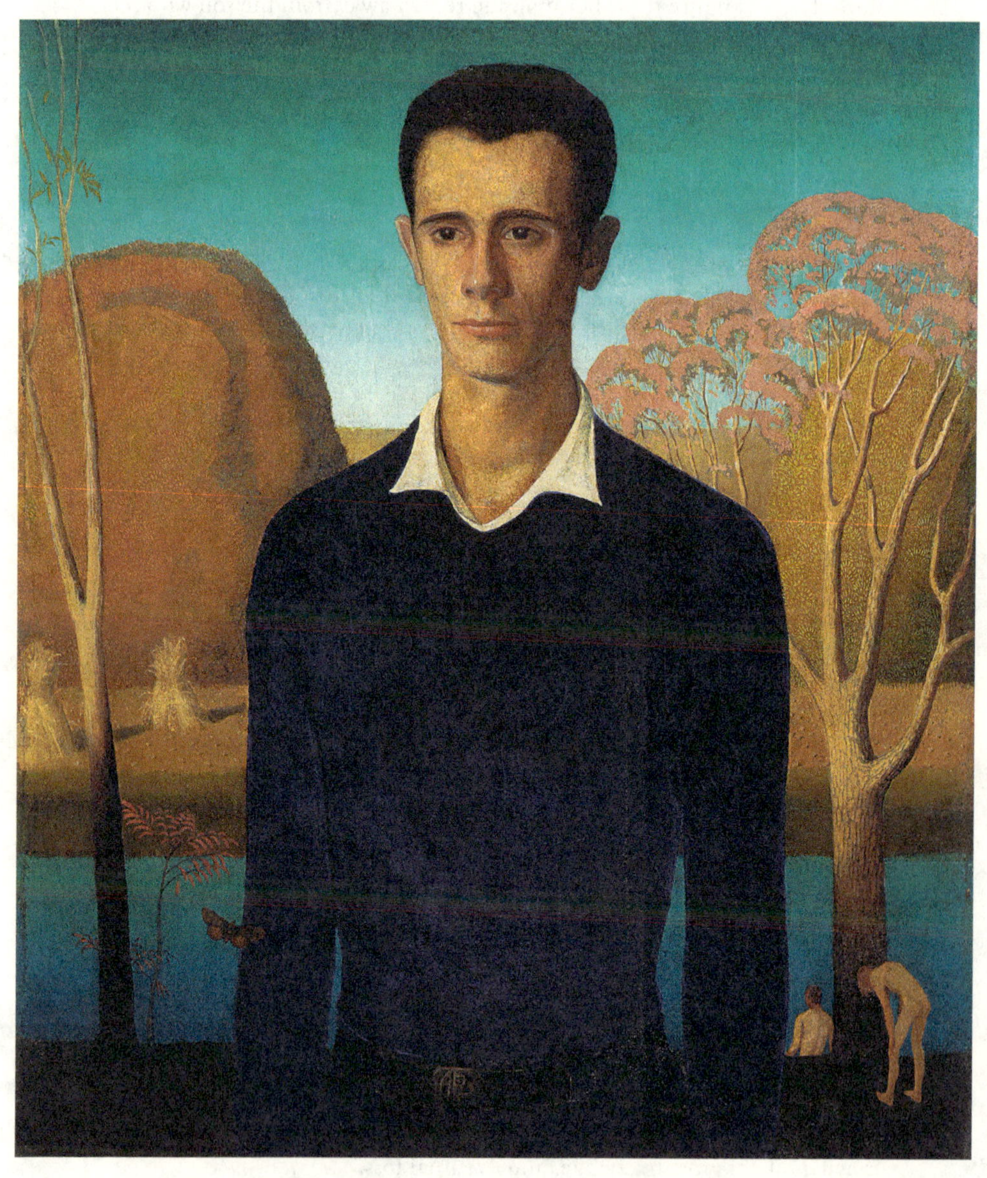

Figs. 2.6 and 2.6A (detail, opposite). Grant Wood,
Arnold Comes of Age (Portrait of Arnold Pyle), 1930.

artist, who was an experienced metalsmith and designer of original lamps, tea kettles, and jewelry.[24] Indeed, the very portrait itself is a testament to Wood's generous love for his erstwhile pupil. Although, as Wanda Corn points out, "Wood was often pressed into painting portraits . . . sometimes because he needed the money and sometimes because he found it hard to say no to friends," he never took great pleasure in it and curtailed his production when he had other sources of income.[25] Distinct from depictions of his patrons or their children done on commission, *Arnold Comes of Age* is one of only three portrait paintings Wood undertook on his own initiative during his lifetime, out of sheer devotion to the subject. The other two honor his mother and sister, respectively. Wood had a theory of portraiture that centered on intimacy between the artist and his sitter, and the artist's ability to "see below the surface":

> There . . . are two kinds of portrait painters. One kind can paint anybody—any time—and creates a good photographic likeness even though the painter has never before seen the subject. The other kind has to acquaint himself profoundly with his subject, or have a personal knowledge of him as a type, and has to know what his subject thinks and feels as well as how he looks. This second kind of painter puts a whole philosophy into his picture, not just a set of features and a complexion. His work has depth.[26]

Wood embodied both kinds of portrait painters, depending on the occasion, although he gives himself great latitude with that qualifying phrase about personal knowledge of the sitter as a type. Presumably, this kind of typological understanding would give desirable depth to any of his depictions of Midwesterners because he himself was one, or to his depictions of children because he had been one. As reflected in his art, he had limited knowledge or experience of an intimate kind with women apart from his mother and sister.

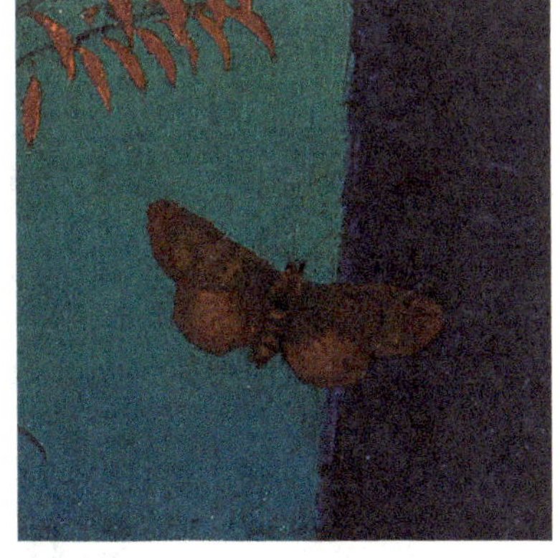

He was never moved to paint a portrait of his wife, Sara Sherman, even during their courtship, nor of his longtime supporter and supervising school principal Frances Prescott, though Rinard remembered that Wood "was absolutely fascinated with Miss Prescott [and] thought she was about the greatest ever."[27] A flattering female portrait Wood created in 1929 seems the exception that proves the rule. *Portrait of Frances Fiske Marshall* (Fig. 2.7) depicts a slender young woman, lovely in her red floral shawl, with thick auburn hair styled in a fashionable bob. Set against a brown background, her elegant figure is bathed in warm raking light. But it is a posthumous portrait, painted at the behest of

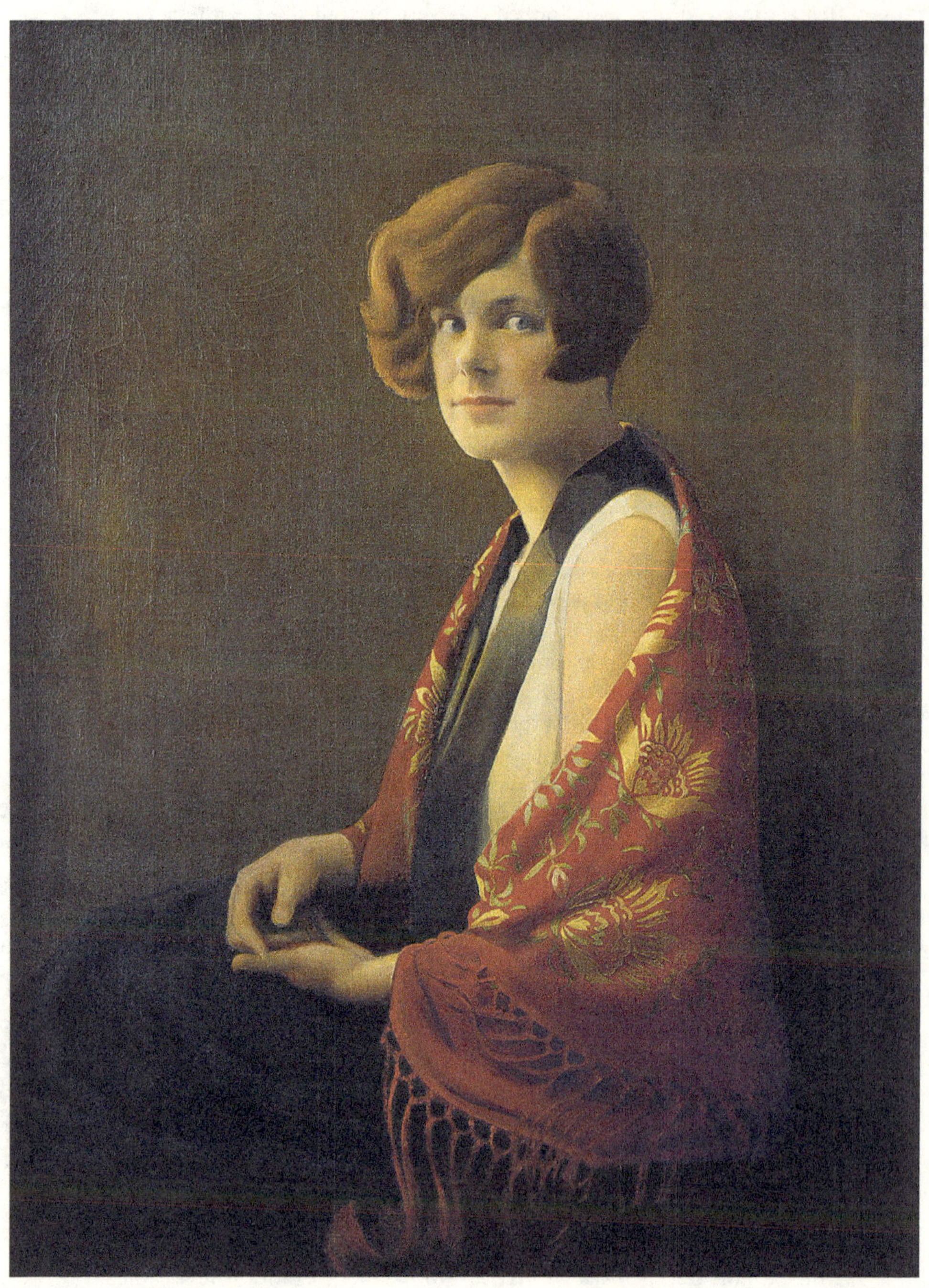

Fig. 2.7. Grant Wood, *Portrait of Frances Fiske Marshall*, 1929.

the subject's husband, Verne Marshall, editor of the *Cedar Rapids Gazette*. According to Graham, Wood resisted the commission, insisting that "he did not care to paint beautiful women, but Marshall prevailed upon him," providing a portrait miniature for the artist to reproduce as an easel picture.[28] Thus, Wood worked from an image, not a model. Although his anxieties about the female body could be elided in this case of a subject safely dead, Wood was incapable of fulfilling his community's more general expectations about how he might represent the women of his region. "Artists Have Neglected One of Iowa's Great Assets," complained a writer for the *Gazette* in 1933, "Its Pretty and Healthy Farm Girls . . . A Tip to Grant Wood."[29] Wood could only ignore the boosterish challenge. It is not surprising that such heteronormative pressures, exerted upon him from every corner and even on the public stage, bewildered him, exacerbating his alienation and social discomfort.

GYNOPHOBIA

Although he enjoyed friendly social intercourse with all kinds of female students, colleagues, and patrons, these relations were never erotically charged. His awkwardness around attractive women is painfully clear in photographs that appeared in *Life Magazine* in 1938 (Fig. 2.8), when he, Thomas Hart Benton, and John Steuart Curry judged the best costumes at the Kansas City Beaux-Arts Ball. A photo of the three artists among a bevy of

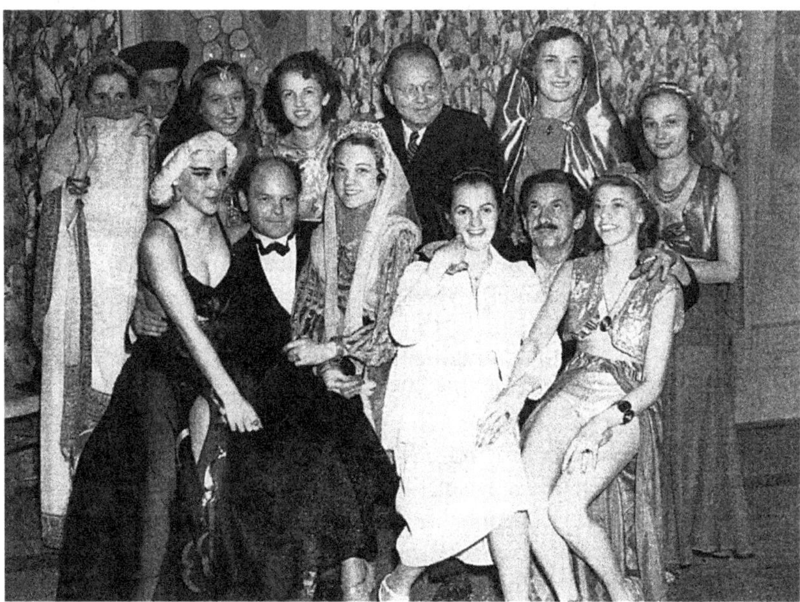

Fig. 2.8. Grant Wood (back row, center), John Steuart Curry (front row, second from left), and Thomas Hart Benton (front row, second from right), with guests at the Kansas City Beaux-Arts Ball, 1938.

female contestants shows Benton and Curry seated happily with women on their knees, while Wood stands uncomfortably in the background, shoulders hunched, wearing an embarrassed grin.[30] On another occasion, accompanying Leata Rowan, acting director of the Little Gallery in Cedar Rapids, to a holiday party, he fled her at the first opportunity. Writing shortly after New Year's in 1934 to her out-of-town husband, Rowan marveled at Wood as "the most reserved gentleman imaginable. Fact is he hardly says boo. And at Lenders' [party] he never got further than the bar—never got any supper and I only saw him to take him home. Which suited me well."[31] Uncertain what to do in the company of his date, the "shy bachelor," as he was so often called, recoiled. With Sherman, who had experienced sex during her first marriage as sordid and repellent, and was searching for "peace and contentment" in a new relationship, Wood likely entered a mutually beneficial platonic arrangement. She recalled how it was a moment of candor and modesty on her part that "decided Grant that I was the gal he had been looking for and that I realized his inhibitions and would never make a point of it."[32]

He could wall himself off, though, with behavior bordering on the bizarre. A strange incident reported by his friend Marvin Cone's wife, Winnifred, suggests the sometimes incapacitating quality of Wood's unease around women. He had asked her to pose for one of the four "Fruits of Iowa" murals (1932) that he was making for the Hotel Montrose in Cedar Rapids. "Grant used lights a lot," she remembered, "this bright light was shining on me, and so I just fainted dead away. And I was so embarrassed. And Mrs. Wood [i.e., Hattie] was running around trying to comfort me. But Grant—the nicest thing about Grant—he never batted an eye; he just went right on drawing."[33] Confronted by a physical female body with frailties and needs, Wood could not even acknowledge his model's distress. He responded similarly when Sherman, according to her memoir, suffered a coronary occlusion brought on by the emotional discord that was ending their marriage.[34] Wood was mowing the lawn when the ambulance arrived, and, ignoring the crisis, he continued mowing as the ambulance carried her away from their Iowa City home.[35] They never saw each other again.

In life as in art, women were sometimes collateral damage resulting not from Wood's queerness per se, but from his tragic inability to be himself, to embody his own sexual truth. His resentments needn't be glossed over; they were, understandably, functions of his particular social and psychic realities. Yet, like Winnifred Cone, who excused Wood's cold neglect of her as "the nicest thing," apologists may sugarcoat misogynist examples in his art as "affectionate."[36] The gleeful mockery and derision seen in *Daughters of Revolution* (1932, Fig. 2.9) was famously vengeful and righteous: the Daughters of the American Revolution had objected to the manufacture of Wood's Veterans *Memorial Window* in Germany, a recent U.S. enemy, and he took them on in this work as ugly, self-satisfied, small-minded patriots and isolationists.

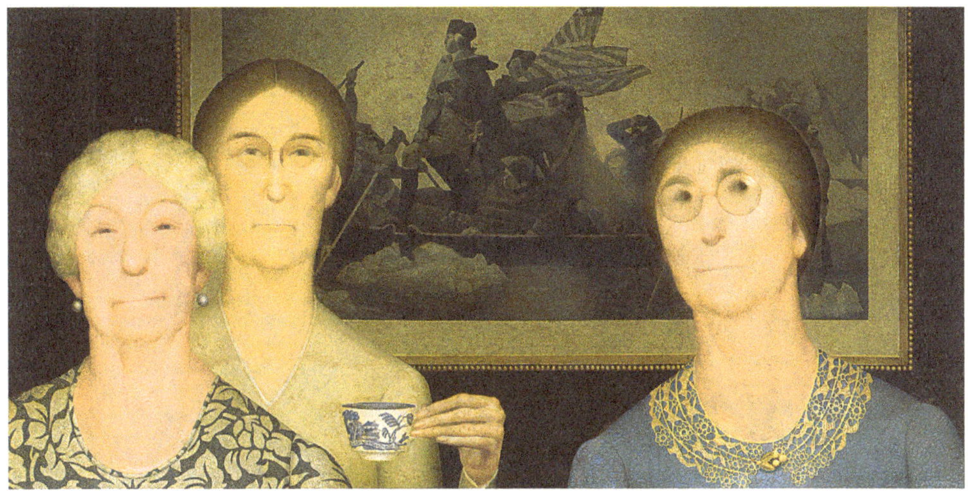

Fig. 2.9. Grant Wood, *Daughters of Revolution*, 1932.

But his mean-spiritedness is somewhat harder to celebrate in *Victorian Survival* (1931, Fig. 2.10), which riffs on a photographic portrait (Fig. 2.11) of Wood's own ancestral relative, Matilda Weaver Peet (1825–1905). A comparison of the painting with the tintype reveals the cruelty in his transformation of a benign-looking gentlewoman with open arms, worried and world-weary, into a beady-eyed avatar of rigid—or better, frigid—inhibition and rectitude. Akin to *American Gothic* in its retaliatory send-up of a personality Wood experienced as a repressive influence, the painting I want to call "Victorian Gothic" performs visually what Jay Sigmund undertook in his fiery protest poem "The Serpent" (1922); Wood was surely familiar with this savage assault on hypocrisy by his fellow Iowan in Waubeek. Both works, painting and poem, attack a type of self-appointed, pietistic, and judgmental monitor of small-town mores. In the painting, the telephone is the instrument and symbol of the woman's controlling preoccupation: gossip. In the poem, Sigmund addresses the "sexless spinster" with her finger in a Bible: "I behold your shriveled soul, / Brown and dry and unlovely. . . . / And I shudder." He calls her "the arch-assassin of reputation," lying in wait for innocence, and compares her to a fanged serpent, "A crawling reptile, / With venom / Spouting from a lightning tongue." In the final stanza, Sigmund imagines a violent revenge on his hated nemesis in the name of a beneficent paternal power:

> I would nail your putrid spirit
> To a cross of flame—
> I would bare it and burn it—
> And so purify
> A world created sweet
> By the Great All-Father![37]

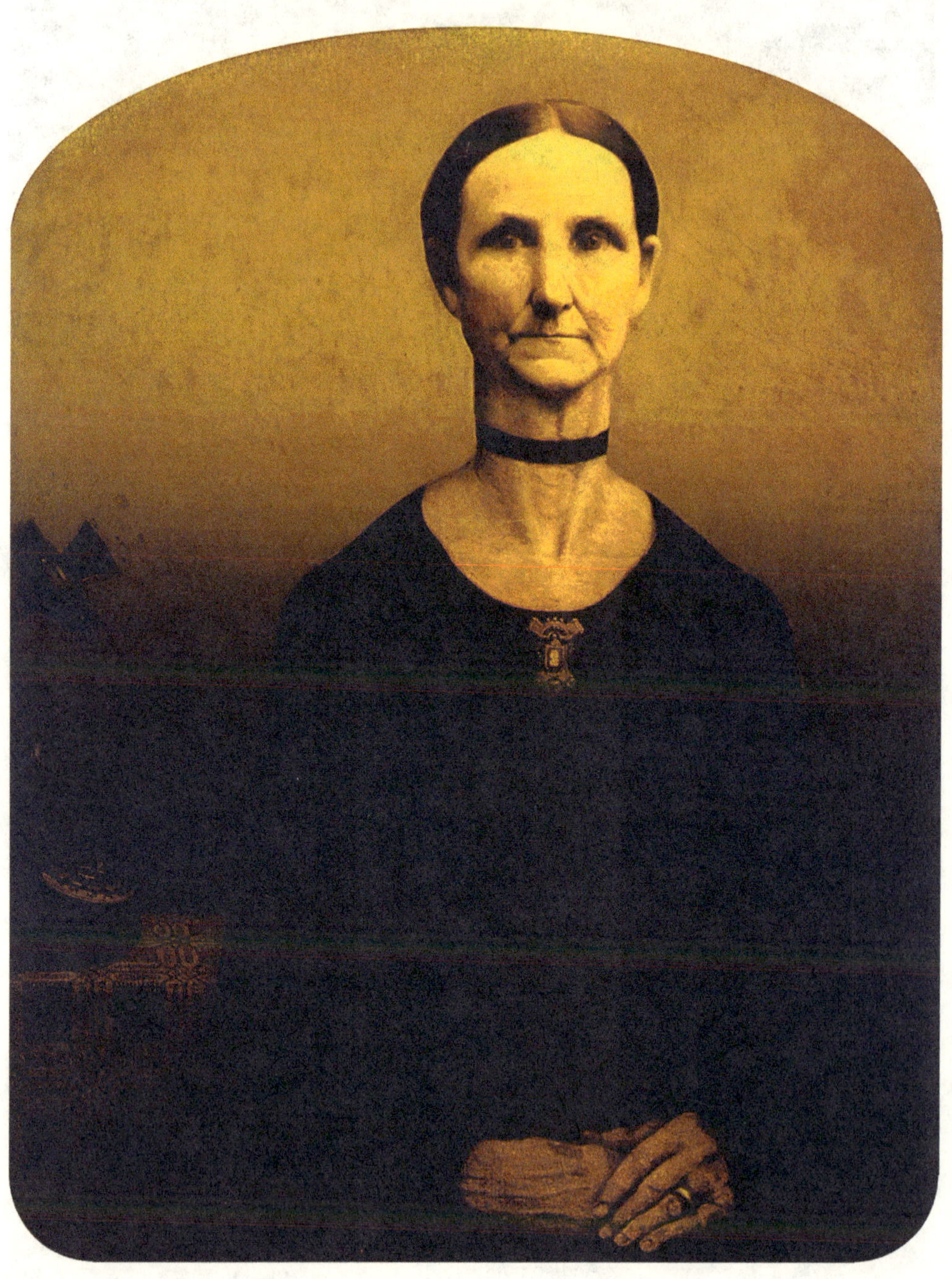

Fig. 2.10. Grant Wood, *Victorian Survival*, 1931.

Victorian Survival is infused with a wicked humor not found in the impassioned poem, and, though sexless like Sigmund's serpent-spinster, Wood's black-garbed widow wears a wedding ring, as Hattie does in *Woman with Plants*. Indeed, it is as if Wood has here reimagined his mother-portrait set in a dull interior, with the woman in *Victorian Survival* also wearing a distinctive brooch (both pins are now in the collection of the Figge Art Museum in Davenport, Iowa), hands similarly folded across her lap, and a symbolic attribute at her left. The candlestick telephone suggests to Corn a confrontational theme: modernity represented by the phone clashes with the vanishing world of the old crone. Corn's description of Wood's picture captures the aggression he enacts on his auntly figure, "with eyes like glazed marbles" and mouth "firmly gagged":

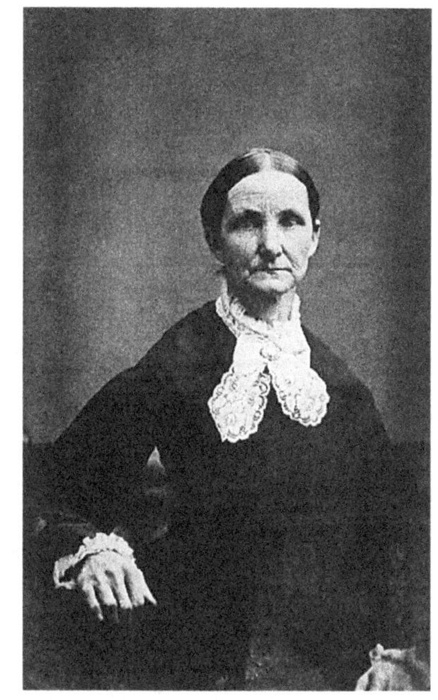
Fig. 2.11. Matilda Weaver Peet, n.d.

> Other details dissect this Victorian body. The part in her straight black hair, slightly off center, is a knife cut, slicing through the silken hair mass to the whiteness of the skull. Around her exceedingly long neck a black ribbon, tight and taut, throttles her pronounced muscles and vocal cords. This choker cuts across the woman's thick neck like the blade of a guillotine. All of these bodily incisions add tension and darkness to this figure from the past. Her surface correctness is over drawn, her gentility tinged with meanness and intolerance.[38]

I think the meanness here belongs to Wood, and all the violence Corn perceptively discerns—the dissecting, slicing, throttling, and cutting—is his, too. Phallic in overall form like the telephone that dates and mocks her but also serves her, the woman with the ribbon severing her head from her body becomes the very image of castration. The most conspicuous and unlikely invention in the painting relative to the tintype, the choker (which Corn compares to a blade and Evans to a cock ring)[39] puns verbally on what Wood wishes to do to this figure who stirs in him unconscious fears for his own bodily integrity. Painted in sepia tones, moreover, and framed like a giant daguerreotype, *Victorian Survival* points insistently to the past, preserving a disturbing buried memory—of child Wood's unwelcome discovery of sexual difference. It is a classic Freudian formation, in which the little boy's recognition of his mother's apparently castrated condition, and the possibility of loss it suggests *for him*, provokes a desperate disavowal of the mother's lack in the creation of a fetish, a fantasy substitute for the missing maternal phallus. The vigorous sansevieria in *Woman with Plants* and the candlestick phone in *Victorian Survival* function in this compensatory fashion. In the latter picture, the woman is punished for her imagined lack, as Wood's displaced hostility plays out on a likeness of his mother's surrogate—her aunt—whose keepsake photograph, Corn reminds us, he always treasured.[40] In the image of the symbolically decapitated Victorian woman, phallicized in her rigidity, Wood conflates his anxiety problem and its fetishistic solution.

Contemporary psychoanalytic thinking on castration transcends the literal anatomical meaning it held for Freud to elaborate its metaphorical valence in psychic reality, wherein threats to object relations, individuation, or selfhood, not simply to body parts, may arouse castration anxiety, in both sexes.[41] Whether or what kind of disempowerment or loss may have threatened Wood as he conjured his matronly fetish figure is hard to know, but his sister's imminent move to Albuquerque with her husband around this time probably wounded him deeply, breaking up the vestige of his family—the intimate circle of mother, sister, and self—that survived in Cedar Rapids. The maternal associations of *Victorian Survival* are also telling—again, his mother's brooch, the tintype memento of her forebear, a composition that repeats that of the mother-portrait *Woman with Plants*, whose dark counterpart this picture may in fact represent—casting Wood as the "hypocrite" who nurses unconscious resentments beneath a loving and genial facade. Moreover, the figure's stiff posture resonates with the way Hattie defended herself in the midst of emotional loss, when she was deserted, for example, by her youngest son. Graham described her mother's stubbornly unyielding attitude about John's estrangement from the family: though he continued to live in Cedar Rapids, and "once in a while we'd glimpse him in the distance, . . . mother said 'I didn't do anything to him, if he comes home, I'll welcome him, if he doesn't, I won't.' And that was that."[42] With her daughter's departure for the Southwest, Hattie's long-suffering resignation to the ongoing disintegration of her family could have impressed Wood as admirably stoic while secretly stirring in him grief and irrational anger. His own greatest loss remained the loss of his father, whom Hattie had outlived—a Victorian survivor. If on some level Wood blamed her for this, he could punish her in fantasy, prosecuting her substitute in his aggressively hostile image of a castrated/castrating old biddy.

This psychic drama operates in the painting simultaneously with the artist's manifest program as an "uneasy modern," as Corn aptly dubs him, contemplating a new technology in the process of transforming a traditional way of life—with "sped-up communications, intrusive noise, impersonal exchanges."[43] Back then, the telephone signaled rapid change; in 1931, the upright device in *Victorian Survival* was itself being eclipsed by the handset that integrated receiver and transmitter in one unit. Already a staple feature in homes across the U.S. in the twenties and thirties, including Wood's own, the telephone was gendered feminine by virtue of an exclusively female workforce of switchboard operators, the hundreds of thousands of young women or "Hello Girls" who gave a human voice to the inanimate object.[44] Popular images like George Petty's pinups (Fig. 2.12), or those of Alberto Vargas, Petty's successor at *Esquire* magazine, portrayed this feminine voice in sexualized fantasies that would have been utterly alien to the painter of *Victorian Survival*—but with similarly long, hard, taut forms strategically placed to ward off the same emasculating fears. Wood repudiated the fashionable body type celebrated in the glamorously modern Petty Girl and Vargas Girl, frowning on what he called in the *Cedar Rapids Gazette* "the streamlined, serpentine charmers of today."[45]

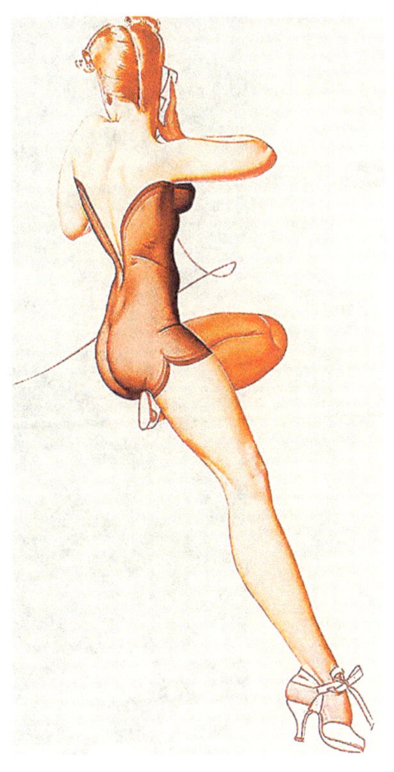

Fig. 2.12. George Petty, "I'm the one with the part in the back," *Esquire Magazine*, April 1941.

With its dangerous connotations, "serpentine" recalls the only extant painting of a female nude that Wood produced (Fig. 2.13). He created it spontaneously, in September 1937, maybe in a mildly intoxicated state, to amuse a group of friends. In the company of his fellow artists Benton and Curry and their wives, Wood was a guest at Dr. Wellwood Nesbit's home in Madison, Wisconsin, when someone proposed the postprandial decoration of the host's liquor cabinet. Nesbit's sister-in-law, Blanche, suggested to Curry the subject of a pink elephant, which the artist duly executed, complete with female circus rider on its back and ice skates on its feet, on the cabinet's left interior panel. Benton then added the image of a painter's palette with a cryptic inscription below Curry's cartoon.[46] According to Blanche, "Grant Wood came next and he asked no one's opinion. He painted on the right panel a woman with a snake coiled around her. He called it the 'Evil of Drink.'"[47] His slim, stylized yellow-haired nude with upturned face and arms held stiffly out from her body resembles the very "dieted debutantes" he would rail against to the *Gazette*. She stares mesmerized at the head of the snake with its open red jaws and forked tongue. Like Eve in the Garden, she surrenders to a sinister temptation, apparently levitating under the serpent's power. But Wood's title is of course ironic, as he was very fond of alcohol, and the overall configuration of his woman-with-snake mimics the rod of Asclepius, symbol of the

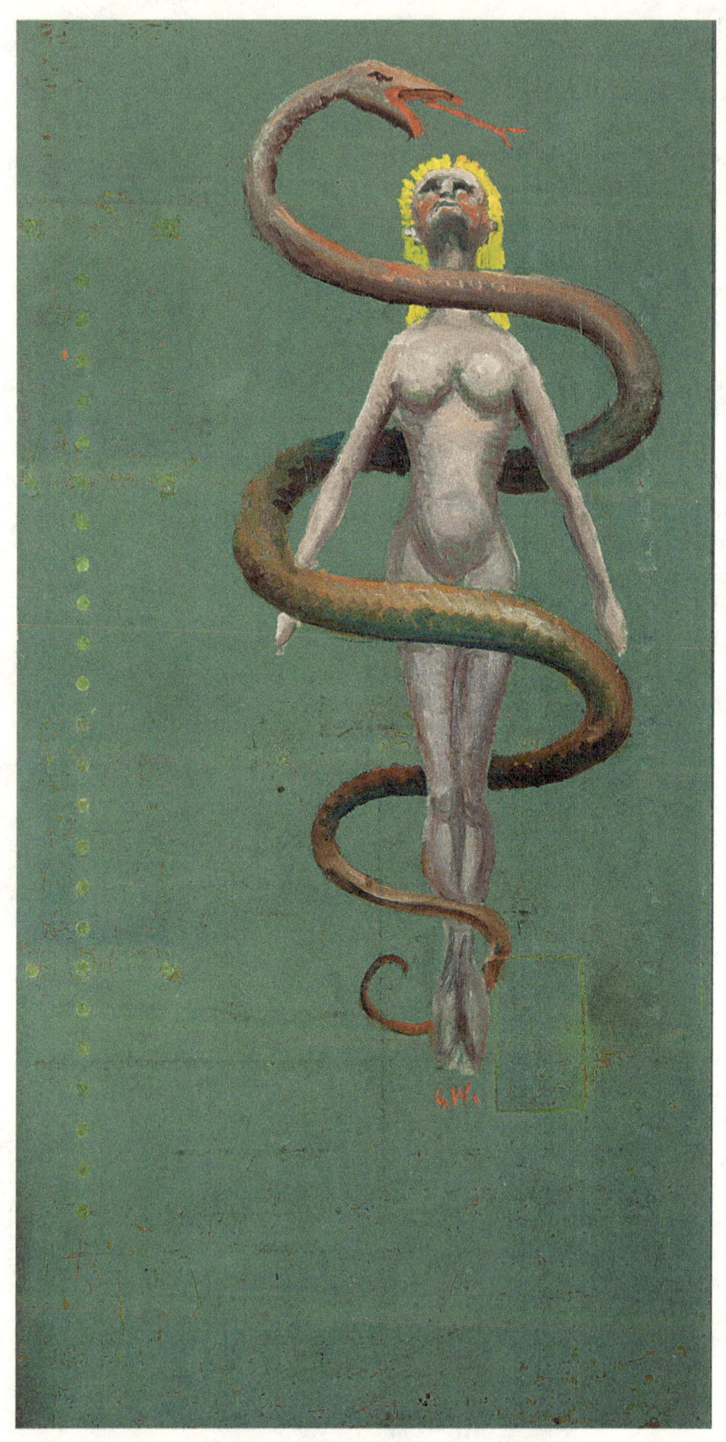

Fig. 2.13. Grant Wood, *The Evil of Drink*, 1937.

healing arts. The image collapses contradictory points of view about drink: it is poisonous as venom, salutary like medicine.

In terms of the possible latent content of this curious work created in an unguarded moment, the serpent is an overdetermined symbol whose precise meaning may be difficult to discern. In the autobiographical "Return from Bohemia," as we've seen in Chapter 1, Wood associates it with his own genital sexuality; playing with the magical joint snake signifies masturbation and arouses guilt. But in the liquor cabinet panel, the snake takes on a different kind of significance, less phallic than devouring, linked with female sexuality and the fantasy of a *vagina dentata*. At stake seems to be a fear not only of castration—hence the hard, statuesque, fetish-like form of the woman—but also of incorporation, for snakes swallow living things and some strangle their prey. Interpreting this predatory-type snake common in myths of many cultures and in schizophrenic fantasies, Philip Slater finds encapsulated in it the fears of an oral-narcissistic dilemma, emerging from the opposing desires for fusion with and separation from the mother. Originating in "the insatiable hunger of the child itself—the desire to gobble up the mother and keep her forever inside," the fantasy of fusion with the maternal body becomes a fear of being consumed by her, and the snake represents "the entangling, smothering, devouring mother who destroys the boundary between the child and the external world and returns him to a quiescent state of non-being [. . .] whence he came."[48]

Two other recorded female nudes Wood created reflect these very life and death concerns, of orality and fusion on the one hand, and of death and destruction on the other. Wood biographer Darrell Garwood reported the young artist's fascination (circa 1916) with the sight of his friend Paul Hanson's wife, Vida, breastfeeding their newborn child.

> He would stare at Vida when she was nursing [. . .] until she became ill at ease. Then one day he asked her to pose for a mother-and-child figure, which seemed to explain his unusual interest, and she agreed. For several days, at nursing hours, she sat at a window with her back partly turned and the light across her while he worked on a figure so small that he could cover it with his hand. He wouldn't let her see it, and when it was done he took it home with him. A week later he brought it back and placed it on the table. What he had done was a mother-and-child nude. Vida was embarrassed and angry. Yet she could see that it was a finely done thing.
>
> She didn't destroy it intentionally. It was in plaster, covered with gilt bedstead paint, and was accidentally knocked to the floor and broken. Grant said it didn't make any difference. Vida thought he had decided it wasn't the right thing to do.[49]

If the ill-conceived little scene of the child suckling memorialized Wood's own archaic needs and oral satisfactions, he never returned to the

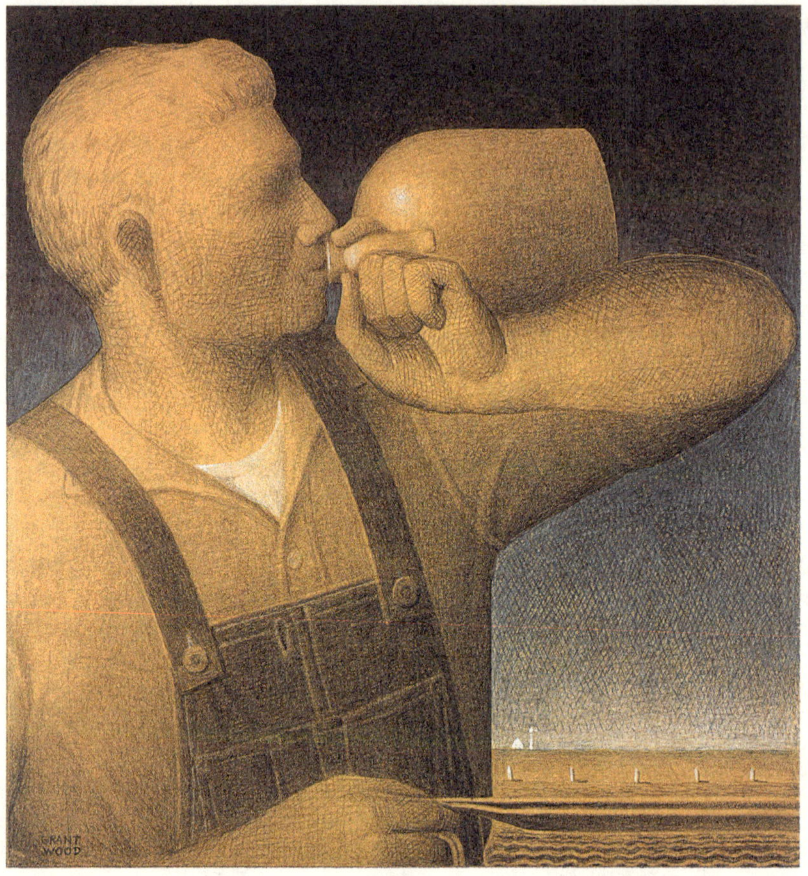

Fig. 2.14. Grant Wood, *Plowing on Sunday*, 1934.

theme so directly in his art. There is, however, the beautiful drawing (1934, Fig. 2.14) for the frontispiece of Sterling North's *Plowing on Sunday*, which supplants the breast with the euphemistic jug. From this novel of 265 pages, Wood chose to illustrate the passage in which the protagonist, Stanley "Stud" Brailsford, momentarily gives over his active, phallic striving for a passive pleasure: "One must," thinks Stud, "throw down the shining tobacco hatchet beside the shagbark hickory, snatch up the heavy, brown-earthenware jug, tip it deftly over the shoulder and slosh long, cool swigs of cider down one's parched and dusty throat."[50] A fantasy of fellatio may have lurked too near the surface of Wood's composition, with its suggestive juxtaposition of jug handle, fingers, and spout with the young man's lips. Wood obscured this detail when he repeated the motif of the farmer slaking his thirst in the mural *Breaking the Prairie* (1936–37, Fig. 2.15) for Iowa State University. That tableau, flanked on either side by an image of a pioneer vigorously chopping down a tree with an ax (see Fig. 2.28), also includes the

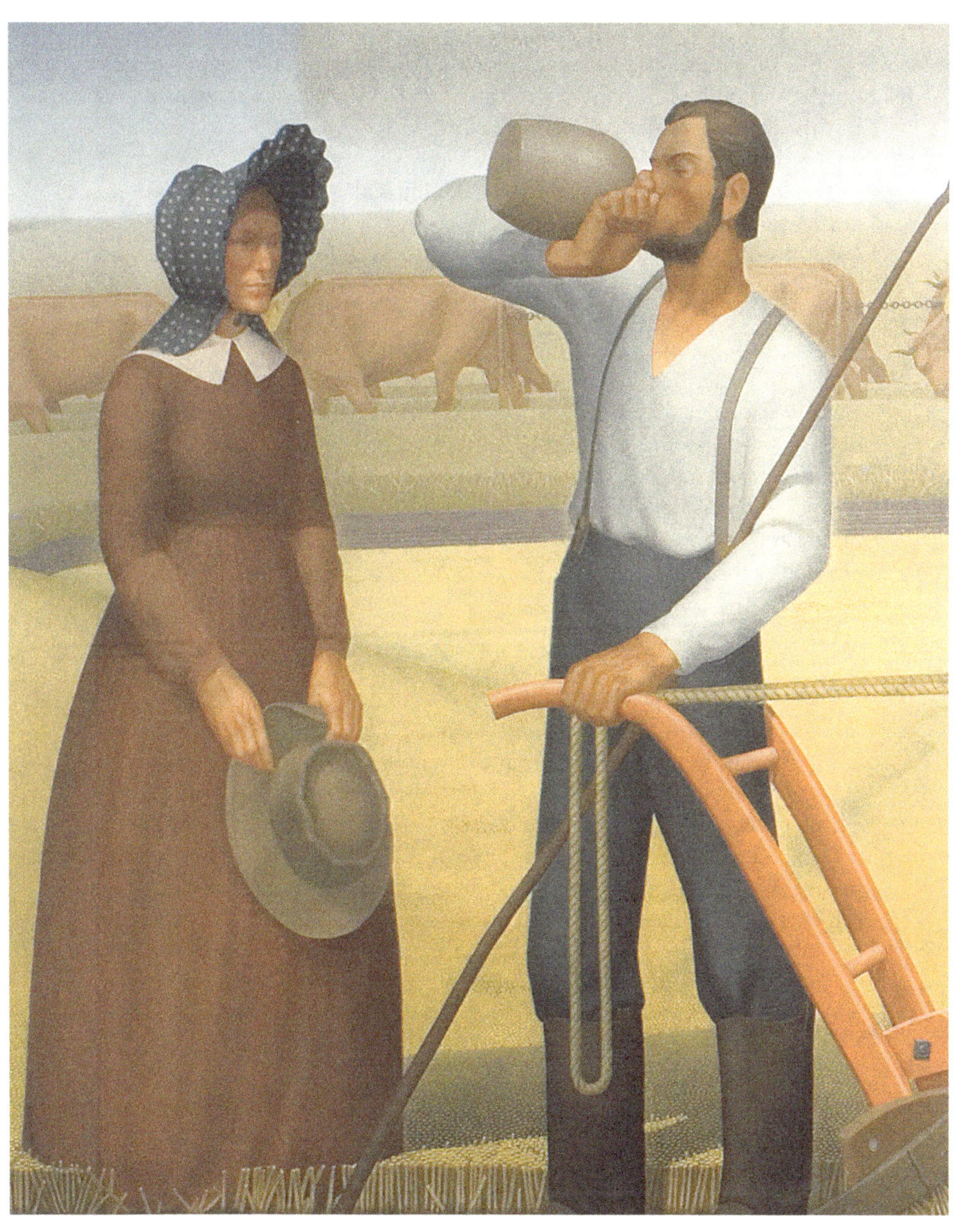

Fig. 2.15. Grant Wood (designer), *Breaking the Prairie* (detail of central panel), 1936–37.

woman who has brought the jug to the plowman. Here Wood limns an antidote to the wished for/fear of fusion with the powerful mother. The woman, blandly modest and submissive, stands near the drinking farmer, who is defended in his separation and self-sufficiency by all manner of manly trappings: suspender straps, rope, a long stick for whipping his horses, the rigid plow handle strategically placed at the level of his crotch. In this way, he maintains his precarious autonomy while still taking satisfaction in what the woman provides.

The fear of returning to the maternal body is also a fear of annihilation or death, and the other rare instance in which Wood conjured a female nude was indeed associated with a near fatality. In 1933, to cheer Sigmund when he had been injured in the automobile accident that inspired *Death on the Ridge Road*, Wood presented him with a scrapbook that included "a humorous drawing of a female nude in pretzel-like twists" ironically titled *Repose* and inscribed "to be carved in Stone City limestone."[51] Privately held and inaccessible today, the drawing that so few have ever seen is a mere footnote in Wood studies. Like the destroyed nursing nude and *The Evil of Drink*, it represents an obscure anomaly in the artist's oeuvre from which we can nevertheless deduce certain attitudes about the female body. The male nudes are another story altogether, and the remainder of this chapter is devoted to them.

A CHERISHED *ACADÉMIE*

Disparaged by early critics and generally neglected in the literature, the handsome studio nude, or *académie*, titled *The Spotted Man* (1924, Fig. 2.16) is the only figure painting and the only interior scene that survives among the host of landscapes and city views Wood painted in Europe. Those *plein-air* pictures, rendered in oil on handy composition board, are small studies. *The Spotted Man* is large in comparison, thirty-two by twenty inches. Wood created it at the Académie Julian, where he had the opportunity to paint, on canvas from the nude model, in the time-honored tradition of the life class. In 1924, however, the male nude was largely a relict of a past age, superseded in the nineteenth century by its female counterpart, with rare exceptions—for example in a few very distinctive bathing pictures by Frédéric Bazille (1868) and Gustave Caillebotte (1884),[52] which *The Spotted Man* belatedly resembles. Stylistically, with the conservative, quasi-Impressionist technique that inspired its title, Wood's *académie* stands apart from canonical developments continuing in Paris in the early twenties, such as Synthetic Cubism, which he purposely ignored. It differs as well from his own contemporaneous paintings, which are much more brightly hued, broadly brushed and scumbled with lively surface emphases. *The Spotted Man* is notable for its careful restraint and the rather crepuscular space that envelops the figure.

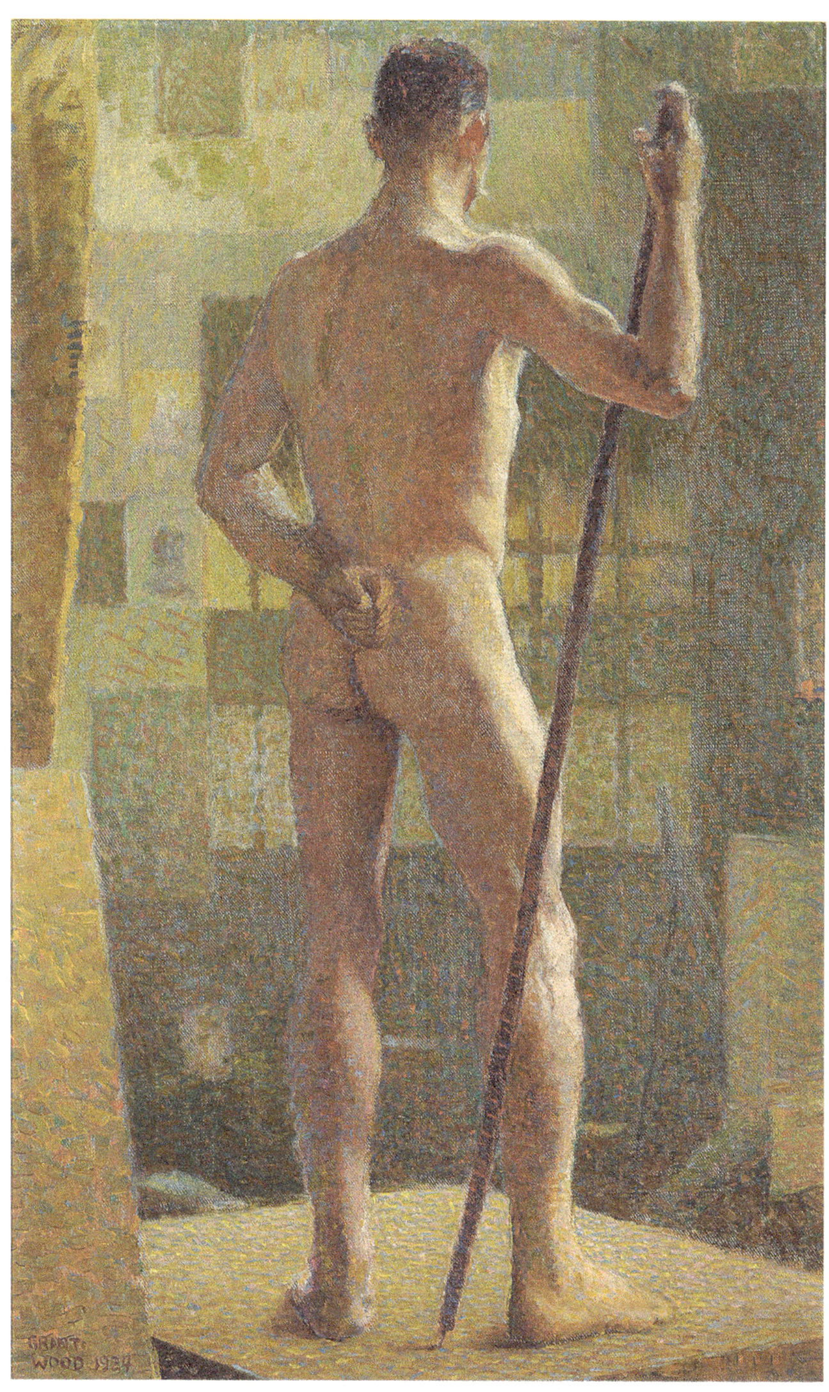

Fig. 2.16. Grant Wood, *The Spotted Man*, 1924.

From his position behind and slightly below the model in the atelier, surrounded by the easels of other painters, Wood framed the man's muscular body with insistently geometric shapes: the square dais on which he stands, rectangular canvases on either side of him in foreground and background, and, on the rear wall, pictures pinned up around what seems to be a gridded screen or window. The bit of golden drapery hanging at the left and the tall staff the model holds with his right hand to maintain his pose, both common studio props with practical functions, help situate his virile body safely in the realm of Art. Most compelling is the white light bathing the model from the upper right. Wood follows it along the radiant contour of the man's right side, from the slope of the neck to the lower leg. Shoulder blades, spine, and the cleft of the buttocks are indicated along the shadowed rear of the body, and the loose fist resting at the small of the back forms a suggestively dark opening around which the fingers curl. Because the man's face is averted, the observer's gaze can linger at leisure over his nudity. Seeing and longing are the salient subtexts in this image of a man "spotted," that is, espied, picked out.

Likely a working-class man posing in his spare time,[53] the model also offered Wood an imagined subjectivity and ideal masculinity with which he might have yearned to identify. His pleasure with this picture was such that he never parted with it. "It was the first of his works in fifteen years . . . that he decided to keep for himself," Garwood marveled, after insulting the painting as "ungainly" and "ugly," which it is not, and characterizing Wood's fondness for it as "perverse."[54] If in European art in the first half of the twentieth century the *académie* represented a waning but once esteemed tradition, in Iowa it had no such context and could only raise prudish hackles and eyebrows. Wood had to participate in the denigration of his painting to protect himself from its erotic implications. He offered the picture as a parody, circulating the tale that, in order to mock Impressionism, he had "slapped on great splotches of red, leaving spaces for greens and yellows," and that the "ghastly" result prompted his expulsion from the Académie.[55] All this was patently untrue. The tiny strokes of paint, in shades of orange and olive, suggest a methodical surface decoration, patiently applied. The muted colors and the pictorial arrangement—a central, static figure amidst a linear scaffolding—recall Cubist painting of the previous decade while rebuking it with realist readability. In Paris, Wood had been well aware of Picasso's work and was even cowed by it as he plunged into a spell of dispirited self-doubt, from which he eventually emerged with a greater sense of self-acceptance and clarity.[56] In *The Spotted Man*, we see him in the process of discovering his own artistic, and perhaps sexual, orientation. Stylistically, he moved toward the tidy control that would characterize his mature work. Thematically, he brought into focus in this sensitive, rear-view study of the male body an erotic fascination that expressed itself periodically throughout his career.

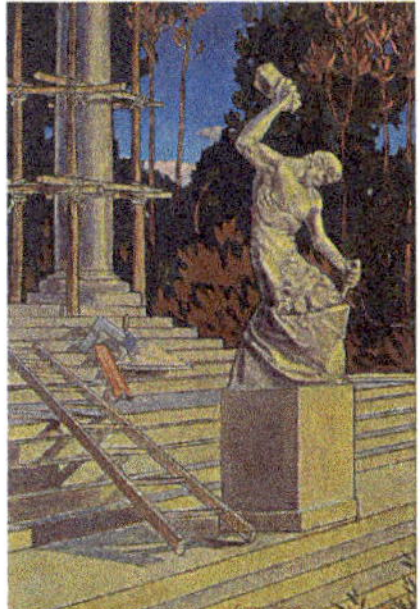
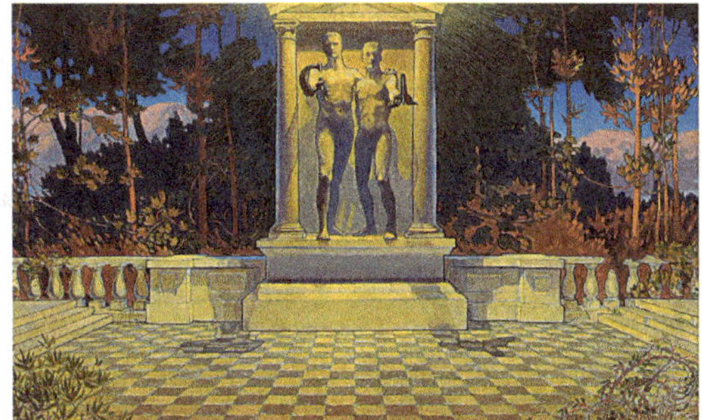
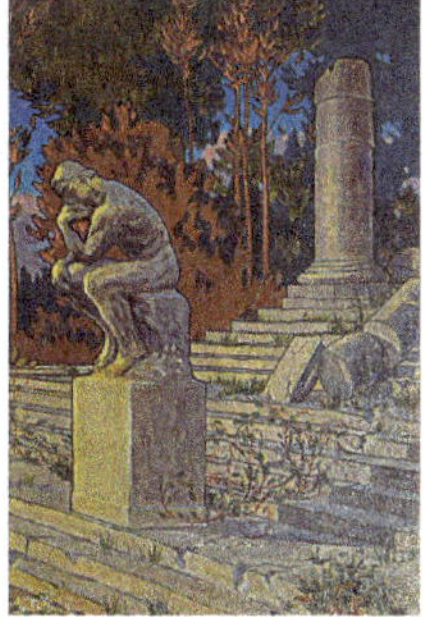

Fig. 2.17. Grant Wood, *First Three Degrees of Free Masonry*, 1921.

REFUGE IN THE CLASSICS

A tentative early example of that fascination dates to his 1921 commission, *First Three Degrees of Free Masonry* (Fig. 2.17), which includes four male nudes. Wood was inducted into the Cedar Rapids Mt. Hermon Masonic Lodge No. 263 that year and created the picture at the direction of former Grand Master George L. Schoonover.[57] As an age-old, homosocial society—devoid of women, founded on craft, and operating in open secrecy—Freemasonry must have represented a kind of paradise to Wood. His triptych, with its arcane subject matter, depicts a tiled plaza flanked by staircases with a low balustrade separating it from a deciduous forest in the background. Featured on each panel is a sculpture representing one of the Masonic degrees: from left to right, Entered Apprentice, Fellowcraft, and Master Mason. Traditional Masonic motifs associated with buildings also appear: pillars, a trowel, an L-shaped square, as well as the ladder and construction scaffold, and, prominently displayed by the two central figures, the sacred "G" for geometry and an old-fashioned level with plumb. Resorting to chilly sculptural forms in which passion could be safely disavowed, Wood modeled the painting's four male nudes on icons of art history at a time when art students' training still familiarized them with plaster casts and reproductive engravings of the corpus of classical statuary. Most easily recognizable even today is a modern addition to the canon, Rodin's *Thinker*, standing for the highest of the three Masonic degrees, shown ruminating here on his plinth in the right-hand panel.[58] His thoughtful quietude complements the vigorous action of the figure in the opposite panel, representing the Apprentice; the sculpture Wood depicted here is *Man Carving His Own Destiny* (1907) by Albin Polasek (1879–1965), who had arrived to teach at the School of the Art Institute of Chicago while Wood was studying there in 1916 (Fig. 2.18). Wielding a mallet and chisel, Polasek's heroic man is caught in the process of carving himself free from the stone. The conceit follows Michelangelo's famous claim, so beautifully embodied in his slaves for the Julius tomb, that the sculptor releases the vital

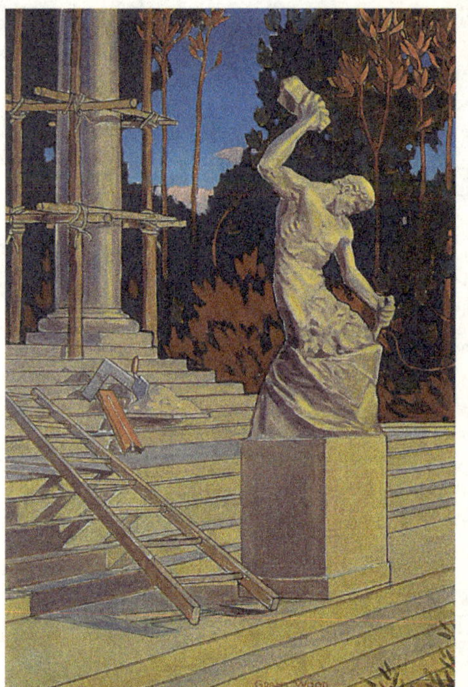

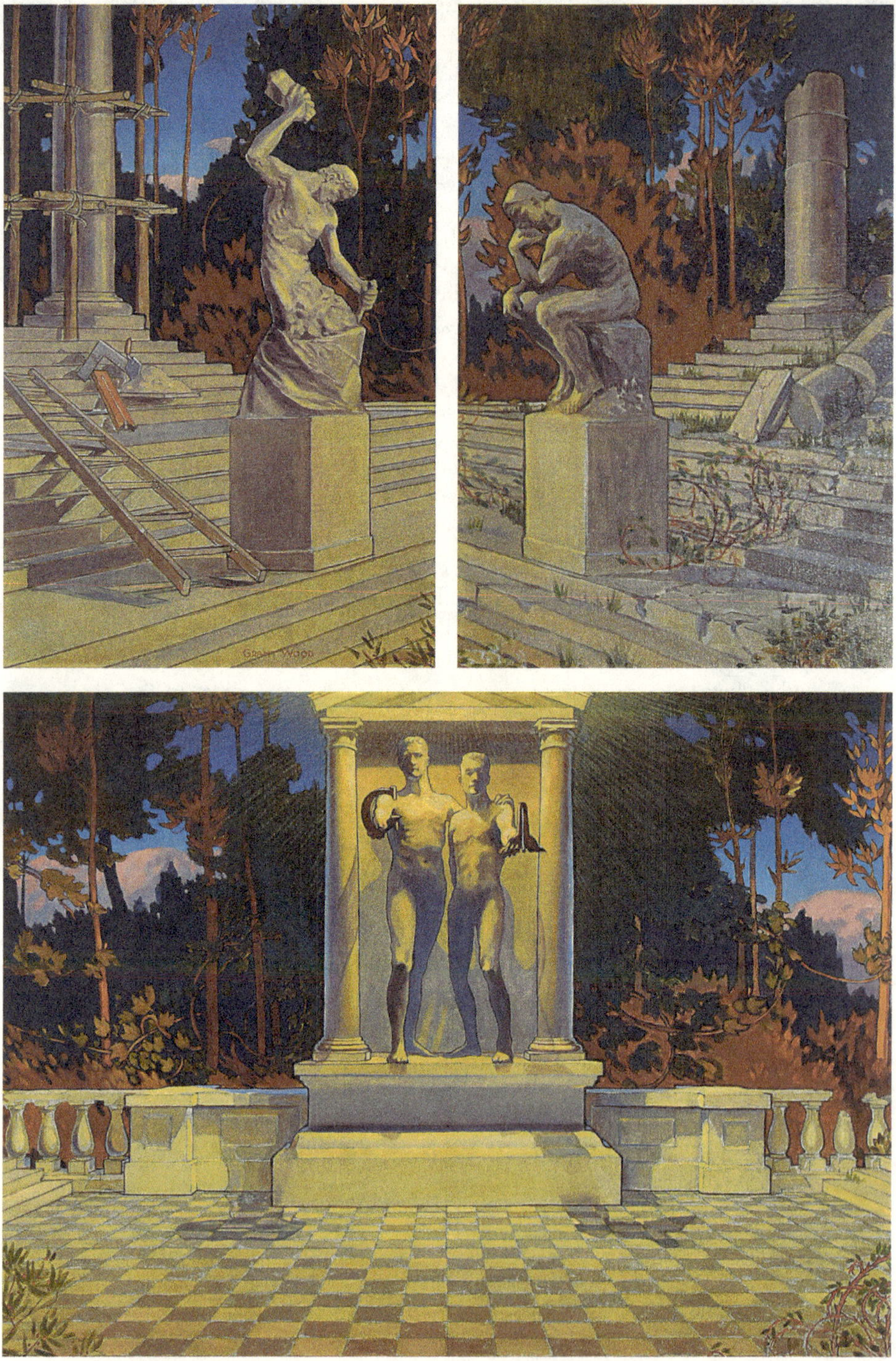

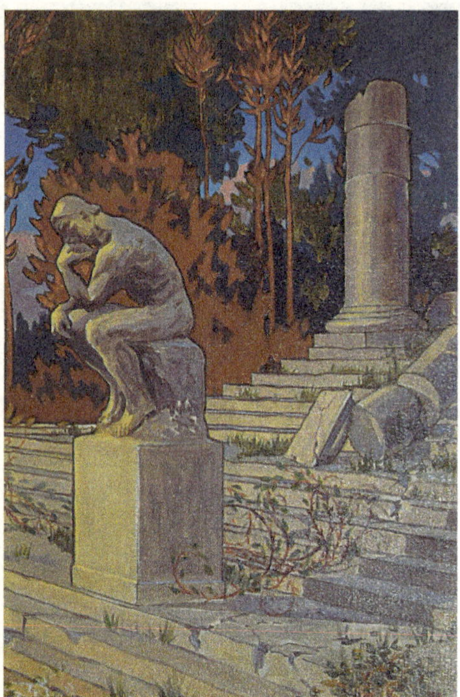

Figs. 2.17A–C (details). Grant Wood, *First Three Degrees of Free Masonry*, 1921.

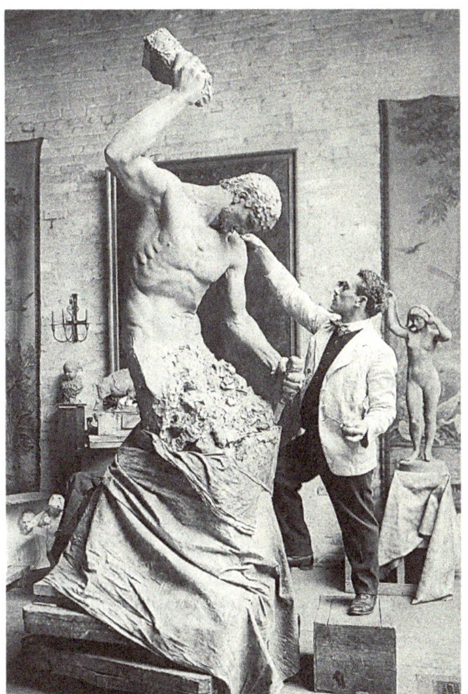

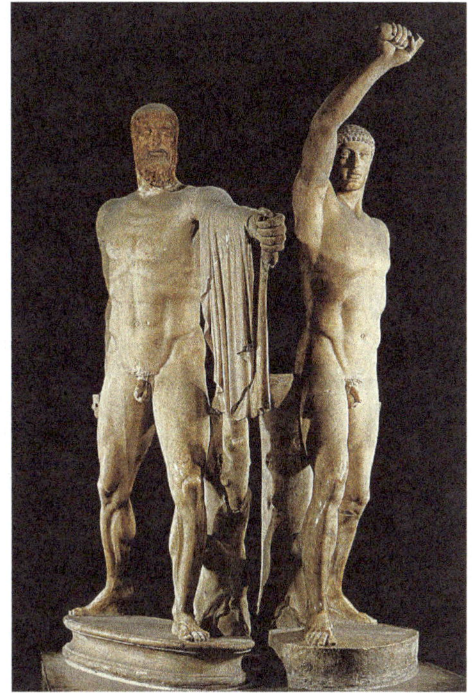

Fig. 2.18 (left). Albin Polasek (1879–1965) modeling *Man Carving His Own Destiny*, c. 1916.

Fig. 2.19 (right). Roman, *The Tyrannicides (Harmodius and Aristogeiton)*, 477–76 BCE, after the Athenian version by Kritios and Nesiotes.

form imprisoned in the block, but Polasek added a new level of meaning in his fantasy of artistic self-creation.

In the central, Fellowcraft panel stands the personification of ideal brotherhood, a pair of frontal nudes flanked by classical columns and locked together in a fraternal embrace. Each figure steps confidently forward, with the foot of his outer leg protruding beyond the edge of the sheltering niche. Importantly, Evans has discovered Wood's inspiration for this proud pair in a lost but widely copied sculpture by Kritios and Nesiotes from the fifth century BCE,[59] which Wood knew of even before he had the opportunity to see a Roman copy of it (Fig. 2.19) in the Neapolitan National Archaeological Museum near Sorrento in 1924. The heroic subjects of that work, Aristogeiton and Harmodius, were celebrated in songs and vase paintings in the ancient world as "The Tyrannicides," assassins of one Hipparchus of Athens.[60] They were also, as Evans notes, lovers, as famous for "their sexual fidelity to one another as they were for their bravery."[61] Homoeroticism thus hides in plain sight in Wood's unimpeachably chaste painting, in which he was careful to cloak the male lovers' genitals, frankly exposed in the classical monument, in discreet shadow. Instead of positioning the heroes back to back as in the original sculpture, he rendered them side by side, a likely indication that his immediate source was a two-dimensional illustration, perhaps in a book, that included for clarity's sake two views of the sculpture, the Aristogeiton side and the Harmodius side respectively. The new arrangement allowed Wood to drape each figure's left arm around the other's shoulder, foregrounding the pair's friendship more than their daring exploits. He equipped them with Masonic symbols instead of the swords long lost but once brandished by the heroes in the ancient monument.

Altogether repressed by these transformations in Wood's picture is a primary reason for Aristogeiton's and Harmodius's notoriety and for his interest in them: their crime. An atmosphere of classical calm pervades *First Three Degrees of Free Masonry*, an almost uncanny stillness, with figures frozen in stone masking the latent content of the painting's central image—the violence of regicide, the filial revolt against the tyrannical father. Hailed in antiquity as liberators, Aristogeiton and Harmodius are here understood as liberated themselves, libertine in their same-sex love and triumphant over the despotic rule of law. They are made modern by Wood, clean-shaven and wholesomely handsome, ensconced in their pristine columned shelter just as the artist constructed in this work a protective edifice of allegory and Art in which to sequester his own rebellious yearnings, "taking refuge," as he himself would later aptly describe it, "in the classics."[62] Read from left to right, his three Masonic panels trace not only an aspirational progression of status within the secret society Wood had just joined, but also a son's emotionally fraught development: from an active struggle for personal freedom and autonomy in the self-fashioning figure, to a conspiratorial victory over the hated father, and finally, in the wake of the tyrant's assassination, to a guilty remorse in the brooding image of *The Thinker*. Choosing an outdoor sculpture gallery set somewhere in the remote past and far from Iowa as the subject for his fraternal order commission, Wood fossilized his feelings and made them publicly presentable, while on the surface, his dreamlike scene exudes a serenity untroubled by patricidal wishes or carnal desire.

In the tradition of the great homosexual art theorist J. J. Winckelmann before him, Wood at this period in his career found in statuary the perfect vehicle for "imaginative projections of identity and desire,"[63] and gravitated to it in other pictures such as the exuberant *Runners, Luxembourg Gardens, Paris* (1924, Fig. 2.20). One wonders if he saw in those lithe bronze nudes balanced gracefully on their plinth an idealized embodiment of the companionship he sought during that second European sojourn. In 1920, he had traveled abroad with his high school friend Cone, who spoke French and had previously studied at the Ecole des Beaux-Arts in Montpellier. This time, in 1923–24, Wood did not have Cone to rely on but formed relationships with other artists and expats, such as Rolf Armstrong and Lee "Jeff" Jeffries (Fig. 2.21), and with Marcel Bordet, the English-speaking Frenchman

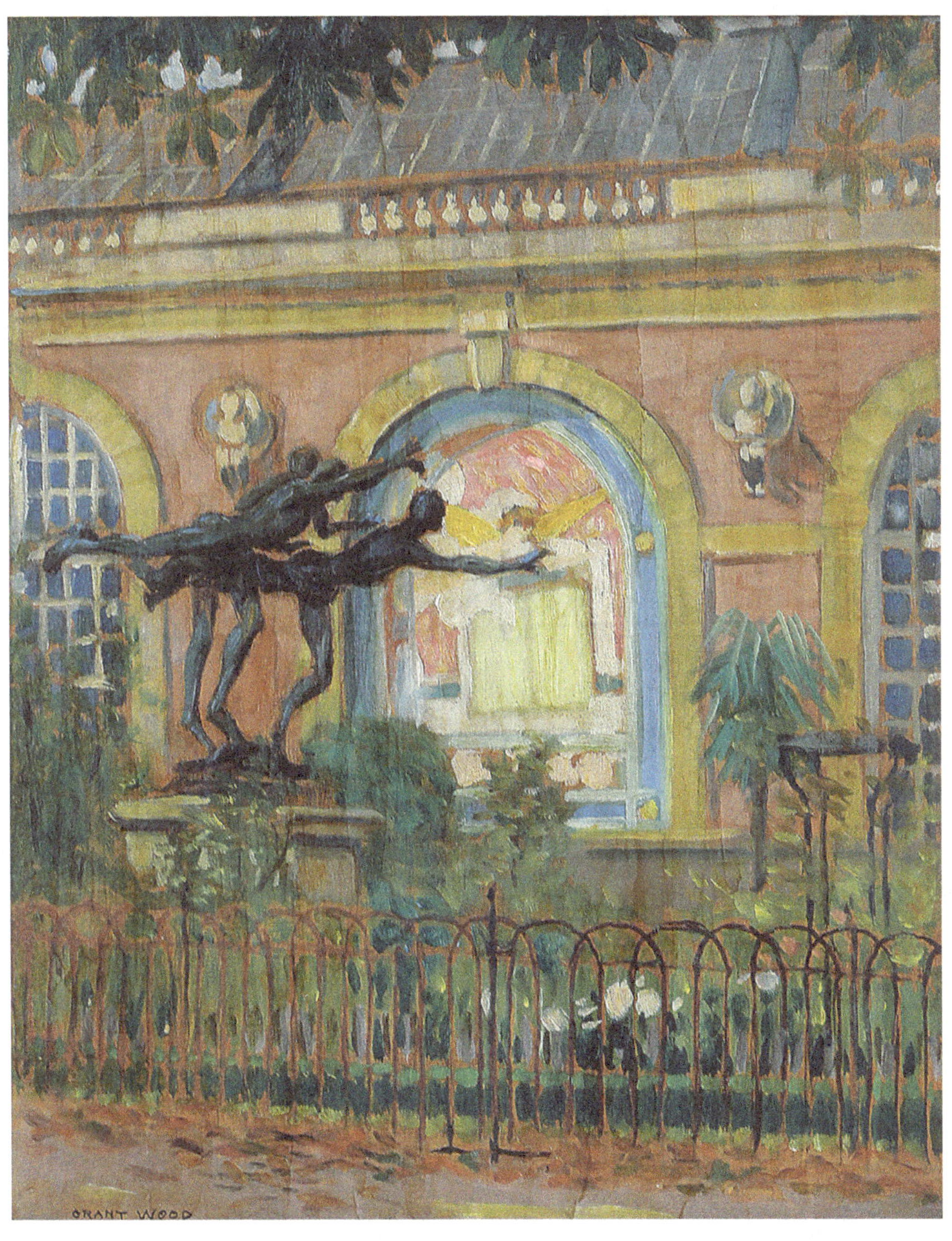

Fig. 2.20. Grant Wood, *The Runners, Luxembourg Gardens, Paris*, 1924.

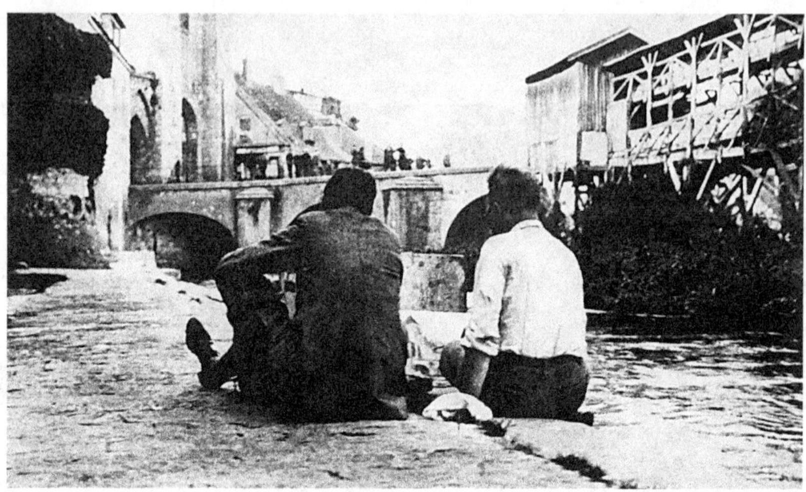

Fig. 2.21. Grant Wood with Lee Jeffries, Paris(?), 1923–24 or 1926.

who, according to Garwood, introduced Wood to Paris nightlife.[64] Apparently smitten, Wood wanted to bring Bordet home with him to Cedar Rapids but was unable to realize his impractical plan. For a while at least, the artist seems to have experienced a veritable heyday of male camaraderie, and in this milieu of happy attachments he created *The Runners*, adopting a warm palette of pink, yellow, and brown that contrasts with the decidedly cooler tones of *First Three Degrees of Free Masonry*. Here, a tight-knit group of sculpted bodies, joyously unconstrained, inhabit a protected corner of nature. The sun-drenched scene, with its overhanging vegetation and blossoming white flowers just beyond a low wicket fence, presents an artistically mediated fantasy of what literary scholar Byrne Fone has characterized as "blissful habitation in the garden."[65]

ARCADIA AND NARCISSISTIC DESIRE

In his classic essay on "Arcadia and the Homosexual Imagination," Fone claims a literary tradition from Virgil to Whitman, Wilde, and Gore Vidal in which a metaphorical park, forest, or glen provides a haven for "the loving and sexual fraternity of men" apart from any fear of punishment or social scorn. Often the protected enclave includes a watery element for symbolically washing away societal guilt, as was invariably the case when Wood dared to render the naked male body, rather than its sculptural surrogate, in nature. He had for example in 1920 created the idyllic *Peter Funcke at Indian Creek* (Fig. 2.22), depicting his sixteen-year-old Cedar Rapids neighbor on the bank of a secluded stream. The first of Wood's extant male nudes,[66] the picture was probably conceived shortly after his initial French trip, when he was undoubtedly emboldened by exposure to a culture where the nude was a commonplace not only in museums but also in sculptural form throughout the city. Back in Iowa, he teetered between newfound possibility and familiar constraint, and did not exhibit *Peter Funcke* publicly. It is a sensitive, somewhat tentatively painted image of the boy seated in profile, amidst summer foliage, on what appears to be a black cloth on the ground. The model is about to remove his sock; his other garments are nowhere to be seen. Despite the specificity of its current title (in the past the work was known simply as *Nude Bather*), Wood strove for a timeless atmosphere by eliminating details of contemporary clothing and avoiding any sense of portraiture. His treatment of the boy's face in lost profile was also a way of preserving the anonymity he had promised Funcke when he asked him to pose.[67] The painting exhibits the same tripartite arrangement the artist would employ in *First Three Degrees of Free Masonry*, where it has an obvious logic in relation to its subject matter. Here, however, the rationale for multiple panels seems unclear, even arbitrary, given the unity of the scene.

Perhaps the triptych format carried hallowed associations for Wood, and he used it as a device to elevate or sacralize his subject. His inclusion of several white flowers at the right of the composition adds a suggestion of purity, as if subtly to deny any prurient intention. An etherealizing blue permeates the scene, defining sky and water and caressing the figure's foot, arm, and back, like moonlight falling on the body of Endymion. Indeed, in its pastoral tranquility *Peter Funcke* recalls the image of a shepherd boy at rest. There is scant precedent for it in American art. Lost in moody self-absorption, Wood's bather bears little comparison, for example, with the group of dynamic young men in Thomas Eakins's homosocial *Swimming* (1885). In that painting of naked open-air sport, the artist had overcome his own need for "refuge in the classics," evinced just a few years prior by his pan-piping nudes in the Corot-like *Arcadia* (c. 1883). More than any counterpart in Eakins, Wood's ephebic Funcke sits close to the picture plane. His proximity to the viewer is akin to that of another lone male nude, similarly passive and withdrawn from the world, Hippolyte Flandrin's much-copied figure study (1835, Fig. 2.23) in the Louvre, already established in the nineteenth century as an icon of homosexual desire and also, in some interpretations, of shame.[68] Though not a reprise of the Flandrin, Wood's image shares with it the low horizon, the discreet profile view with hidden face and genitals, the cloth on which the figure rests, as well as his isolation in nature and sense of inwardness. Funcke's indistinct facial features and his spatial affinity with the artist/viewer foster an identification, as if Wood were both desiring and being the boy he depicts, in a tender idealization of his own youth.

The boy's solipsistic solitude conjures the memorable opening tableau of the autobiographical "Return from Bohemia," with the child Wood sitting "on an island of sod beneath an enormous cottonwood tree," an oasis in the coolness of the leafy shade (Appendix, p. 195). "The scene is as clear to me

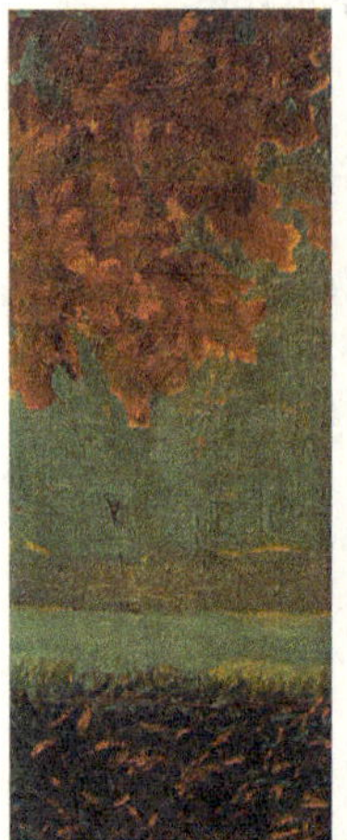
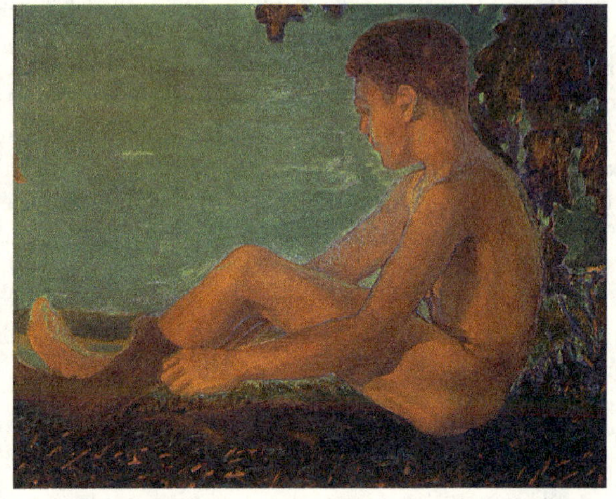

Fig. 2.22. Grant Wood, *Peter Funcke at Indian Creek*, c. 1920.

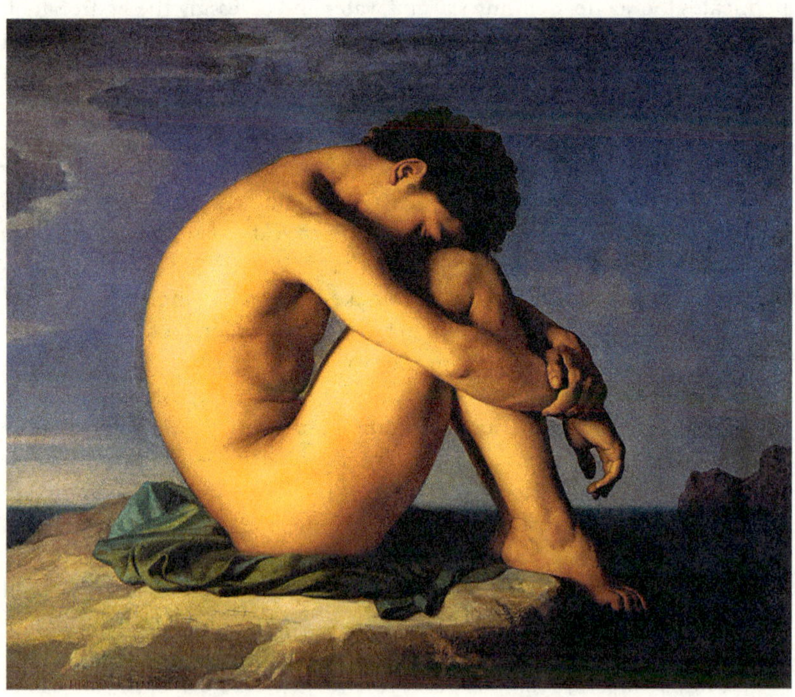

Fig. 2.23. Hippolyte Flandrin, *Figure d'étude* or *Jeune homme nu au bord de la mer* (Figure Study or Nude Boy by the Sea), 1835.

as a passage out of a singularly vivid dream," Wood claimed of this summery recollection, the latent content of which is sexual: his boyhood self is mesmerized by "the mysteries of a garter-snake that lay writhing and spitting on the fresh earth of a molehill." The child's fascination with the phallic snake in suggestive juxtaposition with an underground burrow renders every "problem in heaven or earth" nonexistent for him, while the whole countryside is "fixed for an intense, breathless moment in the sleeping lull of noon." (The soporific daytime lassitude could be a disguise, as sometimes emerges in the dreamwork, for its opposite, vigorous waking activity at night.) But the happy boy is soon interrupted by a paternal interdiction: "Presently I heard the rattle of the harness and father's 'Whoa!'" Maryville has arrived with his plow horses. The first word he utters in Wood's memoir, directed on the narrative surface at his team, represents in the context of the child's onanistic reverie a sexual prohibition, and the harness stands for the father's perceived control of his son's (animalistic) behavior. "Whoa!" instantly signals Maryville's terse, censorious authority; at the same time, the word puns on what his life and death so often meant to his ambivalent artist son—woe. Mother Hattie immediately echoes her husband's disapproval of the child's pleasure, albeit indirectly on the conscious level of Wood's text, where dinner preparations now drive the action along. Once Maryville enters the scene with his curt command, Hattie issues one of her own. She instructs Frank, Wood's older brother, "Go find Grant," then orders a pail of water, as if the guilty child needed to be found (out) and washed clean. Indeed, Maryville urges Grant, "Hurry up and get washed, son."

Water's purifying connotation helps explain Wood's need to situate *Peter Funcke* on the shore of Indian Creek. While the littoral setting provides a convenient pretext for the boy's nudity in Cedar Rapids, functioning in a protective way as the life class would for *The Spotted Man* in Paris, it also implies a cleansing baptism of the type noted by Fone in his homosexual Arcadia. The solitary youth's heavy-lidded gaze in the painting, transfixed on the water, renders him a modern-day Narcissus in Iowa—a model of male homoeroticism in which the object of desire is a mirror image of the self. Theorizing this kind of libidinal attraction in his essay "On Narcissicism" (1914), Freud differentiated it from the anaclitic sort, which "leans on" prior satisfactions associated with caretakers in infancy "and the succession of [parental] substitutes who take their place."[69] According to this reasoning, desiring narcissistically, a man may love another as a version of himself, as part of himself, or as what he once was or would like to be. Accordingly, in *Peter Funcke*, and in the many crushes Wood developed on younger men throughout his life, his object choice recapitulates less his archaic love for his mother than his mother's adoring love for him in his childhood. He desires, then, from the imagined position of the mother, and projects this narcissistic attitude onto the reflective boy in his painting.

THE BOLDEST NUDE

Given the reticence with which Wood treated the vulnerable body exposed in this early work, it is remarkable to consider his stunning miscalculation in another *plein-air* nude, the late lithograph *Sultry Night*, published in 1939 (Fig. 2.24).[70] The unfortunate fate of this extraordinary picture, which shows Wood at the height of his artistic powers, is well known. It was among the nineteen otherwise highly successful lithographs he produced with Associated American Artists (AAA), which marketed 250 impressions of each print at its Manhattan gallery and through its mail-order catalogue. AAA's master lithographer George Miller pulled fifty impressions at a time from stones Wood sent him from Iowa until each edition was complete. In the case of *Sultry Night*, however, production stopped at one hundred impressions when the U.S. Post Office forced the withdrawal of the image from sale on the charge of obscenity. Both Wood and his AAA dealer/publisher Reeves Lewenthal were taken aback by this development. Over the telephone, they had initially discussed the subject of a "farmer cooling off after a hard day, with water from a trough," and Lewenthal approved enthusiastically, believing that "Wood had perfectly captured a genuinely Mid-Western motif."[71]

Encouraged by this support and pleased with his original drawing for the lithograph, Wood replicated the image in a painting, at some point adding two cows and a small pond to the right middleground, for submission to the

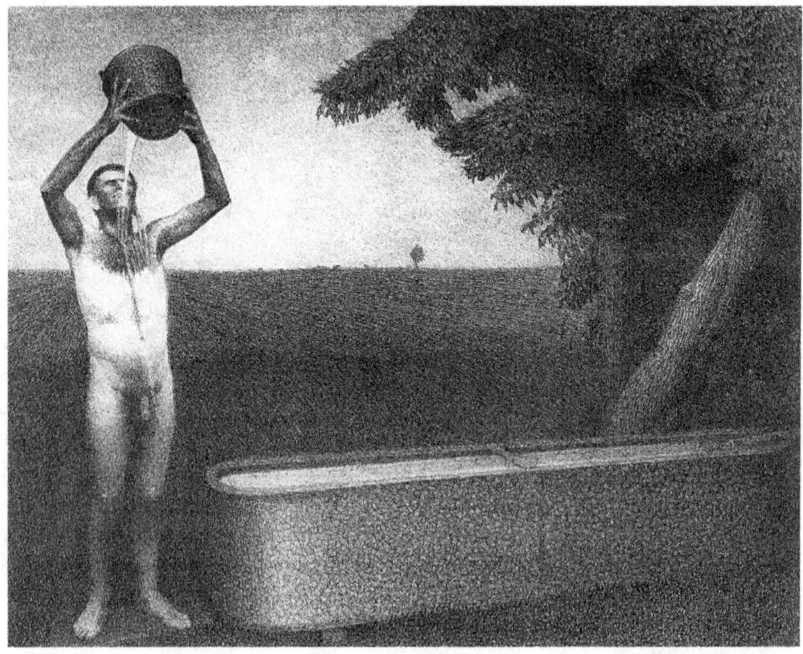

Fig. 2.24. Grant Wood, *Sultry Night*, 1938.

prestigious 1938 Carnegie International Exhibition in Pittsburgh. The glazes were still drying that summer when he wrote confidently to John O'Connor, organizer of the American section, that it was the best picture he had painted for years.[72] But his public was hardly prepared for such a graphic rendering of male frontal nudity. When he unveiled the new painting at his Iowa City home before shipping it to Pittsburgh, many among the fifty-some invited guests, according to Garwood, were deeply embarrassed, especially the men.[73] The picture was refused for the Carnegie International and sent back to Iowa. Wood substituted the only other work he had available, *Woman with Plants*, making him ineligible for a prize since the painting of his mother was by that time nine years old. This was particularly awkward for him, as the International was a veritable "who's who" of American art, and his friends and fellow Regionalists Benton, Curry, Doris Lee, and Arnold Blanch were all represented with current work, Blanch taking third prize. In New York, the collector J. Stanley Resor, who had first option on *Sultry Night*, decided not to purchase it.[74] Then came the postal ban on the print, followed by Wood's self-justifying, ultimately ineffectual efforts at damage control and, finally, his self-punishing surrender: he mutilated the painting.

Sultry Night was most unusual in American art at the time. Although the Carnegie exhibition from which it was omitted displayed nudes aplenty, both European and American, they were all female. A similarly frank treatment of the male body could only be found in works addressed to a small cosmopolitan homosexual subculture—Charles Demuth's contemporaneous watercolors of well-endowed sailors, for example, or George Platt Lynes's searching photographic portraits of gay men. Paul Cadmus created comparably realistic drawings of studio nudes, but when producing a painting for public consumption in *Gilding the Acrobats* (1935, Fig. 2.25), he hid the genitals of his naked circus performer decorously behind the head of a seated stagehand. Similarly, the frolicking naked men in Curry's boldly homosocial outdoor *Bathers* (c. 1928, Fig. 2.26) are discreetly positioned; only the child about to dive into the pool faces the viewer, displaying minute genitals and certainly no pubic hair. One wonders what prompted Wood to display such explicit interest in the male body in *Sultry Night*. Years of his personal and professional experience separate the diffident ephebe in *Peter Funcke* from the unabashedly naked farmhand depicted here. Wood may have believed himself shielded by his national fame, his confidence in the viability of the male nude boosted by *The Spotted Man*'s exhibition in 1935 at the Ferargil Galleries in New York and his election to the National Academy of Design that year. In Iowa, he had worked to spread tolerance for the nude in art. The life drawing class was a regular feature of the curriculum at his Stone City Art Colony in the summers of 1932 and 1933 (Fig. 2.27), where he actively sought to inoculate the surrounding rural community against philistinism by means of public Sunday programs.

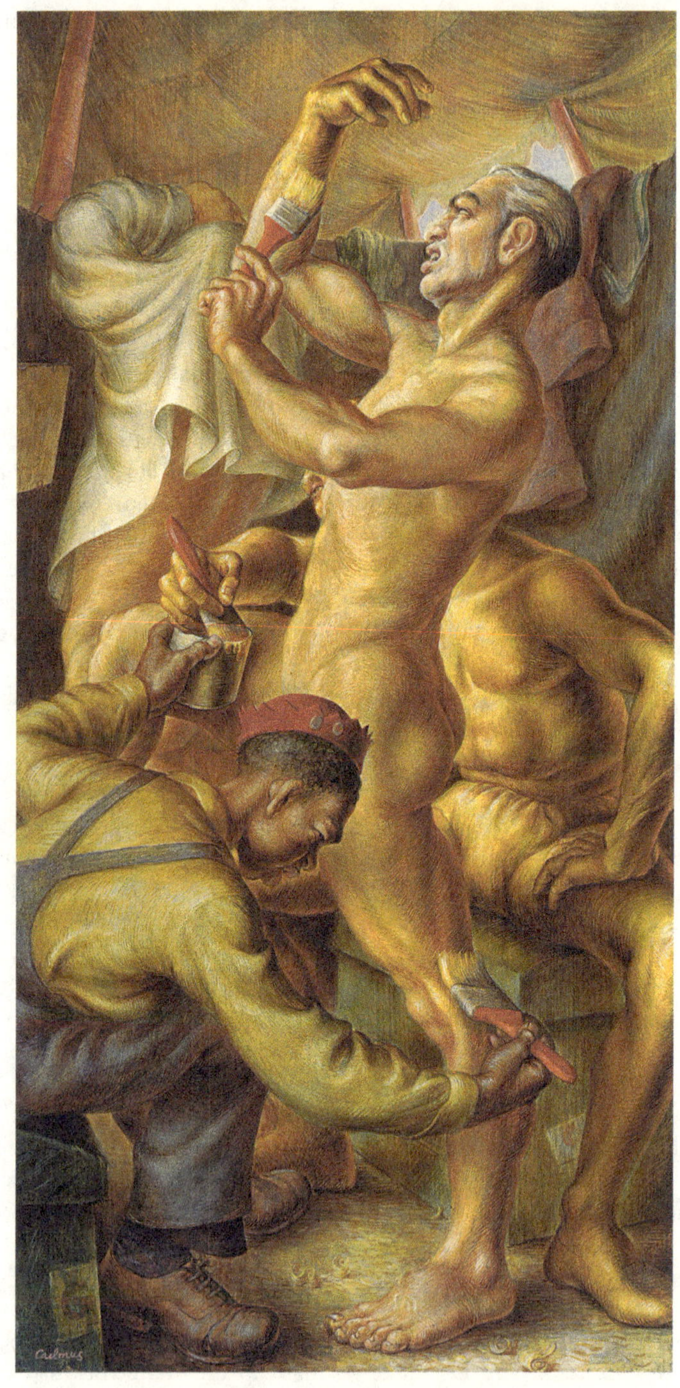

Fig. 2.25. Paul Cadmus, *Gilding the Acrobats*, 1935.

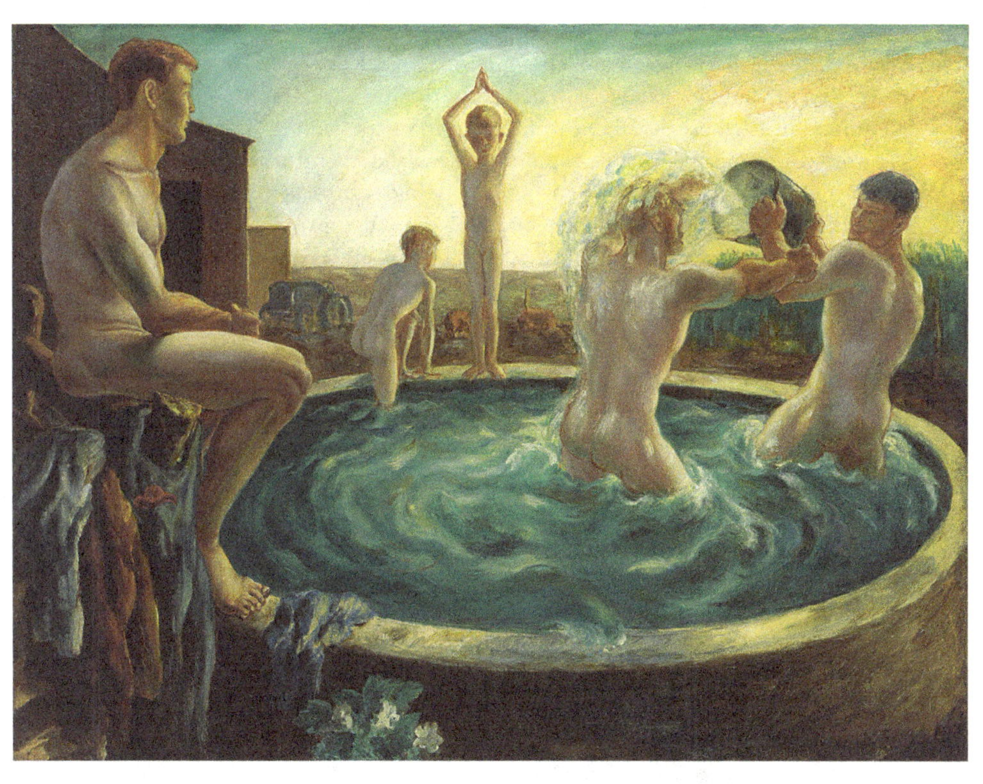

Fig. 2.26. John Steuart Curry, *The Bathers*, c. 1928.

"The crowd that comes are usually expecting to see something freakish," wrote instructor David McCosh from the colony, adding, "Grant is experimenting with nudes which he is slipping into the exhibitions one at a time to break the natives in gradually."[75]

While Wood had painted from the live model, furtively in nature in *Peter Funcke* and matter-of-factly in the atelier in *The Spotted Man*, he worked from photographs for *Sultry Night*. It was a habit he developed in the thirties that would contribute to his difficulties in the art department at the University of Iowa, where his colleagues associated this technique with a presumed inability to draw. For this reason, he was careful not to preserve evidence of his process, and he swore the professional photographers he hired, often the university's photographer Fred Kent or his assistant Ruth Weller, to secrecy.[76] Kent produced a number of photographic studies from which the artist created a large drawing for *Sultry Night*, now lost, in black and red crayon on brown wrapping paper. Had Wood registered Weller's alarm when Rinard scheduled her to photograph the drawing, he might have thought better about proceeding with the print edition and the painting. "I nearly fainted," she recalled. "And here I was with these two fellas, and they thought nothing of it, and of course I had to go ahead and do my thing but I was shocked. It was a shock." The astonished Weller subsequently discovered Kent's nude negatives (or perhaps contact sheets) for the drawing in his files, recognizing the model, whom she identified as a local Iowa City man with the last name of James. It seems to me that this might well have been Howard James, a student of Wood's at the University of Iowa,

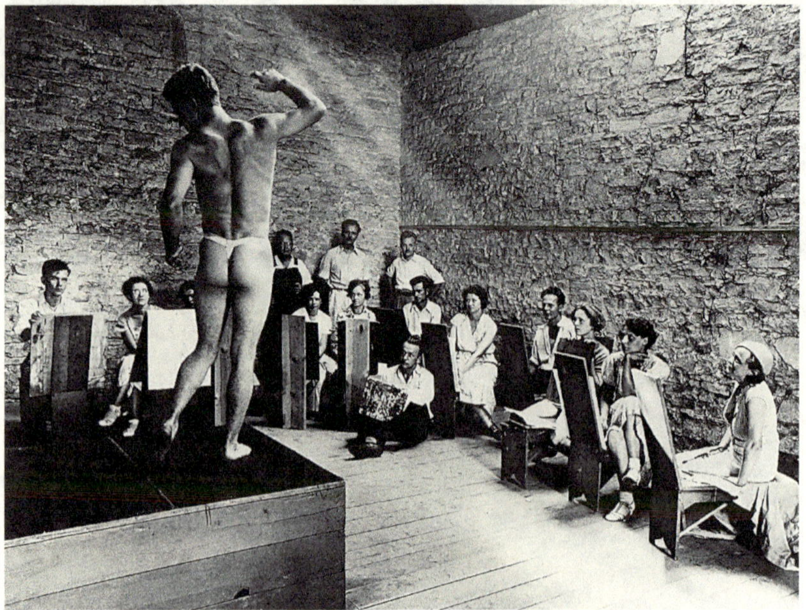

Fig. 2.27. Life class at Stone City Art Colony, 1932 or 1933.

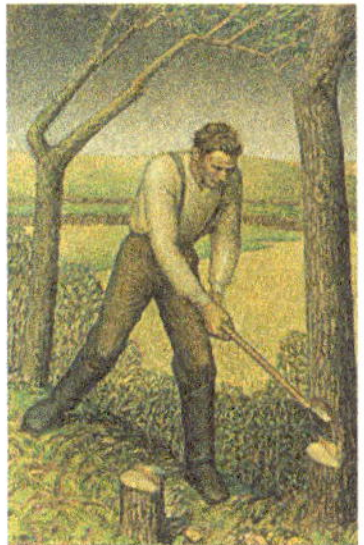
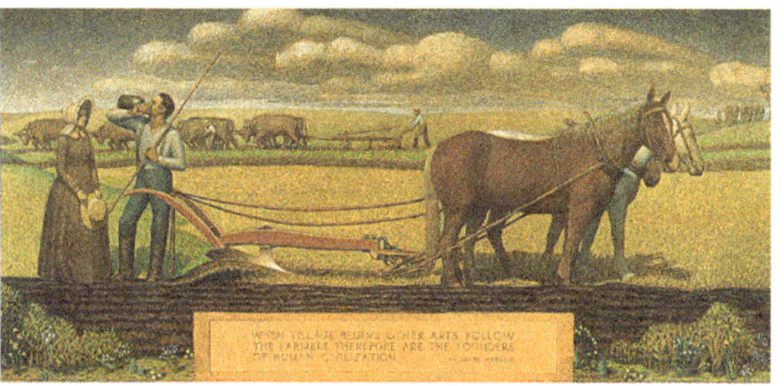
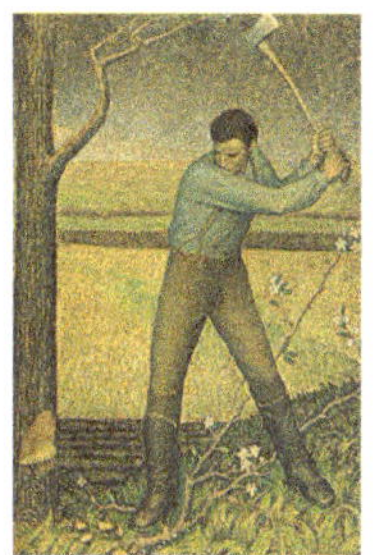

Fig. 2.28. Grant Wood, *Study for Breaking the Prairie*, 1935–39.

one of the team who worked with him on the mural paintings destined for the library at Iowa State University in Ames. James served as the model for the two woodchoppers in the entrance hall mural, *Breaking the Prairie* (1935–37), and for the related, highly finished study (1935–39, Fig. 2.28).[77] The woodchoppers' features are too generalized to draw any definite conclusion about their relationship to the figure in *Sultry Night*, but the tall, slender proportions do conform to the body type seen in the nude. "We weren't used to seeing that in a photograph," Weller explained about the negatives of James she was not supposed to have found, "I was a little surprised that Grant Wood would do that. I didn't believe he'd be interested in doing a shock thing."

From Kent's photographs, probably taken on location in some field outside Iowa City,[78] Wood created the figure of a farm laborer stripped down at the end of the day, pouring water over his face and chest from a bucket held aloft. As in *Peter Funcke*, the figure's shed clothing is absent from the composition. With both arms raised, standing in slight contrapposto with his weight on his right foot, the farmhand in *Sultry Night* seems a male reprise of Jean-Auguste-Dominique Ingres's allegorical *Source* with her upturned urn (1856),[79] and other variants of the Venus *anadyomène*, rising from the sea, with all the attendant associations of beauty, fertility, and love. Wood situated his nude in the dim light of an Iowa evening, before a vast furrowed field with a single tree on the otherwise flat horizon. He divided his composition into thirds both vertically and laterally, as was often his wont with landscapes:[80] from top to bottom, sky, field, then trough; from left to right, farmer, field, then tree. Adeptly with the litho crayon, he created a plethora of sensuous textures, from the smooth core and downy limbs of the body to bristling grass, foliage, tree bark, and the hammered metal of the trough.[81] Most impressive is Wood's calculated manipulation of chiaroscuro effects, making the man's white torso gleam against the dark field and his tanned arms and face stand out starkly against the pale cloudless sky.

Every element in the picture responds to the naked figure, whose chest is neatly bisected at the tan line by the level of the horizon. Wood placed the

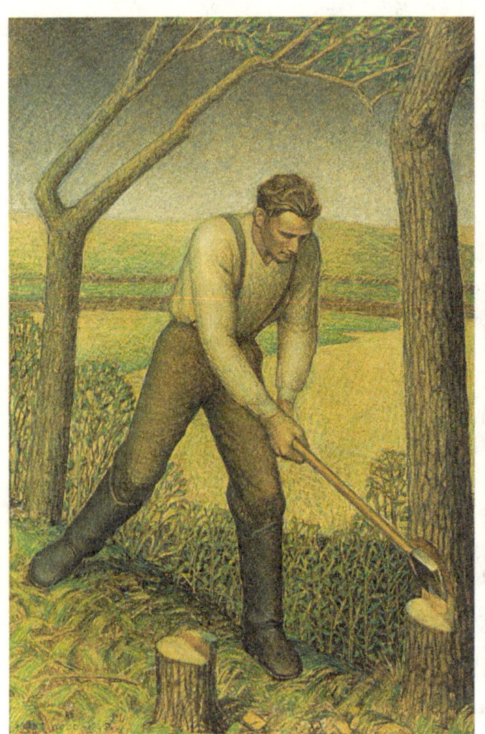
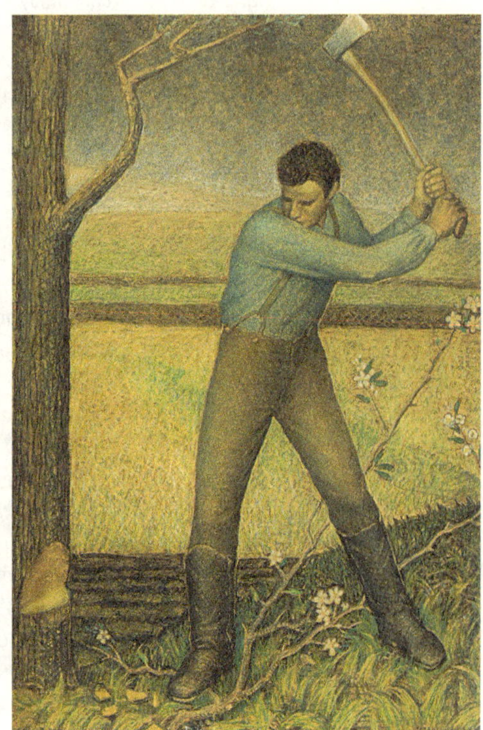

Figs. 2.28A–B (details). Grant Wood, *Study for Breaking the Prairie*, 1935–39.

vanishing point of the composition behind and just above the man's sternum; the receding orthogonals of the plowed field thus rush toward the place his heart would be. The trough, and the long spigot of the (invisible) water pump that replenishes it, emerge from the shadows at the far right to carry our attention in his direction, just as the leafy upper branches of the tree gesture toward him like the fingers of a great hand. The knotty, anthropomorphic trunk seems to lean back in awe at the sight of this body, hardly able to support its own giant erection in the curious upright post that stands at the convergence of the diagonal strokes delineating the earth and those articulating the tree bark. These subliminal, animistic signs of desire may have helped stoke the reaction of viewers unprepared for a male figure so starkly revealed at his toilet, feminized in his specularity.

MAKING APOLOGIES

Garwood's report that the male guests at Wood's unveiling of the painted version of *Sultry Night* were most disconcerted by it suggests not only homosexual panic—men recoiling from the very possibility of their own same-sex desire—but also a fearful realization that masculinity itself might be made vulnerable in such a way. Viewers outside of Wood's most intimate circle were forced to recognize in their midst a person capable of such a vision, heterosexuality encountering "the close proximity of its terrifying (homo)-sexual other."[82] Although Wood had naturalized his nude, creating a scene that the imagined spectator apparently happens upon unintentionally, this strategy failed to protect the image from opprobrium, especially given the (ill-advised) sexy title. Unlike other descriptive phrases he could have selected—"Summer Night," "Muggy Night," or simply "Farmhand Bathing"—"Sultry Night" carries with it associations not just of heat and humidity but also of passion and lust. Though an early defender of the picture, critic John Selby, attempted to ennoble the naked figure by comparing him to a statue of Apollo,[83] already it was too late. According to Graham, "Grant was bothered by the thought that some detractor might try to create evil where there was none. He sawed off the portion [of the painting] that portrayed the nude farm hand and burned it."[84]

He also spun defensive explanations placing the nude in the context of his youthful, firsthand experience on the farm: "In my boyhood," he said, "no farms had tile and chromium bathrooms. After a long day in the dust of the fields, after the chores were done, we used to go down to the horse tank with a pail. The sun would have taken the chill off the top layer of water. We would dip up pails full and drench ourselves."[85] This is a familiar, even banal kind of nostalgic formulation, which the artist hoped might strike a chord in Iowa: life was rough back then without modern conveniences, people worked hard and had wholesome fun. This was somewhat disingenuous. Wood was only ten when his family left the farm, and he had not worked the fields as he claimed here. There is a notable disjunction, moreover, between his putative recollection and the image it sought to redeem. Cannily, he recalled several boys rather than a single adult male and omitted any mention of undressing, appealing to a popular vision of childhood as uncorrupted and asexual. I think he may have realized the weakness of his position and attempted further to buttress it with another work of art. The charcoal drawing *Saturday Night Bath* (Fig. 2.29) seems to me a veritable illustration of Wood's verbal apologia for *Sultry Night*. The drawing repeats the format of the destroyed painting, with its arched top,[86] bowdlerizes its objectionable title and subject matter, and replaces a moment of visual and sensual pleasure centered on the body with a scene of nonchalant camaraderie. If this drawing does indeed represent, as I understand it, a kind of peace offering to audiences offended by *Sultry Night*, then the date of 1937 traditionally ascribed to it needs to be revised to a more likely date of 1938 or 1939.[87]

Eschewing frontal nudity in *Saturday Night Bath*, Wood shows one boy bather decorously positioned behind a trough from which he skims a pail of water, the other with his back turned, pulling off his shirt. Art historian Luciano Cheles has recently proposed a source for the disrobing boy, head hidden in his garments, in a similar figure in Piero della Francesca's *Baptism of Christ* (c. 1448–50), which Wood reversed in his composition.[88] This is an intriguing possibility, especially if Wood's project was indeed to convey in this drawing the purity and innocence of his subjects. With the inclusion of horses, fences, and barn, *Saturday Night Bath* reads as the very type of guileless genre scene that the haunting, moody *Sultry Night* exceeds. And this is despite the charcoal's unfortunate phallic log, draped at one end with a towel as if with a foreskin and seeming to eye the empty bucket beside it. A piece of conscious propaganda for the artist's own virtuous intentions—with a snide or perhaps inadvertently and unconscious subversive sexual symbol erupting in plain sight—*Saturday Night Bath* lacks the deeply emotional and erotic investment of the lithograph and is, it seems to me, much less successful aesthetically. It is a reaction to a reaction in the vexed back-and-forth between Wood and his puritanical audience.

Did he himself perhaps judge the drawing a failure? He did not translate the image into a painting or a print as he so often did with finished drawings. Instead, retreating even further from the danger he had risked with the nude in *Sultry Night*, he reworked the charcoal composition into the lithograph *Fertility* (1939, Fig. 2.30), supplanting the male figures with tidy rows of corn in the foreground and introducing the quaint *American Gothic* house into the middleground. Suppressing any possible anecdote, trading night for day with the starkest contrasts of bright light and shadow, and closing up tight the gaping hayloft door of the drawing, Wood made everything in this image stand rigid and alert, as if ready to pass inspection.

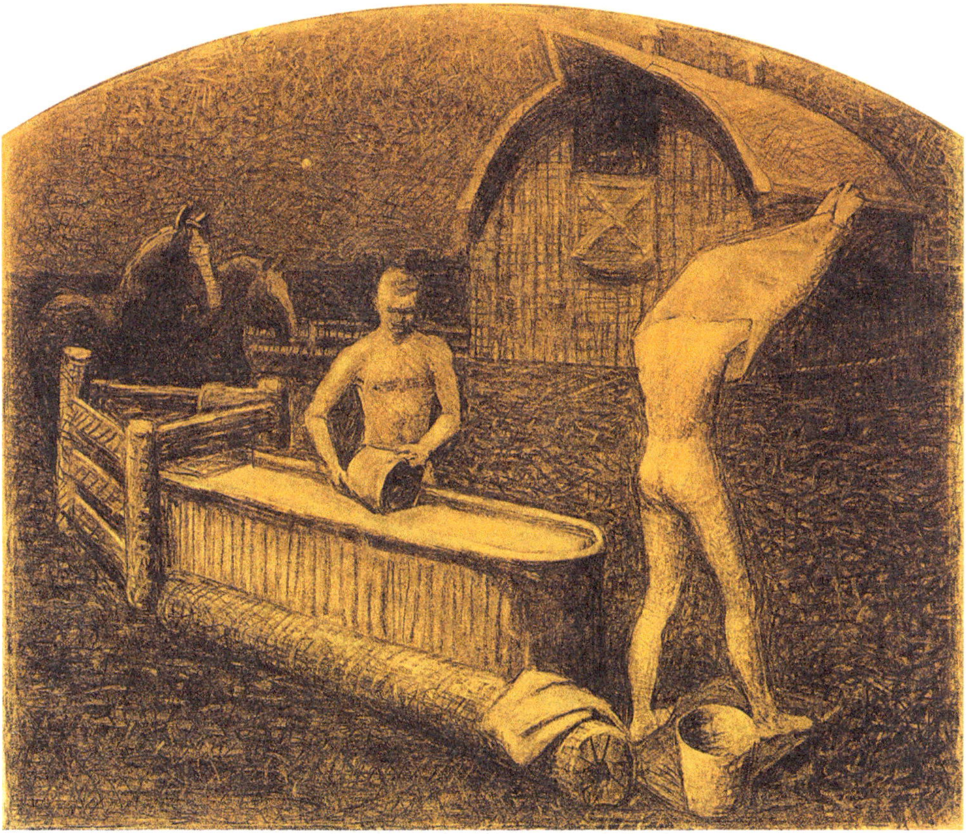

Fig. 2.29. Grant Wood, *Saturday Night Bath*, 1937.

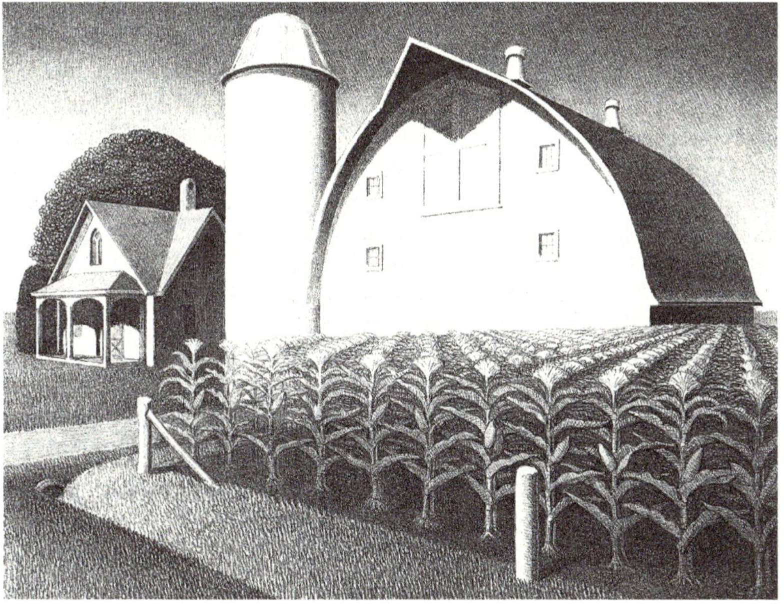

Fig. 2.30. Grant Wood, *Fertility*, 1939.

Here is a scene buttoned up, holding in its very breath. Yet while all is regimented and under control, the pneumatic silo and the incessant repetition of bristling verticals everywhere suggest the potential return of the repressed in this manifest celebration of agrarian productivity.

THE HIRED MAN

Ever vigilant about Wood's reputation, Graham joined her brother in his nervous backpedaling after he had let himself be carried away so injudiciously in *Sultry Night*. Her explication of the image as a genuine reflection of farm life was surely just a repetition of what Wood told her, since she had been a mere two years old when the family decamped from Anamosa for Cedar Rapids. "When Grant was a boy on the farm," she instructed, "hired men were given no facilities. Nights, they slept in the hay. Baths were drawn from the watering trough after the sun had warmed the water all day long. The men carefully dipped buckets in the water to avoid stirring up the settlings on the bottom. Horses are very particular and won't drink water that isn't clean. The hard-working men looked forward to sultry nights as those were considered best for bathing."[89] Complete with its picturesque details, Graham's testimonial complements Wood's and helps provide a backstory for *Sultry Night*, a haunting tableau that has fundamentally to do, I believe, with the artist's struggle to understand the enigma of his own sexuality. Although the image was perfectly plausible as a contemporary scene in the late 1930s, Wood in his rationalizing statements projected it backward in time, to his youth, and indeed the perspective in the lithograph is that of a child, looking slightly up at the nude bather. In this voyeuristic scheme, Wood rehearsed the boyhood fascination he also conveyed in "Return from Bohemia" with the taciturn farmhand the family employed in Anamosa, David Zephaniah Peters. "Everything about the hired man," Wood recalled, "was tinged with mystery" (App., 197), and part of the mystery is coded in the narrative as sexual.

We meet this strange man at the very beginning of the memoir, just after the child Wood reluctantly leaves off playing with his garter snake. Like the figure in *Sultry Night*, though not in physical appearance, the red-bearded Peters in this initial scene is juxtaposed with water, standing "over by the rain-barrel" (App., 197). In the course of the story, Wood described him as seasoned and capable, adept at braiding bullwhips and carving things of wood and bone. Peters is a necessary fixture on the farm; at the same time, he represents the possibility of adventure in the wider world, for he had been a Mississippi bargeman, a sheepherder, and, Wood and his brother Frank suspect, an Indian fighter. His eventual departure one Sunday for his hometown of Cairo, Illinois,[90] while the family is away at church, leaves everyone dismayed and bereft. Wood's own feelings about him are a complex mixture of awe, curiosity, and fear. At times the hired man seems predatory, with his "hawk-like face," "talon-like hands," and "condor-eyes" (App., 197, 212, 238, respectively), and he terrifies Grant and Frank with tales of Indian massacres: "The hired man gouged out the bloody details so vividly that Frank and I were fairly popeyed," Wood reported in fraught language, adding how later he had still "shivered with fright, and snuggled closer to [his] brother" in bed (App., 213). Peters's vague association with things Native American makes him an emissary in "Return from Bohemia" of something the boys imagine as savage and exotic. He thrills Grant with the gift of an arrowhead, which the child mistakes for a rock and which his father has to explain to him. At the county fair, much is made of Peters's recruitment as a local agent by the Indian medicine man to distribute a "celebrated elixir" (App., 254).

Wood did not call the elixir snake oil, but he did implicate Peters as the generator of his guilt-inducing snake fantasy, which his child self indulges, as described in the preceding chapter, in church:

> While the congregation grappled with problems of original sin and eternal damnation, my mind reverted to the topic that was of greatest importance to me at the time—namely, joint snakes. For several days, I had been able to think of little else. It had all started one evening the week before when Dave Peters had told my brothers and me about an actual experience he had once with a joint snake. As the minister's voice writhed on, I seemed to hear the hired man telling the story, paring his fingernails with his jackknife as he talked [App., 232–33].

Peters, whose very name points to his phallic influence, initiates the boys into the mysteries of the mythical joint snake. His revelations to them consist of showing as well as telling. In his very first appearance in the narrative, he displays to Frank "some kind of chain puzzle carved out of wood" (App., 195). The symbolic "puzzle," something to be figured out, has length and woodenness, a disguised erection. Among the brothers, Grant is the one for whom all this becomes an obsession. His raging fantasies, as we've seen, lead to trouble, for just as the church minister promised that "the Lord rained upon Sodom and upon Gomorrah brimstone and fire" (App., 233), a grassfire besets the Wood farm. The family emerges unscathed from the conflagration—except for Grant and Peters. The boy's hand is burned and the hired man's beard singed in the backfire. They are secret sharers in blame. Alarmed by the preacher's animadversions, Wood's tormented child-self had worried in the pew, "Oh, why had I been so foolish as to offend the Lord?" (App., 233), and even the mature Wood seems on some level to have preserved the awful threat of fiery chastisement. His burning of the excised figure of the farmhand from the painted version of *Sultry Night* suggests as much. It was not enough for him simply to reuse the panel or to discard it, nor even just to cut it up; he had to slice off the guilty part and subject it masochistically to the flames. And he allowed the tragic remaining fragment to survive, even framing it, as a monument to the whole explosive affair (Fig. 2.31).

It seems to me that the offending nude, modeled on Mr. James in Iowa City, harbored the memory for Wood of a hired man in Anamosa. Indeed, Wood may have traced the very nature of his erotic desire back to Peters, believing his own sexuality to have been indelibly imprinted at an early age by whatever contact had occurred between them. At a time when homosexuality was considered a psychiatric disorder, Wood's insistence, invoked in the introduction to this book, that "psychologists tell us that we're conditioned in the first 12 years of our lives"[91] could have been his way of accounting to himself for the development and character of his libido as well as his art. Perhaps this was the sexual secret he confided to Kantor amidst the rumors of his preference for a particular kind of "emolument," as Kantor euphemistically put it. Whether Wood had actually been seduced as a child can of course never be known, though it remains a possibility.[92] Regardless of whether it was guiltily remembered or retrospectively imagined, a formative encounter with the farmhand seems implicit in various passages in "Return from Bohemia" and is movingly memorialized in *Sultry Night* and its misfortunes.

ERASING HOMOSEXUAL DESIRE

Positioning Wood's contribution within a larger cultural context, James Dennis described the naked man in the lithograph *Sultry Night* as an elemental "American Adam," casting the picture as a culmination of the artist's "agrarian myth of plenitude."[93] The image may also distill another origin myth—that of Wood's personal homoeroticism. In his mutilation of the painting, Wood enacted a harsh kind of repression, removing the overt figure of his desire. The Arcadian scene that remains to us on this panel, with its now softly rising green hills and resting animals, is sometimes known as *Sultry Night with Cattle*, incongruously so because it is barely evening on the farm and there is little sultriness in its mood or atmosphere. But in this poignant fragment, Wood (perhaps unwittingly) preserved the content of his sexual fantasy, camouflaged as a spooky farm-"hand" in the foliage of the tree, reaching out with leafy fingers to caress the symbolic "wood" of the trunk below. As in a dream, in an ostensibly innocent scene of uncanny stillness, the repressed wish emerges in ingenious disguise.

Although the painting is small, less than twenty inches tall without its frame, it looms large as a veritable monument to the self-censorship historically imposed on homosexual artists, to the forced erasure of their experience and desire. And as a mere part for the whole, *Sultry Night with Cattle* allegorizes the limited concept of Wood's oeuvre that prevailed for six decades in the history of American art, until scholars such as Wallach and Adams began to respond to evidence that was always there, in Wood's biography, the

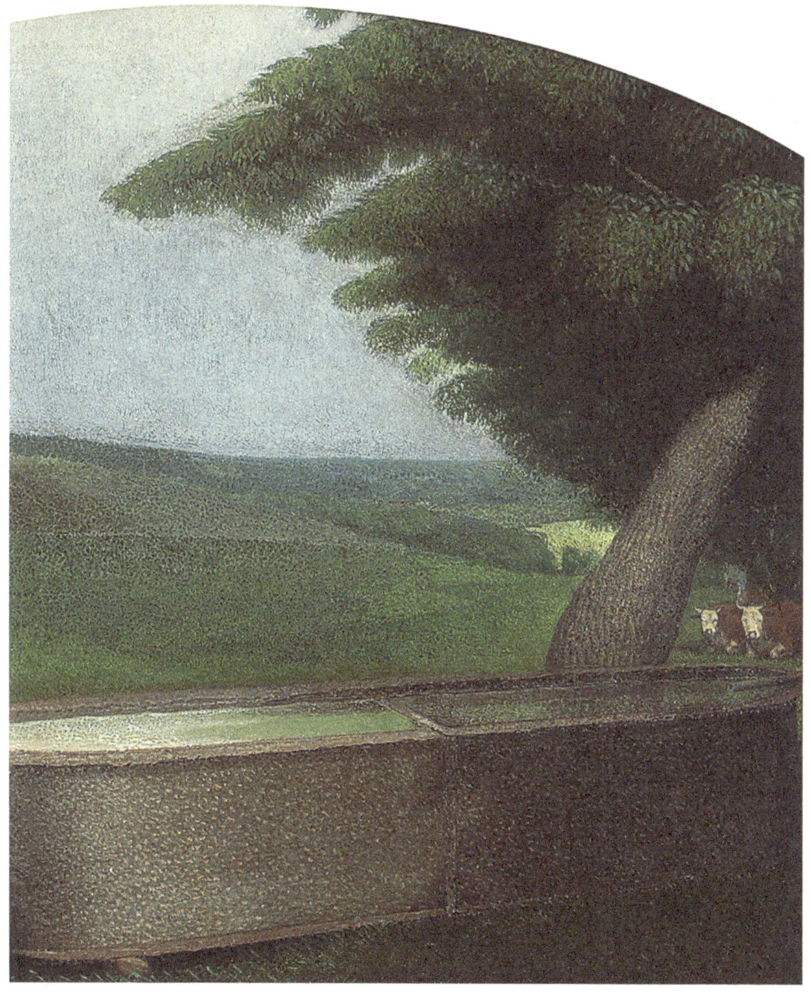

Fig. 2.31. Grant Wood, *Sultry Night*, 1938.

documents, and the work itself. The peculiar shape of this painting, with the top arc halted on its gentle descent to the left, signals a redaction and compels us imaginatively to reconstruct the expurgated object of Wood's desire. As we attempt to recuperate an artistic project formed under a powerful regime of social (and psychic) censorship, I like to imagine the artist triumphant, secretly enjoying the last word in putting the finishing touches on *Sultry Night with Cattle*. Absent in the original lithograph and possibly too in the initial version of the painting, the resting cows provide a charming anecdotal detail, similar to the two horses watching the nude boys in *Saturday Night Bath*. The eponymous cattle here rehearse the activity of Wood's viewers, who may stare dumbly without comprehension at half a picture. If he intended the joke, it is a deliciously tendentious one and points to his brilliantly rebellious humor, explored in depth in the next chapter.

❖ CHAPTER 3 ❖

Queer Habits of Dissembling

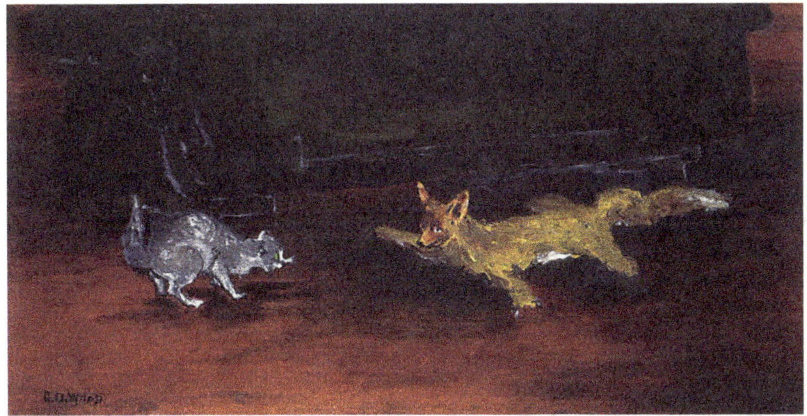

Fig. 3.1. Grant Wood, *Cat with Fox Rug*, 1905.

GRANT WOOD PAINTED *Cat with Fox Rug* (1905, Fig. 3.1) when he was fourteen years old. In this beguiling bit of juvenilia, a gray kitten, back arched and tail bristling, recoils in alarm from the spread-eagled rug. Juxtaposing domestic and wild, one lively thing and the other inert, the picture predicts the many "narratives of confrontation" Wanda Corn has identified in Wood's mature work, for example, where newfangled technology meets old-fashioned prudery in *Victorian Survival* (Fig. 2.10) or country type encounters city type in *Appraisal* (1931, see Fig. 3.20).[1] But the little animal painting also announces another, overarching theme in Wood's art and life—that things are not always what they seem. The cat is duped. There is pleasure to be had for viewers in her simple naïveté, to be sure, but there is also more. Who, after all, uses a flayed fox as a rug? We should expect a bear, but Wood gives us instead the wily creature fabled for his devious schemes.

Could the fox be *posing* as a rug? How would we know? Does the cat sense something that we don't? If the fox is indeed only a rug, then his canny ability to deceive endures even in death, rendering his presence uncanny. The scene, I believe, inadvertently allegorizes the future relation of Wood to his public. Clever like a fox, the artist would engage in all kinds of plots and hoaxes throughout his career. He became a poseur in life and bequeathed a legacy where fact is sometimes inseparable from fiction.

A curious letter to Wood when he was a senior at Washington High School in Cedar Rapids suggests how serious a prankster he was even as a youth, implicating him in an elaborate fraud. Dated November 14, 1909, the missive from Iowa State College in Ames is signed by a suspicious character named Whiting. He greeted the artist as "Dear pal Wood":

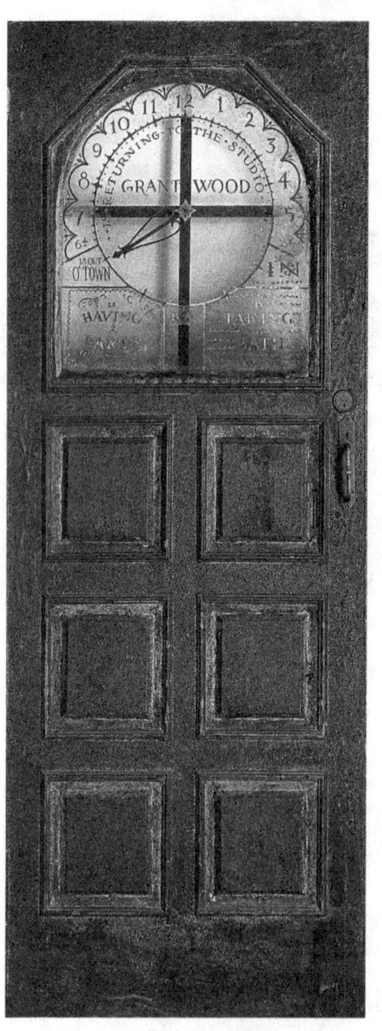

Fig. 3.2. Grant Wood, *Door to 5 Turner Alley*, 1924.

> I was glad to hear from you and to know that you had not given up your persecutions of the honorable gentleman, Gil Fry. He is by no means onto the graft yet and did not even notice the post-mark on your letter though he brought it in himself. I have got him into my confidence pretty well and [he] will show me most of his letters especially from you. He thought you were a very fine fellow to keep that stuff out of the *Pulse* [Wood's school newspaper] but did not see where he could help fight your battles if you got into trouble. By all means send an inquiry from some fake paper as that seemed to worry him most.
>
> Wells got that letter from his cousin but it came very near not working for of course he was not onto it and came near giving things away to Fry. He told Fry all about her tho and now Fry has had nearly everyone he has written to, look her up. So I am afraid he will find out it is a put up job, but you can keep sending them until he does suspect something and then I will let you know. I don't think Jim has written anything about her yet so you had better hustle him up. You send the letters as planned and we will do our part. He received the postal from Waterloo and Marion but not from Chicago and he thinks matters have died down.[2]

One wonders if the hapless Fry caught on to the scheme and what precise role Wood played in conning him and to what end.

While the intrigue may be dismissed as a case of boys being boys, it helps sensitize us to other ruses, side steps, and manipulations that Wood carried out through the years. Unremarkable in themselves, these incidents pile up to suggest a wily character, often delighting in pulling the wool over the eyes of his mark.

He could work the system, or get around it, as in 1911 when, commuting thrice weekly from Cedar Rapids to Iowa City, he posed as a registered student in Charles Cumming's drawing class at the University of Iowa, bypassing prerequisites and fees by pretending to have forgotten his documents. "You were a swindler," critic Thomas Craven later chided him about not having paid his tuition. Wood offered a bogus justification about not having learned anything and thus owing nothing in return.[3] He could be elusive, renting private digs he called his hideaway in an old Cedar Rapids office building; not even his mother or sister knew the location.[4] His celebrated studio door at 5 Turner Alley, fashioned from a windowed coffin lid he acquired from mortician Dave Turner, announced whether the artist was in or out by means of an arrow indicating his hour of return or if he was "out of town," "having a party," or "taking a bath" (Fig. 3.2). According to Wood's friend MacKinlay Kantor, there was also a trick code: when the arrow was in a certain position, "it meant that [Wood] was turning the public at large away from his door, but would be happy to receive intimates."[5]

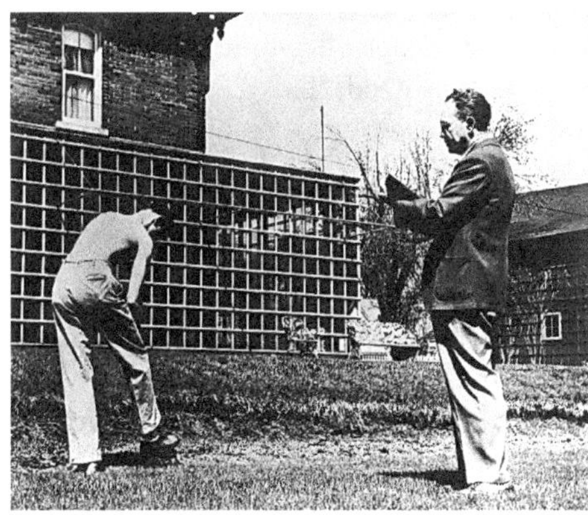
Fig. 3.3. Grant Wood sketching, Iowa City, 1941.

As he gained renown, Wood became adept at managing his image. Though he claimed not to enjoy public speaking, he traveled tirelessly to lecture about his work and to promote the Regionalist cause, with Lee Keedick, a professional agent in New York, booking national venues for him and providing advance publicity. At each lecture stop, Wood gave interviews to the local press, disingenuously reiterating how he was just a simple man, a farmer from Iowa. He courted the media assiduously, to the point that Lester Longman, his jealous department chair at the University of Iowa, ascribed Wood's fame to stories he planted in the newspapers. Cannily, when Wood was said by fellow faculty in the art department to rely on photographs to produce his paintings—an accurate and, at that time in Iowa, scandalous accusation—he made sure he was photographed in the act of drawing from life (Fig. 3.3).[6] It is no surprise that he was consistently characterized as shrewd, both by friends and in the press, a claim that amused him but incensed his sister, who feared that his integrity was impugned.

LIVING UNDER THREAT

Wood's cultivation of an admiring audience and his maintenance of a kind of false self surely gratified certain psychic needs, to be analyzed presently, but central to his chronic dissembling, it seems to me, was his homosexuality, which placed him constantly at risk in a way hardly imaginable today. He had a secret to hide and suspicions to deflect by any means necessary. Beginning in 1892, the year after his birth, sodomy laws in Iowa prescribed imprisonment for offenders for at least one year and up to ten years, then became even more oppressive as Wood came of age. In 1911, when he was twenty, the legislature enacted a statute providing that inmates of state institutions deemed "moral or sexual perverts" could be sterilized. This law was expanded two years later to include "criminals, rapists, idiots, feeble-minded, imbeciles, lunatics, drunkards, drug fiends, epileptics, syphilitics, moral and sexual perverts, and diseased and degenerate persons."[7] Although due process guarantees were grudgingly added to this law in 1915, forty-nine Iowans were sterilized from 1911 through 1921. With the passage of a harsher statute in 1929, no actual "crime" was necessary to justify sterilization, but only the perception by the state's board of eugenics that a so-called pervert was a "menace to society." Ninety-five Iowans were accordingly sterilized over the next five years. Of these unfortunates, fifty-seven were male offenders—for whom sterilization meant surgical removal of the testes.[8]

Such were the draconian conditions under which Wood lived, and even if he did not consider himself immediately menaced by the state apparatus, he could not escape the pervasive social attitudes that underpinned the official abuse of homosexuals. At the very least, he suffered from the kind of small-town gossip that Jay Sigmund excoriated in his poem "The Serpent" and that Wood himself skewered in *Victorian Survival* and *The Good Influence* (1936, Fig. 3.4). The latter work, one of his illustrations for a special 1937 edition of *Main Street*, depicts Sinclair Lewis's malicious Ma Bogart, purveyor of gossip and nosy monitor of community morals. In the novel, she succeeds in banishing the lively young high school instructor by spreading false rumors about her; Fern Mullins is unable to find another teaching job after her forced resignation and exile from the town of Gopher Prairie. In his drawing, Wood stations Bogart, "The Good Influence," before the town's Baptist church, providing an institutional backdrop for her self-righteous prosecutions, and he endows her with a perfectly self-satisfied expression. She flashes a devious smile and a look, aimed directly at the viewer, that promises "I'll get *you* next." Of the seven characters Wood chose to portray for the *Main Street* project—such as protagonist Carol Kennicott (*The Perfectionist*) or Miles Bjornstam (*The Radical*)—Mrs. Bogart is the only one whose sobriquet is ironic and the one whom Wood treats with the least sympathy.

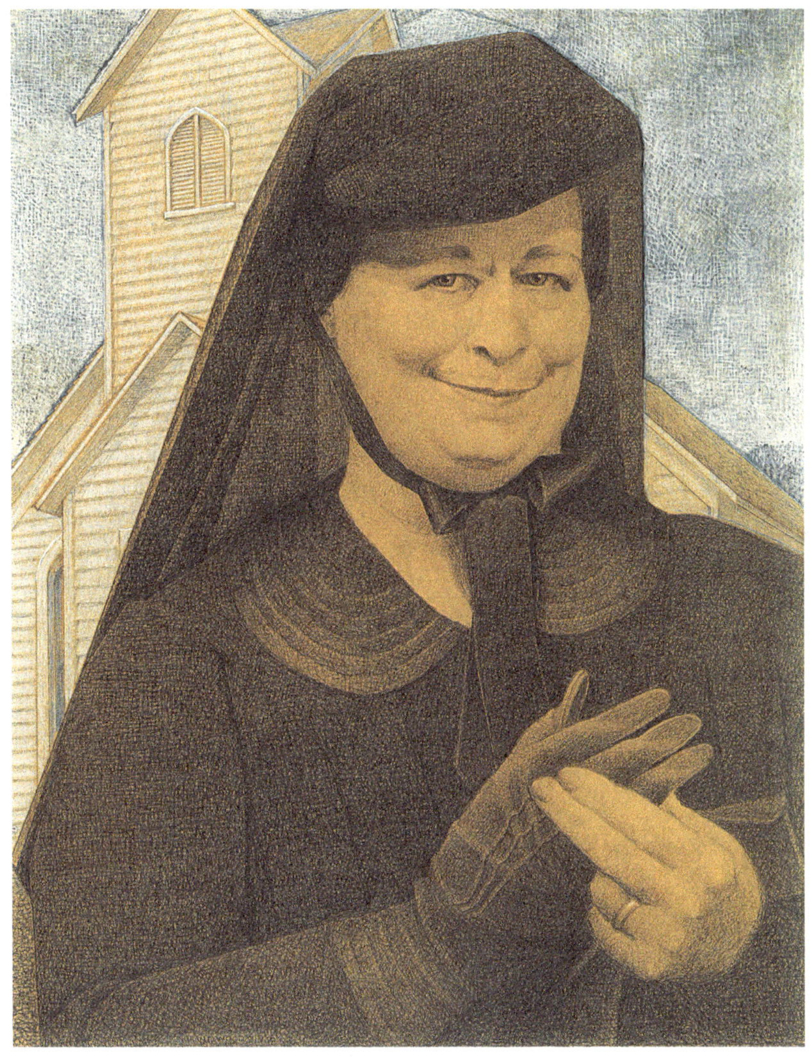

Fig. 3.4. Grant Wood, *The Good Influence*, 1936.

If he was moved by her innocent victim's ostracism, what did he make of the awful fate of another school teacher fallen from grace, Wing Biddlebaum in *Winesburg, Ohio*, Sherwood Anderson's penetrating treatment of small-town American life with which Wood's own work was often compared? A correspondent of Sigmund's, Anderson was also among the literary guest speakers Wood's friend Frank Luther Mott brought to the University of Iowa. In the story of Biddlebaum, Anderson portrays a sensitive soul destroyed by homophobic violence. Nervous and distracted, the broken Biddlebaum is forty years old when we meet him but appears sixty-five. He is a mystery to the people of Winesburg, who tease and cruelly mock him. When a young newspaper reporter befriends him, we learn about his tragic past and the reason for his alienation. His real name is Adolph Myers. In Pennsylvania, where he once taught, he had become the target of "hideous accusations" by one of the youths in his charge, who nursed a mad crush on him. Anderson leaves the verity of the accusations in question, but the townspeople's doubts—already aroused by the teacher's gentle demeanor and his tenderness toward his students—quickly "galvanized into beliefs." Brutally beaten in broad daylight in the schoolyard, Myers was later awakened in the night by a lynch mob and only narrowly escaped hanging, pelted with sticks, mud, and insults as he ran terrified and screaming out of town.

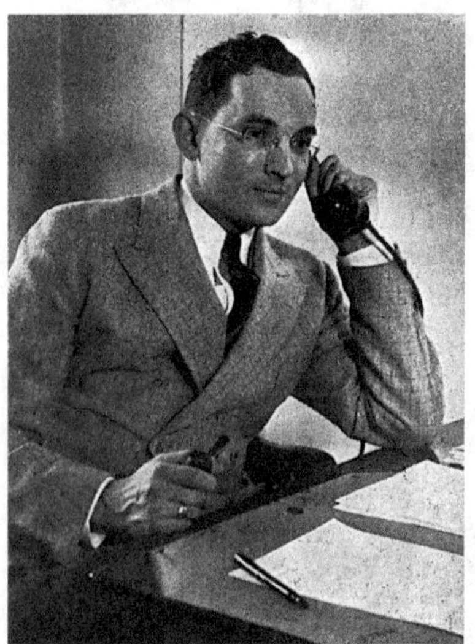

Fig. 3.5. Lester Longman, Iowa City, 1938.

As a teacher himself, first at Rosedale Country School, then at Jackson Junior High School, McKinley Junior High, and finally at the state university, Wood could have empathized with the character of Myers and internalized the danger of violence perpetrated against homosexuals. In actuality, the possibility of exposure always hung over him, threatening his emotional equilibrium and his career if not his person, reaching a climax in 1940 and 1941 and possibly hastening his early death. I have already alluded to the antagonistic state of affairs in the university's Department of Graphic and Plastic Arts, where Wood's commitment to Regionalism and his teaching style came into conflict with the progressive modernist ambitions of other faculty. Unapologetically anti-Semitic as well as racist and homophobic, Longman (1905–1987, Fig. 3.5), a Princeton PhD in art history, was relentless in his efforts to discredit Wood, a product of art schools without proper academic credentials notwithstanding his several honorary degrees.[9] Longman and Fletcher Martin, the painter hired as Wood's sabbatical replacement in 1940, broadcast their contempt for Wood and his work within and beyond the university. They alleged that he could not draw (citing as evidence his use of photographs), that he did not like Picasso, that he locked his studio door and had students paint his pictures for him—and that he was a homosexual, involved with Park Rinard.[10] Rumors spread as far as Chicago and New York, so that in November 1940, while Wood was on leave preparing for an exhibition with Associated American Artists, *Time Magazine* correspondent Eleanor Welch came to Iowa City to inquire about the charges against him.

The university administration became embroiled, with countless conferences, internal memos, and letters to and from Wood, who involved his lawyer, Dan Dutcher, and sought "vindication" from the attacks on his "reputation as an artist and personal character."[11] Welch did not in the end cover the affair for *Time*, but during her probe Longman prepared a written statement for her, aimed on the surface at damage control while actually defaming his nemesis. He explained that Wood had not been dismissed from the faculty as rumored but was on professional leave, and pretended to believe that differences of artistic opinion and taste made for a healthy department. Knowing full well that calling attention to Wood's sexual orientation would injure him, Longman hypocritically proclaimed the irrelevance of "Mr. Wood's personal persuasions," and condescendingly asserted that the artist would be welcomed back into "this liberal circle should he find it possible to resume his teaching."[12] Further, behind Wood's back, Longman was polling prominent museum curators, critics, and educators across the country for negative assessments of the artist's contributions to American art, which he then shared with the administration.

Outraged and humiliated, Wood made it known that he might not return to the university and that he wanted Longman fired or at least demoted from his position as department chair. Wood's situation was precarious: his production was slow and his finances were in disarray since his recent divorce; he needed the job. His national fame proved a double-edged sword, providing leverage in his negotiations with the administration but also making him vulnerable to unwelcome scrutiny from all corners. Shrewdly, as always, he importuned his longtime patron John Reid (1877–1968), President of the National Oats Company in Cedar Rapids, to intervene on his behalf. As a member of the Iowa State Board of Regents, Reid was in a position to lobby for Wood by pressuring university president Virgil Hancher, advising him that "Mr. Longman should not go unscathed for the needless and vicious criticism (particularly that portion casting reflection on Mr. Wood's morals) which he had directed against Mr. Wood."[13] Despite Wood's demands, Longman was not fired, nor was Wood granted the administrative control he sought, but the issue was settled in June 1941 when he was removed from Longman's supervision. Wood was named Professor of Fine Arts, reporting thereafter to the director of the School of Fine Arts and to the dean of the College of Liberal Arts.

This compromise brought an end to Wood's *annus terribilis,* and he was able to resume his painting and to enjoy the summer with Rinard at Clear Lake, Iowa.[14] While the battle was raging, however, he had fallen into an emotional abyss. Over the phone in April 1941, Wood told Hancher that the arrival of the *Time* reporter in Iowa City had upset him so much that he could not work; his upcoming exhibition would likely have to be postponed.[15] During this creative block, Wood escaped to Key West. It was not his first trip (Fig. 3.6) to that tropical Florida enclave of artists, writers, sailors, and tourists on "America's outer limits of sexuality and sensibility."[16] His colleague Adrian Dornbush (1900–1970) from the Stone City Art Colony, a homosexual like Wood, had relocated to the island in 1933, and Wood was already known there as a habitué of certain bars, also frequented by Tennessee Williams.[17] On this particular trip, exhausted by the Longman ordeal and affected by his turn to alcohol, Wood was a visible wreck. Williams described him as "a rather dumpy little man with a white shock of hair. . . . Quite flushed in the face all the time, and not from embarrassment either," while poet Elizabeth Bishop wrote to a friend that "he is too depressing, very much like one of his D.A.R. Matrons."[18] Although Wood reassured his sister that he was feeling better after the vacation, he continued to self-medicate on his return to Iowa. In May, Hancher heard "that Grant Wood was rapidly drinking himself to death."[19] One witness to the artist's despair at the time was Bill McKim, a recent student of Thomas Hart Benton's at the Kansas City Art Institute, who stopped to see Wood in Iowa City. McKim described this visit years later to Henry Adams. "Wood was extremely angry and upset," Adams reports, "over his treatment by the faculty at the University of Iowa. The entertainment consisted of drinking, which went on from late afternoon until about two in the morning. Wood drank two entire bottles of scotch and McKim drank gin and bitters until they both passed out together in Wood's bedroom, on the bed with their clothes on."[20]

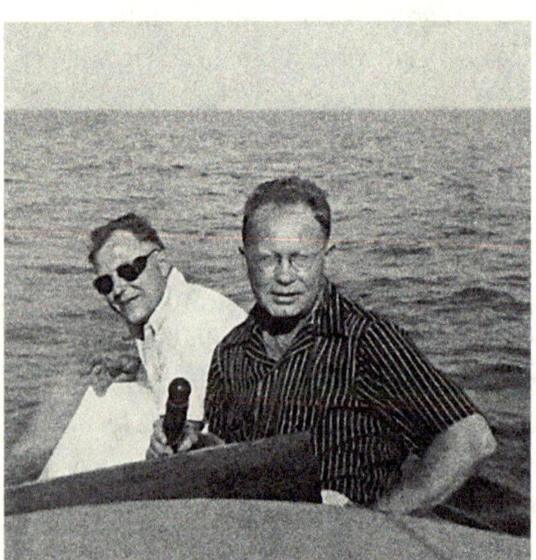

Fig. 3.6. Grant Wood and an unidentified friend, Key West, Florida, c. 1936.

Saddest of all and perhaps most telling is that this binge occurred on Mother's Day. Hattie had been dead four-and-a-half years, and Wood still mourned her passing. He had been her favorite son, but it was not clear that the version of sibling rivalry being played out at the university would have a similarly triumphant outcome. Wood had already been on the faculty for two years in 1936 when Longman, fifteen years his junior, was appointed department chair, at age thirty. The newly arrived upstart was Wood's worst nightmare, at once a younger, jealous brother who displaced him in the limelight *and* a tyrannical father. He had to be overthrown. Thus the artist's unreasonably stubborn insistence during negotiations with his deans that he be made art department chair in Longman's stead, or at least that the department be divided in two, with himself installed as "Creative Head." Wood's exasperated and hostile feelings about Longman are reflected in several curious drawings, apparently done in preparation for a painting or print project never realized, in which he allegorized his own victimization and hoped-for vindication.[21] He selected two of Aesop's fables to illustrate, "The Wolf and the Lamb" and "The Fox and the Lion," each featuring the confrontation between a pair of emblematic animals.[22] For the first image (c. 1940–41, Fig. 3.7), Wood made four studies, copying out on two of them the entire text of the fable in his own hand:

> Once upon a time a Wolf was lapping at a spring when, looking up, he saw a Lamb just beginning to drink. "There is my supper," thought the Wolf, "if I can only find some excuse to seize it." Then he called out to the Lamb "How dare you to muddle the water from which I am drinking?" "Nay, master, Nay," said the Lamb, "if the water be muddy up there, I cannot be the cause of it, for the spring runs down from you to me." "Well then," said the Wolf, "Why did you call me bad names this time last year?" "That cannot be," said the Lamb; "I am only six months old." "I don't care," snarled the Wolf; "if it was not you it was your father," and with that he rushed upon the poor Lamb and ate him up. But before the Lamb died he gasped "Any excuse will serve a tyrant!"

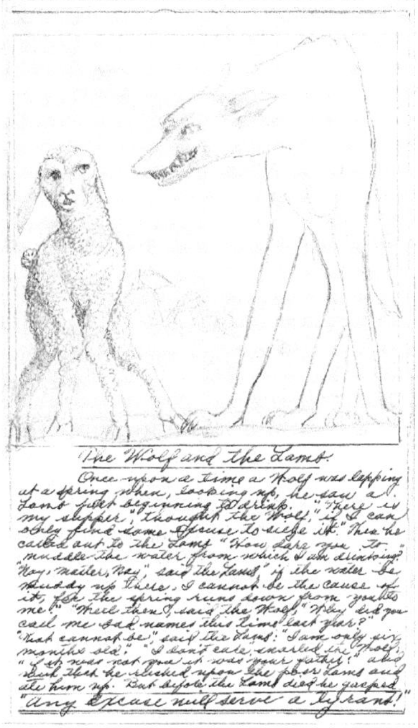

Fig. 3.7. Grant Wood, *The Wolf and the Lamb*, c. 1940–41.

With his capricious rationalizing, the predatory Wolf corresponds to Wood's perception of Longman as "neurotically vicious."[23] In the drawing, the innocent Lamb, doe-eyed and knock-kneed, cringes in a corner of the composition, while the lanky, hulking Wolf, baring his teeth in the Lamb's direction, occupies the entire height of the frame and two-thirds of its width.

Wood countered this sense of a victim overpowered in an untitled study for "The Fox and the Lion" (c. 1940–41, Fig. 3.8). On this sheet, though the Lion maintains the advantage in size, the Fox is not intimidated. The fable, in fact, reveals the Fox's increasing nonchalance vis-à-vis the King of Beasts. When the Fox first sees the Lion, he runs away frightened; the next time he sees the Lion, he stops and watches him from a safe distance; on the third encounter,

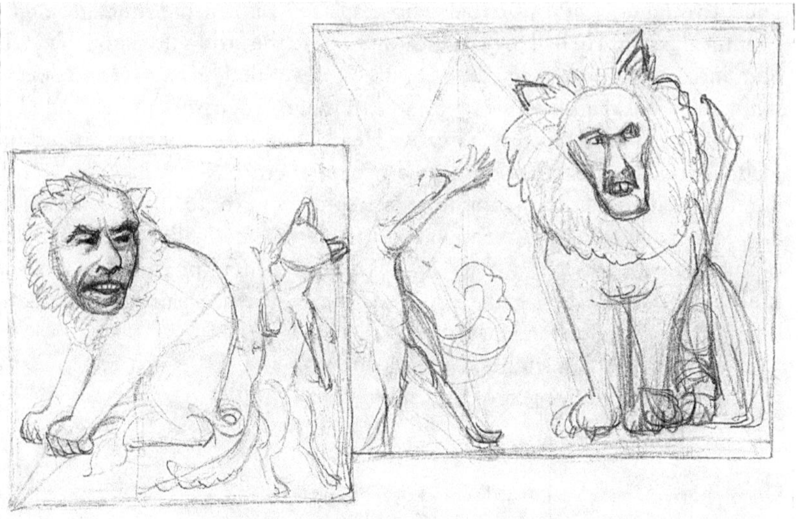

Fig. 3.8. Grant Wood, *Untitled (The Lion and the Fox)*, c. 1940–41.

the Fox goes up to the Lion, chats with him casually, then turns and strides off. Aesop's moral is succinct: "Familiarity breeds contempt." This is Wood's desire—that like the Fox, he could shed his fear, walk upright, and thumb his nose at the ruling pretender to authority. In a reworking of the confrontation between fox and cat he had conjured in his little painting of 1905 (Fig. 3.1), Wood here asserts his own wily character in rebellion against the familiar father, Maryville Wood, whose leonine roars were muffled but not silenced in death, echoing now in the growling noises made by Longman. In the fanciful sketch, Wood toys with two different arrangements for his fabled beasts. In each version, he gives the Lion a human face, perhaps remembering Bert Lahr in *The Wizard of Oz* (released in 1939) and through that oblique allusion rendering his Longman-Lion a coward as well as a villain. The penciled vectors that partition each sketch reveal Wood's exacting compositional methods, with careful attention to internal and part-to-whole relationships. On this formal level, Wood could exert a gratifying, orderly control at a moment when he was vulnerable to external attacks he experienced as irrational and gratuitous, just as the subject matter provided him with opportunities for imaginative role-playing and wish fulfillment.

PROTECTIVE RUSES

In November 1940, Longman and Martin discussed the Wood problem with Earl Harper, Director of the School of Fine Arts. At this meeting, according to Harper's notes, Martin "in no uncertain terms branded G.W. as a 'phony' artist, a fake."[24] Martin's framing of his fellow painter as a fraud reverberated among Wood's critics, during the latter artist's lifetime and after. Insincerity became a theme in many incisive accounts of his achievements, as in the case of Lincoln Kirstein who, reviewing Wood's 1935 exhibition at the Ferargil Galleries, found him "cagey," employing stylistic mannerisms that "destroyed his integrity."[25] This assessment reached its apogee with the Modernist critic Hilton Kramer in the 1980s. For Kramer, Wood's art was "abysmally phony," "a calculated lie from start to finish," and the artist himself an example of "peculiar psychological deformation."[26] Negative conclusions aside, these critical insights point to something fundamental and fascinating about Wood. And with the decline of Modernism's insistence, à la Martin and Kramer, on authenticity as a sine qua non of artistic quality, we are better positioned now to appreciate Wood's ingenuity and artifice, which functioned on various levels—pragmatic, artistic, and psychological.

Foremost, he was faced with the necessity of passing for straight. Once he made the decision to return from a European Bohemia to Iowa, his conscious goal was to fit in. This meant downplaying his differences, both as a homosexual and as an artist; accommodation became a significant subtext in his story. Introducing him to New York audiences on the occasion of his above-mentioned Ferargil exhibition, his dealer Frederic Newlin Price wrote of Wood's Regionalist determination to settle in with his neighbors: "So he thought: 'I shall adjust myself to the home town of Cedar Rapids and try to get along.' From then on it was a-building with his own people. . . . His real fight was adjustment, to get villagers to think him a real person."[27] At the Stone City Art Colony, Wood advocated accommodation energetically to his students. Robert Proost (1914–1982), a student at the colony from Clinton, Iowa, recalled "Wood's fine philosophy" and its strategic success: "He said being artists didn't make us a bunch of freaks, and if we dressed as the farmers and the people of the community did, we and those people would feel much more at ease with each other. He was proved right when those people met us as friends and gave us more cooperation than we ever could have hoped for in our wildest dreams."[28] Wood's own overalls (Fig. 3.9) were of course such a costume, a kind of camouflage declaring his ostensible but in reality deeply ambivalent allegiance to a culture that produced, delighted, and oppressed him. Until things began to fall apart for him at the university—that is, for nearly all his life—he relied successfully on a highly functional repertoire of clever scams. His ingenious fabrications

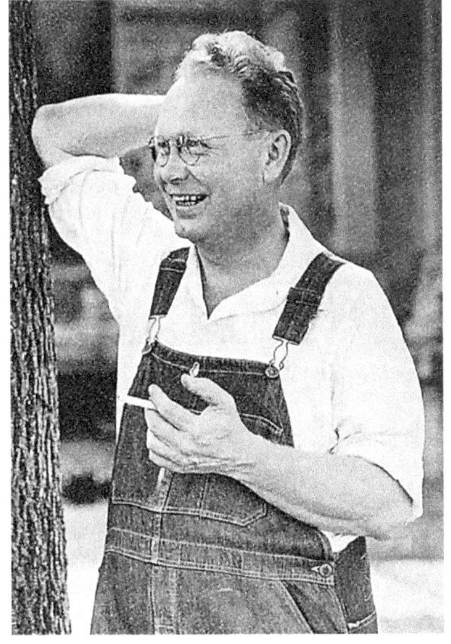

Fig. 3.9. Grant Wood at Stone City, Iowa, 1933.

fooled his contemporaries and remained effective even after his death, taken until very recently at face value in the literature.

Only R. Tripp Evans has seen through Wood's ruse of a putative love child, a mysterious young man who appeared one day at the studio door on Turner Alley to announce that his mother, conveniently deceased, had once told him about his illustrious Wood parentage. The success of this tall tale is confirmed by its unquestioning rehearsal in several sources, including a Wood biography by Hazel Brown, where Bruce McKay, a Cedar Rapids architect, recalls how worried his artist friend had been by the alleged visit. McKay did his best to calm Wood, who then, curiously, "never spoke of the matter again."[29] Pointing to the absurdity of the various versions of this event and Wood's alarmed reaction, Evans suggests an attempt at homosexual blackmail—which the nervous artist then disguised as a different kind of affair.[30] Whether or not Wood planted the tale in response to such a threat, and it does seem plausible, his pretense of possible paternity helped broadcast a conventional heterosexual persona. His sister was among those who loved to repeat the yarn,[31] which entered the Wood lore as colorful evidence of both the price he paid for his fame and the randy adventures of his young manhood.

To his sister, Wood's deceptions were welcome truths. Desperate to disavow his homosexuality, Nan Wood Graham searched for years after his demise for details about Margaret Whittlesy, the young woman Wood professed to have fallen in love with in Paris in 1923.[32] This proved to be a wild goose chase. Nevertheless, Graham held tightly to her brother's story about how he had planned to marry the girl until, learning that she was rich, he rejected her, nobly refusing "to live off a woman's money."[33] Margaret allegedly died of tuberculosis shortly thereafter; Graham wondered if a broken heart had been a factor. With her tragic death, Margaret conforms to the type of "good girl fiancée" frequently conjured by gay bachelors of the period to justify their single status, an ideal lost love whom a man could never betray by becoming involved with another woman.[34] By enshrining Margaret in this way, Wood concluded a period of sexual uncertainty and deflected pressures to resolve his predicament as the only unmarried brother of three.[35]

Graham enlisted this storied heterosexual romance in her lifelong effort to efface the one fact about her brother she could not abide. "Grant pursued his art, never speaking of Margaret," she wrote, while still pretending that "without a question, he thought of her often."[36] Perhaps to reassure herself of this fantasy as much as to control his posthumous public image, Graham repeatedly sought to verify Wood's engagement to Margaret, writing journalist William Shirer when in a 1976 memoir he remembered his old friendship with the artist in Paris. Shirer responded that he had never met the woman, nor had Wood ever mentioned the relationship.[37] By some means, Graham managed to locate Margaret's nephew, and he told her that the affair was a product of her imagination, which infuriated her.[38] She was similarly disappointed by Rinard, whom she pressed for information about Margaret that he might have gleaned from Wood for the abortive biography. "I went over it again and again with him," Rinard explained to her, "knowing his reticence and sensitiveness about such things, in an effort to get it in the proper proportion. However, there was never a single line from her or a single reference about her in any of his correspondence."[39] Seduced nonetheless by her brother's schemes, Graham went so far as to devise her own.

Among the papers she donated in 1984 to the Davenport Municipal Art Gallery (now the Figge Art Museum) is a dubious document she seems purposely to have planted for posterity. Ostensibly from Rinard, the letter dated January 20, 1944 is filed with many others he wrote to her after Wood's death. But the paper on which this one is typed differs from his regular stationery and, inexplicably cut in half, missing its lower portion, lacks his signature. Adding to these anomalies, Graham penciled "important" in large letters at the top of the page, to call attention, I suspect, to this passage: "[N]othing makes me more furious than the insinuation that Grant was stupid or effeminate because he had such rotten luck with womenfolk and because he didn't get married for so long. Don't worry about this, for it will all be taken care of for [*sic*] once and for all. I have plenty of material to blast any such notion out of existence. By the way, did you know that Grant was engaged to a girl in Paris? Her name was Margaret Whittlesly, and she died of tuberculosis in Europe."[40] The tone contrasts with Rinard's typically measured language but corresponds to Graham's indignant posturing in her brother's defense, as when, on the title page of her annotated copy of Darrell Garwood's biography of Wood, she inscribed contemptuously beneath the author's name, "Who wasn't fit to spit on. The worst liar on earth."[41]

Negotiating a thicket of deceptions and false evidence, Wood scholars face thorny interpretive challenges. Evans speculates that "Margaret" was Wood's pseudonym for a man, one who resembled the artist's preferred "type"—youthful, dark, and slender.[42] I imagine the good girl fiancée as something of a composite of the woman Wood invoked by name and the man Evans detects beneath the ruse. And the real illness of a friend provided the artist material for the rejected lover's demise, evinced by a postcard in the Figge Art Museum's archives of December 19, 1924, penned in a tiny hand by someone Wood had known in Paris. Unsigned, the card was sent from Switzerland, where a five-story sanatorium for tuberculosis patients overlooked the alpine village of Leysin.[43] The note reads:

> Dear Grant, I hope this reaches you no idea of your street Happy New Year and best wishes always I'm thinking of you, Marcel and Paris so much—you must be in the same boat. So awful to taste something and lose it. Switz is gorgeous [illegible] but this is no way to appreciate. Resting and stagnating with <u>one</u> view every day, all day, no music, no nothing, except reading and even that being [illegible]

and subjective. Do you find work that pleases you? Do you have time to paint for yourself? If you have a moment to drag a line, I'd be so glad of your news. Chas. seems happier now, tho' N.Y. is not P. is it?[44]

Invoking Marcel in the same breath as "you," the lonely patient seems to pine not so much for a onetime betrothed as for a shared camaraderie that Wood must also miss. Marcel, last name Bordet, was the Frenchman mentioned in Chapter 2 who Wood had hoped might return home with him to Iowa. With the final reference in the postcard to another correspondent, Charles, the Paris heyday Wood experienced in his early thirties emerges as a scene of memorable male companionship rather than of heterosexual love. Still a mystery is whether Wood did "drag a line" to his ailing friend, and whether that friend survived Leysin or succumbed to the fate Wood ascribed to his putative fiancée, dying of tuberculosis in Europe.

THE DOUBLE MAN

Clinging doggedly to the Margaret myth, Graham conspired with Wood to maintain a position for him that would later be called "closeted." Critic Robert Hughes was the first to apply the term to Wood, tagging him from the vantage point of the 1990s as "timid" and his work as "the expression of a gay sensibility so cautious that it can hardly bring itself to mock its subjects openly."[45] The critic was wrong in this bold assessment to imply a failure of nerve on Wood's part, as if the artist's necessary vigilance was a character flaw to be despised. Hughes's view altogether ignores the real dangers Wood faced in Iowa and the brilliantly resourceful ways he coped with them. In this he was hardly uncommon, for, as John Howard notes, many homosexual men in rural America, "though sometimes subjected to intimidation and violence, . . . proved adept at maneuvering through hostile terrain."[46] Wood's deft machinations in art and in life ought to be seen in this light, as "queer habits of dissembling, long inculcated as second nature."[47] It is no wonder that he came perforce to experience himself as a double man.

Grasping the implications of this divided condition for Wood's art, Evans finds a significant, recurring "thematic polarization," even in cheerful exercises such as the decorative floral lithographs of 1939, *Wild Flowers* and *Tame Flowers*, with their unavoidable gender associations (including the prominent potted pansy in the latter image), and the pair of oval charcoal-and-chalk drawings *Draft Horse* and *Race Horse* (1932, Figs. 3.10 and 3.11 respectively).[48] Like cameos of different types of masculinity, these last two drawings match their respective horses with similarly distinctive men. The draft animal, with the massive proportions of a Clydesdale, is led by a sturdy farmhand in overalls; the Arabian thoroughbred, streamlined and fleet, poses with a jockey before a festooned grandstand. A study in contrasts, the vignettes of barnyard and racetrack bring to mind that well-worn metaphor

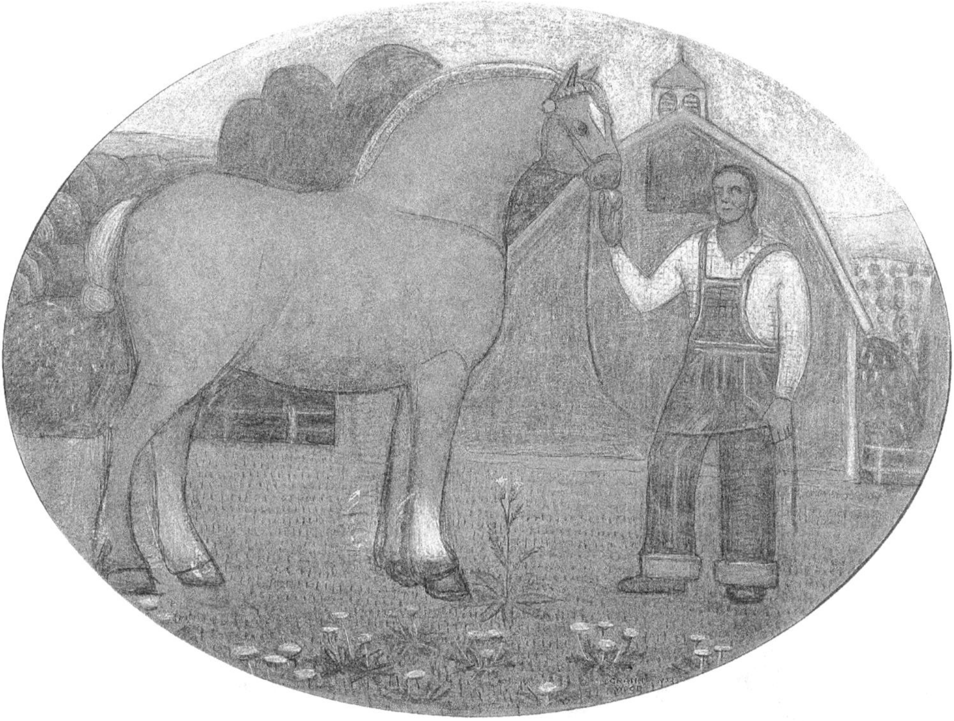

Fig. 3.10. Grant Wood, *Study for Draft Horse*, 1932.

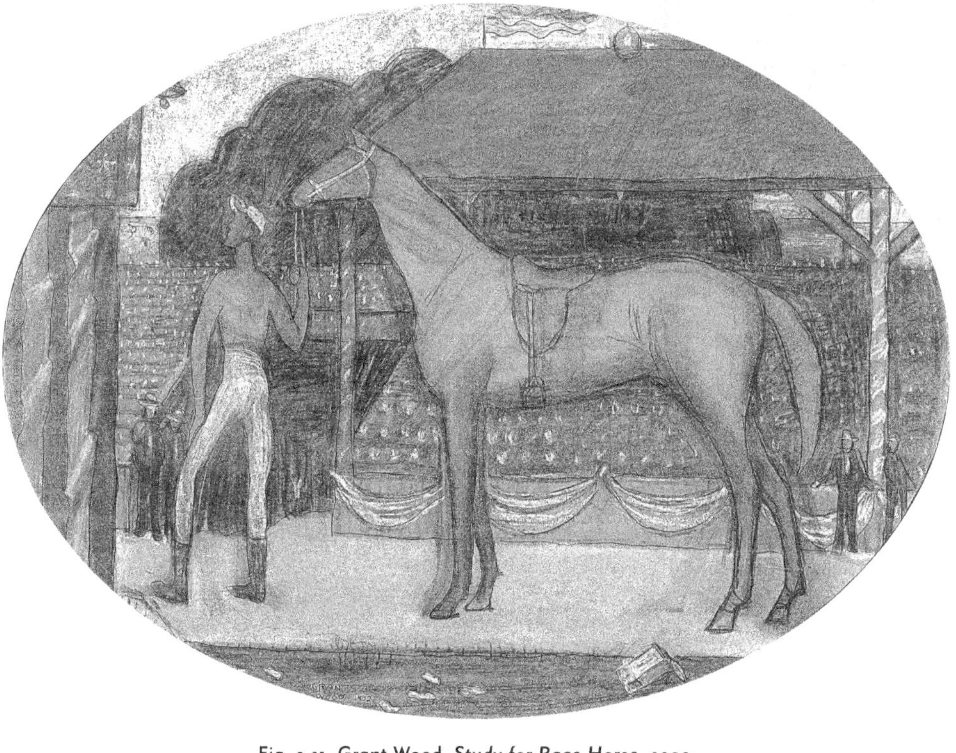

Fig. 3.11. Grant Wood, *Study for Race Horse*, 1932.

for pure alterity, "a horse of a different color," yet both represent aspects of Wood's own identity. The farm locale of course points to his rural heritage and his Regionalism, while the track symbolizes a professional world of training and competition, like the one he had entered with his art, complete with an audience of excited viewers and the Stars and Stripes in the left foreground to suggest the national scope of his ambitions.

Evans observes how both the "mincing" jockey and his mount "are suspiciously aware of their own beauty,"[49] evoking an arena of artifice and spectacle opposed to the "natural" world of agrarian labor. Reading *Race Horse* in this way, one thinks of how Carson McCullers would presently portray the jockey in her eponymous 1941 short story, with his proud hauteur and rarefied manners and taste.[50] McCullers's protagonist sports a Chinese silk suit with a yellow shirt, a pastel striped tie, and a gold link bracelet; he speaks with "dandified courtesy" in a high, prim voice. He is among the many powerful misfits created by this eccentric author, and she presents his fierce love of a fellow jockey in this story as homosexual, not by stating anything overtly but by repeating a secret code word: the men are "particular friends," "particular pals."

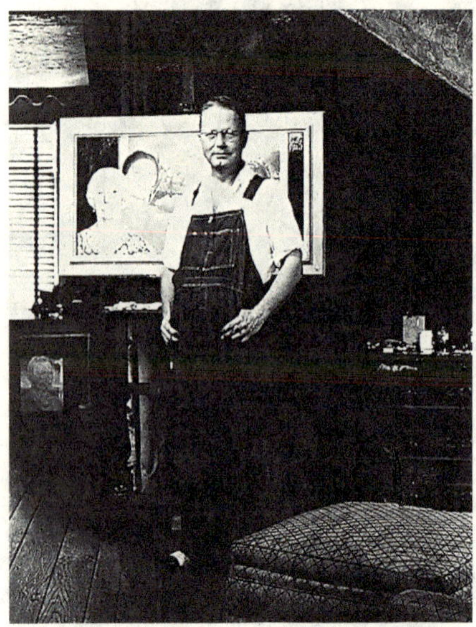

Fig. 3.12. Grant Wood at 5 Turner Alley, Cedar Rapids, 1932.

With a foot in each of the camps depicted in his pair of horse drawings, Wood performed his double nature in a photograph of 1932, wearing his workaday bib overalls in unlikely combination with debonair duotone wingtip shoes (Fig. 3.12).[51] Posing before his easel in the Turner Alley loft, Wood shows himself as farmer and dandy in the hybrid person of the artist. Around this time, too, he had hatched the idea of a picture of a Janus-faced character that surely expressed his own split self. Graham recalled her brother's amused fascination when, before the repeal of Prohibition in 1933, they saw from the loft window a nearby diner that served bootlegged liquor smoke-bombed by a passing carload of mobsters. In response to the excitement, according to Graham, "Grant said he was going to paint a double-faced man. One side would be a minister, and the other side would be a gangster."[52] Wood never followed through with this painting of the good/bad man, but we find this theme of dual identity in his peculiar claim to have a mysterious double, who was often seen in places Wood was not.

In the late 1930s, he wrote to Graham describing this doppelgänger, supposedly spotted and taken for the artist by their Aunt Jeanette: "She is entirely mistaken in thinking that I have been in Omaha recently, and the matter makes me feel a little queer because the man who resembles me so closely that he fools my friends was here in Iowa City a week or so ago and added to the confusion by wearing an overcoat and hat like mine."[53] If Graham marveled at this revelation of an uncanny twin, she still accepted Wood's ruse as fact, as if her brother's reddish hair, cherubic face, and dimpled chin were as common as men's department store coats and hats. She thought it merely owing to his fame that "someone impersonated him in Chicago and charged some purchases to him,"[54] but from these anecdotes shades emerge of the junior con man addressed in the conspiratorial letter from Whiting. "Say you are Grant Wood," the artist advised his sculptor friend Lawrence Tenney Stevens in 1940, when the latter was denied a seat on the train from Iowa City to Chicago, having neglected to reserve ahead.[55] Wood had accompanied his old chum to the station after an overnight visit; Stevens was traveling east from his Wyoming ranch and, despite his conspicuous western outfit, ten-gallon hat, and full beard, the ploy worked: "I am not good at lying," Stevens later confessed about posing as Wood, "but I was desperate. . . . The conductor took charge of me and with much apology and sweat, they at last found me a seat."

More calculated was Wood's scheme to deflect attention from his Iowa City household. During his marriage and for several years after his divorce, his wife's son, daughter-in-law, and granddaughter lived upstairs in the large Wood home on Court Street. The artist doted on his adoptive grandchild, Sally (Fig. 3.13), who remembers how protective he was of her and

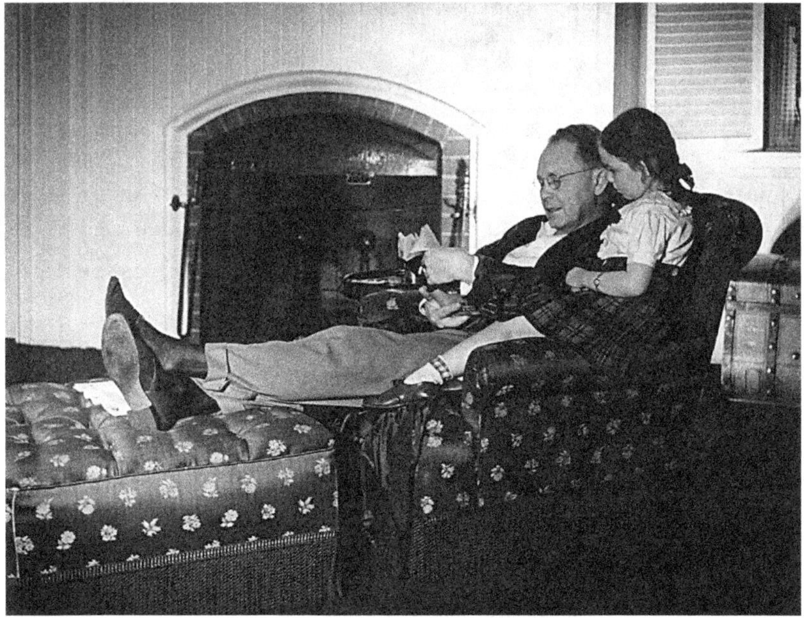

Fig. 3.13. Grant Wood with Sally Maxon, Iowa City, c. 1939.

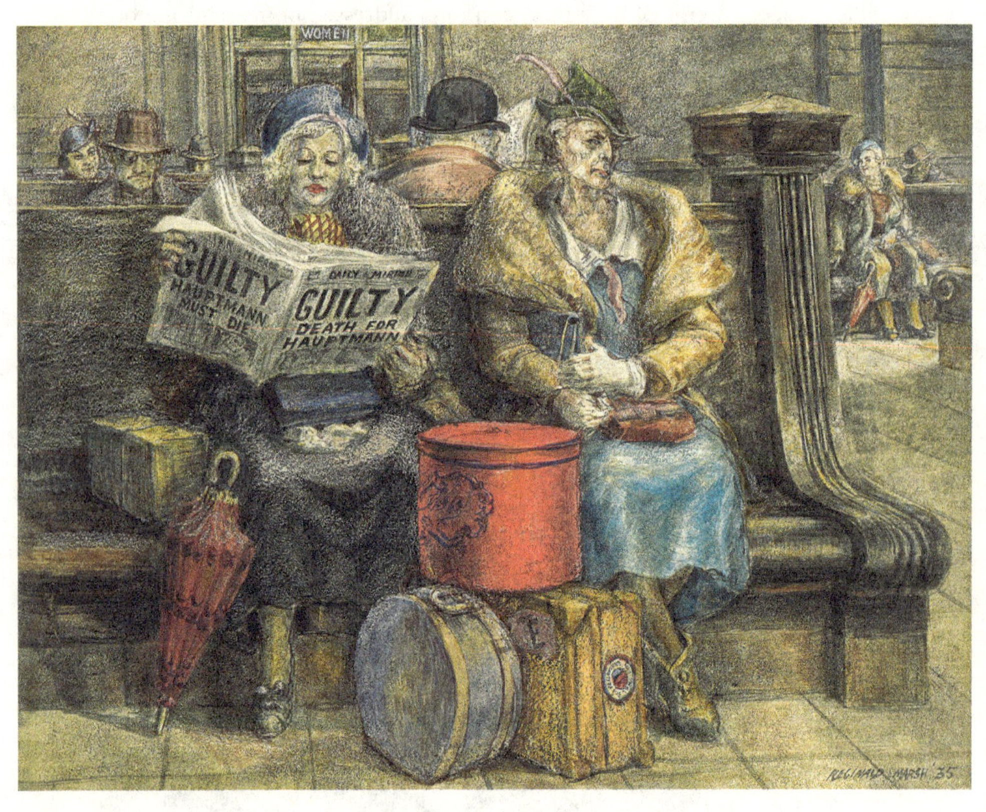

Fig. 3.14. Reginald Marsh, *Hauptmann Must Die*, 1935.

how, fearing that she might be kidnapped, he hired someone to impersonate him, a literal impostor.[56] The tragic Lindbergh baby case may have been on Wood's mind: although the infant had gone missing in 1932, his alleged murderer, Bruno Hauptmann, was convicted in 1935 and executed in 1936, so that the crime lived on in the news—as seen in Reginald Marsh's contemporaneous painting *Hauptmann Must Die* (1935, Fig. 3.14), with its topical inclusion of sensational tabloid headlines.[57] Whether or not Wood was overreacting to the threat that he imagined his own renown brought upon those close to him, the preventive solution he purportedly devised was certainly unusual—or was the impostor perhaps already in place when this perceived need arose?

THE ARTIST AS IMPOSTOR

In her studies of pathological imposture, psychoanalyst Phyllis Greenacre discerned in clinical cases and in celebrated historical examples of great frauds a set of recurring conditions as well as a particular pattern of psychological development. The conditions Greenacre enumerated are three: a dominant and active family romance, a disturbance in the sense of identity, and a malformed superego "involving both conscience and ideals."[58] Wood was by no means a pathological fraud; if there exists a spectrum of imposture, however, and we are all to some extent and from time to time "normal impostors" pretending to match our ego ideals,[59] he was driven toward the inauthentic extreme. Further, it is striking how the characteristic predicament of Greenacre's impostor within the oedipal triangle parallels Wood's situation. As a child, the impostor-to-be (always male) is so profoundly attached to his mother that he fails to develop a clear sense of a separate self. He is unable to identify with his father, whose death or desertion exacerbates the parental imbalance: without a struggle, the child supersedes the father "even though he is maturationally incapable of filling the role."[60] As a result, his infantile narcissism is intensified, and the oedipal conflict remains insoluble, with a lingering, "aggravated fear of the father based on hostility unrelieved by any possibility of positive identification with him."[61] Against this psychological background, Greenacre interprets the phenomenon of pathological imposture (emphases in the original):

> It is the living out of an oedipal conflict through revival of the earliest definite image of the father. Insofar as *the imposture* is accomplished, *it is the killing of the father through the complete displacement of him. It further serves to give a temporary feeling of identity* (sense of self) that can be more nearly achieved in this way than in the ordinary life of the individual so impaired from having been psychologically incorporated by his mother. As part of this imposturous impersonation there is a seemingly paradoxical heightening of his feeling of integrity and reality. This is certainly reinforced and sustained by the sense of being

believed in by others and, with the intoxication of being in the limelight (which reproduces the infantile situation with the general public taking the place of the mother), furnishes a most powerful incentive for endless repetition of this special type of gratification.[62]

Seen in this light, wearing overalls for Wood and insisting to the press that he was just a simple farmer was more than a self-conscious pose tailored to endear him to his community and to express his allegiance to Regionalism—though it was always also that to be sure. Impersonating his father in this way *as an image*, Wood could unconsciously, and perhaps compulsively, displace and vanquish him again and again.

Although Kramer hated Wood's art, he intuited all this keenly in the early 1980s, writing that, after Maryville's death in 1901, "the protracted Oedipal idyll that was the dominant emotional experience of the artist's life unfolded without further conflict."[63] Mocking the way Wood later "liked to dress up as his father, . . . donning farmers' overalls whenever it came time to play the Regionalist painter in public," Kramer found it "hard to know where the family romance ends and the calculations of the shrewd careerist take over." In fact, I hardly think they are separable. As Greenacre observes, moreover, an artist typically resembles the impostor in that he has both a personal self and a creative, public self.[64] This duality was further complicated in Wood's case by his sexual personae: privately and among a trusted few, he was a homosexual, while outwardly he appeared as a conventionally masculine sower of wild oats, an erstwhile fiancée, and an eventual husband, albeit a late and unlucky one. Living the double life, he shifted between these different personae, becoming a man, as Benton described him, "of many curious and illusory fancies" concerning his own identity.[65] On his deathbed but still hoping to recover, Wood shared with Benton plans "to change his name, go where nobody knew him, and start all over again with a new style of painting." His final fantasy was of shedding his past self and relocating—much like, it seems to me, Adolph Myers, a.k.a. Wing Biddlebaum, in *Winesburg, Ohio*.

An impostor's "disturbance in identity" played out in Wood's creative environment, where he projected his duplicitous mode of being onto inanimate objects, one thing made to pass for another in often delightful and imaginative ways. Shape-shifting transformations characterized his whole world. During the cash-strapped winter of 1916, he disguised a piece of round steak as a Christmas duck for himself and his mother, carving the fowl's head from a stick. In the faux potted plants he depicted in the 1920s, playfully titled *Lilies of the Alley* (Fig. 3.15), painted clothespins, bottle caps, discarded gears, and wires became the stems, leaves, and blossoms of hybrid houseplants that needed no watering. These assemblages of cast-off junk transmuted into art decorated Wood's celebrated home and studio at Turner Alley (see Fig. 1.9), where tables and beds, neatly folded or rolled away, disappeared into built-in closets, and the fireplace hood was a metal bushel basket turned upside down.[66] *Trompe-l'oeil* surfaces everywhere advertised this pervasive philosophy of inventively making do. Wood plastered cupboard doors with cut-up overalls and painted and antiqued them to appear rough and weather-worn. Learning that the loft floor would not support the weight of ceramic tiles, Wood substituted the "imaginary tiled floors" of his dreams.[67] He had seen them before his eyes, he said, in black and gold, and set to work incising the floorboards to resemble individual tile squares, employing a cutting tool of his own design, then painted the squares in a checkerboard pattern. The effect fooled visitors, including an astonished Kantor, who remembered the fake tiles years later, still impressed with the seductive simulation (see Fig. 3.29).

Wood enjoyed the impostor's delight in fooling others, which extended to gags such as the rubber cigarette he tucked in among a packet of real ones he

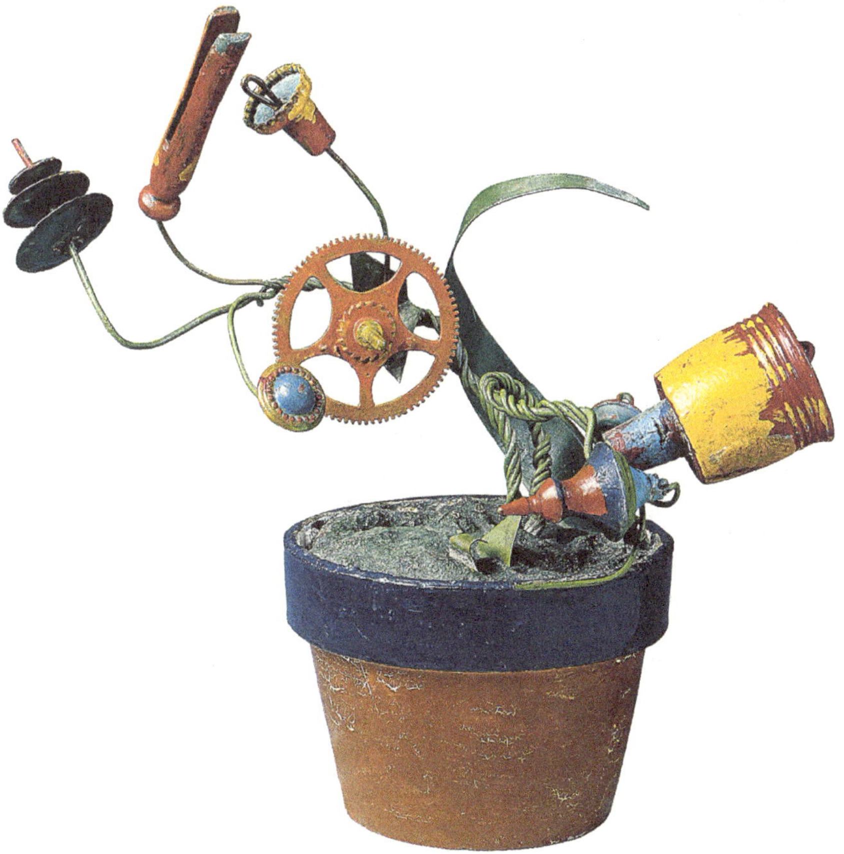

Fig. 3.15. Grant Wood, *Lilies of the Alley*, 1925.

offered to guests. A photograph of him at Clear Lake, which he had made into a postcard to send to friends,[68] captures this amusing and highly significant aspect of his personality (1941, Fig. 3.16). Immersed up to his belly in the water, hair wet and sans glasses, Wood offers a cracker to one of two friendly ducks that turn out to be, like him, wood impostors—painted decoys. Wood staged this ostensibly candid picture himself, draping his arm and shoulder with seaweed as if he had just emerged from a dive, then having to be handed a dry box of crackers by Rinard, his collaborating assistant, who held the camera. Though relaxed and funny, the image is as revelatory as any of the formal artistic self-portraits Wood painted, sculpted, or drew. The viewer is both charmed by the illusion Wood has created—satisfying the goal of all his painting—and in this instance is let in on the trick, as if allowed a privileged peek at the scheming man behind the curtain.

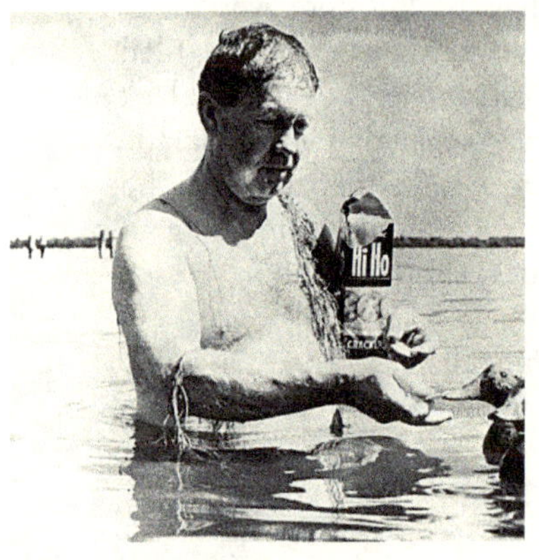

Fig. 3.16. Grant Wood at Clear Lake, Iowa, 1941.

INNER TRIUMPH

Greenacre notes how "enjoyment of the limelight and an inner triumph of 'putting something over,' seem inherent" to the impostor.[69] We get an inkling of such gratifications for Wood in his mischievously vengeful *Daughters of Revolution* of 1932 (Fig. 2.9), a satire of small-minded patriotism in which the artist clearly takes pleasure in making fools of his enemies. Although conceived in reaction to the many patriotic celebrations during the bicentennial year of George Washington's birth, the picture gave vent to feelings Wood had been harboring for some time, since the Cedar Rapids chapter of the Daughters of the American Revolution had alienated him by their angry response to his 1928 Veterans *Memorial Window*. Wood's own status as a member of the American Legion, which had commissioned the work, did not temper xenophobic community outrage over the window's foreign manufacture. Writing in *Scribner's Magazine* in 1937, Craven gave a colorful account of the D.A.R.'s vilification of Wood for having collaborated with German craftsmen in Munich in the wake of the Great War:

> After two years of backbreaking labor, the window was completed and ready for dedication. Whereupon some crank notified the Legion that the glass had been manufactured in Germany, an insult to the flag and to American workmen. The ensuing commotion was terrific. The Legion was rocked by intestine [*sic*] disputes, and to make matters worse, a ranking busybody of the D.A.R. incited the convulsive

Daughters to defamatory gossip. Neither organization, however, registered a formal protest, and the Legion, to its credit, appealed to the artist to state his case at a public hearing. The more soreheaded jingoists were out to exterminate him, but Wood handed them a telling blow, explaining that the window had been made in Germany for reasons of economy of manufacture, and that his net returns from the commission were less than $800. The antagonism subsided, but the ceremony was postponed—and to this day the window has never been dedicated. A less controlled artist would long ago have riddled it with brickbats.[70]

Indignant on behalf of the beleaguered artist, Craven imagined an enraged Wood reacting in precisely the way he would in 1939 to the repudiation of his painting *Sultry Night* (Fig. 2.31), masochistically destroying his own work while rescinding from his obtusely offended audience the fruits of his labor and his talent. In this case, however, Wood weathered the attacks and channeled his hurt creatively, taking the offensive in a belatedly retaliatory image of, in Craven's words, "three aristocratic hussies." Ignoring the Legionnaires who put him on trial, Wood took a symbolic brickbat instead to his female antagonists, beating them into a most unkind, unflattering representation. In the painting, the mannish old crones with their predilection for colonial tea parties pose before a framed print of *Washington Crossing the Delaware*. Primly decked out, with their pulled-back hair, saggy necks, and smug, thin-lipped smiles, the ladies radiate self-satisfaction. The contrast between their comfortable world of blue-and-white porcelain, pearls, and lace and Washington's freezing struggles against the enemy and the elements reveals the absurdity of the women's pride in heroic achievements in no way their own. Wood ridicules the Daughters on many levels, most cleverly and insidiously by planting in their midst a venerable American icon they adore while they remain oblivious to its German origins: Emanuel Gottlieb Leutze painted his original masterpiece in Düsseldorf in 1851.

The situation Wood sets up, mocking the clubwomen who are unaware that something they love is inflected by something they hate, echoes his relation to his broader Iowa community, contemptuous of "sissies" on the one hand but proud to have a famous (unbeknownst to them, homosexual) artist as their native son. Wood, moreover, discharges his hostility in a misogynist image often described as portraying three men in drag, mean-spirited in the way gay humor can sometimes be toward women. Like the tendentious jokes analyzed by Freud, Wood's satire has an aggressive purpose: it turns a neutral third party, the audience, "indifferent to begin with, into a co-hater or co-despiser, and creates for the enemy a host of opponents where at first there was only one."[71] At stake in the painting is a kind of secret knowledge used against an antagonistic party who then become the butt of a joke among those who are in on the game. Artworld viewers of *Daughters of Revolution* possess information the Daughters themselves do

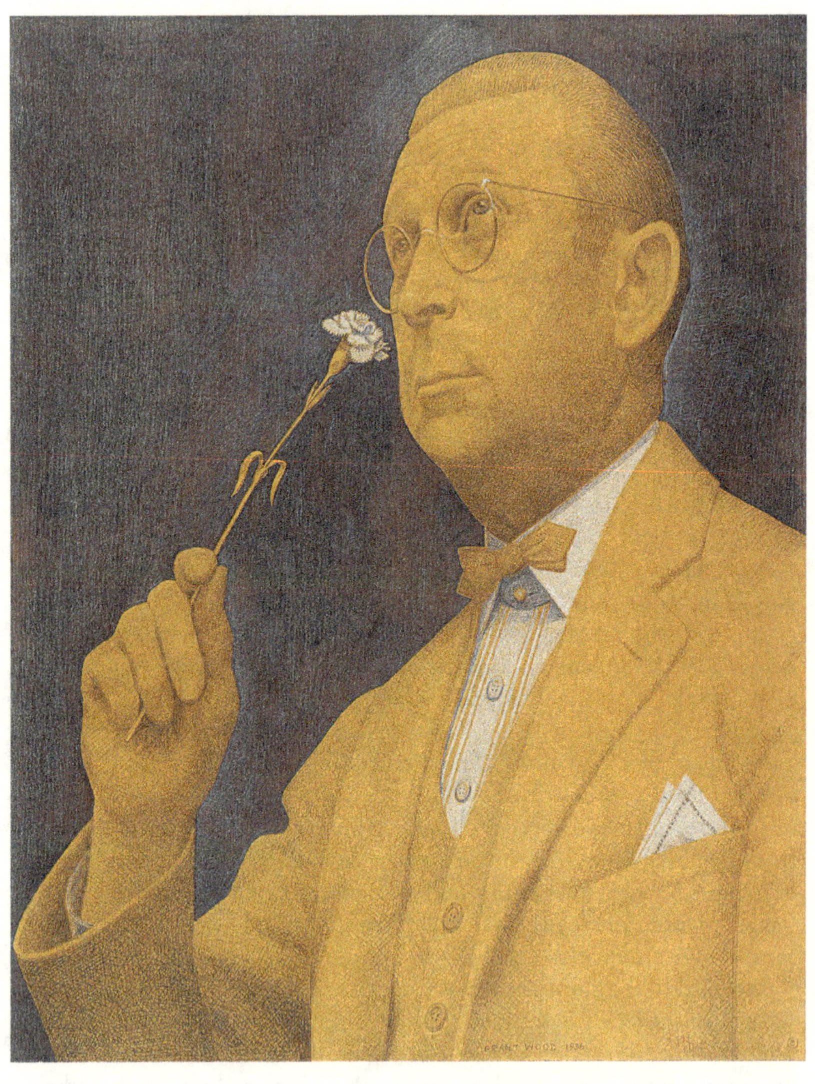

Fig. 3.17. Grant Wood, *Sentimental Yearner*, 1936.

not share about the foreign authorship of the patriotic picture within Wood's picture; this exclusive knowledge creates an in-group and positions the artist's adversaries as naïfs.

Similarly, passing for straight—a necessary disguise and means of survival—establishes a world of dupes outside the circle of those in the know, subverting the social order of an oppressed minority and dominant majority by means of a private language and cryptic codes. An evolving semiotics of homosexual identity and desire, developed under pressure of censorship, has historically ensured that certain meanings remain unavailable to all but the privileged few. In the nineteenth century, for instance, a green carnation worn on the lapel signaled one's homosexual tastes, a device promoted by Oscar Wilde and made scandalous by an eponymous novel by Robert Hichens in 1894. Wood may indeed have referenced this symbol in one of his illustrations for *Main Street*, *Sentimental Yearner*, endowing the foppish shoe salesman Raymond P. Wutherspoon with such a flower, though it appears nowhere in Lewis's narrative. Art historians have erroneously assumed the carnation to be pink, which is not the case; in the original drawing on brown kraft paper (1936, Fig. 3.17) the carnation does appear to be tinged the palest shade of green. In the twentieth century, during Wood's time, secret homosexual symbols included the red tie, pinky ring, or smoking of Pall Mall cigarettes, whose pack bore the slogan "wherever particular people congregate." One suspects that among Wood's contemporaries in Iowa there was a small coterie of informed insiders, including, for example, the writer for the *Sioux City Tribune* who reported on the artist's decoration of the local Hotel Martin's Corn Room in 1926. The journalist took pains to inform readers that the painter and his assistant on the hotel project, Edgar Britton, were not long-haired freaks in berets but "men whose outward appearance does not differ greatly from that of any dozen men of their age picked out at random in the Martin lobby."[72] After reassuring a general readership in this way, the reporter tipped a more select group with a peculiar non-sequitur in his elbow-nudging final sentence: "And both smoke a very familiar brand of cigarets [*sic*]." The editor who then recycled this article in the *Cedar Rapids Republican* (Fig. 3.18) juxtaposed headshots of the two artists in such a way as to indicate Wood's interest in his handsome young assistant.

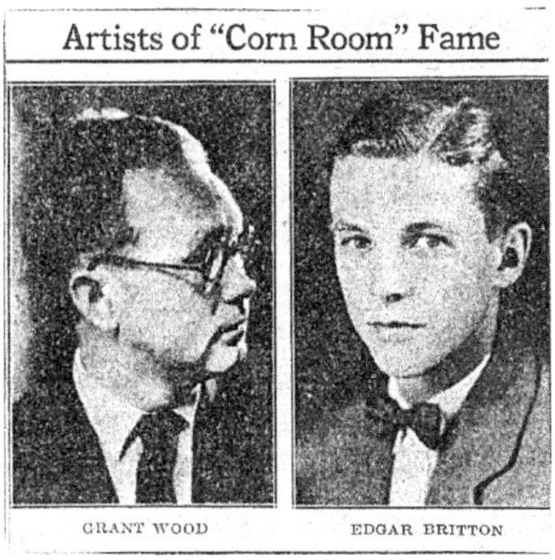

Artists of "Corn Room" Fame

GRANT WOOD EDGAR BRITTON

Fig. 3.18. From "Eppley Hotels Magazine Praises Grant Wood and Edgar Britton for Work," *Cedar Rapids Republican*, October 17, 1926.

So subtle must these in-group messages be that there is always the possibility of missing or doubting their true significance. Looking back in time, moreover, it is hard to know precisely when particular codes gained currency. Critic Hal Fischer describes a highly developed set of signals involving handkerchiefs that was in use by the 1970s, in which a man's availability and preferred role (aggressive or passive) was designated by a bandana's red or blue color and the side of the body on which it was worn.[73] Whether men of Wood's generation employed the hanky code is unclear, but the red kerchief in the youth's right hip pocket in *Farmer with Corn and Pigs* (1932, Fig. 3.19) seems intriguing. In this image, which Wood painted for the "Fruits of Iowa" series in the Hotel Montrose in Cedar Rapids, Evans identifies a "brawny masculinity" in the figure's muscular proportions and in "the oversized ears of corn emerging from his basket." Evans interprets the corn, positioned at the man's groin, symbolically, observing that "this impressive bushel indicates the man's sexual potency in an almost comical fashion."[74] Indeed, "basket," according to Bruce Rodgers's classic gay lexicon, is slang for the bulge of a man's genitals in his pants, and a "basketeer" is one who ogles men's crotches.[75] Following Evans's intuition that Wood is here playing with symbols, it might even be possible to read the pair of pigs—one tough-looking, one meek and on the side of the daisies—as top and bottom respectively. All this is guesswork on account of the necessarily clandestine nature of the signs, if they *are* signs; only members of the endangered subculture would know. When Tennessee Williams in his 1972 memoir recalled Wood in Key West, describing him winkingly (and redundantly) as "very, very friendly," the playwright outed the artist to some readers but not to most, shielding a fellow homosexual even posthumously from hostile outside awareness.

A private message of a different sort informed Wood's conception of the remarkable *Appraisal* (Fig. 3.20), a confrontation of urban and rural in which the artist's sympathies of course favor the latter. This beautifully composed, richly detailed image of a well-heeled city woman come to buy a cockerel from the farm hides a mean prank. The artist wanted to get over on his colleague Edward Rowan (1898–1946, Fig. 3.21), the Harvard-educated director of the Little Gallery in Cedar Rapids, for a perceived slight: Wood had proposed a show of regional artists at the gallery and Rowan was slow in scheduling it, busy as he was hosting traveling exhibitions to fulfill his educational mission. According to biographer Brown, whose partner, Mary Lackersteen, posed for the portly, fur-clad woman in *Appraisal*, Wood cast Rowan vicariously as the other female figure. "I came across a teacher over at Grant School who looks exactly like Ed Rowan," the artist reportedly told Lackersteen,[76] intending to present an image of the good-looking gallery director in drag. The actual model for the painting was Bette Rupke (Fig. 3.22), later Sanbourne, a pretty and talented art teacher and friend of the artist's family in Cedar Rapids.[77] With her dark-brown eyes, classic features, and dimpled chin, she provided Wood both a surrogate for Rowan and an attractive avatar of the hardy farmwoman about to surrender a prized fowl to the overdressed urbanite. Supplemented with this backstory of Wood's intended swipe at his

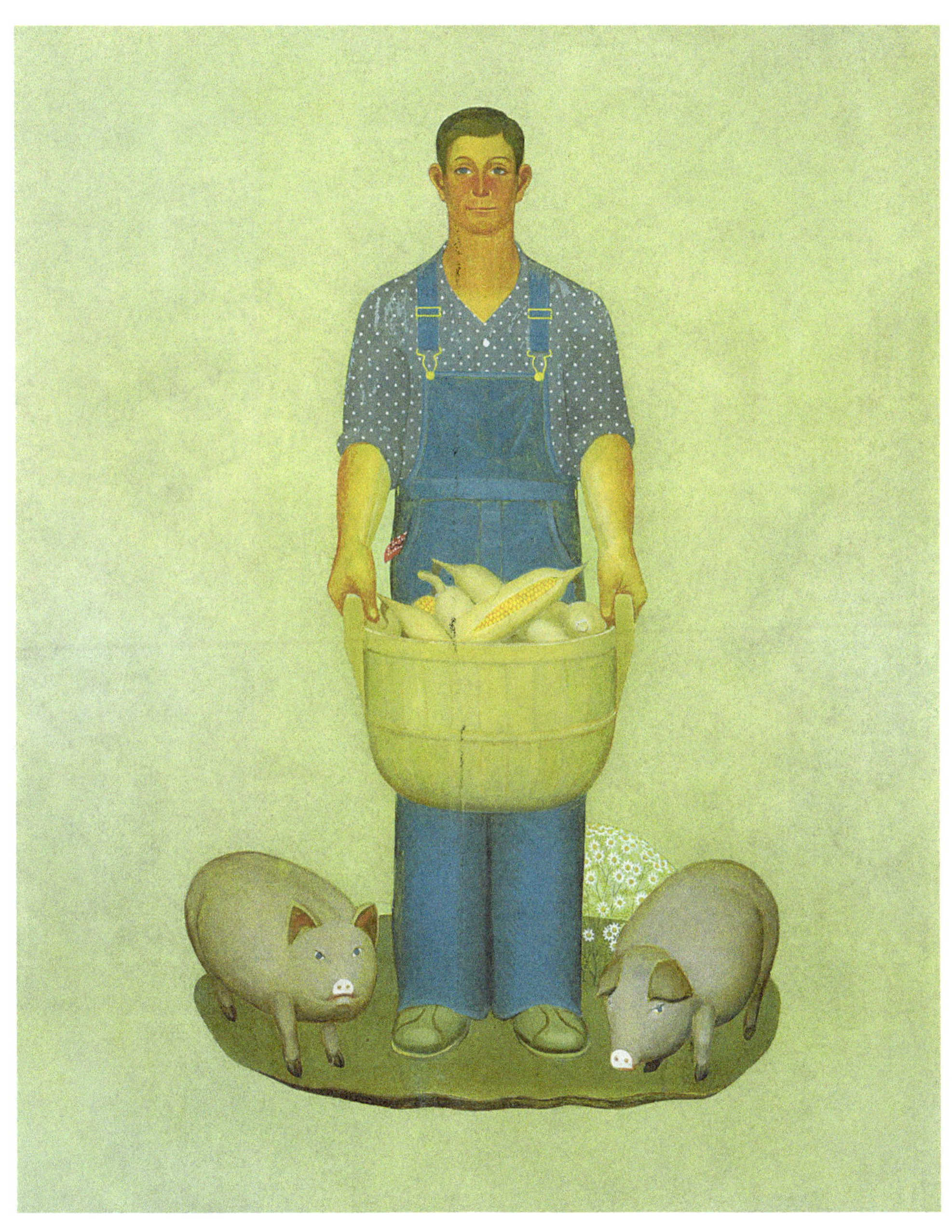

Fig. 3.19. Grant Wood, *Farmer with Pigs and Corn*, 1932.

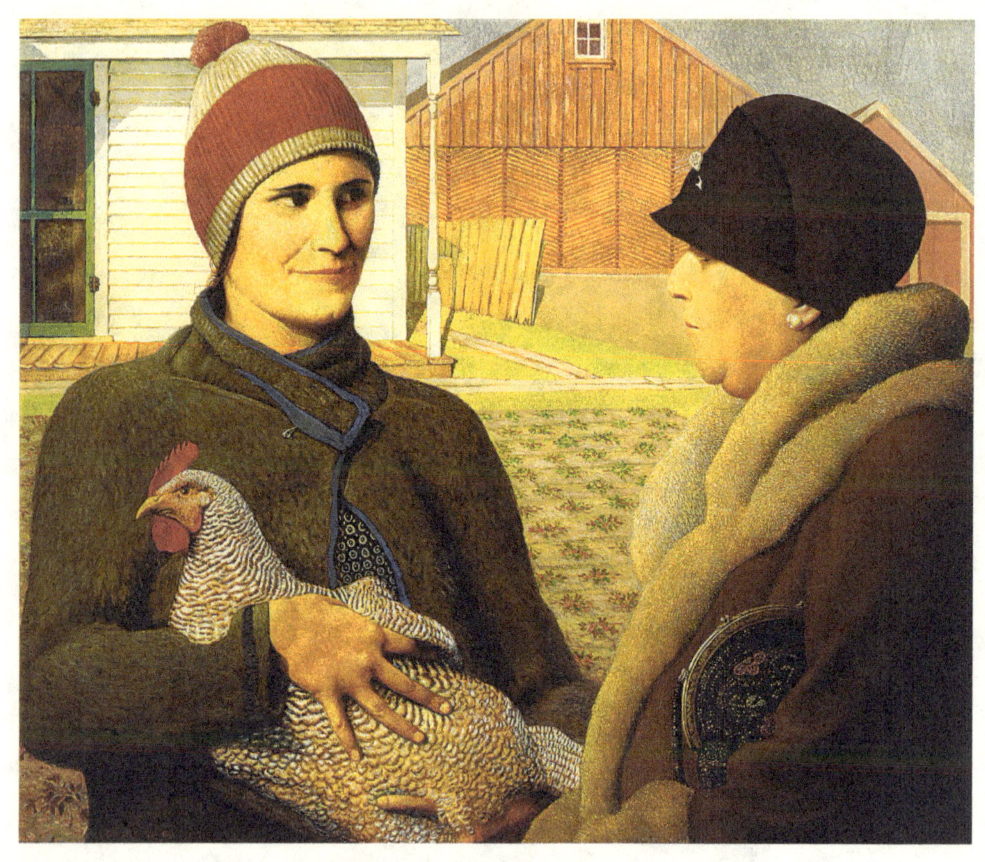

Fig. 3.20. Grant Wood, *Appraisal*, 1931.

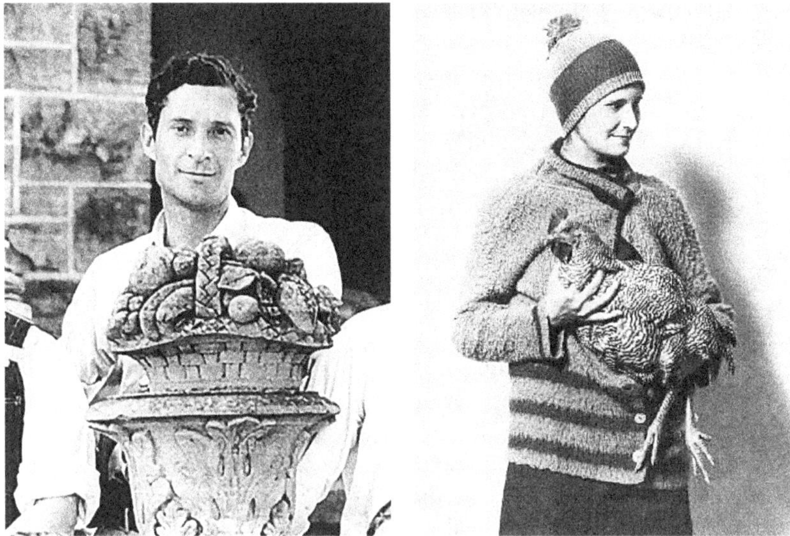

Fig. 3.21 (left). Edward Rowan at Stone City Art Colony, 1932.

Fig. 3.22 (right). Bette Rupke Sanbourne modeling for *Appraisal*, 1930.

artworld colleague, *Appraisal* yields multiple narratives—a public, time-honored, and even universal one concerning the difference between and interdependence of city and country, and a private, circumstantially specific, and retaliatory one that casts Rowan as a sham Regionalist "selling out" in his art programming to an alien elite.

CHICKENS

The secret send-up of Rowan is among several anecdotes passed down about *Appraisal*. Wood had kept the depicted Plymouth Rock rooster in his Turner Alley studio while the painting was in progress, calling it "good old boy" while it annoyed both household and neighborhood with its loud early morning crowing.[78] The picture's format was at first vertical, showing three-quarter-length figures, the cockerel's dangling feet, and a chicken-wire fence running parallel to the picture plane.[79] After the painting won the sweepstakes award at the 1931 Iowa State Fair, Wood cut about ten inches off the bottom and retitled it *Clothes*, perhaps backing off his negative "appraisal" of Rowan, with whom Brown and Lackersteen had encouraged him to patch things up. Although his public never embraced the new title, one can see why Wood proposed it, as the women's clothing conveys much of the work's content. The cloche hat worn by the lady visitor, her pearl earrings, fur-trimmed coat, and clasp handbag, all were fashions of the moment, and Wood rendered them with loving exactitude to create an image of indulgent comfort. The photograph of Rupke shows how he manipulated his source material, changing the light color of her jacket to a deep olive green while retaining its wooly texture, dispensing with the buttons and relocating the eloquent detail of the makeshift safety-pin closure. Beneath the jacket, he added the familiar dot-and-circle-patterned apron. This was his first painting after *American Gothic* (Fig. 1.2), and, in addition to the apron, he borrowed from that earlier work the Eldon house porch, complete with slender support post and green-trimmed screen door. The white porch effectively frames the farmwoman's handsome head, whose cap, with its red stripe and pom-pom, seems color-coordinated with the comb and wattle of the bird she cradles. In an engaging ricochet of gazes, she looks searchingly at the city woman, who in turn eyes the cock, who glares directly at the viewer of the painting.

Adjusting the bird's position in the picture, Wood painted it in profile rather than in three-quarter view. In the photograph, Rupke supports the rooster's breast with one hand and grasps its thigh with the other; in the painting, the farmwoman clutches the bird possessively, with arm and hands encircling its body. Was there another photograph mirroring the painting, or did Wood invent the rather lewd detail of a single finger protruding penis-like through the cockerel's gorgeous brown and white feathers? Evans connects this "small phallus" to the relationship between the two women in the painting, in light of "Rowan's gender-crossed figure in this work, as well as the period's stereotypes concerning 'butch' women like Lackersteen," who, again, modeled the stout urbanite.[80] Perhaps the pointing finger/little penis is a sign, whether conscious or unconscious, underscoring the bird's role as an object of desire. In the overt narrative of market exchange, the farmwoman's prized poultry will be sized up, purchased, and consumed, but other forms of having and wanting may operate sub rosa in the painting. "Chicken" is gay slang for a beautiful young boy,[81] an object of homosexual interest. And on the most literal level, the poking finger evokes an unmentionable fact of rural life: the sexual use of animals, reported to Alfred Kinsey in 1948 by about one-third of his male subjects who grew up on the farm.[82] Thus, Wood's celebration of the Plymouth Rock chickens in "Return from Bohemia" as "friendly, human and just the right size" (Appendix, p. 217) reads as a bizarre and unfortunate choice of words. Rinard thought so too; in his lightly edited version of the manuscript, the breed is hailed instead as "friendly and communicative."[83]

Wood's first biographer identified chickens as the preferred subject matter of the artist as a preschooler, claiming that "he drew them on all occasions—roosters crowing, roosters fighting, hens on eggs."[84] That the chicken was a kind of totem animal for Wood we learn from his own childhood recollections as well as from another picture, the comical and poignant *Adolescence*. This image, rendered as a highly finished drawing (1933) and later as a painting (1940, Fig. 3.23), depicts a molting young bird between two adults on a rooftop, exposed to the chill air of dawn or dusk. Wood asserts in "Return from Bohemia" that chickens were his favorite animals; it was his chore on the farm

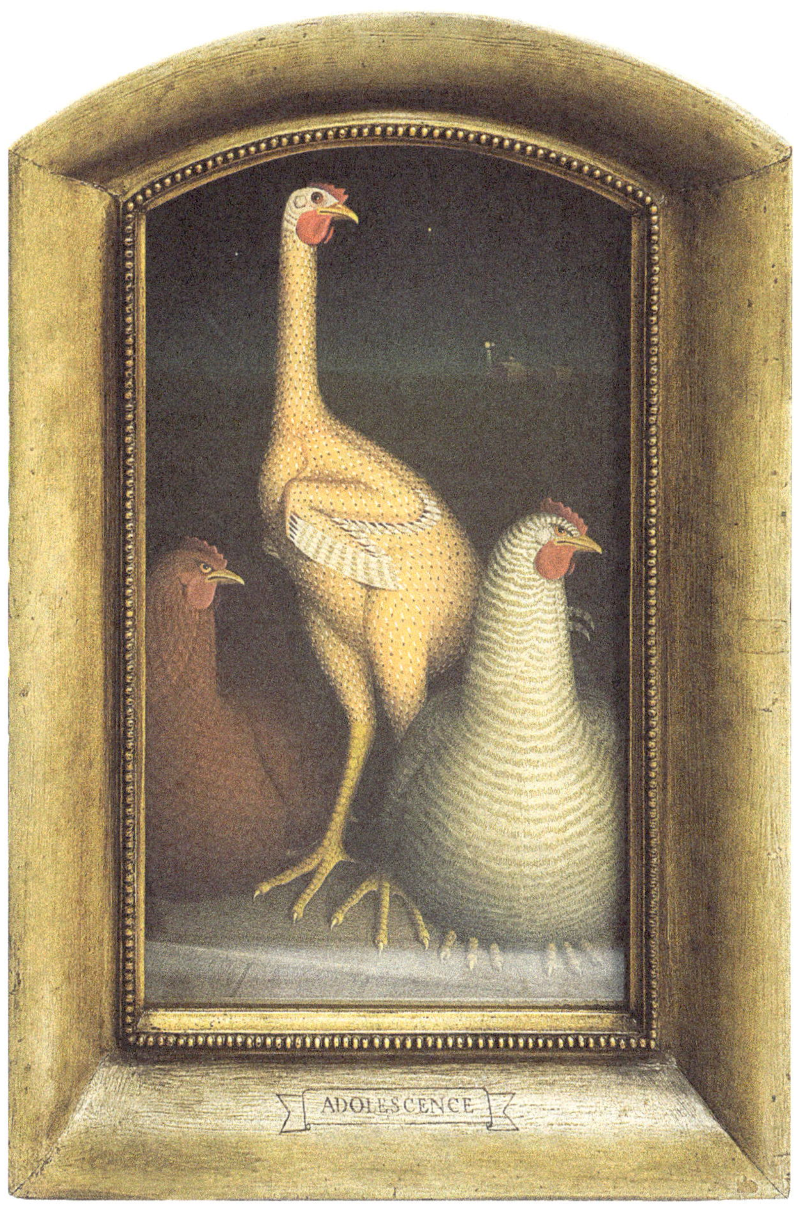

Fig. 3.23. Grant Wood, *Adolescence*, 1940.

to feed them and to collect their eggs. "I had watched them hatch and grow up," he explains fondly, "and when they had been in the featherless, adolescent stage, I had even gone so far as to rub mutton tallow on their wings to relieve sun-burn" (App., 231). He imbues his picture with similar empathy. Capturing the discomfiture of puberty in an image of a gawky bird with its surly elders, Wood touches on everyone's remembered teenage insecurities and on his own personal sense of estrangement. The fowl's elongated gullet, more goose- than chicken-like, conveys its mutant condition and conjures the uncommon breed known as the Naked Neck or "turken." Often mistaken for a cross between a turkey and a chicken, the odd-looking turken is bred for easy plucking. Wood's naked bird epitomizes a hybrid, intermediate condition, poised not just between youth and maturity, but, with a hen on one side and the larger rooster on the other, literally between female and male.

Wood's artistic insistence on drawing something instructive from a chicken's life finds a hilarious negative counterpart in Sherwood Anderson's existential ruminations in "The Egg," an autobiographical short story published in 1921. "I am a gloomy man," Anderson broods, "inclined to see the darker side of life, [and] I attribute it to the fact that what should have been the happy joyous days of childhood were spent on a chicken farm."[85] From his firsthand observations, the author could only conclude that the fowl's is a pitiful existence:

> One unversed in such matters can have no notion of the many and tragic things that can happen to a chicken. It is born out of an egg, lives for a few weeks as a tiny fluffy thing such as you will see pictured on Easter cards, then becomes hideously naked, eats quantities of corn and meal bought by the sweat of your father's brow, gets diseases called pip, cholera, and other names, stands looking with stupid eyes at the sun, becomes sick and dies. A few hens and now and then a rooster, intended to serve God's mysterious ends, struggle through to maturity. The hens lay eggs out of which come other chickens and the dreadful cycle is thus made complete. It is all unbelievably complex. Most philosophers must have been raised on chicken farms. One hopes for so much from a chicken and is so dreadfully disillusioned. Small chickens, just setting out on the journey of life, look so bright and alert and they are in fact so dreadfully stupid. They are so much like people they mix one up in one's judgments of life. If disease does not kill them they wait until your expectations are thoroughly aroused and then walk under the wheels of a wagon—to go squashed and dead back to their maker.[86]

Chickens teach us, according to Anderson, all about grief, and in this pathetic round of life and death, the poor rooster is only a hapless instrument of the cycle's pointless continuation.

In Wood's *Adolescence*, the cockerel becomes the very image of vulnerability. Henry Adams detected an irony in the composition, suggesting that while "the chickens are grouped together into the shape of an erect phallus," the picture itself "is about being emasculated."[87] Indeed, long-necked and beady-eyed like the skinny, chokered figure in *Victorian Survival*, Wood's pinfeathered bird is similarly threatened, the distant horizon line cutting visually across its attenuated throat. And strange to say—but surely a barnyard fact known to Wood—despite the swaggering phallic connotations of the very terms "cock" and "cocky," roosters do not have penises, but mate by means of a cloaca, presenting a somewhat confusing example of sexual difference and procreation to an impressionable child on the farm. A curious chicken tale in "Return from Bohemia" captures boy Wood's naïve struggle to puzzle it all out. Finding one of the family's young cockerels lying inert on the ground after school one day, Grant determines to resurrect it. He models his intervention on the hired man's account of how first lady Ida McKinley had been "brought back to life by *an injection of salt in the arm*" (emphasis in the original, App., 231). Grant secretly attempts to duplicate this miracle, with brother Jack as co-conspirator:

> Luckily, mother was down [in the] cellar when I came into the kitchen. I got a fistful of salt from the jar over the stove and took father's carving knife out of the china cupboard drawer. When I returned to the scene of the tragedy, Jack was shaking the chicken's head, trying to get him to open his eyes.
>
> We took the body around to the side of the house where no-one would be likely to see us. Then I cut a long slit in the flesh of the cockerel's wing and rubbed the salt into the wound.
>
> "What will that do?" asked Jack wonderingly.
>
> "Bring him back to life," I said with complete confidence. . . .
>
> I had the idea that the salt treatment was a sort of magic that would work better if we didn't watch it, so we forced ourselves to stay away all that evening.
>
> But the next morning, the first thing we did was to rush out to see how the chicken was. I arrived at the scene first. . . .
>
> "He's gone!" I cried. Jack and Frank came running to see. "Gone!" they echoed. We all danced about, hysterical with delight [App., 231–32].

With the fundamental problem of life and death at its core, this episode suggests the sexual researches of children: the clandestine operation, modeled on a procedure dimly understood through hearsay to have been performed on the president's *wife*, is carried out with the *father's* knife on a passive male chicken. One thinks of Freud's Little Hans and his desire to comprehend his parent's relations and his own place and that of his baby sister within the family, with little to go on save the nonsense about storks that was given him.[88] In his anxiously uncertain state, Hans developed an irrational fear of horses; his lesser-known little contemporary Arpád became obsessed with chickens. Sándor Ferenczi published Arpád's case as "A Little Chanticleer," interpreting the five-year-old's fascination with "the goings-on in the fowl-yard" as a similarly insistent wish for knowledge.[89] Arpád "could conveniently observe in the hen-coop all the secrets of his own family about which no information was vouchsafed to him," Ferenczi noted; "the 'helpful animals' shewed him in an unconcealed way everything he wanted to see, especially the continual sexual activity between cock and hen, the laying of eggs, and the creeping out of the young brood." Arpád also loved to watch when poultry were killed and prepared for dinner. For a time, he lost his speech and only cackled and crowed, often for hours on end. Once he began to speak again, it was always of chickens. A budding artist, he made small newspaper sculptures of cocks and hens, which he pretended to sell and to slaughter with a knife; he could draw with patience and skill, but only birds, with big beaks.

Triggering this behavior was the child's recollection (or fantasy) that a fowl had snapped at his penis one day as he urinated in the chicken coop. From the family, moreover, Ferenczi discovered that in order to discourage Arpád's masturbation, someone had "jokingly" threatened him with castration. The boy became terrified of roosters. The whole syndrome, Ferenczi reasoned, was a reaction to the fear that the scolding threat had inspired. "Now I will stick this dead fowl's blind eyes," Arpád announced in the kitchen, armed with his own castrating intentions and a curling iron; at other times, "he would kiss and stroke the slaughtered animal," clucking to it tenderly. As if envisioning a variation on *Adolescence* in advance of its artist, Arpád declared: "I should like to have a live plucked cock. He must have no wings, no feathers, and no tail, only a comb, and he must be able to walk like that."[90] Expressing all manner of violent, cannibalistic, and masochistic desires to his family, their servants, and his playmates, the boy blurted out one day, "My father is the cock!" And he imagined surpassing the father, in a dream of superior power and masculinity: "Now I am small, now I am a chicken," he explained. "When I get bigger I shall be a fowl. When I am bigger still I shall be a cock. When I am biggest of all I shall be a coachman."[91]

For Freud, the salient features of Little Chanticleer's case were his "complete identification with his totem animal and his ambivalent emotional attitude to it."[92] Arpád's obsession with the chicken replicates the clan's exaltation of the totem, which links all members of the group to their common ancestor—the primal father, symbolized by the animal that is venerated, feared, and ritually slaughtered. The castration anxiety that gave rise to Arpád's totemism haunts the image of the long-necked fowl in Wood's *Adolescence*, where the horizon mimics the edge of a chopping block, a literal dividing line between life and death.

Garwood claimed that Wood drew *Adolescence* from the corpse of a pet chicken at 5 Turner Alley, the erstwhile hatchling depicted in *Portrait of Nan* (Fig. 1.8), which had choked in the studio on a rubber cigarette.[93] As is so often the case with Wood legend, it's hard to know if that is true: Graham said she cried when the bird swallowed the cigarette for a worm, and had "thought the chick was a goner, but it survived."[94] Another time, she remembered her brother's earlier remorse for smashing a trespassing chicken in the kitchen door (they ate it for dinner),[95] yet his ostensible compassion is countered by the sadistic disgust he confessed to Sara Sherman on the subject of chickens: "He told me," she wrote of the boyhood reminiscences her onetime husband had shared, "how he loathed the feeling of the still-warm eggs, sometimes slippery and offal-spattered, as he lifted them out of the nests."[96] Wood's private confession to Sherman reveals a destructive origin myth that inverts the good intentions of his childish chicken rescue story in "Return from Bohemia":

> One day, in a fit of fury and self-loathing, he picked up a brooding hen and flung it on the ground, breaking her neck. And after he had done this, he said, he had a wonderful [impression of the] beautiful, brown glossy feathers of the fowl and then, without knowing why, he carefully plucked a few of the feathers from the dead body and went home.
>
> A few days later, with a discarded paint box of his sisters [*sic*] and using the chicken feathers as a brush, he painted his first picture of a chic[ken].

Here Wood's totem animal incites hatred, destruction, awe, and, ultimately, the urge to create art. He identifies with the chicken, for he punishes it out of *self*-loathing. Its death casts a spell on him—he preserves its feathers without knowing why. Its femaleness in this instance, and his appropriation of a girl's paint box, implicate Wood's feminine side in his artistic creativity.

Though this tale dates his initial chicken painting to early adolescence (eight years his sister's senior, he would have been at least thirteen or so before she discarded a paint box), in "Return from Bohemia" he is preoccupied with the subject much earlier. His very first efforts at drawing, with pencil or crayon on cardboard from a cracker box, are devoted to chickens: dressed in his nightgown and lying under the kitchen table, he renders a setting Plymouth Rock hen (App., 198–99). Hidden for the moment from his father, who has commanded that the child should be in bed, Grant thinks of his drawing as an illicit activity. Though Maryville indeed disapproves, both parents marvel at his picture, with its impressive number of eggs. Here, art-making confronts the mystery of life's beginnings, the chicken/egg conundrum; in the parable Wood told Sherman, the very act of painting commemorates a death, one he brought on himself. Like Arpád, he figures out familial roles and relationships by referring to what he observes among the chickens and projects onto them feelings both affectionate and murderous, wanting to be the cock, wanting to kill the cock—read the father, sacrificed for art. Looking back as a mature artist through a veil of oedipal guilt at his own featherless/fatherless adolescence, Wood created a tragicomic self-portrait in his painting of a molting chicken.

The image grew from unconscious conflict, familial feeling, and quotidian experience, enabled by Wood's encyclopedic store of art historical material. In the 1950s, his onetime colleague and antagonist at the university, art historian

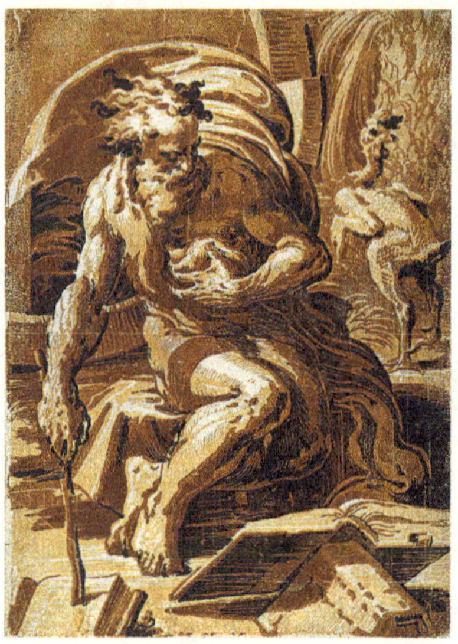

Fig. 3.24. Ugo da Carpi, after Parmigianino, *Diogenes*, c. 1524–27.

Horst W. Janson, pointed to an arcane iconographical source for Wood's naked chicken in a sixteenth-century print by Ugo da Carpi, *Diogenes* (Fig. 3.24).[97] Janson discovered the original motif in a work that reproduces a drawing by Parmigianino of the fourth-century Greek philosopher, and he proposed that Wood could easily have seen the image almost anywhere, since Ugo's print has been widely illustrated in textbooks on the graphic arts as an example of the chiaroscuro woodcut technique.[98] Making a convincing formal comparison between the two pictures of plucked birds with bodies facing left and profile heads twisting to the right, Janson interposed the woodcut as a kind of reference point between the dead pet chicken Garwood described in his biography and Wood's vivified if highly stylized depiction of it in *Adolescence*.

TRUTH AND FALSEHOOD

Although Janson did not consider the meaning that Ugo's image may have had for Wood beyond a merely formal model, I think we may credit the artist with at least a passing interest in the subject matter of his Renaissance source. Janson assumed, whether justly or not, that Wood was unaware of the motif of the naked chicken as a reference to Diogenes's mocking retort to Plato's idea of man as a "featherless biped." Celebrated for his witty aphorisms, Diogenes rejected convention and exalted nature as a model for simple living, reportedly making his home in a wine vessel, shown in the print as an upended wooden vat in the background. Perhaps Wood recognized in this figure of the legendary Cynic a kindred spirit and fellow satirist, a kind of Mark Twain of the ancient world. Certainly the story of the eccentric philosopher going around with a lamp in broad daylight in search of an honest man was common currency in Wood's time, evinced by William Gropper's self-portrait as *Diogenes* (1945) and the several lithographs he made after it, one of which was published and marketed like Wood's own graphics by Associated American Artists.[99] But honesty in the literal sense was, as we've seen, a virtue Wood could not himself practice. Registering his queer habits of dissembling illuminates in a fascinating way his late masterpiece and largest easel painting ever, *Parson Weems' Fable* (1939, Fig. 3.25). It is a tongue-in-cheek treatment of the parable of an exemplary boy who could not tell a lie by a man who could not risk telling the truth.

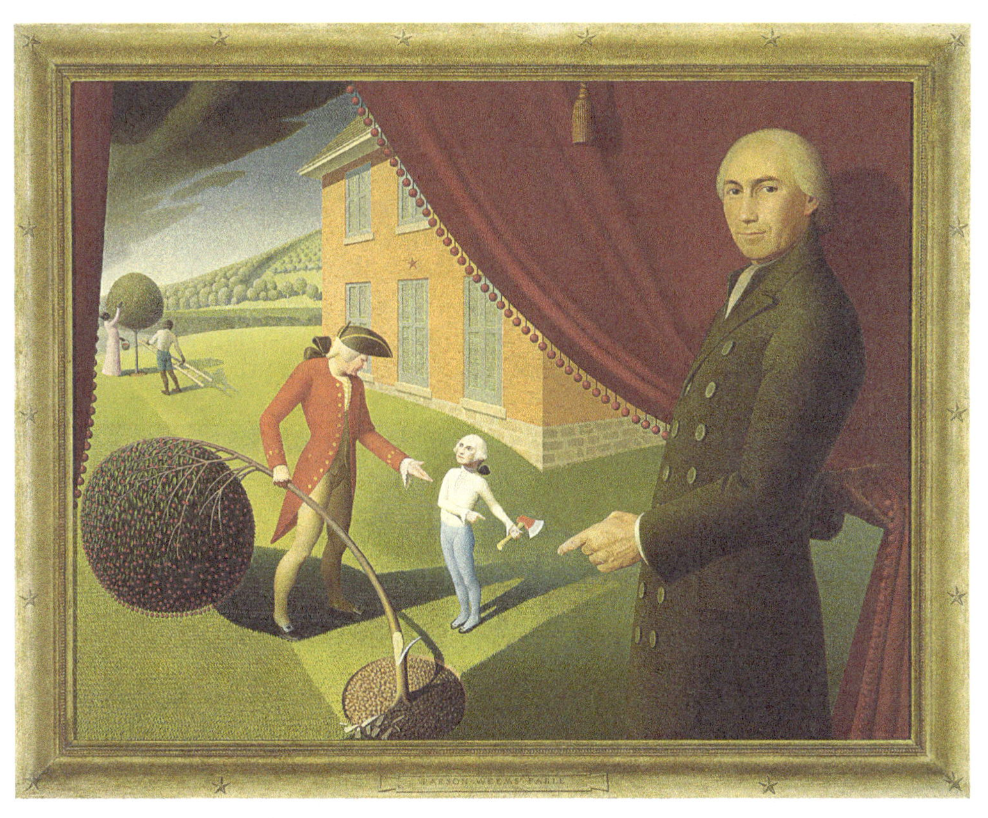

Fig. 3.25. Grant Wood, *Parson Weems' Fable*, 1939.

In the painting, Wood shows little George Washington admitting to his father how he had plied his new hatchet on a prized cherry tree. Mason Locke Weems introduced this incident in his 1806 biography of Washington; by the 1930s, the fable was widely recognized as such—not historical fact, but an inspirational invention by an engaging storyteller, whose narrating figure appears prominently in the foreground of Wood's picture. The public context for the artist's choice of a Washingtonian subject in 1939 involved both the sesquicentennial of the first president's inauguration and an anxious national mood: the rise of fascism in Europe had triggered concerns in the U.S. over whether American patriotism would be sufficiently vigorous to counter threats from abroad.[100] When Associated American Artists unveiled *Parson Weems' Fable* at its New York gallery on December 30 that year, promotional materials included a poster of the image with the pertinent excerpt from Weems's *Life of Washington, the Great*, and, a few days later, an artist statement in which Wood professed dismay over contemporary historians' tendency to discredit such valuable examples of American folktale as that of the cherry tree. "In our present unsettled times," he wrote, "when democracy is threatened on all sides, the preservation of our folklore is more important than is generally realized."[101] This preservationist ambition, of a piece with Wood's preoccupation with the past, can be seen as well in his loving restoration of the Federal revival-style house in

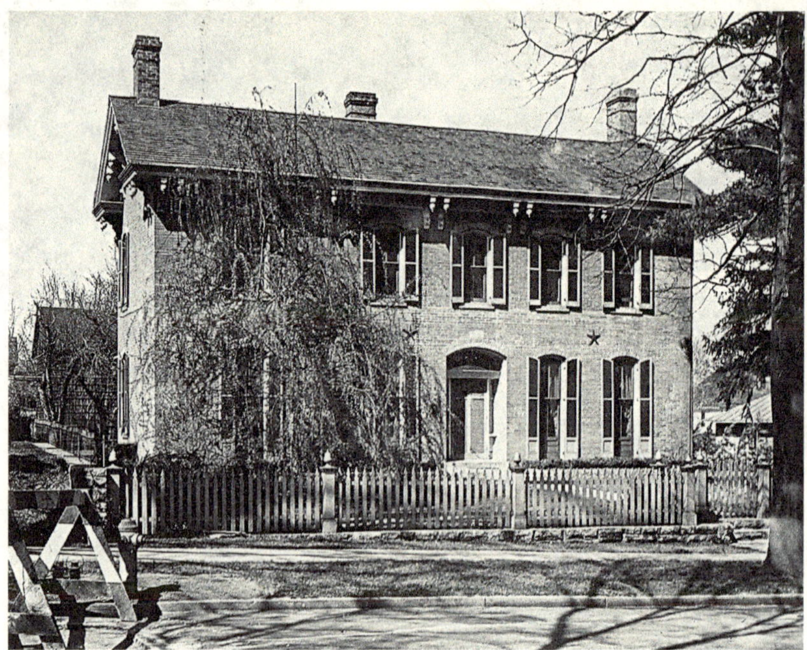

Fig. 3.26. The 1858 Oakes House at 1142 East Court Street, Iowa City, where Wood lived from 1935 to 1942.

Iowa City he and Sherman had purchased four years earlier (Fig. 3.26), and in his collection of Midwestern antiques, Currier and Ives prints, and other Americana.[102]

Yet the comic aspect of *Parson Weems' Fable* puts it at odds with the earnest tone Wood assumed in his public statement, and it is not surprising that the painting elicited indignation along with more commonly appreciative amusement.[103] If he regretted the original story's modern debunking, Wood's response was to re-bunk it rather than attempt to recuperate an irretrievably innocent account. Far from a straightforward patriotic homily to an endangered democracy, the image reads as a highly sophisticated and self-conscious joke. At the very center of the ingeniously ordered composition, with its powerful diagonal emphasis and pleasing formal repetitions, appears an outrageously ridiculous element: the child protagonist wears the head of a senescent Washington, obviously lifted from the Gilbert Stuart portrait reproduced on the dollar bill. Wood's foregrounding of Parson Weems as presenter of the scene places the cherry tree episode in quotation marks, reminding us how the tale of young George's honesty was made up by his eulogist out of whole cloth. The painting thus troubles the nature of historical truth, of mythmaking and its relationship to outright falsehood, all beautifully expressed in the positioning of Weems's conjuring hands—one fully illuminated, the other sneaky-looking, in the shadows behind his back.

The pointing figure of Weems derives from similar Renaissance devices—angels, saints, or donors who draw the viewer's attention to some instructive pictorial event—but Wood's more immediate visual sources were American. Art historians recognize his painting's debt to Charles Willson Peale's standing self-portrait, *The Artist in His Museum* (1822, Fig. 3.27), in which Peale draws back a fringed red drape to reveal his taxonomic collection of scientific and cultural curiosities, from mastodon bones to colonial portrait paintings including his own. Between the curtain-lifting characters of Peale and Weems, we may interpolate the presence of Wood himself: all three famous Americans were showmen of sorts and teachers, entertaining and informing an audience. To model the figure of Weems, Wood chose an educator and historian, John Ely Briggs, professor of political science at the University of Iowa and editor of the *Palimpsest*, a journal of the Iowa State Historical Society. (Briggs's daughter was at the time a student of Wood's in the art department.)

Another visual source for *Parson Weems' Fable* must have been a nineteenth-century painting that circulated in a popular print by John C. McRae, *"Father, I Cannot Tell a Lie: I Cut the Tree"* (1889, Fig. 3.28). Wanda Corn identified this image as a progenitor of Wood's composition, noting "the same setting and cast of characters: the family home, an orchard, black slaves working in the yard, the offended tree, a hatchet, and the son confessing to his father in the foreground."[104] One might add the

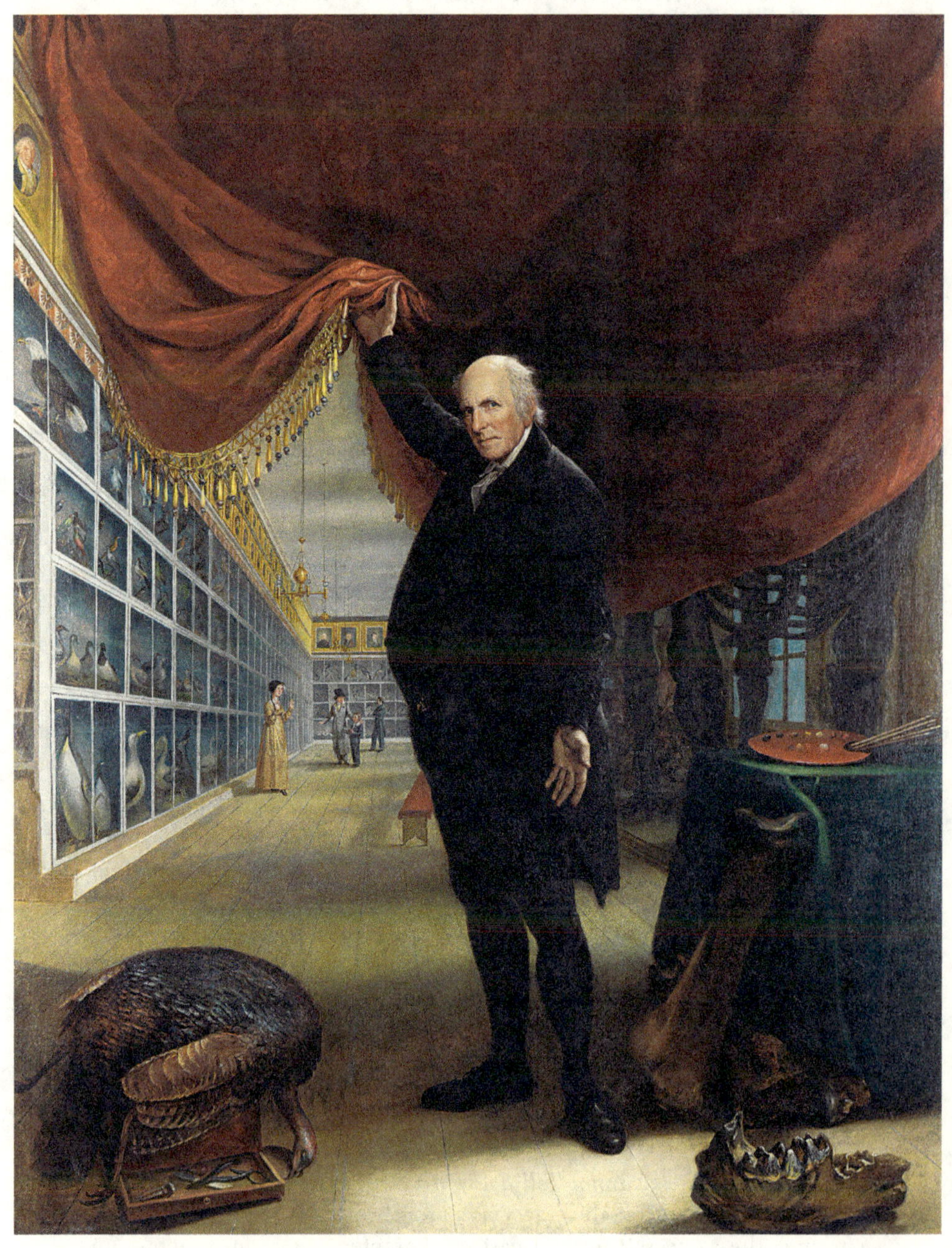

Fig. 3.27. Charles Willson Peale, *The Artist in His Museum*, 1822.

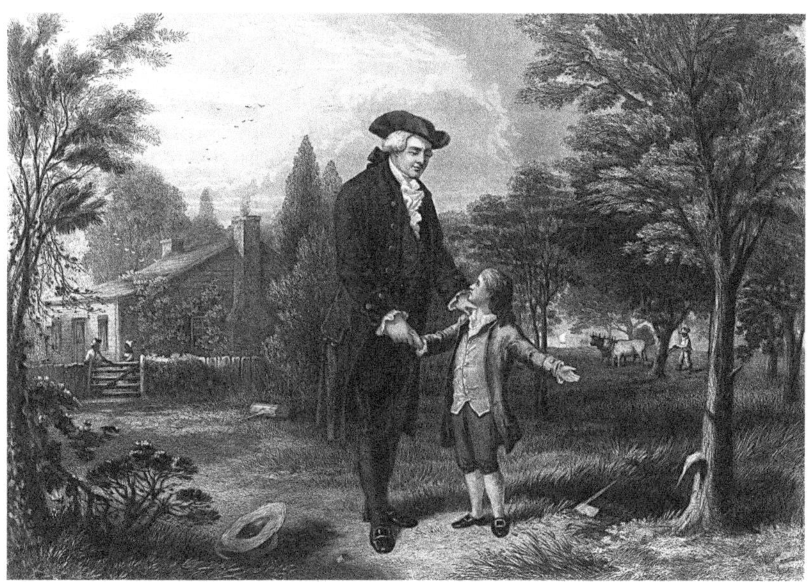

Fig. 3.28. John C. McRae (engraver), George. G. White (painter), *"Father, I Cannot Tell a Lie: I Cut the Tree,"* 1889.

similar positioning of the house at a forty-five degree angle to the picture plane as well as the related diagonal recession from right to left, which leads the eye in both cases from the child to the man to the slave couple in the background. Remarkable in Wood's adaptation of the earlier image, however, is his complete transformation of its content—from a scene of tender reconciliation, where the kindly father forgives a repentant son, to one of paternal anger and filial defiance. The dynamic interplay of gestures in *Parson Weems' Fable* pantomimes conflict, not contrition. The parson's extended finger directs our focus to the cut in the tree; we follow the slender trunk up to the weirdest detail in the painting, Augustine Washington's blood-red, gloved fist beneath a scalloped white cuff, while his other (ungloved) hand, palm upturned, demands the ax, to which the naughty child points with his right hand and holds *away* from his father with his left. In the McRae print, the boy's ax lay abandoned on the ground; here he grasps it still, refusing its surrender. Contradicting everything about the moralizing myth he resurrects for public, putatively patriotic ends, Wood creates a dream of private significance in which the guilty son remains intractable. Moreover, with the gestural momentum in the painting continuing through the ax blade back to Weems's pointing hand, the sequence of misbehavior, parental disapproval, and recalcitrance is never resolved but becomes cyclical and unending.

With *Parson Weems* centering on a patriarchal appeal for honesty, it is notable how much Wood made of his own father's insistence on the supreme value of truth. In "Return from Bohemia," he opposed Maryville's rejection of imaginative fantasy with his own earliest art-making, and it is not hard to detect in this scenario a juvenile ego's struggle against the imposition of the reality principle. Pondering the boy's setting-hen drawing, Maryville (App., 199) asks his wife, "You don't think this will put mischief into the youngster's head?" Hattie responds (mistakenly) that drawing is only a childish enthusiasm soon to be outgrown: "Frank used to like to draw when he was that age too." Still dubious, Maryville then remembers a book of fairy tales given to his children by a well-meaning neighbor and instructs his eldest son to return it. "Oh, gee, pa," Frank objects, "We've only started it." Unmoved, Maryville explains, "*We Quakers can read only true things*" (emphasis in original). Graham invoked this truth-dogma in her account of *Parson Weems' Fable*, asserting, "Grant and I both had good reason to be curious about myths, fables, and fairy tales, all proscribed by our Quaker upbringing."[105] In contrast to all such fiction, Maryville himself read only informative and practical materials—the local newspaper, *Wallace's Farmer*, and history books, including biographies of Abraham Lincoln and William Penn (App., 200). Weems's fable thus provided the perfect vehicle for Wood to undermine his father's values, inoculating as it does serious American history with something entirely fanciful. And Wood goes further still, perverting the fable itself, converting a celebration of filial conscience into an image of stubborn bad behavior. Inserting his own family drama into the fantastical/historical scene, he models the Washington home on his handsome house on Court Street (see Fig. 3.26), where, after laboring for four months on a preliminary drawing, he finished *Parson Weems' Fable* in six weeks, culminating in a manic twenty-two-hour campaign.[106]

Above all, the artist identifies strongly with the little miscreant in his picture (Evans observes how Wood shared Washington's initials and birth month),[107] and in so doing enjoys a last laugh on his father. Funny and fey in his light-blue tights and silver-buckled black slippers, the boy in the painting wears a mask that renders him a strange double of himself. In this uncanny figure, Wood collapses his childhood self, intimidated by a punishing father, and his triumphant adult self, successful and famous beyond anything Maryville could have expected, just as George heroically surpassed Augustine Washington, earning distinction and becoming not simply a patrician farmer-father but father of his country. Wood's unconscious aim in undertaking the subject was, I suspect, once again to defeat his father, an archaic desire revived in 1939 by the struggles with Longman at the university. Although it baffled his first biographer to report it—"people were inclined to think," Garwood wrote, "that Grant Wood had gone out of his mind"—the artist's stated intention to portray Washington *fils* as "the smuggest darn little kid you ever saw"[108] signaled a wish to emerge from his own contest with paternal authority victorious and exultant.

ALL IS THEATER

The presidential facemask that obscures one identity and reveals another is but one element in Wood's self-conscious adaptation of Weems's fable as stage drama. The stylized forms, intense raking light, histrionic pantomime, and especially the parted curtains cast the figure of Weems as master of ceremonies and the other men and woman as players. It is striking to discover how the teaching of history and inculcation of patriotism were similarly theatricalized during Wood's youth in Iowa public schools. A pamphlet issued at the turn of the century by the Iowa Department of Education exhorted the state's grade school teachers that "the anniversary of the birth of Washington [should] be set apart for special patriotic exercises."[109] Classroom exercises compiled in the pamphlet include playlets, music, and poetry recitations, for example "Little Minute Men," a "song and drill with hatchets for little boys."[110] Borrowed from a book or journal of *Primary Education*, instructions for this performance recommend "as much red, white and blue in costumes as possible. . . . Each [boy] carries a hatchet cut from stiff paste board." The prescribed lyrics follow (to be sung to the tune of the "Battle Hymn of the Republic"):

> Let us sing you once again, sir, of the days of Washington,
> Of the loyal Minute Men, sir, armed with knapsack and with gun,
> To do battle, now, as then, sir, in this Nineteen Hundred One,
> We're little Minute Men.
>
> CHORUS:
> So, we've chosen this small hatchet,
> From our ranks no foe shall snatch it,
> As a weapon none can match it—
> We're little Minute Men.
>
> Such a record it has made, sir, we are proud to lift it high,
> Of but one thing it's afraid, sir, it's afraid to tell a lie,
> So, it is the safest blade, sir, for such boys as you and I—
> We're little Minute Men.
>
> CHORUS

Directions indicate at which moments in their song the boys should "give military salute, with left hand to audience," "lift hatchet high; look up at it, smiling," "bring hatchets down," "lift and strike to left," and "march about stage." Elsewhere in the pamphlet, the frontispiece of which reproduces Leutze's *Washington Crossing the Delaware*, are colorful anecdotes about the first president, including a long metrical version of the cherry tree

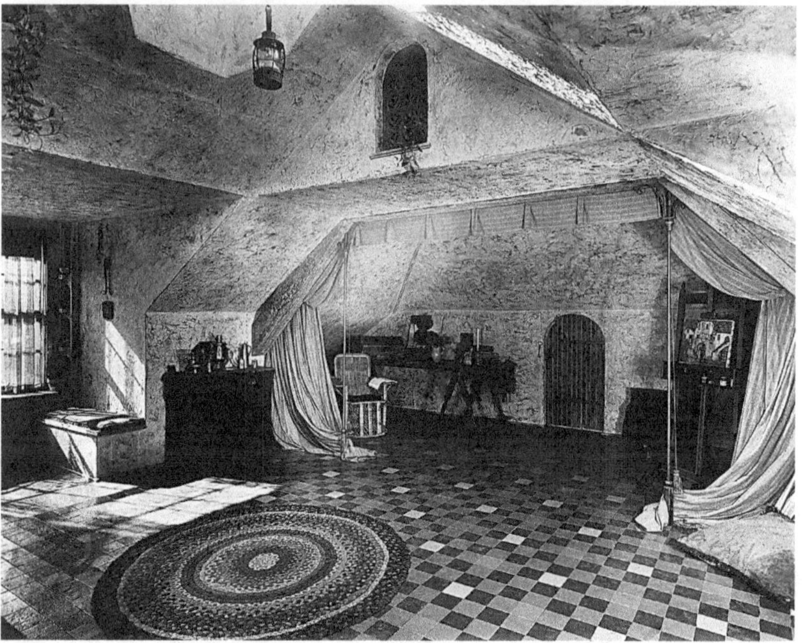

Fig. 3.29. Interior of 5 Turner Alley, Cedar Rapids, Iowa, c. 1925.

episode and a dialogue for five boys about it. All of this suggests that Wood's education on the subject of Washington may well have been infused from the very beginning with a performative flavor.

Wood himself dabbled in various aspects of drama, including playwriting, performing, and set design. His lifelong enthusiasm for theater, with its engaging scenes and the crafty machinations behind those scenes, perfectly suited his own creativity and psychology. In high school, he co-wrote the farcical *Strings* with his pal Marvin Cone, and in 1935, he co-wrote the one-act *They That Mourn* with poet Jewell Bothwell Tull (1889–1963). Both of these attempts at humor sadly fall flat, relying on embarrassing gender and racial stereotypes typical for their time. More successfully in the 1920s, Wood helped found the Cedar Rapids Community Players, whose first performance, at his suggestion, was of George Bernard Shaw's comedic *Androcles and the Lion*, with Wood as the lion. The company presented their fledgling productions in Wood's Turner Alley studio, which he equipped with a valance and curtains to create a makeshift stage (Fig. 3.29) for a crowded audience of fifty, and later they performed in the basement of the Congregational Church or in the auditorium at McKinley Junior High School.[111] Wood painted scenery for the group and, at McKinley, a stage backdrop over thirty feet long depicting a rolling Iowa landscape.

Given his conception of *Parson Weems' Fable* as a theatrical episode, the artist's selection of a colleague in the university's drama department, Professor

Vance Mulock Morton, as a model for the figure of Washington senior seems apposite; the professor's nine-year-old son, James Parks Morton, posed for the boy. Further, it makes sense that in composing his picture Wood held in visual memory the celebration of a distinctively American theatrical event—the 1932 revival of Florenz Ziegfeld's long-running 1927 musical *Show Boat* in a painting by Wood's friend and fellow Regionalist Doris Lee (1905–1983). In 1939, when *Life* magazine commissioned the image from Lee for its "Modern History" series (Fig. 3.30), the wildly popular Broadway play based on Edna Ferber's novel was about to be released for the third time as a movie. Reproducing Lee's painting in a two-page color spread on November 27 of that year, *Life* hailed *Show Boat* as a national treasure, advertising Rudyard Kipling's claim "that it was the best thing out of America since Mark Twain."[112] And *Show Boat* itself commemorates an indigenous American tradition—the floating theaters that flourished in the late nineteenth and early twentieth centuries, bringing dramatic performances to remote towns along the Mississippi, Missouri, and Ohio Rivers, just as Wood's Community Players and the Cedar Rapids Little Gallery promoted cultural opportunities for audiences in the heartland.

Lee's charming rendition of *Show Boat* depicts a dress rehearsal by a group of performers in a musical about another troupe of theatrical players. Several elements in her composition suggest that it appeared in Wood's mind's eye as he began to lay out *Parson Weems' Fable*. Unlike the Peale self-portrait, for example, the *Show Boat* painting, which shows a stage, includes red curtains on either side, and Wood strengthens his allusion to theater in *Parson Weems* by also adding a bit of drapery along the left edge. His placement of a built structure to the right of the main action, in his case

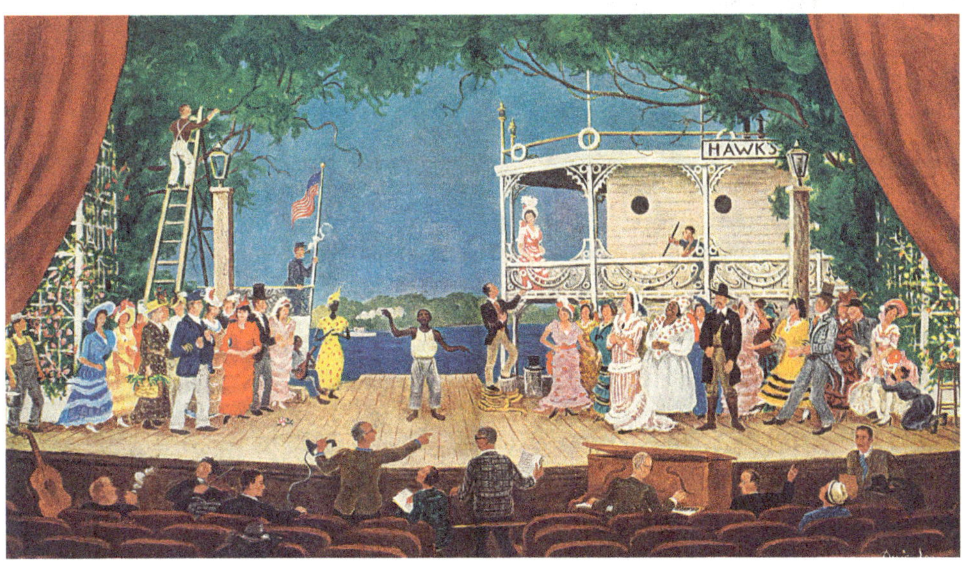

Fig. 3.30. Doris Lee, *Show Boat*, as reproduced in *Life*, November 27, 1939.

Washington's house, parallels the position in Lee's painting of Cap'n Andy Hawk's Cotton Blossom Floating Palace Theater. In both pictures, in the right background, we find a man with a ladder attending to a tree. Because Wood's preparatory drawing for *Parson Weems* was already finished and his canvas well under way when the *Life* feature appeared, he must have seen Lee's original painting, or a study or photograph of it, sometime during the first half of 1939. Lee and her husband, Arnold Blanch, visited Wood regularly in Iowa City, and traded prints with him for an impression of his 1939 lithograph *Wild Flowers* (Fig. 3.31).[113] I suspect that Lee's delightful, folkish painting *Thanksgiving*, showing busy women preparing the holiday meal, had either inspired or derived from Wood's *Dinner for Threshers* in 1934 (Figs. 3.32 and 3.33, respectively). Both images feature a rear wall parallel to the picture plane, a hanging ceiling fixture at the center, and quaint details such as the aproned women, open china storage, old-fashioned wood stove, and tawny housecat. Lee's kitchen scene caused quite a stir when it won the Logan Prize at the Art Institute of Chicago in 1935; Wood may have been aware of it when it was in progress even as he looked to Italian Renaissance paintings of the Last Supper as sanctifying prototypes for his depiction of the gathering of hungry farmhands that had so thrilled him as a little boy.[114] His and Lee's fondness for each other's art registers in interesting ways in his own work, though not as a matter of obvious influence.

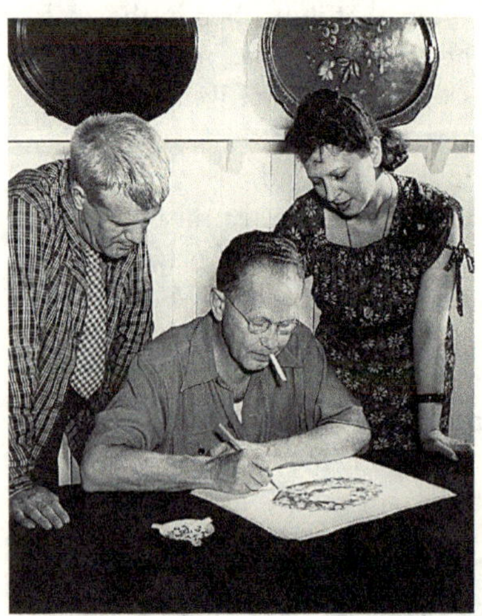

Fig. 3.31. Grant Wood signing an impression of his print *Wild Flowers* (1939) for Arnold Blanch and Doris Lee.

One feature of Lee's *Show Boat* that reinforces its resonance for *Parson Weems* is the theme of race relations; four Black figures appear among the white crowd on the *Show Boat* stage, including Joe the dock worker at the center and his wife, Queenie the cook, standing center-right, next to the sheriff. African American figures also appear in the McRae print, to be sure (see Fig. 3.28), three slaves in the background helping to locate the cherry tree episode in time and place. But Lee's image in which Blacks and whites appear together in a dramatic setting had additional, deeply personal relevance for Wood, recalling his very own first experience of theater—when his Aunt Sarah (Fig. 3.34) took the impressionable Grant and his brother Frank to the opera house in Anamosa to see another mixed-race performance, *Uncle Tom's Cabin*.[115] Like her brother Maryville, Sarah normally disapproved of theater, but, believing that this particular play was "something every Christian ought to see" (App., 248), she persuaded him to let the boys attend. As described in "Return from Bohemia," the violent melodrama has a thrilling effect on Grant, with the

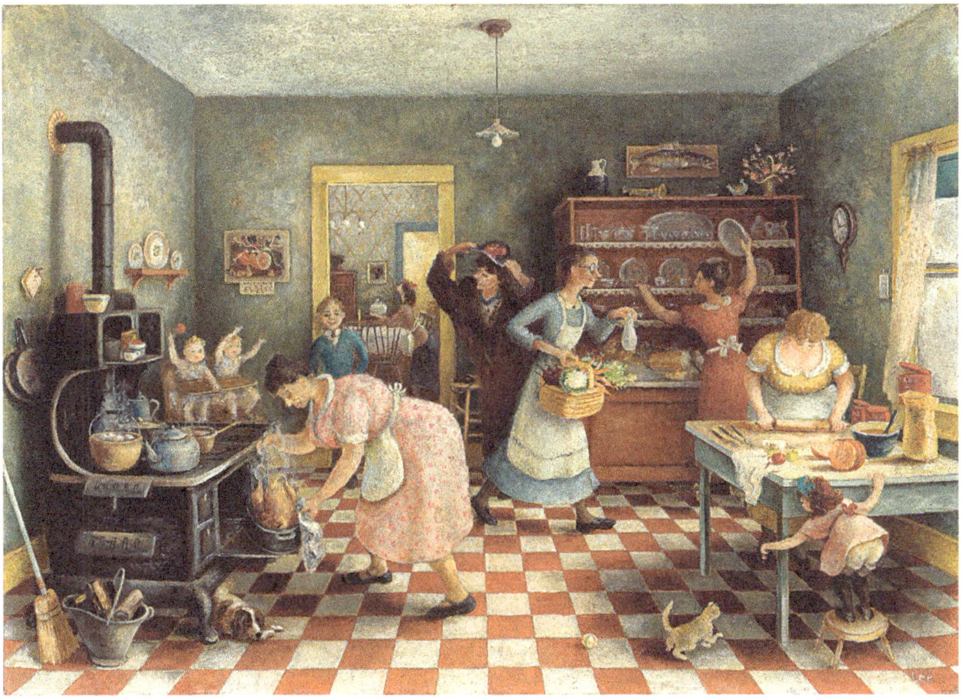

Fig. 3.32). Doris Lee, *Thanksgiving*, c. 1935.

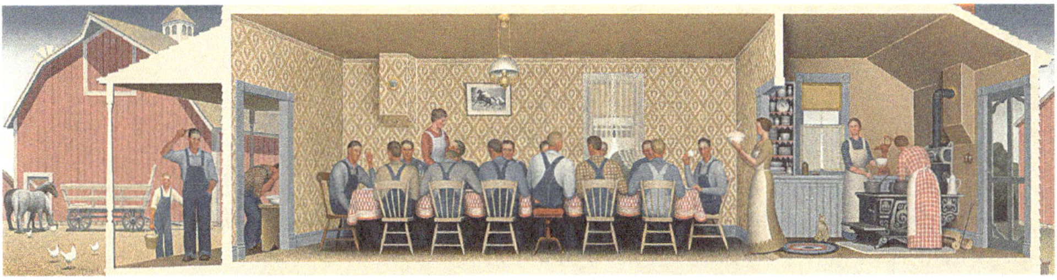

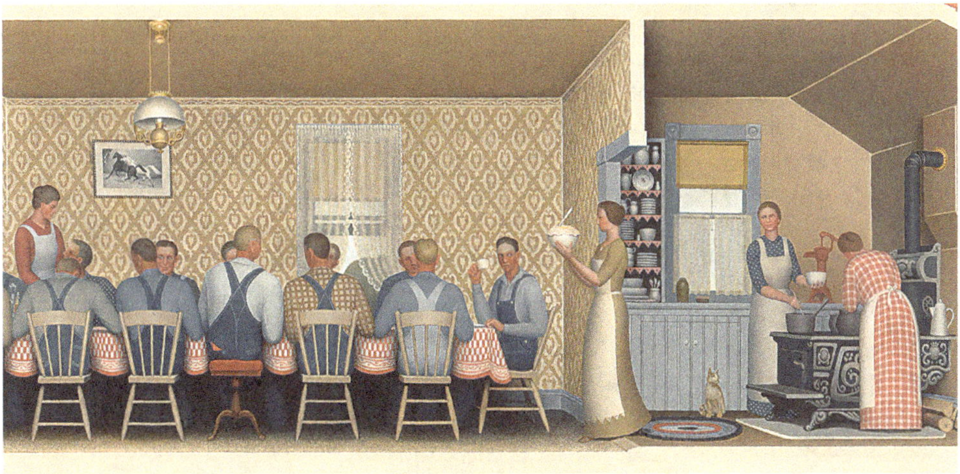

Fig. 3.33 (center) and 3.33A (detail, above). Grant Wood, *Dinner for Threshers*, 1934.

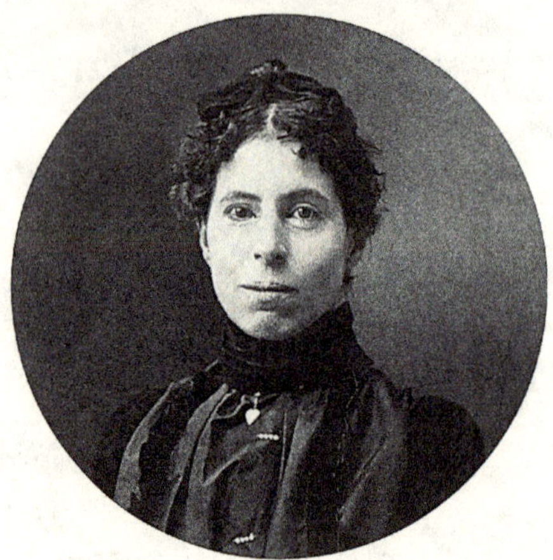

Fig. 3.34. Sarah Wood, c. 1900.

atmosphere of the opera house itself arousing in him a "strange excitement" that is altogether new. "I was fascinated by the stage," he recalled, "once I had set eyes on it, I could not look elsewhere." Velvet curtains part to reveal yet another curtain, painted with a moonlit Venetian boating scene and surrounded by advertisements. Behind this, Wood reported, "was the enchanted world of make-believe, a world I little knew, but longed for with immeasurable yearning."

FANTASY IN THE DARK

"Lights out, the play begins," and Grant enters eagerly into this alternate world. The episodes in *Uncle Tom's Cabin* that elicit passionate reactions from him are: Eliza escaping over the ice with her son in her arms (Grant whoops loudly), Simon Legree repeatedly striking Tom with his whip (Grant screams out, "You stop that!"), and Little Eva soaring to heaven (Grant's "mouth and eyes stretch wide open"). This last celestial scene, which takes place amidst "gorgeous pink clouds," promises to clarify a mystery—"I have always wondered about heaven," he avers—but is suddenly interrupted when Sarah decides it is time to go. They exit the theater with Grant in tears, wailing loudly, "I want to see heaven!" As narrated by Wood in "Return from Bohemia," the sequence is psychologically suggestive, consisting of a mother in jeopardy, a beating, and clouds framing paradise, the ultimate resolution of which he is not permitted to see. All of this takes place in the dark, peaks his curiosity, and agitates him emotionally, such that the entire reminiscence seems to me a distortion of the primal scene—that is, the memory or retrospective fantasy of parental intercourse.

This common and typically repressed childhood experience, the upsetting discovery of sexual relations between the parents, may involve an aural or visual shock, as when the infant sleeping in the parents' bedroom is awakened during their lovemaking, or when an older child interrupts them *in flagrante delicto* or witnesses the birth of a sibling or bloody signs of a miscarriage. Overhearing or seeing his parents' sexual activity, the little observer may misinterpret it as a struggle, or believe that mother or father is sick, or injured. For a child on the farm, the disturbing event may be related to strong impressions "of animals copulating, giving birth, or being castrated. Such impressions," as Greenacre explains, "become agglomerated with real or imagined experiences regarding parental behavior, and it is difficult to determine which came first."[116] Greenacre notes that early exposure to the primal scene, before the third year, produces especially powerful emotional responses in the infant and "body memories" that may later find nonverbal expression. Wood's odd habit even in adulthood of swaying back and forth, which, according to Garwood, "never left him,"[117] might have been a conversion symptom, a physical reenactment of the rhythmic movement he had sensed as an infant in the vicinity of parental coitus. He was two years old when his brother Jack was born but eight when sister Nan arrived; by that time, he had consciously to determine whence she came, with the primal scene deduced regardless of whether or not he had any firsthand knowledge of it.

Perhaps the best-known case of a disguised image of the primal scene is the anxiety dream of Freud's Wolfman, riveted by his vision of the eponymous wolves staring at him from a tree outside his window.[118] It was nighttime in his dream; the window at the foot of his bed opened of its own accord to reveal the frightening prospect, symbolic of his parents' perceived "animalistic" activity and so terrifying to him that he woke up, screaming. In other instances, among Melanie Klein's many child analysands, for example, the scene is disguised as a theatrical show or concert: ". . . in fact," Klein asserts, "any performance where there is something to be seen or heard always stands [in the child's dream or imagination] for parental coitus—listening and watching standing for observation [of sexual relations] in fact or phantasy—while the falling curtain stands for objects which hinder observation, such as bedclothes, the side of the bed, etc."[119] The motif of the *parting* curtain externalizes the sleeping child's eyes opening onto the unsettling action, and notable in all of these cases is the appearance of the dreamer him- or herself in the dream as a witness or attendee at the performance. The unacceptable sexual content of the scene is invariably obscured by the dreamwork.

What mesmerizes little Grant in *Uncle Tom's Cabin*—for he can't tear his eyes away—suggests a repressed misapprehension of the mother in danger, like Eliza being pursued by bloodhounds, and subjected to some kind of horrible fury, like Tom being beaten, in the primal scene, with the snarling Legree's "great whip," symbolizing the father's penis. The pink clouds represent the female genitals, unfathomable to the little boy for whom the very facts of life, including pregnancy and birth, seem to be at stake. A common association of sleep, death, and intrauterine existence[120] permits us to interpret Grant's intense interest in heaven, that blissful realm beyond the clouds, as a child's curiosity about the prenatal state in the womb; heaven in *Uncle Tom's Cabin* belongs to Eva, who shares a name with the primal mother. Finally, Aunt Sarah's abrupt hustling of Grant and his brother out of the theater, *in res medias*, may duplicate Grant's hasty expulsion from his parents' bedroom if indeed he had actually come upon them at an inappropriate moment. His confusion over the whole affair is blamed on Sarah, who "never explained," he lamented, "why she jerked us away from the gates of paradise." She frustrates him in the manifest content of his memory of the play, while serving the function of the superego in his need to deny and defend against the carnal knowledge presented to him in the scene that the theatrical performance came unconsciously to signify.

In describing his first visit to the opera house, Wood offered us a screen memory, seizing on the recollection of his attendance of *Uncle Tom's Cabin* and substituting it for another, repressed childhood experience. Like a dream, a screen memory is subject to all the mechanisms of the dreamwork (condensation, displacement, distortion, symbolization, secondary revision); it has "high valence for the individual," as psychoanalyst John Gedo explained, and a latent meaning with "applicability to a broad area of the child's inner life."[121] Wood's fixation on the primal scene reemerged, I think, in another screen memory detailed in "Return from Bohemia," where feelings of alienation produced by the sight or fantasy of the parents' union are strongly negated. Suffused with a sense of joy and well-being, this golden moment occurs for Grant as he watches his father in the barn, scraping a wood plane over the pine board that will be a wash bench for Hattie (App., 199). Wood's word choice is evocative—one thinks of a "pine box"—but this worked-over plank will support a tub. The board is a metonym as well as a metaphor for his mother.

Grant thinks how, unlike Frank or Dave Peters, who were competent to do other things, only Maryville could do *this* thing, this thing meant for Hattie. Wood's ascription to Maryville of an air of detachment in this passage is belied by what follows: "As he leaned over the saw-horse now," Wood continued, "sweat dripped from his face and the veins stood out in his arms. He worked hard and expertly and not without pleasure in his task." Amidst this strenuous manly effort, a glorious intrusion—Hattie appears at the door, bearing milk and cookies, with the exterior light creating "a blurred gold outline around her brown hair" (App., 200). Imagining his mother literally haloed, Wood denied his impressions of her debasement in the primal scene, of which this treasured memory is a gross distortion. "I thought she must be the most beautiful lady in all the world," he asserted, in an obvious overvaluation that may mask other, unconscious, impermissible thoughts. As Hattie and Grant observe Maryville planing the bench, the child luxuriates in their wonderful triadic togetherness (unencumbered by siblings who are nowhere in this idyllic tableau): "It was as if we three had been drawn together in that place and moment," he concluded, "to create an image that would be remembered in after time."

Importantly, this visual image takes shape in the dark: we are repeatedly referred to "the dusky corner of the barn," "the big, dark barn," "the musty half-light of the barn," "the generous twilight of the barn." Wood's recollection, moreover, possesses the vivid quality typical of screen memories and involves various senses. "I can still smell the fragrance of the pine shavings," he marveled, "hear the whistling of my father's plane, feel the presence of my mother at my side." It is an apparent wish fulfillment, the satisfaction of his desire to participate in the scene of his parents' love. The sheer happiness Wood conveyed in this passage, so distant from and so unlike the distress usually aroused by the primal scene, conforms to what psychoanalyst Bertram Lewin termed a "screen affect." Just as in the service of repression "the screen memory is a 'real' memory that conceals another real memory," Lewin stated, "the screen affect feels real, but it conceals another real feeling."[122] Both screen memory and screen affect are a kind of dissembling—in the psychic realm.

Wood's love of theater and even of art itself represents a splendid sublimation of the particular libidinous fixation encoded in his reminiscence of the golden moment in the barn. Indeed, it is as if he inscribed his very destiny as an artist within this textual reconstruction of the primal scene—namely, from the haunting vision of his parents together, "to create an image that would be remembered in after time." He did this spectacularly in *American Gothic* but in other pictures as well, including, as we shall see, the highly theatrical *Parson Weems' Fable*. In light of his fixation, we may detect an intriguing subtext in his restaging of certain components of his primal fantasy, in which he takes the place of his father—in fashioning a wooden bench (see Fig. 1.7), for example, which he tellingly crowned with a commemorative trio of heads: those of father, mother, and child. Or, assuming a place onstage as a devouring lion in the first production of his Community Players, he identified with the beastly father and also dislodged him, compulsively revisiting and revising the original drama, whose primary actors were his parents, with an audience of one. When he attempted in reality to imitate his father's role as a husband, Wood married an *actress*; her name, Sara, evoked the aunt who first exposed him to the "world of make-believe" that screened what he had imagined or observed, and then repressed.

Backstage left in *Parson Weems' Fable*, we encounter once more the return in disguised form of that which has been repressed. The man and woman picking cherries in master Washington's orchard, the only African American figures Wood ever depicted, recall Adam and Eve plucking fruit in the Lord's garden. Read with the biblical first parents in mind, the idyllic vignette becomes a scene of forbidden knowledge and culpability. Indeed, Evans has interpreted the image as "a coded scene of sexual union"; the symbolism of the woman's cherry basket and the man's ladder pointing in her direction is patent and reminds us of the appearance in dreams of steps, staircases, and ladders—all of them means of climbing or mounting—as signifiers of sexual activity.[123] In Evans's view, the fantasized union is an incestuous one between mother and son; to my mind, it involves the parents. But given the child's triangulation within the primal scene, his yearning to take the place of the father with the mother or of the mother with the father, Evans's and my respective ideas about the meaning of this vignette may be less contradictory than complementary. Perhaps the short pants worn by the ladder-man for Evans (and for James Dennis before him) cast him as a son,[124] though the figure is taller than his female companion and is just as conceivably her husband. The ambiguity is telling. And although on the surface the docile couple appears as a "model of good conduct" for Dennis,[125] more sinister possibilities may have lurked in the artist's unconscious. One wonders whether, on some level, Wood associated his black figures with literal darkness—the darkness of night—or with shadowy characters, with bodies glimpsed in the dark, models not of good conduct but of illicit behavior. Dark clouds hover menacingly above them in the painting, and we are reminded how their counterparts in Genesis were expelled from Eden by a wrathful God for violating a certain interdiction, ever after to till the hard soil in the wake of their original sin.

A scandalous secret in *Show Boat* leads to a similar expulsion: Julie Laverne and Steve Baker are ejected from the *Cotton Blossom* when it is discovered that their marriage is interracial, and therefore illegal, for Julie is a mulatto passing for white. In Lee's painting (see Fig. 3.30), the couple appears stage left, Julie in a red dress and Steve the top-hatted man at her side, across from the sheriff who comes to arrest them. Did Wood perhaps see the play on one of his many trips to New York? Or catch one of its movie versions in the Midwest, or read Ferber's novel,[126] or talk with Lee about her research for the *Life* commission? Had he any of these opportunities, he might have found *Show Boat* to be, like his memory of the performance of *Uncle Tom's Cabin* that hypnotized him as a child, "racy" in a double sense. Ultimately in *Show Boat*, Julie is tragically abandoned by Steve, as Hattie was by Maryville, whose angry ghost comes back to confront his guilty son (passing, like Julie, though with a different kind of secret) in the middleground of *Parson Weems' Fable*. Here, the anxiety aroused by the primal scene inflects an endless intergenerational struggle: boy George holds onto his misused ax while Augustine remains a menace, gripping the wounded sapling with what looks like a blood-soaked right hand, his phallic aggression vividly expressed in the bladelike points of his stiff red coattail and projecting tricorn hat.

CAMPING IT UP

The reiteration of red cherries harvested in the orchard, dangling from Augustine's prized tree, and reappearing as ball fringe on Weems's curtain is a brilliant conceit, helping both to unify the composition and to ironize the scene. Doubled and decorative, the cherry motif is more than droll; it calls attention to the overall artifice of *Parson Weems' Fable*, with its carefully rendered details (down to individual blades of regimented grass) and specially crafted, star-studded wooden frame (see Fig. 3.25). With a title-bearing pseudo-plaque built right into that frame, the artwork winkingly anticipates its own future as a museum masterpiece, while the ornamental stars around its periphery mimic both the virtual one on Washington's house and the real cast-iron medallions on the facade of Wood's Iowa City home (see Fig. 3.26)—where he painted *Parson Weems* in his second-floor bedroom studio.[127] His artistic vision was all-encompassing and his materials—not just paint, or charcoal, graphite, and chalk, but also stained glass, wrought iron, wood, stucco, copper, brass—were many. As a decorator, he transformed numerous Iowa interiors beginning in the 1920s. Jane Milosch's research traces his many commissions, both the famous and the forgotten: the Submarine Sweet Shop in Waterloo; Eppley Hotels in Cedar Rapids, Council Bluffs, and Sioux City; the Turner Mortuary; and private residences belonging to the Armstrong, Douglas, Hamilton, and Van Vechten-Shaffer families in Cedar Rapids.[128] Wood lavished similar beautifying care on his own domestic environments, always oriented to past styles and resisting the modern.

On one occasion, in 1935, he treated his decorating scheme ironically in an over-the-top Victorian revival style for the headquarters of the Society for the Prevention of Cruelty to Speakers (SPCS) in Iowa City. Wood founded the society with Frank Luther Mott (1886–1964), a professor of English and journalism at the University of Iowa and, as editor of *The Midland* magazine, a promoter of Midwestern culture. Through his Times Club, Mott brought noted writers and musicians to lecture at the university, such as Sherwood Anderson, as mentioned above, as well as critic Gilbert Seldes, composer W. C. Handy, poets Stephen Vincent Benét and Langston Hughes, and others. The auxiliary SPCS responded to a felt need to host these guests, unforgettably, "in a typical Iowa setting."[129] Together, Wood and Mott had cast about for an appropriate space. They considered remodeling a disused country schoolhouse near town, a barn, and an old flour mill, but settled on rooms offered to them by Roland Smith, owner of Smitty's Cafe, where the two friends lunched every Tuesday. Flush from investments in Texas oil wells, Smith gave over to the club the entire floor above his restaurant and paid the utilities. As a lark, Wood created an old-fashioned dining room and parlor with patterned carpet and flowered wallpaper, hung with pictures and needlework one imagines might have been dear to his mother or his aunts.

We decorated with Currier and Ives prints [Mott recalled]; a fine chromo of that old favorite, "Rock of Ages," in which a lady clings to the foot of a cross on a great rock lashed by foam-tipped waves from the sea; embroidered mottoes, "God Bless Our Home," "Peace Be With You," and so on; and certain designs under glass formed from the hair of some dear departed. In the dining-room section a big table was covered with a red-and-white checkered cloth, and a bulging sideboard stood in one corner. In the parlor was much red plush and walnut furniture—Boston rockers, and love seats on either side of the marble fireplace. One big chair was made of steers' horns, with seat, back, and tassels of green plush. A cottage organ, with elaborately carved walnut case and music rack, proved highly useful at our parties.[130]

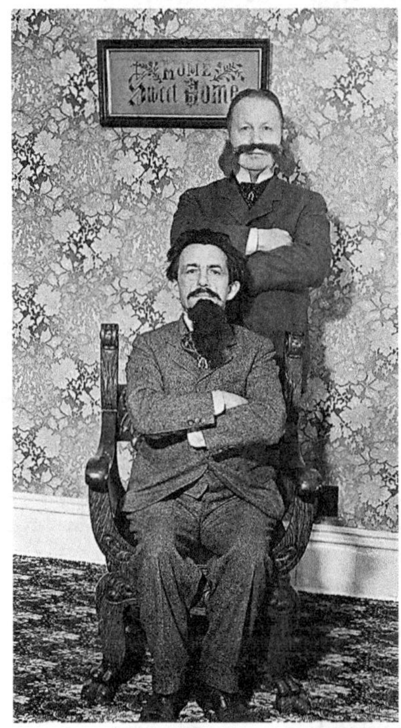

Fig. 3.35. Grant Wood and Thomas Hart Benton at the Society for the Prevention of Cruelty to Speakers, Iowa City, 1935.

Wood's mocking celebration of the sentimental and the outmoded in this project achieved the desired effect. "Almost always," Mott reported, "conversation began with our guests' exclamations about the furnishings of our rooms. 'Oh my aunt had a decoration piece of peacock feathers just like that in her front parlor! And it was set on just such a marble-topped stand!'"[131] In these period rooms, SPCS members and guests donned period accessories to pose for photographs for the society's red plush commemorative album, choosing from the assortment of fake mustaches and beards provided, as well as from vintage coats, hats, ties, and detachable collars (Fig. 3.35). Lovingly attending to every detail of his make-believe setting, Wood claimed to have emulated "the worst style of the late Victorian period,"[132] thoroughly enjoying himself yet maintaining an ironic distance. Just so, he praised and pilloried Aunt Sarah in "Return from Bohemia," adoring the skill with which she transformed the front yard with Japanese lanterns strung up in the pines or pruned an arbor vitae to resemble a giant rooster, while he also characterized her as a pretentious old bore (App., 247). Wood was accustomed to speaking this way, out of both sides of his mouth. For him, the SPCS could be a funhouse of too-muchness and bad taste, a stage set for camping it up with his fellows and, privately, a venerable shrine to decorous old mothers and maiden aunts.

The irony informing his spirited shenanigans at the SPCS and pervading *Parson Weems' Fable* and other pictures seems to be the overall defining characteristic of much of his art—along with theatricality, artifice, and humor, all qualities associated with camp.[133] When Henry Adams first recognized Wood's campiness as such, he pointed to the relevance of Susan Sontag's "Notes on Camp" for a more complete grasp of the artist's expression and taste: "To perceive Camp in objects and persons," Sontag had suggested, "is to understand Being-as-Playing-a-Role. It is the farthest extension, in sensibility, of the metaphor of life as theater."[134] On the psychic level, Wood's dedication to theater related to the primal scene, his imposture to a durable and prominent family romance. In the social realm, he was primed for theater and a campy perspective by the necessity of accommodating through pretense and charade to a hostile homophobic environment. Camp is of course associated with a homosexual subculture, that of an oppressed minority resorting creatively to mimicry and humor, often devastatingly defiant. Moreover, "the art of passing," as queer theorist Jack Babuscio observes, "is an acting art: to pass is to be 'on stage,' to impersonate heterosexual citizenry."[135] One hopes that it may be a dying art, but in Wood's time and place it was a rigorous requirement for men like him.

His favorite play, according to Garwood, was *Androcles and the Lion*, and he read and reread George Bernard Shaw's lengthy preface to the drama,[136] a critical discussion of Jesus, the confusing accounts of him in the Gospels, and the principles and "prospects" of Christianity. *Androcles* addresses the Roman persecution of early Christians and by extension the persecution of all dissenting minorities—"My martyrs," Shaw declared, "are the martyrs of all time, and my persecutors the persecutors of all time."[137] Wood surely could not have overlooked the rousing appendix to what the playwright subtitled his "Fable Play." In that coda, Shaw characterized defenders of established law and order as "pure opportunity Have-and-Holders" and placed them in opposition to eccentrics of all kinds. "People who are shewn by their inner light," he argued, "the possibility of a better world based on the demand of the spirit for a nobler and more abundant life, not for themselves at the expense of others, but for everybody, are naturally dreaded and therefore hated by the Have-and-Holders." Wood had a champion and kindred soul *avant la lettre* in Shaw, who deplored in this inspired tract the manipulation by Have-and-Holders of "that herd instinct which makes men abhor all departures from custom, and, by the most cruel punishments and the wildest calumnies, force[s] eccentric people to behave and profess exactly as other people do."[138] To his own credit, Wood managed to preserve his eccentricity and even to thrive for a brief historical moment against considerable odds. Against those dangerous forces that threatened him—from within and without—he waged, by dissembling, a valiant defense.

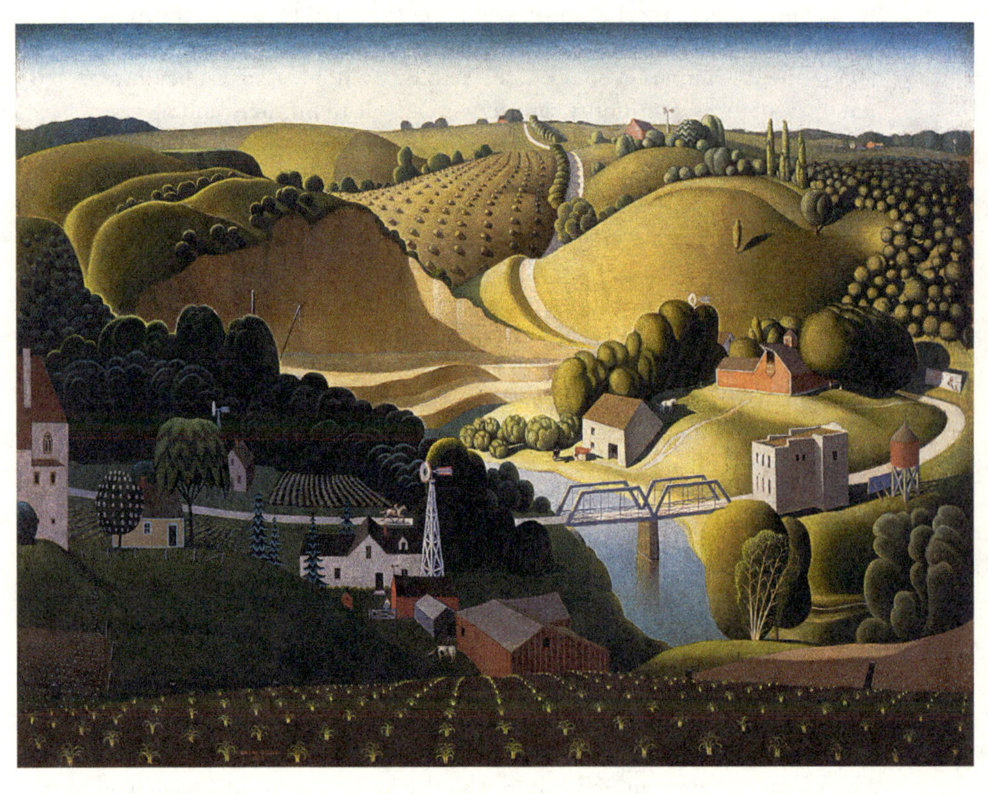

Fig. 4.1. Grant Wood, *Stone City, Iowa*, 1930.

❖ CHAPTER 4 ❖

The Ground Itself

Before he achieved renown as a booster/satirist of Midwestern types, Grant Wood was, as he would always remain, a landscape painter. His early pictures show him searching for ways to transmute sensuous impressions of his rural environment into pleasingly picturesque scenes. Characteristic of these *plein-air* exercises are rustling foliage, dappled sunlight, streams or footpaths, and weathered sheds and barns. It is Iowa that Wood painted, but only incidentally; there is little difference between the tree-flanked meandering stream he captured in *Indian Creek, Midsummer* (1928) in Cedar Rapids and one he depicted in Corot's hometown, *Ville d'Avray* (c. 1924), on a French trip a few years prior. But in the late 1920s, a new vision of landscape began to emerge in his painting. While executing a mural commission for the Pioneer Room at the Hotel Chieftain in Council Bluffs, Iowa (1927), he turned to nineteenth-century vernacular sources to compose images of a frontier settlement spread out on the plains.[1] In one of his cartographic views of Kanesville (as Council Bluffs was first known), Wood showed toy-like log cabins and frame houses, covered wagons, tents, and tipis nestled among softly rolling hills. Within a cartouche identifying town landmarks such as the sawmill and saloon, he acknowledged deriving this composition "From an old Painting dated 1849." He had also consulted engravings in an 1855 travel book and became fascinated with historical maps of his region.[2] Though not well known today, the Hotel Chieftain project represents an important moment in Wood's oeuvre, a move away from the direct observation of nature to an imagined historical past mediated by other works of art and material culture. Wanda Corn has pinpointed this transition in her discussion of the murals: "In taking a theme from local history, borrowing heavily from American artifacts, and, in the townscape, using a bird's-eye view of a panoramic landscape done in a self-consciously primitive style, Wood had invented all the ingredients for a major work like *Stone City, Iowa* (1930, Fig. 4.1) painted three years later."[3]

Stone City is an early example of Wood's mature landscapes, characterized by an acute clarity, with crisp contours and strong cast shadows, and stylized forms. Notable, too, are a lofty point of view and high horizon line. All of Wood's landscapes of the 1930s celebrate the Iowa of yesteryear as a pastoral wonderland. They are anachronistic and, despite their many contributing influences, highly original. Informing their development was Wood's embrace of blue-and-white china as a wellspring of decorative patterns and motifs, where one finds the alien trees with cotton ball, feathery, or flame-like foliage that Wood first adopted in his overdetermined, over-the-top *Overmantel Decoration* (1930, Fig. 4.2), conceived for an interior he designed for clients in Cedar Rapids. In this painting for the Herbert Stamats family's newly built neo-colonial house, the artist again referenced antique engravings that, like those bordering the 1869 Linn County map in the background of Wood's *Portrait of John B. Turner, Pioneer* (1928/30, Cedar Rapids Museum of Art), featured local properties typical of the area surveyed. Other important sources included Currier and Ives prints and, in particular, a Blue Staffordshire platter Wood admired in the Stamats household, probably from the "Beauties of America" series (c. 1817–30) depicting stately mansions or public buildings on neatly manicured grounds.[4]

Imagining his clients as prosperous landowning gentry, Wood showed the family itself at the left of his *Overmantel Decoration*: mother, toddler, and baby in pram, with the father on horseback hailing the group, all curiously decked out in nineteenth-century costumes. Propelling the family back in

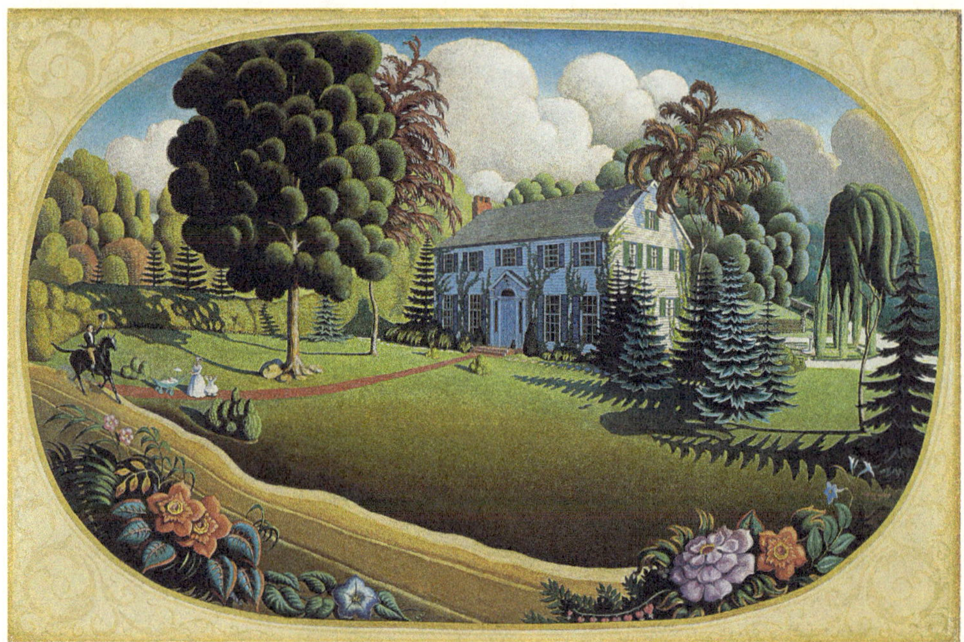

Fig. 4.2. Grant Wood, *Overmantel Decoration*, 1930.

time, Wood fashioned a vision of their home for their home inspired by an object found in their home. For all this hominess, the painting is strange, with ivy tentacles creeping over the house and mutant vegetation surrounding it, eerie shadows impinging on the lawn, and hothouse flowers clustered in the foreground. Behind the house, a tiny sundial encircled by funerary cypresses serves as a memento mori in this peaceful park-like setting, while a black cat contemplates an unsuspecting robin on the grass from the front stoop, biding its time. Tension arises between the manifest charm of the image, with its lovely ornamental mat, and the hallucinatory Magic Realist quality of something apprehended through an aperture of an uneasy dream.

IOWA MEMLING

When Wood applied his new landscape approach to a public work with *Stone City*, he opted for a panoramic vista, highlighting the variety of rich artistic possibilities in the Iowa countryside. Choosing the viewpoint from a hill above the Wapsipinicon River where it meanders through the tiny village, he could include elements he would enumerate in the 1932 prospectus for his Stone City Summer Art Colony: "Within the radius of a few miles," he wrote of the colony's ideal location, "lies the most characteristic and paintable mid-Western landscape, prairie, high bluffs, winding streams, woods, plains, farms and country towns."[5] The shorn hillside in Wood's picture and a bit of abandoned rigging behind the treetops in the left middleground are the only traces of the industrial, limestone-quarrying center that Stone City had once been. Instead, Wood creates a rural idyll, nature transformed by fancy into a tufted "Land of Counterpane" glowing with radiant warm light.[6] Assimilated here are not only nineteenth-century illustrated regional maps but also the beautiful fifteenth-century altarpiece that charmed Wood in 1928: a storiated landscape by Hans Memling, *The Seven Joys of the Virgin* (c. 1480, Fig. 4.3), in the Alte Pinakothek in Munich. The impact on Wood's art of his last European trip is well known; his encounters during his German sojourn with both Northern Renaissance and contemporary New Objectivity painting reportedly led him to his mature hard-edged style. Interviewed in 1932 about his rise to fame after *American Gothic*, the artist explained this epiphany and its deliberately reasoned repercussions:

> Several years ago I went to Munich to have a stained glass window completed. While I was there the annual exhibition at the Glass Palace was in progress. There I found myself experiencing a reaction against so-called Modernism and felt myself strongly drawn toward rationalism. It appeared that the Modernists went to the Primitives for inspiration. I wondered if I could anticipate what was to follow. It seemed to me that the Gothic painters were the next step. I had always admired them, especially Memling, whom I had studied assiduously. . . . So I retained what

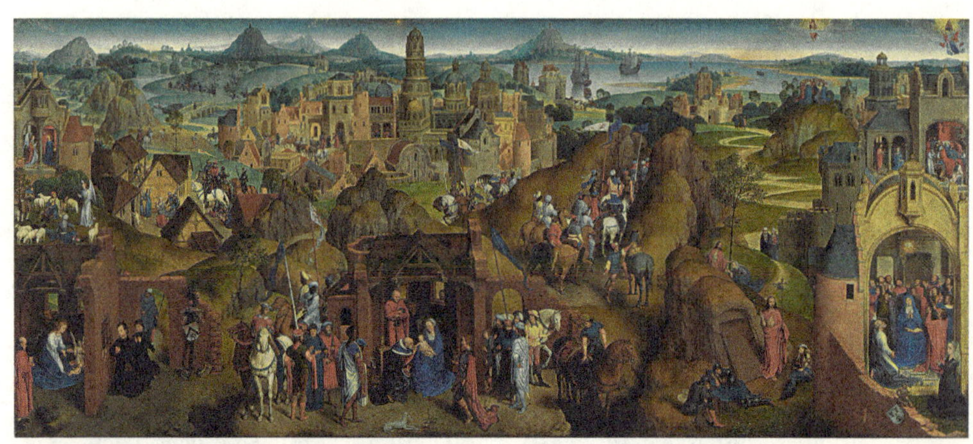

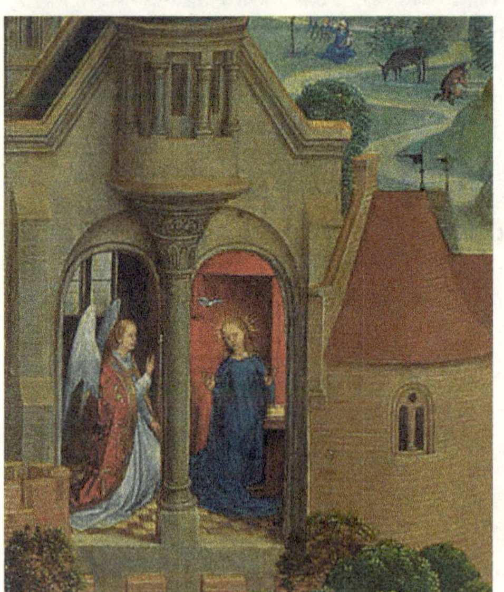

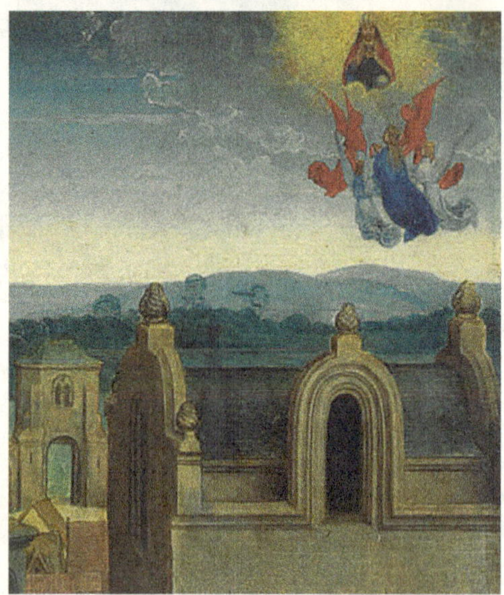

Figs. 4.3 (top) and 4.3A–B (details, above).
Hans Memling, *The Seven Joys of the Virgin*, c. 1480.

I thought was lasting in the Modernistic movement and to it added a story-telling quality as a logical opposition to abstraction. . . .

Here I was on dangerous ground, because story-telling pictures can so easily become illustrative and depend on their titles. For this reason I leaned strongly to the decorative and also, I endeavored to paint types, not individuals. The lovely apparel and accessories of the Gothic period appealed to me so vitally that I longed to see decorative possibilities in our contemporary clothes and articles.[7]

One first notices the implications of all this in the generically titled *Woman with Plants* (1929, Fig. 1.4), which Wood undertook after his return from Germany. The Iowa landscape in the background of the portrait, with its soft hills, clustered trees, corn shocks, windmill, and barn, predicts a number of features soon to be confidently celebrated in *Stone City*. Comparisons are often made, moreover, between *Woman with Plants* and half-length portraits by Memling.[8] In both cases, the compositions consist of a sitter holding a symbolic attribute and occupying a large amount of pictorial space in the immediate foreground, a distant landscape background, and no middleground. But Wood had already studied Memling "assiduously," as he himself acknowledged, before his 1928 epiphany, likely in books and in other European museums. What was it about the Munich trip that suddenly made the long-admired Flemish master available as a practical model for storytelling, landscape, and portraiture in Wood's own painting? One scenario includes the combined impact and interrelationship, in terms of learning as well as feeling, of Wood's visits to the Alte Pinakothek and to the Glaspalast.

What he saw at the "Münchener Kunstausstellung 1928 im Glaspalast" was certainly not Modernism.[9] Nor was it New Objectivity as it was practiced in Berlin, Dresden, or Frankfurt, but rather a very conservative, often religious, sentimental, even reactionary kind of art particular to Southern Germany. Much of the art on view was not even contemporary. A special section of the exhibition devoted to Swiss art included a bacchante by the Symbolist Arnold Böcklin (1827–1901), and among the Germans were nineteenth-century Romantic or Realist artists Wilhelm Leibl, Franz von Lenbach, Carl Spitzweg, and Hans Thoma. Also represented was the Austrian academic painter Hans Makart (1840–1884). Thus, when Wood says he found himself reacting against the Modernists, it was likely Picasso and Matisse he had in mind, artists who had in fact gone to "the Primitives" and whom he associated with abstraction, rather than the examples he had before him in Munich. In those examples, he saw a universal embrace of classical traditions, which he translated as rationalism.

Of the then still-living artists exhibited in the Glaspalast, some had adopted the sharp visual focus (though not the socially critical content) of their better-known peers among the New Objectivity painters who had also, recoiling from Expressionism, turned to old-master techniques. Munich Secessionist Carl Schwalbach (1885–1983), for instance, provided a reminiscence of the veristic

Northern Renaissance or "Gothic" style, as Wood would have had it, and an update of the Memling portrait formula in the image of a modern woman, complete with the requisite symbolic attribute. The clear glass vase at the lower left of Schwalbach's *Bildnis* (Portrait, n.d., Fig. 4.4), which predicts the flowerpot in *Woman with Plants*, may stand for the sitter's purity at the same time that it allows the painter to show off his skill in depicting a transparent object. Amid the many derivative biblical scenes in the Glaspalast—Crucifixions, lugubrious Depositions and Entombments—Schwalbach's image was at least temporally credible in 1928. In it, Wood saw how his love for a fifteenth-century artist might legitimately be put to work for contemporary purposes. He was already applying a detailed realism to the figure in his 1928 *Portrait of John B. Turner*; here was an affirmation of his intuition for portraiture as well as a broad landscape that Wood would associate, overtly in *Woman with Plants* and at least subliminally in all his works, with his mother. Indeed, one reason the Memling in the Alte Pinakothek made such an impression on the artist surely had to do with its Marian subject matter: throughout the rolling topography of *The Seven Joys of the Virgin* are episodes from the life of the quintessential long-suffering Mother, whose very existence was defined in relationship to her adored, one and only Son. From left to right in Memling's picture, we see unfolding simultaneously within a unified landscape scenes from disparate moments in Mary's motherhood, from the angelic Annunciation of her pregnancy to her final Assumption into heaven to join her Son forever after.

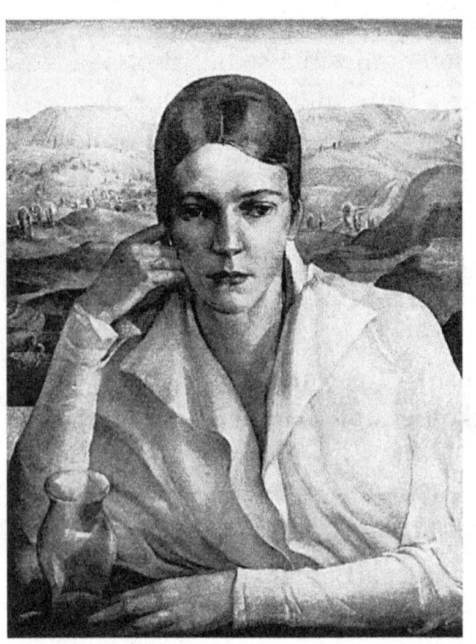

Fig. 4.4. Carl Schwalbach, *Bildnis* (Portrait), n.d.

Wood was not a religious man, certainly not Catholic, yet he was deeply moved by the image of the Madonna, whose name his father bore. In Europe in 1923–24, the artist had acquired a ceramic figurine of the Virgin and Child, which he enshrined like a house goddess in its own niche above the fireplace in his Turner Alley studio in Cedar Rapids (see Fig. 1.9) and depicted in a painting with giant outsize flowers, *Cocks-Combs* (c. 1925–29, Fig. 4.5). In this still life, the artist miniaturized his Madonna relative to the huge cockscombs. The picture becomes an allegory of creativity, where the talismanic presence of mother love assures great and powerful growth. Wood treasured his souvenir statuette always; it passed to his sister when he died.[10] Understandably during his travels, missing his mother, he was attracted to images that reminded him of her. In Munich, while he marveled as an artist at the carefully rendered anecdotal details and panoramic landscape in *The Seven Joys of the Virgin*, I think he also responded as a son to the maternal devotion that marks the painting's theme. In this way, Munich catalyzed the transformation of the subject matter, as well as the style, of his work and was crucial to his sudden success in 1930.

He became a Regionalist, lamenting the years he had spent searching for motifs that looked, in his words, "Europy," and embracing his own "natural tendencies" toward meticulous rendering.[11] After this, no further travel abroad would be necessary. His final return to Iowa had such psychological valence that he would render it legendary. He explained early on to his young friends Arnold Pyle and Park Rinard how familiar everything had appeared to him then, and yet different, and they relayed his impressions in an essay about his work in 1935: "Here [back in Iowa] were the same broad meadows and the same evenly-spaced cornfields. It was a reality he had seen before. But now it had taken on meaning."[12] This strong, self-conscious sense of wondrous recognition seems analogous to the feeling Freud described in certain dreams of landscapes—of having been there before. The analyst interpreted such dreamy localities as symbols of the mother's body: "There is indeed," he observed, "no other place about which one can assert with such conviction that one has been there once before."[13] Arriving at an entirely new

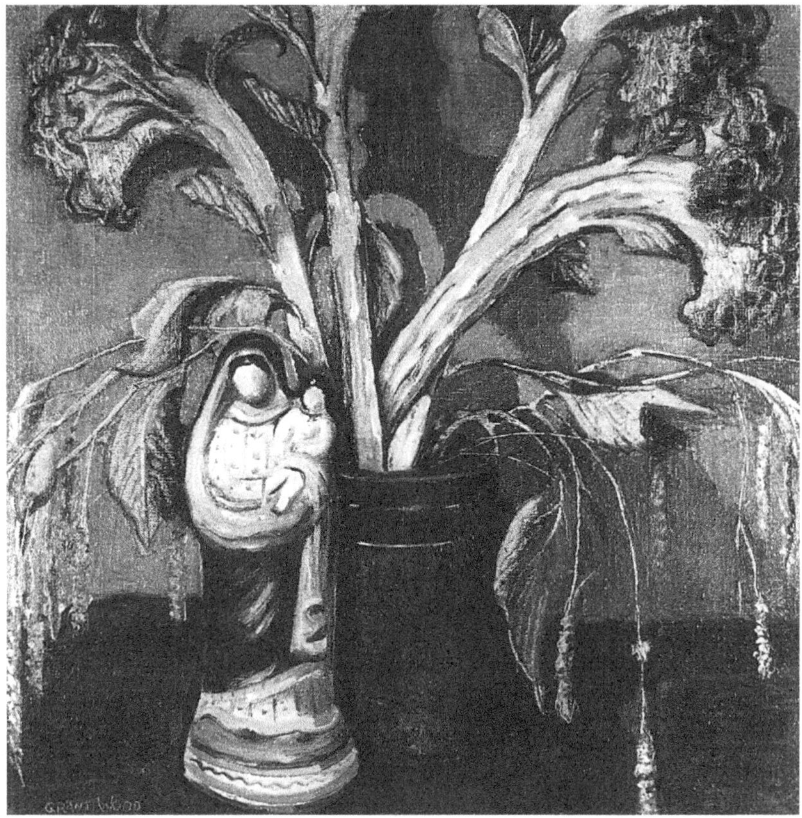

Fig. 4.5. Grant Wood, *Cocks-Combs*, c. 1925–29.

place in his painting, Wood experienced his artistic self-discovery and maturation as a homecoming, and his mother was its emotional guiding spirit.

It would be fascinating to see how he handled the apotheosis of Mother Mary in *The Assumption*, a now lost drawing included in his 1935 retrospective along with *Woman with Plants* and forty other works at the Ferargil Galleries in New York.[14] Reviewing that exhibition and thoroughly grasping the how if not the why of Wood's stylistic development, Lincoln Kirstein dubbed the artist an Iowan Memling. Kirstein did not mean this as a compliment. Asserting that each age must have its own vision and its own technique, he thought contemporary artists should look not to art of the past but to photography and film for qualities of light and perspective unique to modern ways of seeing. Critical of Wood, he nonetheless regarded him with a respectful curiosity, declaring his future production worth watching and cautioning him that to be truly successful, he would "have to deny that very sweetness upon which his prestige is largely based."[15] Kirstein concluded with a reminder to Wood of the harsh realities then afflicting the American landscape, and issued a challenge that the artist could only ignore: "He will have to gain some trace of insight," Kirstein urged, "into the real weather of his Middle West—dust storms and drought, slaughtered pigs, unsown crops, or crops ploughed under. An element of tragedy would make his cleanly farmers less quaint, but closer to the spirit of the Gothic, which is no less beautiful because it is so grim."

AN EDENIC UNREALITY

The fair-weather fairytale that was *Stone City* likely annoyed Kirstein; it was shown in the Ferargil exhibition, as were two landscapes from 1931, *Young Corn* and *Fall Plowing* (Figs. 4.6 and 4.7, respectively). These rhapsodic works predated the severest conditions Kirstein described, but it hardly mattered to his argument: unfazed by critical animadversions, Wood continued to imagine an Edenic Iowa in paintings such as *Spring Turning* (1936, Fig. 4.8), even in the depths of the Depression. He was hardly unaware of the awful realities. The idyllic farm world he limned in his pictures, where nature is invariably benign and technology is limited to the windmill and the walking plow, had in fact always been menaced by natural disasters such as fire and cholera, as Wood himself remembered in "Return from Bohemia." In 1935, he signed Frank Luther Mott's ghostwritten manifesto, *Revolt against the City*, invoking "the drouth of last Summer," including persistent one-hundred-degree temperatures that destroyed half of Iowa's corn crop, and "the great dust storms, the floods following drouth, the milk strikes, the violent protests against foreclosures, the struggles against dry-year pests,"[16] yet he shut his eyes to all such woes in his fantasy landscapes. This distinguished him from his many contemporaries who documented the real plight of American farmers in the thirties: the great photographers, of course, of the Farm

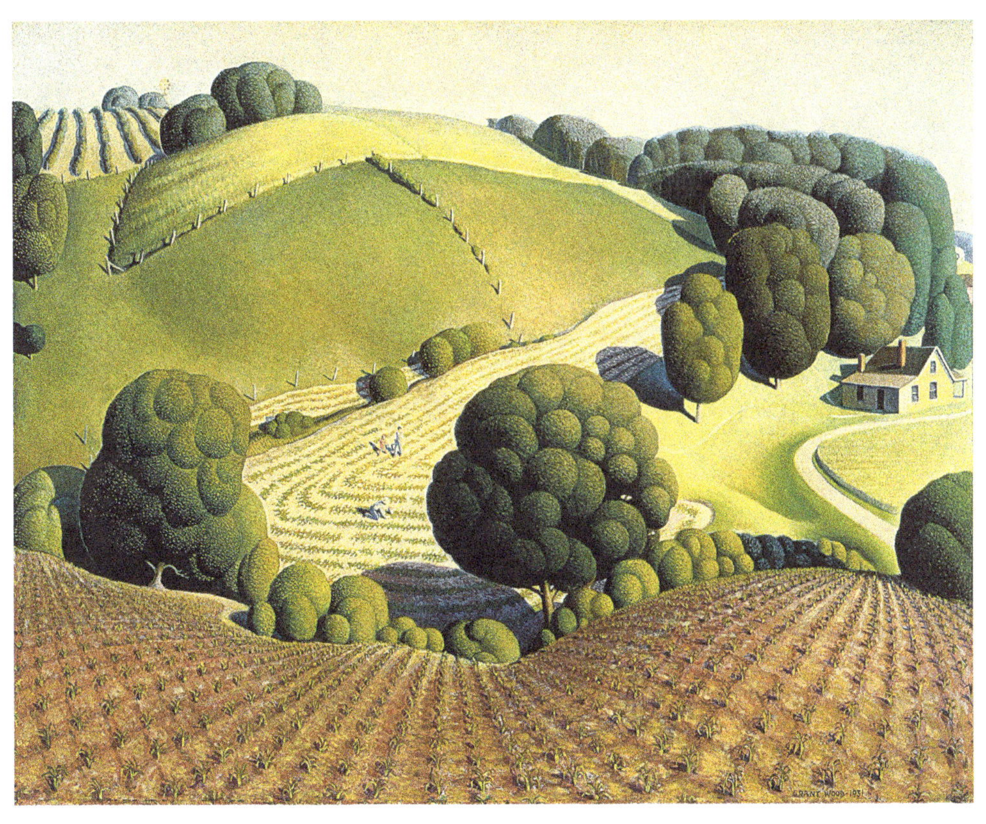

Fig. 4.6. Grant Wood, *Young Corn*, 1931.

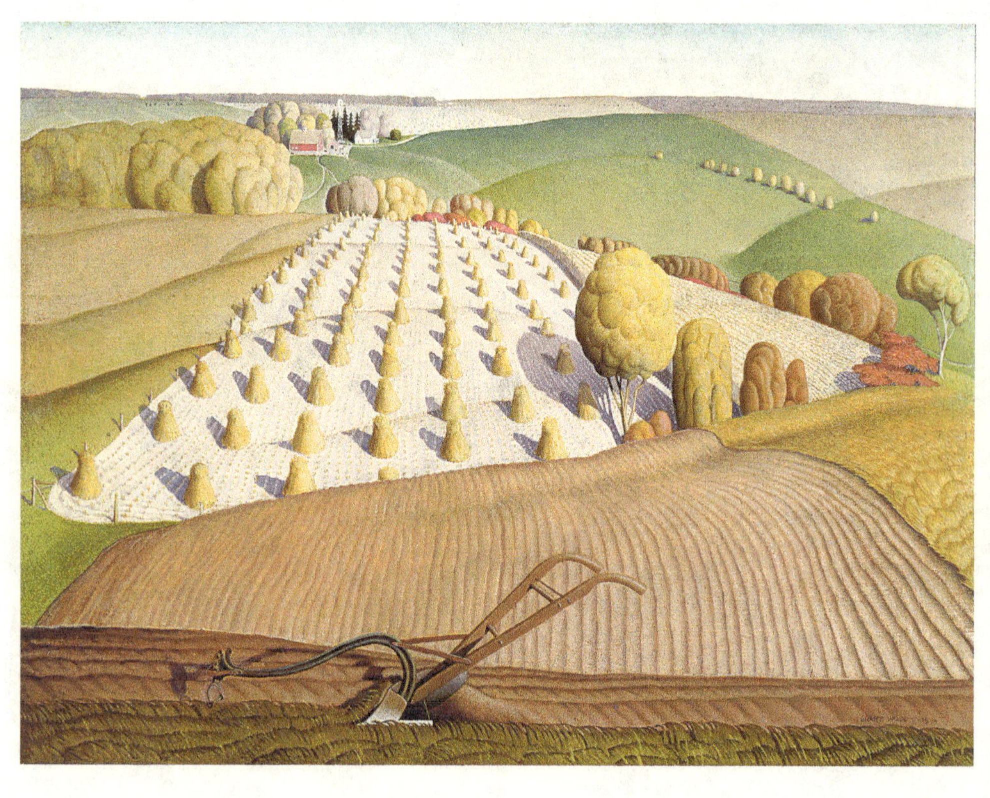

Fig. 4.7. Grant Wood, *Fall Plowing*, 1931.

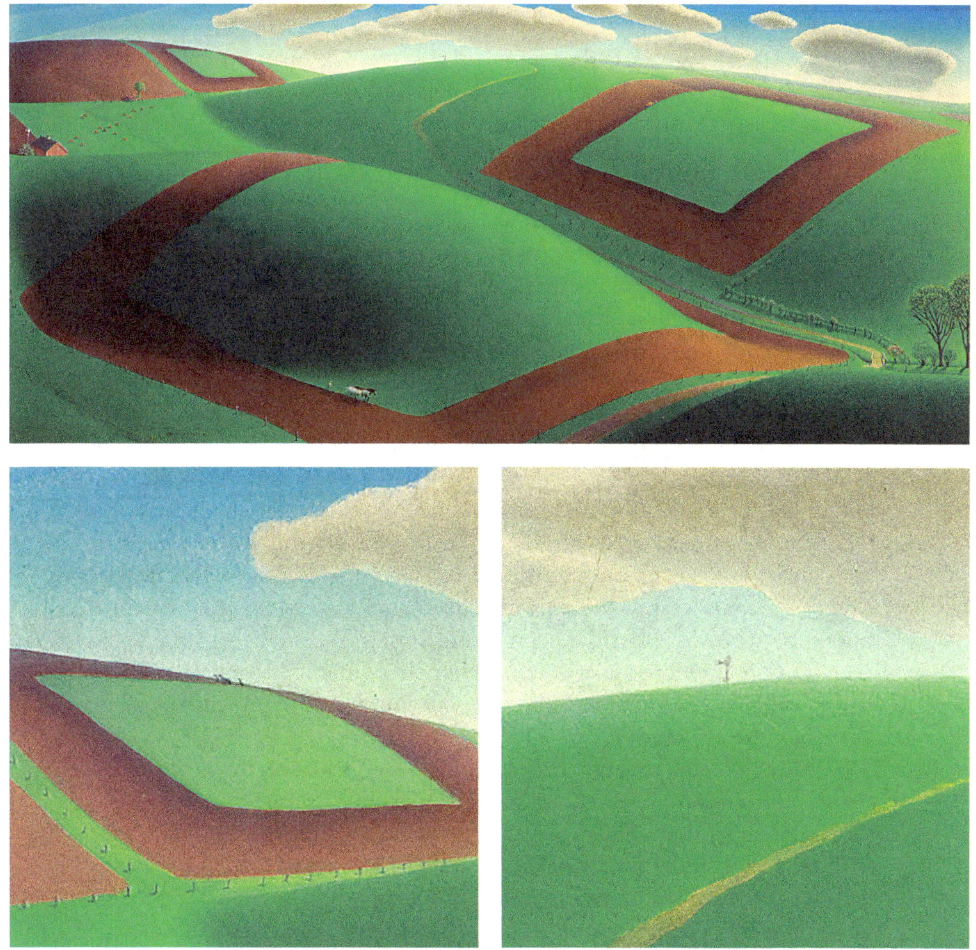

Figs. 4.8 (top) and 4.8A–B (details, above). Grant Wood, *Spring Turning*, 1936.

Security Administration—Walker Evans, Dorothea Lange, Arthur Rothstein—as well as Margaret Bourke-White, but also painters such as Wood's fellow Regionalist John Steuart Curry in his images of floods and tornadoes, or Helen Johnson Hinrichsen of Davenport who memorialized the bloody outcome of a strike by the Iowa Farmers Union in 1932.

Hinrichsen (1896–1988) had trained at the School of the Art Institute of Chicago and at the Art Students League in New York, and was at the Stone City Art Colony with Wood in the summers of 1932 and 1933. In *Farm Holiday* (1932, Fig. 4.9), she depicted a roadblock on a highway to the market in Sioux City, where, withholding milk and produce in the hopes of gaining at least subsistence prices, desperate farmers "smashed windows and headlights, . . . punctured tires with their pitchforks," and ultimately killed a truck driver to prevent him from thwarting their action.[17] The Farm Holiday movement continued at a fever pitch in April of 1933, when 250 farmers seeking a moratorium on mortgage foreclosures dragged an uncooperative judge from his courtroom; the honorable Charles C. Bradley barely escaped lynching by the mob that hauled him to a country crossroads outside the town of LeMars, Iowa.[18]

In her painting, Hinrichsen addressed the social turmoil that resulted from the economic crash of 1929. The ruination of the land itself by mechanized farming techniques and dry windy weather became the subject of Joe Jones's devastating *American Farm* (Fig. 4.10), created in 1936, the year before he departed his native Missouri for New York. Jones envisioned a forlorn house, shed, and windmill perched on an outcrop of denuded land, with no sign of vegetation for miles. The barren vista must be the bleakest Midwestern landscape ever painted and dramatizes by contrast the sheer unreality of Wood's farmland pictures. *Spring Turning*, for instance, is exactly contemporaneous with Jones's hopeless lament, its verdant promise of cyclical beginnings denying the day of deadly reckoning that in *American Farm* has already arrived.

Not that Wood's art should (or could) have been otherwise, *pace* Kirstein's admonitions. Defending Wood's offer of escapist reassurance to a beleaguered population, Corn later aligned his landscapes with those other cultural forms—film, literature, mural painting—that had defied fear during the 1930s in favor of "hopes and dreams," turning to "a usable past of happiness and plenty."[19] This was a classic struggle against the reality principle, a comforting denial of unacceptable fact. Moreover, as nostalgic visions of an idealized, fertile realm, *Young Corn* and *Spring Turning* fail as faithful historical records of Depression-era Iowa but are compellingly truthful in a different, psychological sense. Relative to the artist's own inner life, they may be interpreted, like dreams, as wish fulfillments, disguised expressions of (repressed) desires. They unfold from an unconscious memory of the maternal body, as I've proposed above and as other scholars have implied at least on the level of common metaphor: "mother" nature generates life and

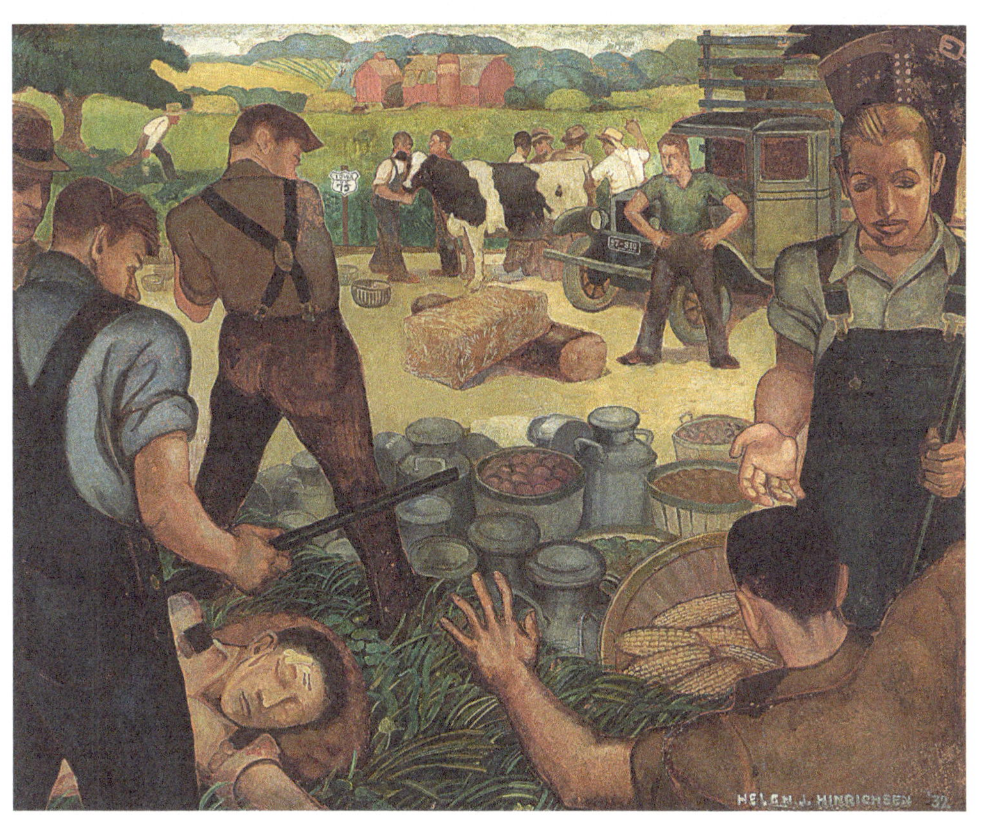

Fig. 4.9. Helen Hinrichsen, *Farmer's Holiday*, 1932.

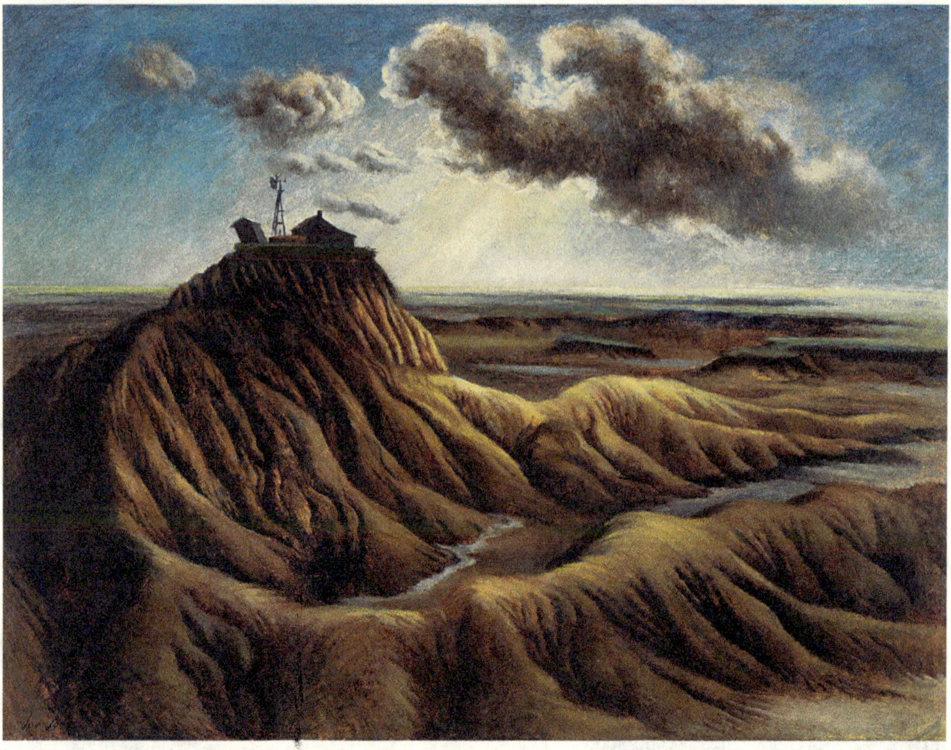

Fig. 4.10. Joe Jones, *American Farm*, 1936.

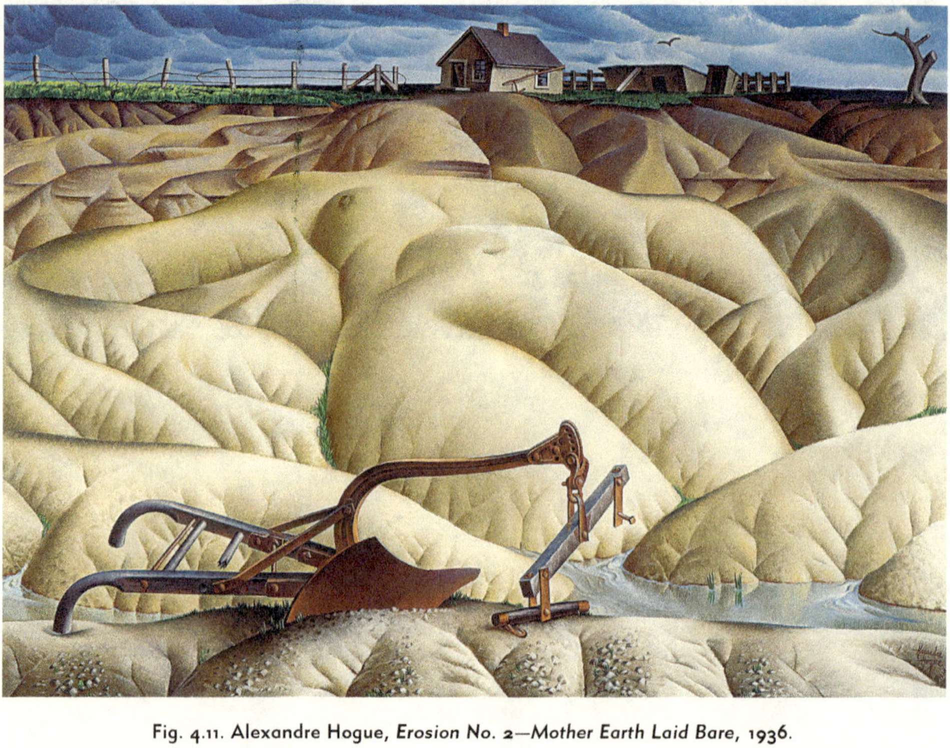

Fig. 4.11. Alexandre Hogue, *Erosion No. 2—Mother Earth Laid Bare*, 1936.

nourishes it; the "swollen" landscape forms in Wood's pictures similarly invite comparison to the pregnant or lactating body. This then is the artist's own personal Eden, an originary scene not just of a charmed childhood in the toy-like setting of *Stone City* but of an even earlier moment, when the neonate is held in a nurturing embrace. The undulating shapes and smooth, stubbly, or spongy textures in *Young Corn* and other Wood pictures echo the expansive mother body experienced by the babe-in-arms who perceives no limits to that body—which seems, like the Iowa landscape, to go on and on. While Wood's placement of his pastoral plots in a former time functioned as a conscious repudiation of the present, with its disastrous economic, technological, and climatic effects, his search for a positive alternative led him back unconsciously to an archaic memory of cradled comfort.

His mature landscapes feature sheltering structures—little houses and barns that announce "homestead"—as well as minuscule figures who crawl upon the great earth like Lilliputians over the body of a captive Gulliver. Anthropomorphized topographies were not unique during the 1930s to Wood's pictures; what he treated only suggestively Alexandre Hogue made explicit in *Erosion No. 2—Mother Earth Laid Bare* (1936, Fig. 4.11), one of a series of six accusatory environmentalist pictures, "Erosion by Wind and by Water" (1932–39), that exposed the consequences of poor agricultural practices.[20] In what could have been a retort to Wood's almost Panglossian paean to farming in *Fall Plowing*, the Missouri-born Hogue, active in Texas, rendered his stricken Mother Earth as a naked, supine victim of the broken plow in the foreground of his picture. His ravished earth goddess, though faceless, emerges carefully delineated amid the gullies and rivulets of the desiccated ground, with anatomical details of nipples and navel. Wood was never so obvious, his pillowy knolls and soft ridges only subtly akin to a series of part-objects, like the "good breast" described by Melanie Klein, introjected by the infant as a source of pure beneficence.[21] From a Kleinian perspective, Wood's landscapes might be seen as the result of a process by which an infantile sense of well-being internalized long ago is now projected outward onto the forms of the external world.

A LOVE AFFAIR WITH THE WORLD

Another pertinent analytic perspective is provided in Phyllis Greenacre's studies of creativity and especially of the childhood of the artist. Greenacre theorized in the potentially gifted infant an acute sensitivity to sensory stimulation, with a precocious awareness of form and rhythm, and, following from this, an intensified experience of the primary object (mother) and soon also of peripheral objects. The latter Greenacre calls "collective alternates," which on some level approximate the mother and which the future artist animates and anthropomorphizes empathically. These imaginative tendencies, lost to most individuals after early childhood, remain active in gifted persons, Greenacre proposed, either in their own right or "in the form of the ease and wealth of symbolization."[22] She explained how this process might emerge:

> The potentially gifted infant would react to the mother's breast with an intensity of the impression of warmth, smell, moisture, the feel of the texture of the skin and the vision of the roundness of form, according to the time and situation of the experience—but more than might be true in the less potentially gifted infant. Such an infant [i.e., the gifted one] would react also more widely and more intensely to any similar smells, touch or taste sensations or visions of rounded form which might come its way. . . . This may be the beginning [for the artist] of the love affair with the world.[23]

Wood's rapturous landscapes evince his ongoing love affair with the mother body as a kind of unconscious anlage for the collective alternates he discovers in nature: "The naked earth," he marveled in his autobiography, "in rounded, massive contours, asserts itself through everything that is laid upon it" (Appendix, p. 194).

His hypersensitivity to form and color, sound, taste, and smell enlivens "Return from Bohemia" at every turn, affirming in his case the special endowment that Greenacre posits. How much he owed Rinard for the specific terms in which he conveyed in his narrative the noises of an autumn evening on the farm (the "rhythmic see-saw of the windmill" and "thinned-out fiddling of the insects") or the mixture of pungent and mealy odors he registered as a boy upon entering the barn (App., 257–58) will never be clear. Yet it is notable how excessive the language waxes whenever sensuous impressions involve the food that mother Hattie prepares: "potatoes, fried brown and crisp, roast pork that crumbled beneath the carving fork, garden vegetables, and thick slices of moist, yeasty bread coated with yellow butter" (App., 257). In another example, keen on the sweet and spicy smells of Hattie's pickling process, young Grant enjoys organizing her canned goods on shelves in the cellar, and composes a veritable color wheel of fruit-filled jars:

> The blue green of stuffed, bull-nosed peppers; light greenish yellow of gooseberries and currants; pale yellow of pears; warmer yellow of apple jelly (each glass with a leaf of rose geranium on the top to give it flavor); the richer yellow of spiced Siberian crab-apples; brownish yellow apple butter and ground cherry preserves; yellow plums with a slight orange tint; great two-quart jars of orange-tinted peaches; the red orange of wild plums; the flecked vermillion of tomatoes; the crimson of strawberries and raspberries; the deeper red of blackberries; red violet of loganberries and pickled beets; the blues and purples of tame plums, given variety and depth with grapes; the varied greens of cucumber pickles, water melon pickles, picallilly [*sic*], green tomato pickles, chow-chow, bread-and-butter pickles; and moss-green dills covered with grape leaves [App., 257].

Arranging the jars according to their "gorgeous, liquid colors," boy Wood mixes up his art-making with Hattie's homemaking, showing how the one proceeds from the other. Nature forms the fundament of both, as in the narrative Grant turns from the canning shelves to admire the raw fruits and vegetables heaped in bins. Wood continued on (and on) for two more paragraphs to enumerate them all, including every one of the nine varieties of apple and their respective hues, finally concluding synaesthetically with how the cellar was permeated with their ripe odors, "mingled with the good, firm smell of sun-washed earth" (App., 257).

For him, the Iowa earth was a kind of first cause, and elsewhere in "Return from Bohemia," Wood proclaimed his own growth from and allegiance to it: "The rhythms of the low hills," he declared, "the patterns of crops upon them, the mystery of the seasons, and above all, a feeling for the integrity of the ground itself—these are my deep-rooted heritage" (App., 194). When he painted the landscape he loved so well, Wood imbued it with conscious and unconscious memories, sensuous appetites, and corporeal pleasures. No wonder that Corn has found eroticism in his pictures or that R. Tripp Evans discerns in them expressions of the artist's homosexual desire—in *Stone City*, for example, whose features for Evans exhibit "the rigid smoothness of an erect penis" and include a pair of upturned male buttocks in the hilly middleground and "a seemingly endless battalion of ejaculatory corn sprouts" in the tilled foreground.[24] Evans's bold reading is underscored by the canny detail he notes at the far right of this scene, near a turn in the country road, a billboard for cigarettes with a smoking man in a red necktie (secret badge of the homosexual) who avows, "They Satisfy."[25] The oral gratifications of Wood's own chain-smoking and addiction to sweets and alcohol are also echoed in his images of farmers in the field drinking from jugs (see Figs. 2.14, 2.15, 2.28). In a late, Neo-Impressionist-style landscape, the dizzyingly vertiginous and bristly *Haying* (1939, Fig. 4.12), no farmer appears, but the jug remains, situated prominently on the ground abutting the picture plane, at the foot of a harvested hill. Corking the jug with a red stopper, which stands out brightly in a green chenille field, Wood conjured the nursing breast with its erect nipple, harking back to a distant pleasurable time before weaning.

A child's polymorphous perversity[26] pervades his feeling for the landscape, and we are reminded of how in Wood's autobiography he connected his youthful autoeroticism to the ground itself, where, seated on the sod, he plays with a garter snake writhing on a molehill (App., 195). Evans calls attention, moreover, in *Spring Turning*, to the anal eroticism latent in the artist's placement of a dark sluice in the cleft between two gently rounded hills that read as buttocks. Although Evans rejects the idea of Mother Earth metaphors in Wood's visions of Iowa farmland in favor of celebrations of male strength and beauty, the sensuality informing these scenes seems to me wide-ranging, encompassing unconscious recollections of infantile enjoyment as well as

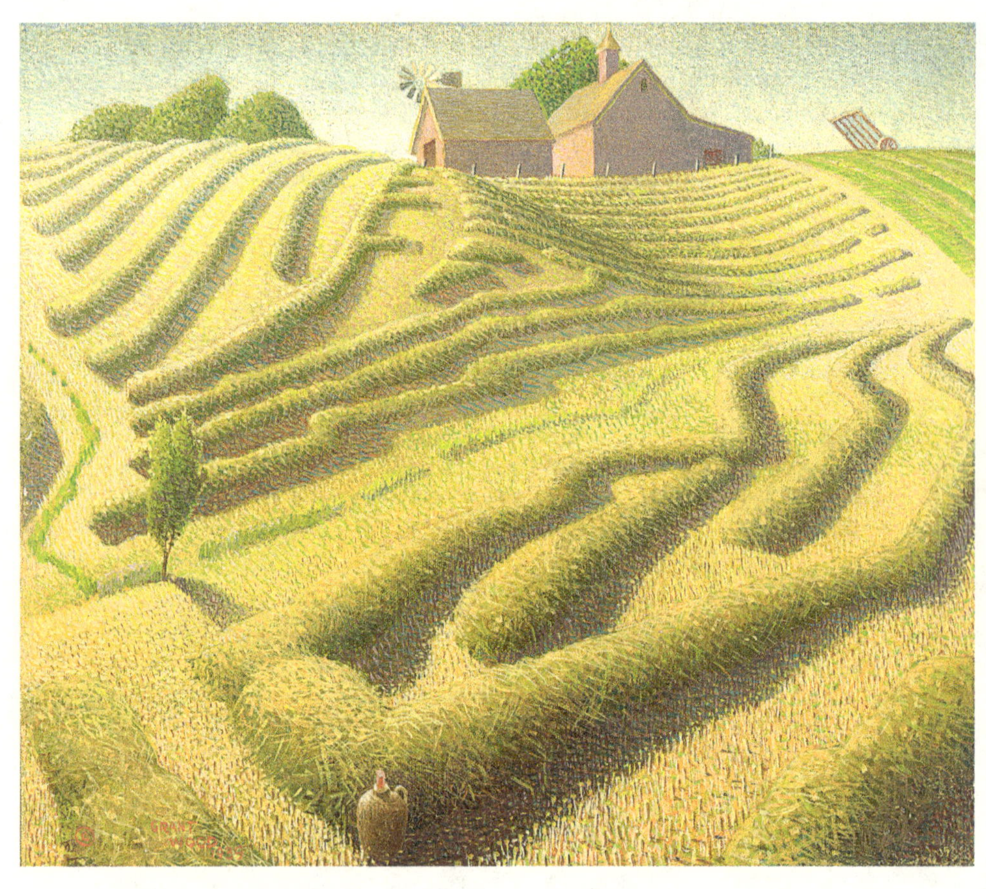

Fig. 4.12. Grant Wood, *Haying*, 1939

adult desire. Importantly, the imagery in *Spring Turning* and *Young Corn* illustrates not merely a body recumbent in nature but a *giant* body, an impression strongly reminiscent of how a baby might perceive the big maternal body that interacts intimately with its small self. The view in *Young Corn*, where massive breast- and belly-like swells define the voluptuous topography, may also convey a masculine awe of pregnancy, perhaps an element as well of Wood's interest in the figure of the Marian Madonna.[27]

To the two complementary possibilities, of the landscape as mother and/or lover, I would add another fantasy not yet considered in analyses of these paintings—a blissful union of one's *own* body with the earth, Wood's "return" to Iowa made literal. Struggling all his life with an extraordinary emotional dependence on his mother and an opposing need for autonomy, he could capitulate safely in imagination to the earth, lie prone upon it and meld with it, in *Spring Turning*. This transcendent vision seems to me especially poignant, painted as it was the year after Hattie died and was herself placed in the earth. Pictured here is a reconciliation with Iowa more profound than anything Wood was able to describe in words, either in his autobiography or in his frequent professions of Regionalist affiliation and affection for his homeland. The image parallels on a vast scale a compelling episode in Iowa writer Robert Boston's account of his own return from a sojourn in Germany as a disillusioned youth, with a stopover in New York. At age fifteen, Boston came home to his family farm:

> After supper, I went into the cornfield south of the barnyard. It was just sunset, and the western sky glowed gold. I lay face down between the rows and stretched my arms full length toward the sun. The earth was warm and soft beneath me, and I breathed deep, smelling, smelling, smelling the heavy smell of earth, tasting earth on my tongue. The new corn rustled slightly in the breeze, and I lay there for a long time. The knowledge surged within me. I dug my fingers deep into the black earth, gripping tightly, pulling myself downward against it. I was of this earth, this earth and no other. Like the corn, I drew my sustenance from it. I belonged to it, and it to me. I felt warm, secure, an infant in my mother's lap.[28]

Rising after a long while from the site of his surrender, the prodigal son looks down and sees the imprint of his body in the ground. In this tableau, as in Wood's paintings, we find the sense of merging with the outer world that Freud's friend Romain Rolland first termed "oceanic." While Rolland understood the phenomenon as a religious experience of eternity, "as of something limitless, unbounded," Freud searched for a materialist explanation, tracing the feeling to that still undifferentiated period in every individual's life before the development of a discrete, seemingly autonomous ego: "An infant at the breast," he wrote, "does not as yet distinguish his ego from the external world as the source of the sensations flowing in upon him."[29] This early, all-embracing feeling may persist for some people in recurring moments in adulthood, Freud speculated, "side by side with the narrower and more sharply demarcated ego-feeling of maturity, like a kind of counterpart to it."[30]

Similarly for Greenacre, who encountered in her analyses of creative individuals strikingly frequent reports of transcendental feelings in childhood of either sharp ecstasy or fusion with nature, the latter, oceanic state "seems derived from re-aroused infantile experiences of nursing."[31] Further, she noted how "a sense of special lightness or airiness may pervade either of these subjective states producing an illusion of flying or floating." This is a remarkable observation given the hovering perspectives in Wood's mature landscapes. His treatment of space in these pictures is such that a susceptible viewer may even share an illusive sensation of flight, as Dennis described for a number of compositions, including *Spring Turning* and the autumnal *Near Sundown* (1933, Fig. 4.13): "As the foreground slope recedes into space, the observer glides aloft, soaring out over the land, visually airborne. Figures and fence posts, farther below than ever, inch along the surface of attenuated hillsides, details of their texture, light, and shadow undiminished regardless of distance."[32] Significantly, in the peaceful *Near Sundown*, where the smooth hills are rendered in warm skin tones, Wood includes a tiny figure on a path at the right of the composition who drives home an orderly line of cows: it is time for milking.

STATES OF AWE AND ENVY

Do the evocative bird's-eye perspectives in such landscapes indicate that Wood had any actual experience of flight? The single documented instance of his air travel postdates these paintings: in 1940, thanks to a commission secured for him by his dealer Reeves Lewenthal, the artist flew by commercial airliner to Hollywood to paint cast members of *The Long Voyage Home* (directed by Walter Wanger and starring John Wayne).[33] There may well have been other, earlier occasions when he traveled by plane, crisscrossing the country on his frequent lecture tours.[34] Regardless, the terrain in Iowa is by no means flat, and so hilltop vistas provided sufficient inspiration. "I liked to stand on the crest of a hill and watch father or Dave Peters plowing in a field below," Wood remembered in "Return from Bohemia," foretelling precisely what he would depict in *Spring Turning*: "They guided the plow parallel to the sides of the rectangular field and progressed concentrically inward, cutting great square patterns with light stubble centers" (App., 214).[35]

This passage refers to the spring of Grant's sixth or seventh year. Liberated from the protective confines of farmyard and house, he enjoyed new horizons, spending free time watching the men labor in the outlying fields. His brother Frank, he recalled, "was old enough to work with them now; I envied him his increased importance" (App., 214). Sibling rivalry is repressed in *Spring Turning*, where the farmers peacefully tilling their plots number three—like the Wood brothers Frank, Grant, and John. With a

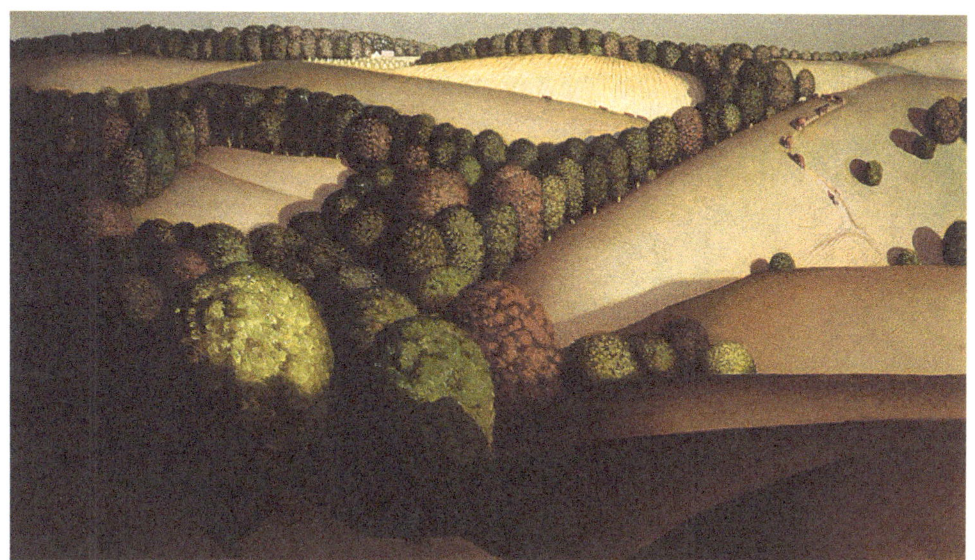

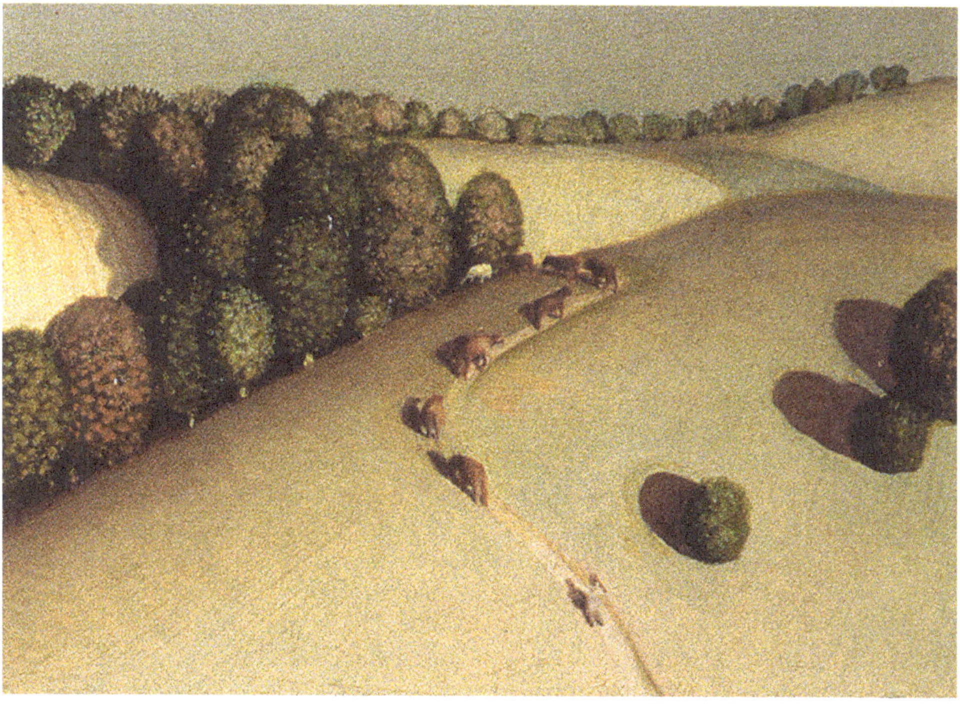

Figs. 4.13 (top) and 4.13A (detail, above). Grant Wood, *Near Sundown*, 1933.

team of white and brown horses, the first of these ant-like toilers on the land appears in the foreground, the second can be picked out in his respective square above right (Fig. 4.8A), while the third is barely discernible on the hilltop at the left. In this reading, the painting presents what would have been Maryville's dream, a future for his sons that conformed to and issued from his own agrarian values and labors. At the same time, *Spring Turning* reproduces, as suggested above, the very image Wood describes in his autobiography, of his father, the hired man, and his older brother in a triumvirate of masculine effort that Grant admires but observes as bystander. In the picture, as in the text, Wood regards the working men "from the crest of a hill," from the position he shares with the viewer of the painting—but also from a panoptic point opposite, in the figure of the windmill (see Fig. 4.8B), his personal symbol, isolated and infinitesimal on the distant horizon.

Impressed by the triumvirate, his superiors in age and ability, Grant registers his awe and envy of their manly endowments. One evening around the supper table, the whole Wood family gets excited over Maryville's report of a tornado that had recently torn roofs from houses and barns and destroyed livestock. The violent scene of phallic power associated with Grant's father is immediately outdone by one described by the hired man. "People nowadays don't know nothing about cyclones," he snorts. His tornado is bigger: "Back in 1860, when I was a kid, a cyclone blowed the whole town of Comanche acrost the river into Illinois" (App., 216). Frank knows about tornadoes, too; he understands that they develop from funnel clouds. "All this talk about cyclones ran wild in my imagination," Wood recalled, as young Grant daydreams a means to overcome what must be anxious feelings of phallic inadequacy. He seizes a heroic figure with whom to identify, the intrepid Paul Revere, introduced to him by Hattie only several nights prior through reading Henry Wadsworth Longfellow's poem. Adapting the tale to his emotional needs, Grant finds in it a formal substitute for the funnel cloud that haunts him—the prominent roof lantern atop the Old North Church—and envisions himself like the historic revolutionary, earning praise and renown by spreading a warning, not of a British arrival by sea but of an impending cyclone. He finds an opportunity for his grandiose ambition the next day at school, when he spies a passing cloud "shaped like the utensil mother used when pouring vinegar into a jug" (App., 216). To his agitated cries of "Teacher! Teacher! There's a cyclone coming," terrified children are rushed out of the schoolhouse down the road toward the storm cellar of a nearby farm. But it is a false alarm. Halfway to the farm, the frazzled teacher notices the fair weather. Grant's funnel cloud, far from blowing away buildings or towns, had only petered out pathetically: "My little cloud," he rues, "had either melted away or taken another shape." Humiliation and punishment ensue.

Such was his chagrin that the artist sought even decades later to redress the injury to his self-esteem, in the peculiar painting alluding to the poem featured in this anecdote—the *Midnight Ride of Paul Revere* (1931, Fig. 4.14).

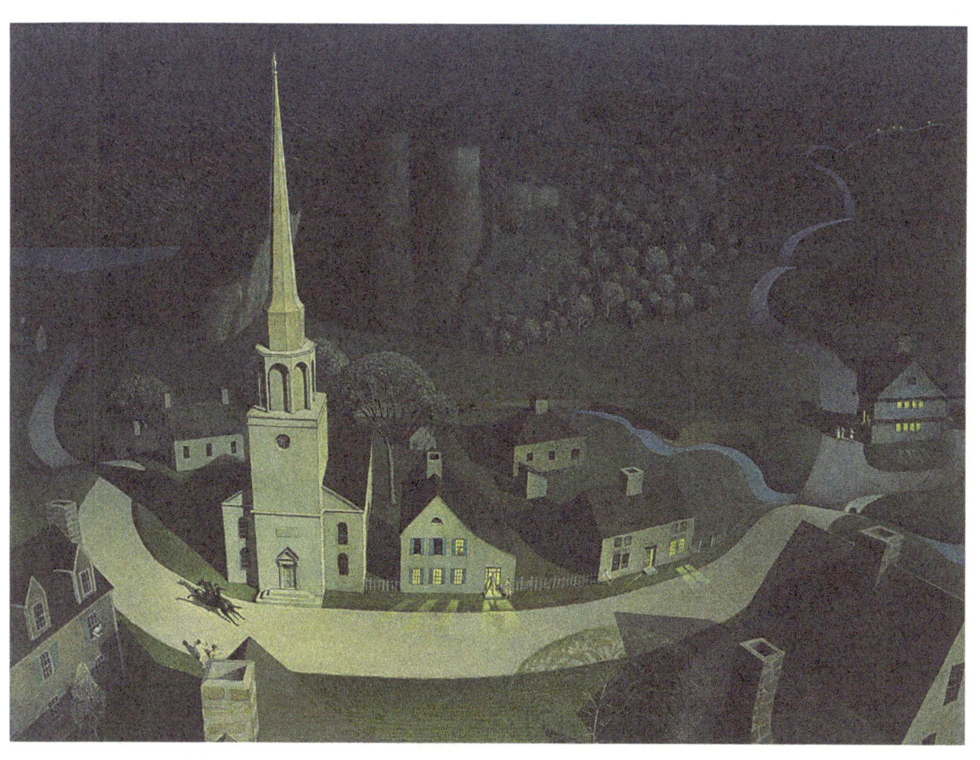

Fig. 4.14. Grant Wood, *Midnight Ride of Paul Revere*, 1931.

The humorous self-deprecation with which Wood presented the embarrassing failure of his boyish striving in the autobiography seems to me a defense (to deny his real pain) only somewhat tempered in this picture, where a hero is celebrated in unheroic terms. Riding through a nocturnal landscape along a moonlit ribbon of road, Revere causes a stir, with astonished townspeople running outside in their nightgowns to receive his news. But the whole adventure unfolds in a dollhouse village, with everything including the hero on his galloping weathervane steed made charmingly toylike. The lofty viewpoint above rooftops and trees is remarkable, helping Wood literally to put things in perspective. He is able to do just that from his position of triumph over the father, whose severe presence is felt in the church steeple looming over the tiny figure of the rebellious Revere. By 1931, when he painted *Midnight Ride*, Wood had realized through his art the praise and renown he once dreamed would compensate for his sense of inferiority in the face of his father's intimidating power.

Like George Washington, another hero of Wood's, Revere had participated in overthrowing the rule of a king. The image of the mounted Revere proclaiming his news represented unconsciously to Wood the defeat of the father and rehearses a motif he had painted a decade before in Paris in *Place de la Concorde* (1920, Fig. 4.15). Rendering the Baroque sculpture by Antoine Coysevox, *La Renommée du roi montée sur Pégase sonnant la*

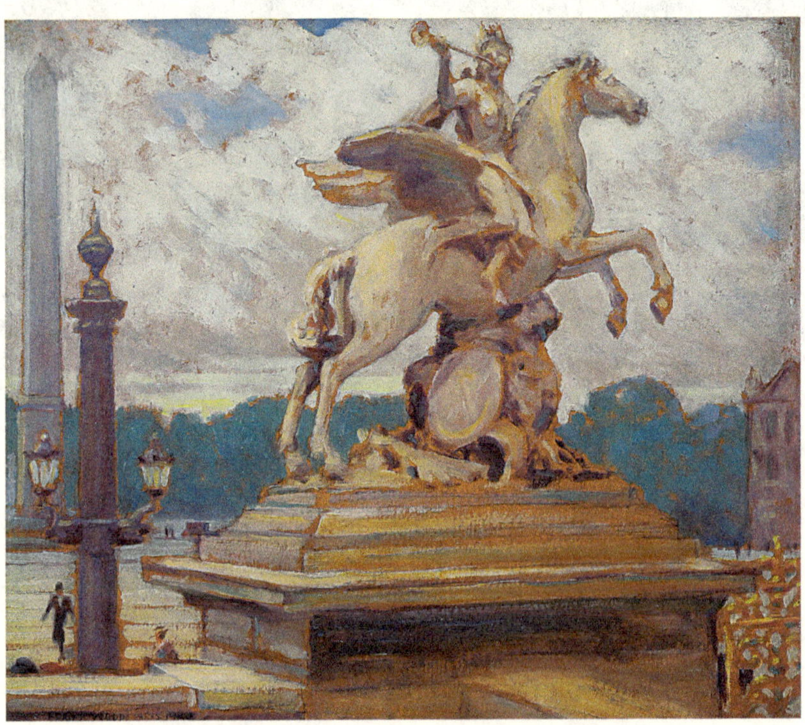

Fig. 4.15. Grant Wood, *Place de la Concorde*, 1920.

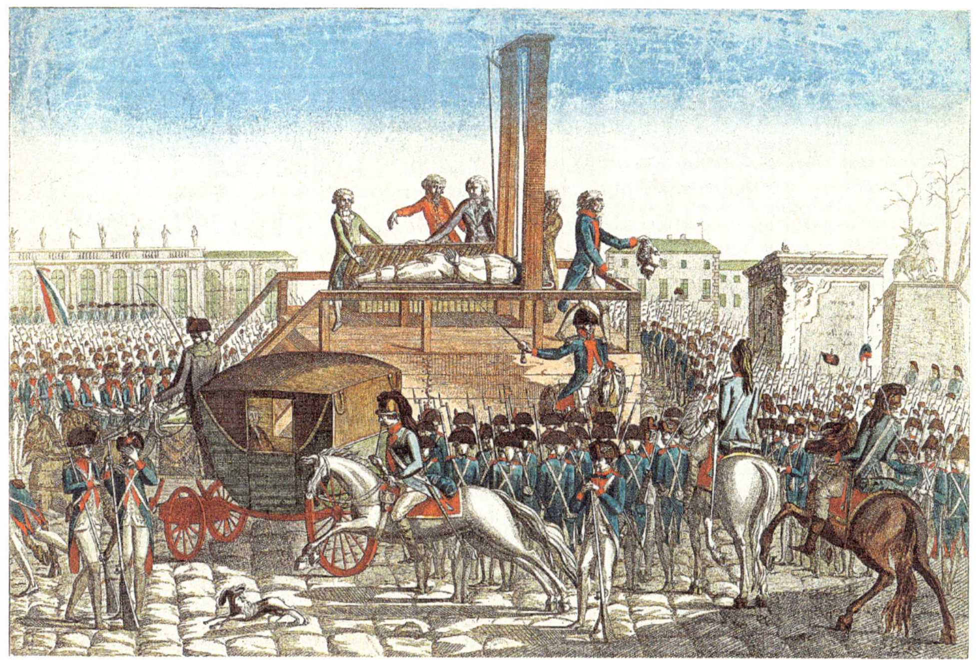

Fig. 4.16. Georg Heinrich Sieveking, *Execution of Louis XVI*, 1793, engraving after an unknown French painter, showing Coysevox sculpture at right later painted by Wood.

trompette (The King's Renown Mounted on Pegasus Sounding the Trumpet, 1701–2), Wood selected a vantage point from which the allegorical monument of regal fame, with his long slender horn, upstages both the Obelisk of Luxor and a columnar fixture with its testicular lamps that dwarf a little man at the left of the composition. *Place de la Concorde* seems to me a murderous fantasy in lovely disguise of Wood's own victory over his oedipal rivals, painted on the historic site of a regicide—Louis XVI was executed here in 1793 by his revolutionary subjects (see Fig. 4.16). With patricide as its latent content, moreover, the image forecasts the passage in "Return from Bohemia" where, after Maryville's demise, a messenger on a rampant white horse brings word of President McKinley's assassination (App., 280).

It is the pattern and repetition of this thematic material that alerts us to its ongoing psychic significance for Wood. He covered it over, just as Parisians cloaked the scene of past crimes in euphemism, renaming what had been known as Revolutionary Square (originally the Place Louis XV) with the French equivalent of "Harmony Plaza." Whether hidden in the tourist view of *Place de la Concorde*, the reprise of an American legend in *Midnight Ride*, or an autobiographical schoolboy escapade, child Wood's evident phallic awe and envy conform to reactions that, according to Greenacre, date to the phallic-oedipal period and are triggered by such experiences as a boy's sight of his father's tumescent penis, exposure to masturbatory exhibitions of an older brother and his friends, or seduction by an older boy or man.[37] The bodily excitement revealed to a little boy in such circumstances "substantiates the strange magical responses which the child is experiencing in himself."[38] Whatever may have transpired in Wood's early life, his penis awe is conveyed more than once in "Return from Bohemia," for example in the exciting spectacle of the hot-air balloon man at the county fair, who sheds his common overalls much to Grant's delight to reveal an "athletic daredevil in black tights and a red waist glittering with silver spangles" (App., 253), cheered wildly by the crowd. In the grandstand with his father and brothers, Grant sees the man's limp balloon grow "bigger and bigger . . . and harder to manage in the breeze," watches him soar, and—"then the miracle"—witnesses his white parachute blossom in the sky while the balloon deflates, leaving a trail of smoke behind.

Also thrilling to Grant is the day the steam-operated threshing machine arrives on the Wood farm, and the men who tend it laugh and spit and swear lustily as they prepare their "dragon" for the task at hand (App., 242). "I was completely awed by the stupendous size and complexity of the threshing equipment," Wood wrote, struck by "the huge body of the separator," its big conveyor belt, innumerable gears, and how when the throttle was thrown open, "the vibrations shook the earth under me." All day long Grant marvels as the machine puffs and roars until, toward evening "the last of our grain dribbled from the separator." The sexual symbolism is so close to the surface—Evans in his reading calls it "unavoidably Freudian"[39]—that one wonders whether Wood was consciously crafting his prose for knowing, inside readers. He concluded his account of the day with a symbolic seduction: shy little Grant is invited by the rakish threshing-machine operator to blow its whistle. The boy grasps the leather thong above the driver's seat and tugs, causing the machine to sound "loudly enough to shake down the strawstack" (App., 245). He lets go in fright, but the friendly man instructs him, "Give her a real yank!" "And what a terrific blast it was," recorded Wood with satisfaction, "that I sent screaming over the dusky countryside!"

IN MEMORIAM

Wood turned the memorable day of manly exertion into a decorous vignette of homosociality in *Dinner for Threshers* (Fig. 3.33), where the workers pause for the midday meal in Hattie's lace-curtained dining room, all passion sublimated and relegated to the print of running horses on the rear wall.[40] Evans interprets this painting convincingly as an homage to Maryville, represented by the central white-shirted figure with his back turned (seated on the piano stool), surrounded Christlike by his fellows at a Last Supper before his sacrificial death.[41] Maryville's demise also forms the buried content in Evans's understanding of *Fall Plowing*, the beautiful

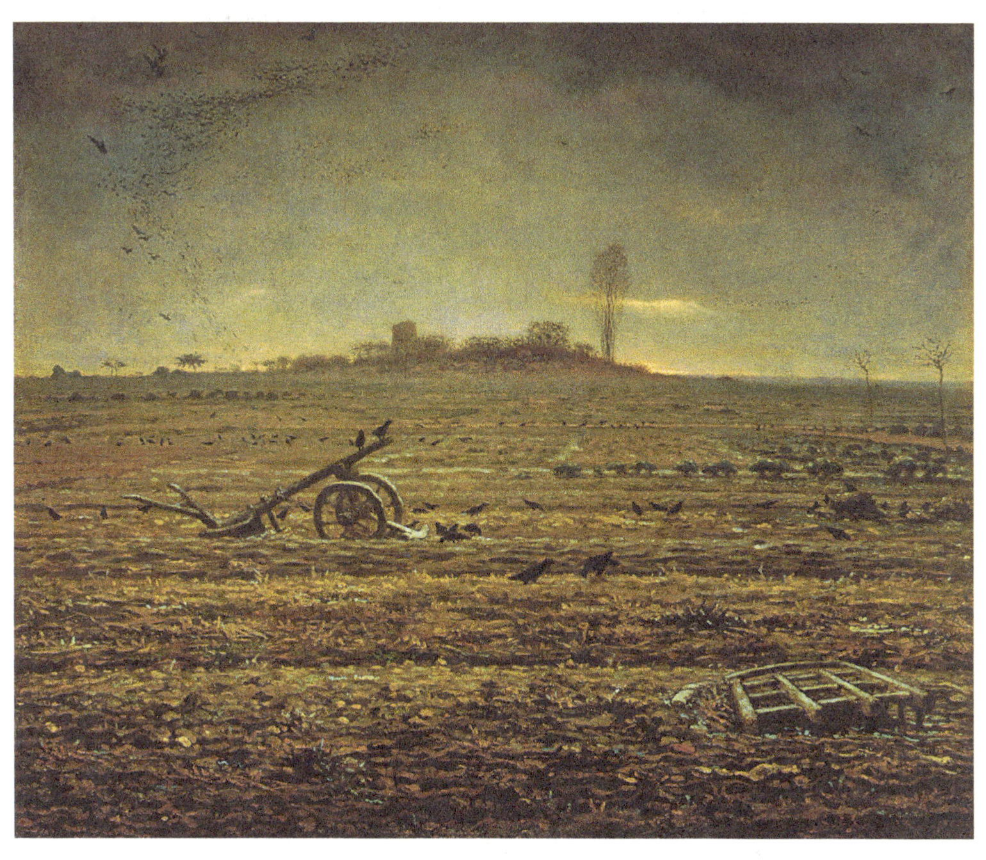

Fig. 4.17. Jean-François Millet, *Plain of Chailly with Harrow and Plough*, 1862.

landscape commemorating the end of the agricultural cycle that begins green and verdant in *Spring Turning*. Wood rehearsed the pageantry of this cycle in loving detail in the very first pages of his autobiography, concluding with the farmer's last tillage before the onset of winter frosts. Similarly elegiac in tone, *Fall Plowing* is set in the past, remote from the realities of Iowa farming in the 1930s, when the tractor was fast supplanting the horse-drawn riding plow, which itself had long since displaced the antique walking plow seen in Wood's picture.[42] Memorializing a bygone method of working the land by hand cultivation, *Fall Plowing* harks back to the nineteenth century in another way as well, evincing Wood's debt to Barbizon painting, in particular to Jean-François Millet, who had affirmed for him the legitimacy of the landscape of agricultural toil as artistic subject matter. One sees this as early as 1924 in *Truck Garden, Moret* (Figge Art Museum), which Wood painted in France, south of Paris near Barbizon, observing a farmer hoeing a field.[43] One of several versions of Millet's *Plain of Chailly with Harrow and Plough* (1862, Fig. 4.17) seems to me to have been a possible inspiration for *Fall Plowing*, with its lone plow set against a harvested stubble field.

Infinitely more idealized, Wood's rendering insists on tidiness—in both farming and painting—as a supreme virtue. The casual neglect implicit in Millet's image of plow and harrow left to the elements contrasts starkly with the meticulous effort everywhere apparent in Wood's scene. While there is a sense of aftermath in Millet's work, conveyed by the crows pecking at the remains of the harvest, *Fall Plowing* is poignant in a different way: the tilling is unfinished, as if suddenly abandoned mid-task, implying, like seventeenth-century Dutch still lifes of the interrupted meal, death's unexpected intrusion. The plow itself becomes a metonym for the departed farmer. Wood pushed the implement into the center foreground of his painting, making it dramatically iconic in a way reminiscent of Willa Cather's unforgettable apotheosis of the motif in *My Antonia*: "Presently we saw a curious thing," narrator Jim Burden reports, in the company of Antonia and three of their friends, "On some upland farm, a plough had been left standing in the field. The sun was sinking just behind it. Magnified across the distance by the horizontal light, it stood out against the sun, was exactly contained within the circle of the disc; the handles, the tongue, the share—black against the molten red. There it was heroic in size, a picture writing on the sun."[44] This vision, which soon vanishes as the sun sets, appears to the young people after Jim attempts to comfort Antonia, who is missing her dead father. They imagine his spirit moving among the Nebraskan woods and fields that had been dear to him. One thinks again of Evans's interpretation of *Fall Plowing*, which conjures a haunted scene, that of Maryville's interment, as Wood described it in "Return from Bohemia," "in the same rich soil, the same rolling hill-land he had farmed from boyhood" (App., 269).[45] The painting becomes a thanatopsis, infused with an element of Eros in the sensual slicing of the earth by the phallic plow, a primal scene opening on the ground itself.

Love, death, and desire contribute to the emotional richness of this work; guilt plays a role as well, perhaps the predominant one. Painted the same year as *Midnight Ride*, from the same position of triumph when Maryville was no longer and his artist son had become nationally renowned, *Fall Plowing* distills Wood's unconscious childhood wish to kill and rob the father as well as his ultimate evasion of filial duty. His failure to follow in father's footsteps, to take his place behind the plow, aborts the agricultural and generational cycles he exalted in his autobiography, and he painted his own absence into the scene as well as his father's, evoking his own oedipal crime and its feared punishment in the same image. The hallucinatory perfection and clarity of the scene, with its sense of arrested motion, render it uncanny, the repressed returning at a moment coinciding with the artist's sudden rise to fame. As an envious child in the grip of magical thinking, Wood had imagined his culpability for Maryville's death (wishing had made it happen), an irrational notion he overcame in his conscious adult mind; but when he realized his secret ambition to surpass his father, those thoughts did seem omnipotent after all. He *was* a guilty patricide, and deserved retribution. "The law of talion," analyst Otto Fenichel contended in this regard, "is so closely interwoven with the world of magical thought which our ego pretends to have conquered, that any sudden warning that magical power might [indeed] be potent is apt to remobilize a latent expectation of punishment."[46] That warning for Wood had arrived with the instant notoriety of *American Gothic* the preceding year and lends an aura of suspense as well as an eerie absence to *Fall Plowing*.

Later in the 1930s, his landscapes became increasingly dark, turbulent, or frozen like the wintry view in *January*, which exists as a charcoal study, a large finished drawing (Fig. 4.18), a lithograph, and an oil painting. Wood conceived the print (1938) for Associated American Artists, along with other lithographs depicting seasonal scenes—*February*, *March*, *July Fifteenth*, *Seedtime and Harvest*, *December Afternoon*—and afterward produced the painting (1940–41, Cleveland Museum of Art), which Lewenthal immediately sold to Hollywood film director King Vidor. Henry Adams's analysis of the rabbit tracks entering an aperture in one of the shocks as a coded reference to "cornholing," or anal intercourse, seems astonishing,[47] yet Wood may indeed have been fully conscious of the joke. He hinted as much to Vidor upon the latter's purchase of the painting, writing of Januaries in Iowa: "The farmhouses are snug, the barns well-stored; it is a land of plenty here which seems to rest, rather than suffer, under the cold. In light of this, it seemed to me that nothing caught the spirit of an Iowan winter more aptly than the familiar scene of a field of corn shocks partly covered with snow. The rabbit tracks, leading into the snug shelter of the shock in the foreground, are a piece of symbolism with which I had some fun."[48] Even if

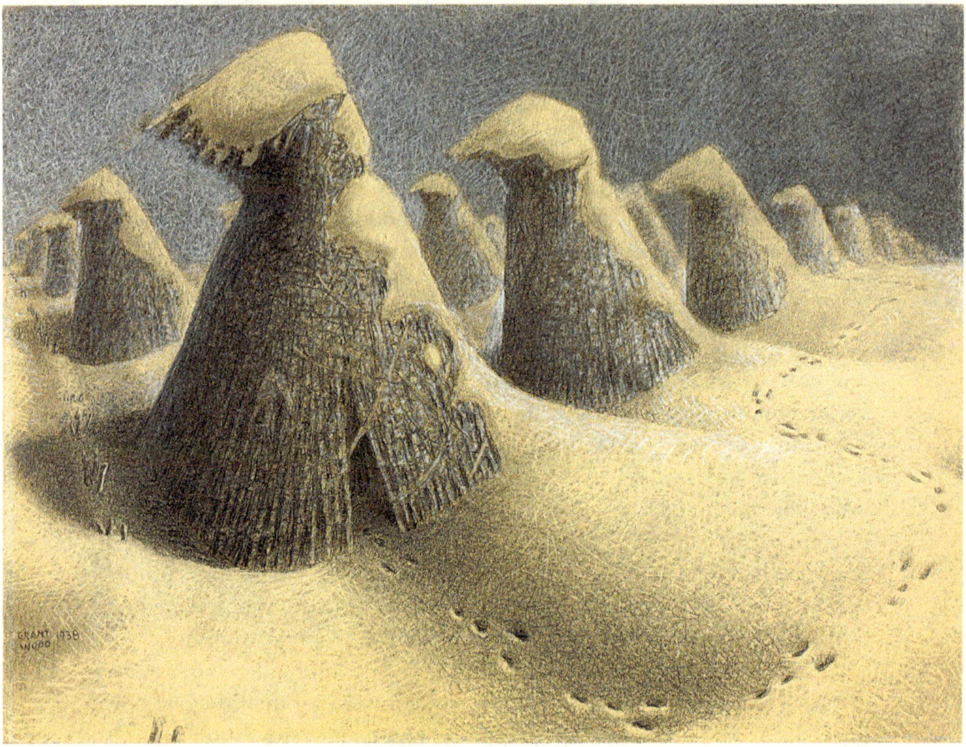

Fig. 4.18. Grant Wood, *January*, 1938.

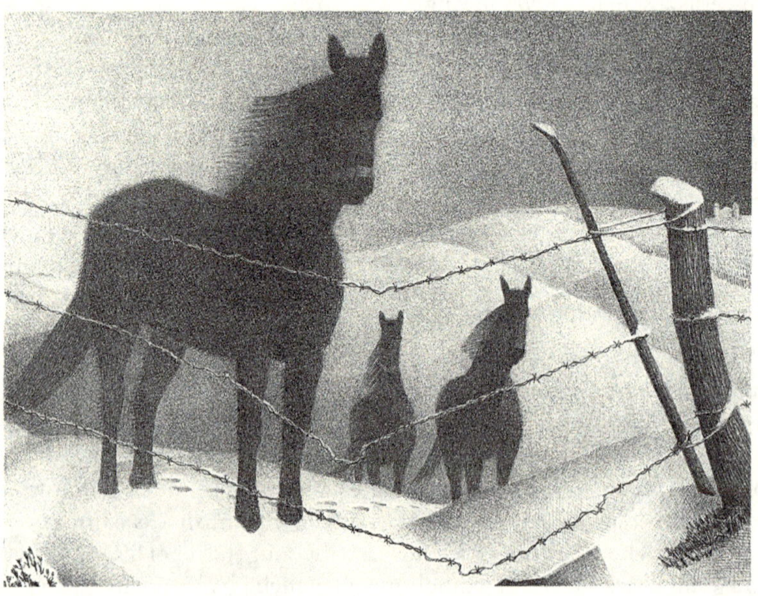

Fig. 4.19. Grant Wood, *February*, 1940.

Adams's interpretation obtains, and I think it does—note the inadvertent repetition of "snug" in Wood's commentary above—it hardly cancels out the mournful aspect of the picture, with the orderly rows of corn shocks taking on the quality of a funeral procession beneath the wintry sky. With their windblown snowy hoods, the anthropomorphized sheaves resemble white-robed monks or the *pleurants* carved on medieval tombs. Wood first envisaged the scene sometime in late 1937 or early 1938, in the wake of his friend Jay Sigmund's tragic end at the age of fifty-one on October 19, 1937. The poet had bled to death as a result of an accidental self-inflicted gunshot wound as he was hunting for rabbits along the Wapsipinicon River in Waubeek. So stricken was Wood by this shock that he could not bring himself to attend the funeral.[49] *January* may well be his memorial to the fellow Regionalist whose poem "Grant Wood" glories in the idea that a native son "dreaming on the plain" might perceive and paint the splendor of Iowa—thwarting all expectations. Sigmund's verse begins:

> Such dull fields; corn shocks
> And drab pasture lands:
> "Beauty cannot spring," they said,
> "From plow-warped hands!"

Sigmund had composed his poem in the late 1920s when he saw an exhibition of Wood's European paintings at the public library in Cedar Rapids. Legend has it that when the artist read this tribute, and its implicit Regionalist challenge, in the local newspaper, the two men met and formed a friendship that lasted until the poet's death. Supportive and encouraging to the younger man, Sigmund urged Wood to devote himself to Midwestern subjects, and though the latter's turn to Regionalism was overdetermined, it is interesting to note that two early paintings of corn shocks date to the time of the poem, which concludes with farmers grateful to an artist giving tint to their world of barns and grainstacks.[50]

The motifs shared by poet and painter include the fatal ridge road, as we have seen in Chapter 1, and the three horses in winter that Wood depicted in the haunting *February* (1940, Fig. 4.19), which conjures the first lines of Sigmund's "Winter Pastoral":

> Out on the winter-battered hills
> The three gray horses paw:
> No harness binds them to the thills;
> The snow is thin; the east wind chills—
> No manger there, no straw.[51]

February in "Return from Bohemia" is for the whole Wood family "the dreariest month of year" (App., 213), and in his print the artist captured his poet friend's similarly dispirited lament: "My winter mood's a smoke-hued one," Sigmund brooded, "I have no heart to sing." Bleak as Sigmund's sunless verse, *February*, with its shadowy chiaroscuro effects and crepuscular atmosphere, includes a frozen farmstead in the distance, at the right edge of the composition. The spooky velvet-black horses, though featureless silhouettes, confront the viewer attentively from behind a barbed-wire fence that has fallen into disrepair. Hoofprints in the snow seem to predict rather than record the movements of the foreground horse, a curious detail that opens the image to the possibility of truly profound content.

By 1940, when he created this lithograph, Wood had faced, in addition to the sudden death of Sigmund, the recent dissolution of his marriage, financial duress, the crushing censure of *Sultry Night*, and the hateful campaign against him at the university. There were bright moments, to be sure—the Hollywood trip and Wood's enthusiastic reception there among the talented movie set—but the artist was under emotional siege and his final illness was looming if not already beginning to take its toll. Producing prints for Associated American Artists and paintings after those prints for Lewenthal to market was an urgent economic, professional, and therapeutic necessity. As Wood searched for inspiration for this project in Sigmund's poetry,[52] he confronted again the devastating loss of his friend, which in turn revived earlier losses, significantly three that haunt *February* with their ghostly symbolic presence: his father, his mother, and his brother John. All awaited him now in the world of the dead, a chilling fact allegorized in Wood's winter pastoral, where the barrier separating the imagined spectator from the three horses' realm is flimsy and provisional. One only need lift the top rope loop from its fence post and raise the leaning stick from the lower loop in order to pass to the other side. It is an invitation, like the one contemplated by Robert Frost stopping by woods on a snowy evening, "to rest, rather than suffer," as Wood put it to Vidor in his description of an Iowa January. Frost in his poem demurs; in *February*, the invitation remains open. Once the flimsy fence is breached, the horses will turn in the direction of the anomalous hoofprints and lead one back inexorably to the sepulchral white homestead on the horizon.

HOMECOMING IN SPRING

Following the publication of *February* by Associated American Artists, Wood produced the lithograph *Approaching Storm* (1940), in which three farm workers hurry to collect sheaves of harvested grain as sheets of rain advance on their field from the background. The foreboding atmosphere of these late images undoubtedly had to do with events beyond Wood's own personal life. War was tearing Europe apart at this time, and we know where his political sympathies lay: he produced a poster for the American charity for British war relief, Bundles for Britain, and refused to do the same for the isolationist, anti-interventionist America First Committee.[53] At a moment of pervasive national anxiety, in what would prove his last major project, Wood conceived a pair of paintings that repeated his turn earlier in the Depression away from harsh reality to peaceful idyll: *Spring in Town* and its companion *Spring in the Country* (both 1941, Figs. 4.20 and 4.21, respectively). He created several preparatory sketches of these works in Iowa City and finished the pictures during a summer vacation with Rinard in the northern Iowa resort town of Clear Lake, where he rented a lakeside cottage and an old disused train depot nearby as a studio.[54]

The first painting, a small-town scene of spring cleaning and gardening, with a church overlooking a tidy neighborhood of single-family houses and a factory in the distance, clearly fulfilled Wood's intention to promote a galvanizing national myth. To fellow artists he had announced, "It is time for us to admit we believe in the value of the goals we mean, in general, when we say 'the American way of life.'"[55] Though two boys in the right background of *Spring in Town* share a common task in beating a rug, other figures in the painting pursue their respective activities independent of the rest, performing a kind of individualism in work and play. So effective was Wood's scene in conveying a happy fantasy of everyday American life that after the U.S. entered World War II, *The Saturday Evening Post* enlisted the picture as magazine cover and propaganda. Totalizing in its presumption of a homogeneous, white, middle-class, Midwestern, non-urban national audience, the *Post* presented the image as a visual response to the question "For What Are We Fighting?"[56]

Spring in Town belies a guilty inner world. Tranquility reigns in the picture that manifests something worth preserving while secretly harboring a disquieting content. Completed while the artist vacationed in a cottage dubbed "No Kare – No More," *Spring in Town* emerged unconsciously from Wood's greatest care of all, whose inescapable reality, as we have seen again and again in his art, weighed so heavily upon him: the loss of his father and his imagined responsibility for it. From photographs documenting how he set about work on this picture, we can date its original conception to early spring of 1941, when no snow was on the ground nor leaves or blossoms yet on the bare trees. Thus, he began sketching out of doors around the time of an anniversary—forty years after Maryville died on March 11, 1901. Wood drew at least two motifs from direct observation in Iowa City for *Spring in Town*, the shirtless gardening boy modeled by George Devine, son of the University of Iowa football coach (Fig. 3.3),[57] and the house in the middleground with its distinctive asymmetrical elevation and window arrangement (Fig. 4.22). That house still stands, in the Goosetown neighborhood about a mile from the university campus. Significantly, it sits at the edge of a cemetery.[58] As he sketched, gravestones dotted the landscape to Wood's right; directly behind him were many more, as the forty-acre cemetery stretches out along a gentle rise. Wood was drawn to the house with the

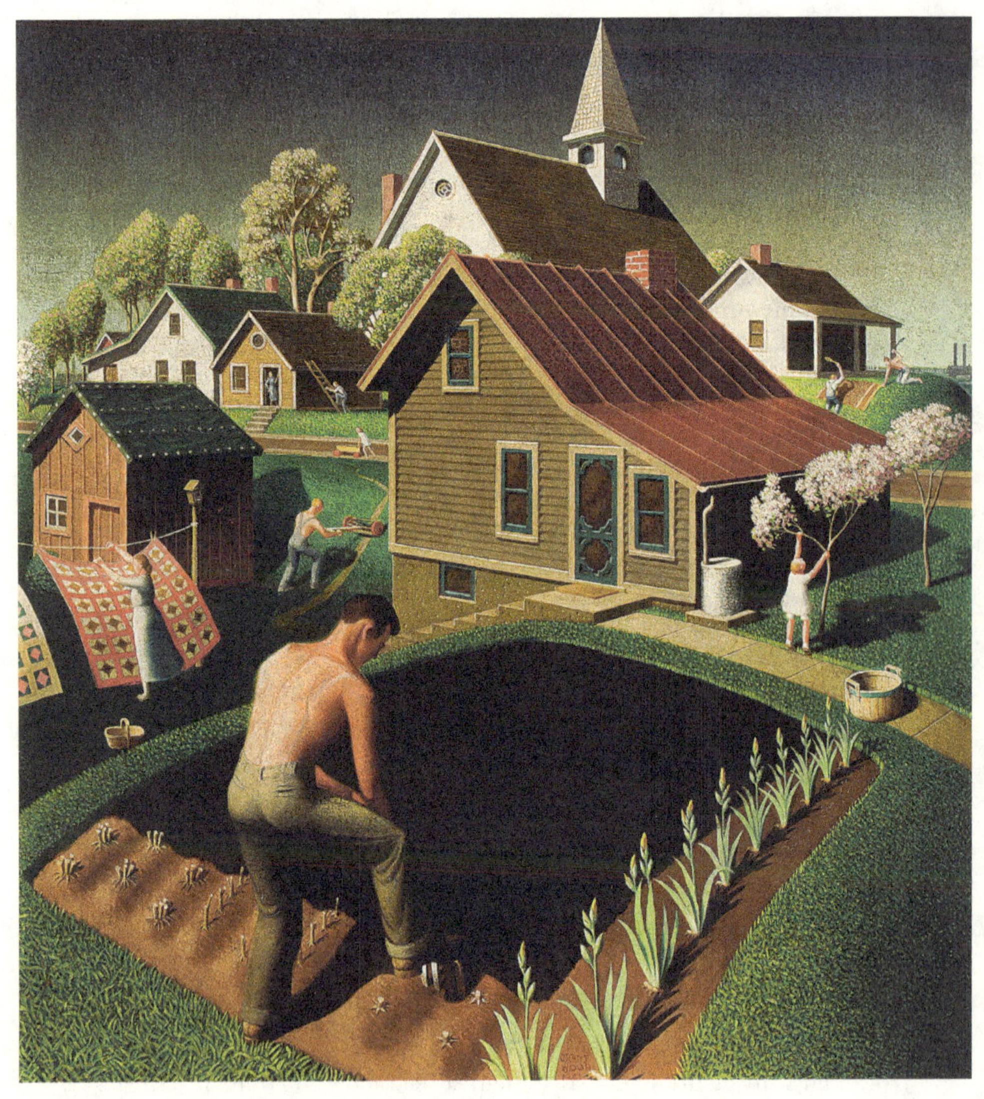

Fig. 4.20. Grant Wood, *Spring in Town*, 1941.

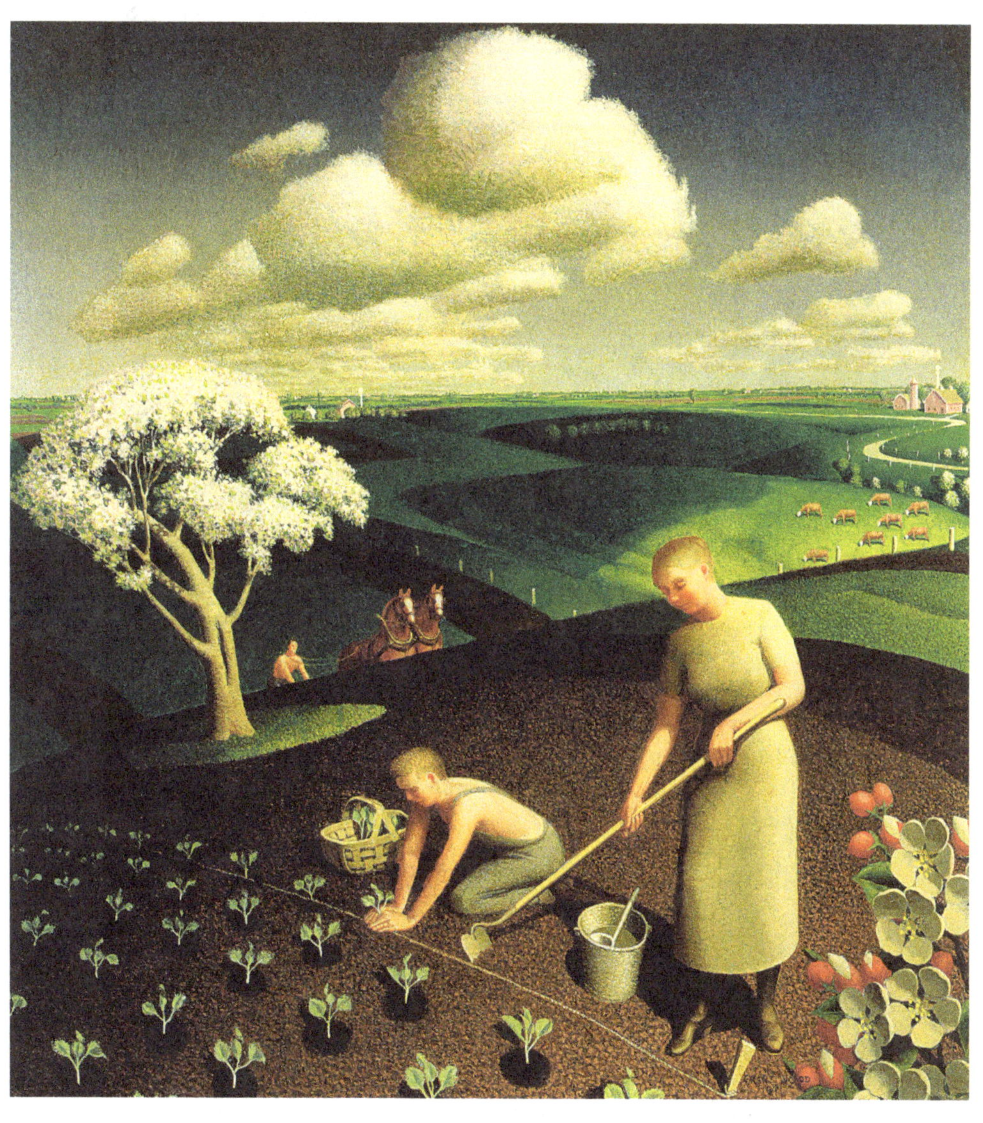

Fig. 4.21. Grant Wood, *Spring in the Country*, 1941.

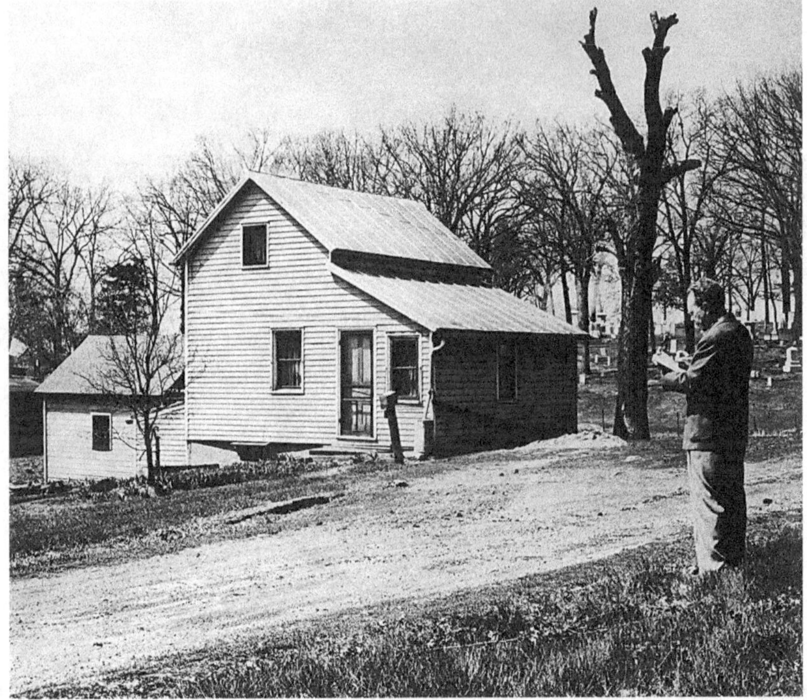

Fig. 4.22. Grant Wood sketching a house for *Spring in Town*, Iowa City, 1941.

conscious purpose of creating a pleasant scene, while death lurked at the periphery of his imagination. The earthen plot that dominates *Spring in Town* doubles in this reading as garden and grave, and the figures around it represent members of Wood's family, who went about life without the father, exiled to Cedar Rapids, to town, after Maryville died and they had to leave their farm.

Wood's big brother Frank (named after Francis Maryville Wood) tends the plot, while Hattie hangs the bedding, John mows the grass, Nan bothers a sapling in bloom, and Grant himself peers out from among the irises, inscribed in the ground itself in the form of his signature at the corner of the plot. The same figures reappear, as if in a recurring dream, in the background of the picture in identical costumes, with Grant's avatar now assuming bodily form, climbing a ladder that leans against his mother's house. Props delineate sexual difference: males are given phallic implements (spading fork, lawn mower, rug beaters, ladder); females are juxtaposed with containers (baskets, barrel, wagon, house). The symbolism in dreams of ladders and staircases, as noted in Chapter 3, is well known. Associated with mounting, exertion, and increasing breathlessness in approaching a summit, they stand for intercourse. Thus, the oedipal vignette in *Spring in Town* of the mother standing at the door of her house, at the top of a stairway, and the son/husband ascending a ladder, encodes a repressed sexual wish and rehearses a similar ambiguous coupling in the left background of *Parson Weems' Fable* (Fig. 3.25). *Spring in Town*, in other words, evokes Wood's familiar family romance: the son's guilty desire to possess the mother as his own requires that the father go away—which he does, permanently. Wood engraves his own anticipated punishment in his signature in the soil, as if masochistically to announce, "Here (too) lies Grant Wood." One wonders, moreover, if in 1941, at age fifty, he felt he was living on borrowed time, having already exceeded Maryville's life span of forty-six years. And indeed, he conceived this painting, recalling the first spring after his father's death, in the last spring of his own life.

Retrospective in its details as in its latent content, *Spring in Town* takes its neighborhood setting from the backyard of Sigmund's summer home in Waubeek,[59] where Wood had often basked in the poet's doting goodwill along with other members of the Sigmund's sophisticated social circle. A beloved father figure to the artist, the late Sigmund haunts this picture as well in the motif of quilts hanging on a clothesline. He had initially scolded Wood for copying French art, pointing the young painter down the street in Waubeek to a pair of quilts hanging on a clothesline as evidence of the kind of beauty available close at hand in Iowa.[60] The small painting Wood created of the poet's exemplary indigenous subject is signed and dated in the lower left corner "Waubeek/1928" (Fig. 4.23). Wood made a gift of it to Sigmund as proof of a lesson learned. The quilts' colors in that early exercise are identical to those shown in *Spring in Town*: orange, green, and white on the left-hand quilt; green, white, and red on the one on the right. Other details in *Spring in Town* are similarly charged with private significance—the birdhouse atop the post anchoring the clothesline recalls the one that Wood had fashioned for the home he built Hattie and himself in the Kenwood area of Cedar Rapids in 1917.[61] Builder, decorator, restorer, as well as a limner of house himself, Wood presents them in *Spring in Town* as emblematic of all things good and comforting about small-town American life. The painting offers a consoling, compensatory fantasy for people and things lost or destroyed, as when one of Melanie Klein's patients, in the throes of a terrible bereavement, "found some relief in looking at nicely situated houses in the country, and in wishing to have such a house of her own." Her solace, Klein concluded, "came from [the mourner's] rebuilding her inner world in her phantasy by means of this interest and also getting satisfaction from the knowledge that other people's houses and good objects existed."[62]

Turning to a time before his family's exile from the garden, Wood resurrected Maryville in the glorious *Spring in the Country*, where his father arrives with his team of plow horses, just as he does in his first appearance in "Return from Bohemia" (App., 195). From the stuff of his own biography, Wood assembled a manifest scene of pure goodness, where clouds float

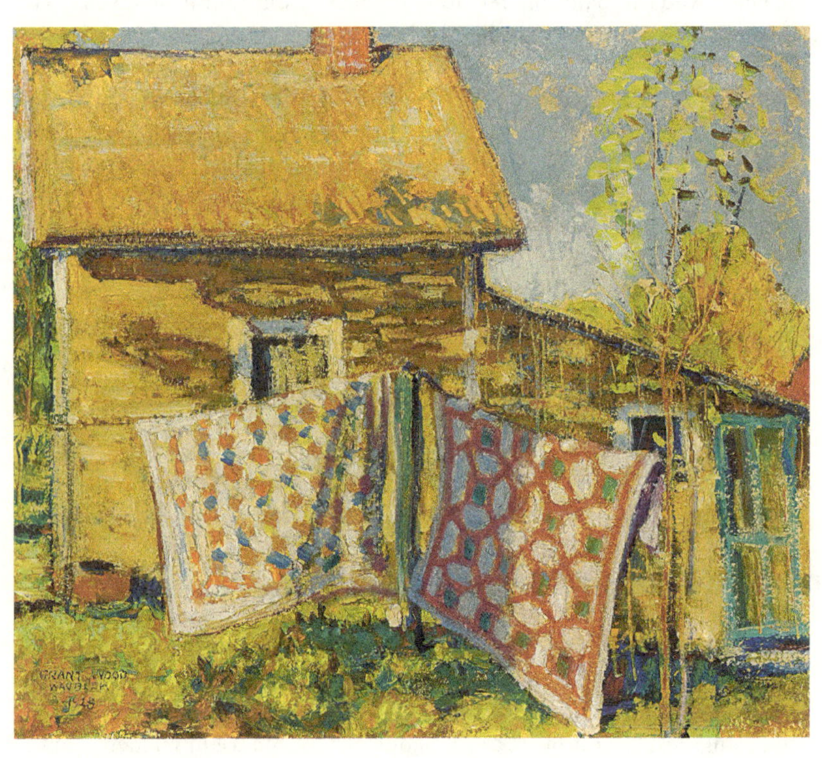

Fig. 4.23. Grant Wood, *Quilts*, 1928.

beneficently above two adjacent farmsteads, the family's own and Grandma Wood's nearby. Undisturbed by siblings in this perfect world, child Wood in his faded blue overalls helps his mother set out cabbage seedlings in neat rows. She shares a wedge of sunlight with a herd of cows grazing in the distance; he is in literal contact with his native soil. *Spring in the Country* responds to the felt need that Wood announced in "Return" when, claiming the ground itself as his heritage, he stated: "I want to tell the story of my father and mother" (App., 194). There is no better description of his artistic enterprise, including the example of *American Gothic*, but now he strips away all irony in envisioning a parental reunion, with his child self inserted at the center. The picture repeats the triadic idyll in "Return," Wood's golden screen memory of Maryville, Hattie, and himself together in the dusky corner of the barn, here brought out into the clear light of day. In *Spring in the Country*, Wood aligns his boyhood self with his mother, reassuringly phallic with her long hoe, the ladle in her bucket, even the stake at her feet. The blossoming apple tree in the middleground evokes a prelapsarian Eden before the child's unwelcome recognition of sexual difference: the heavenly hermaphroditic tree displays a dark vaginal slit at the center of its phallic trunk. "Wounded" in this way, the tree also echoes the sapling in *Parson Weems' Fable*, that damaged cherry tree associated with the oedipal father and his threat of punishment. In *Spring in the Country*, however, this threat is mitigated in an image of paternal disempowerment: the tiny farmer-father with hunched shoulders mirrors the posture of the boy in the foreground—but his arms and legs are cut off by the edge of a hill.

Clustered at the lower right of the composition, pale green blossoms with yellow stamens and red buds remind us of Wood's "unending interest," as he framed it in his autobiography, in native flora, associated with his mother who taught him the names of all the prairie flowers he gathered for her from the fields surrounding their home: Sweet Williams, fireballs, prairie pointers, as well as "Johnny-jump-ups, shooting stars, Black-eyed Susans, jewel weed, milkweed blossoms, Bouncing Betts, gentians, asters, goldenrod," and many others (App., 215). Wood had depicted in the foreground of his *Breaking the Prairie* mural at Iowa State University a veritable herbarium of twenty-four different varieties, all readily identifiable in their characteristic details.[63] Here, in their almost hallucinatory specificity, the blossoms also anchor the vernal country scene firmly in Iowa. They resemble the pink or white flowers of the Iowa crabapple (Malus ioensis), and even more so those of the fragrant wild prairie rose (Rosa pratincola), adopted in 1897 as the Iowa state flower (Fig. 4.24). Tingeing their petals an unnatural green—like those of Oscar Wilde's emblematic carnation—may have been Wood's secret way in *Spring in the Country* of queering Iowa while offering it as a synecdoche for the entire nation. "In making these paintings," he wrote of *Spring in Town* and its prequel, "I had in mind something which I hope to convey to a fairly wide audience in America—

the picture of a country rich in the arts of peace; a homely, lovable nation, infinitely worthy of any sacrifice necessary to its preservation."[64]

To find the lovable ideal he wanted in 1941 to advertise to his countrymen, Wood mined his personal past and the inner world he had constructed of all its introjected elements. Although he would continue to sketch and paint Iowa landscapes during the few months that remained to him, none were so programmatic as these dual apotheoses of springtime in conveying his patriotism, his intense love of a homeland that ultimately represented for him the mother from whom he had issued and in whose arms he had begun to experience his love affair with the world. *Spring in Town* and *Spring in the Country* suggest, respectively, a paradise lost and then regained, an imaginative development enabled by a process of mourning that I believe Wood underwent during the time he worked on these two pictures. He had reached an emotional nadir as a result of the attacks on him at the University of Iowa described in Chapter 3; the painful experiences there reactivated in him past sorrows, including the guilt-inducing loss of his father whose death anniversary informed the genesis of *Spring in Town*. As his feelings of persecution diminished, however, the artist could begin to restore the good objects of his inner world. Klein speaks of how "encountering and overcoming . . . adversity of any kind entails mental work similar to mourning,"[65] and Wood performed that work throughout the summer as he finished *Spring in Town* and embarked on its Proustian counterpart. He accomplished this in the relaxing calm of Clear Lake with Rinard, his most loving and supportive friend, by his side. It was a therapeutic exercise.

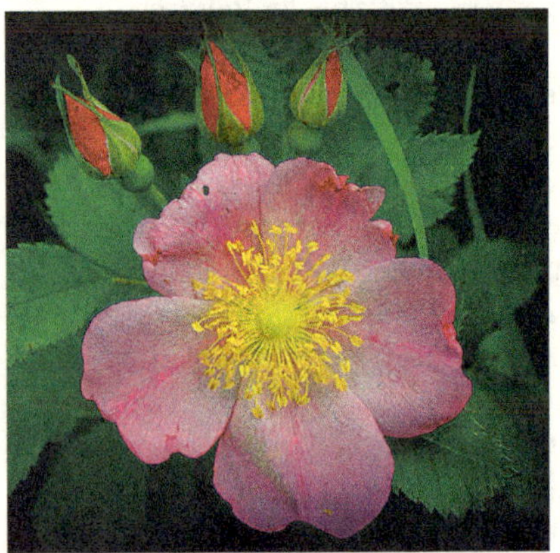

Fig. 4.24. Wild prairie rose (*Rosa pratincola*).

From Klein's perspective, "every advance in the process of mourning results in a deepening in the individual's relation to his inner objects . . . , an increased trust in them and love for them because they proved to be good and helpful after all." In this way, "the love for the lost object wells up and the mourner feels more strongly that life inside and outside will go on after all, and that the loved object[s] can be preserved within."[66] Accompanying his springtime pictures with a public plea for preserving a nation, Wood externalized the preservation project he was conducting in his psychic world. Although life outside did not go on for him much longer, *Spring in the Country* suggests that in his final year, an inner reconciliation was underway.

❖ APPENDIX ❖

"Return from Bohemia"

BACKGROUND NOTE: THE CONUNDRUM OF AUTHORSHIP

In 1935, a would-be author called on Grant Wood as the artist summered with his new wife in Waubeek, Iowa, the home of his friend Jay Sigmund (Fig. A.1). According to Sara Sherman, this "young chap" visiting from New York "had been hired by a publisher to write a book on art, based on Grant's life."[1] Although the details are unclear, at some point the writing project became Wood's own, and Sherman in her memoir claims credit for suggesting the artist's friend and secretary, Park Rinard, as ghostwriter. She would later question the wisdom of her proposal, believing as she did that her husband's intimacy with Rinard helped undermine her marriage. Looking back, probably sometime in the 1950s, Sherman described the genesis of Wood's autobiographical "Return from Bohemia":

> Before we left Waubeek, Malcom Johnston [*sic*], one of the officials of Doubleday Doran wrote me to tell me that he would like very much to have a book on Modern Art based on Grant's experience. Of course, Grant could not write, but I did know a young chap by the name of Park Rinard who was very anxious to give up his job as a bookkeeper and follow through on the course of creative writing which he had had at the University. I went to New York after we were moved [out of 5 Turner Alley] and settled in Iowa City and had a talk with Mr. Johnston, and explained the situation to him. He agreed to have Park do the writing, and advanced $500 to Park so he could give up his job and work with Grant. This arrangement seemed to necessitate my taking Park into our home to live, a circumstance I was later to regret very much. As far as I know the book was never completed, and it is understandable that it was not. My sister, Phoebe, who understood conditions much better than I, had begged me not to marry Grant. Later I realized why.[2]

The official whom Sherman remembered but whose name she misspelled was Malcolm Johnson, a chief editor at Doubleday Doran in the 1930s and 1940s.[3] In the file with the original typescript for "Return from Bohemia" in the Archives of American Art in Washington, D.C., is a small pink slip with a handwritten note that suggests Johnson's assessment of the first installment of the book: "Here are Grant Wood's just 128 pages. You might like to read them for pleasure. I haven't seen better stuff in a long time." This note, signed with a cursive initial J, is addressed to "Mr. Maule," that is, Harry E. Maule, then a senior editor at the publishing house. On the verso of this slip, we have Maule's reply: "Mr. Johnson / Delightful in itself, but I don't quite see how it fits in with a book on the modern school of painting. HEM." That subject would presumably have been addressed in subsequent chapters, Wood intending to discuss the art of Thomas Hart Benton, Charles Burchfield, John Steuart Curry, and Reginald Marsh as well as his own.[4] Perhaps Maule's reaction, however, if it was communicated to Wood and Rinard, threw them for a loop, caused them to reconsider their approach and wonder how to proceed, the disconnect between what Maule expected and what he and Johnson had received contributing to the project's ultimate failure.

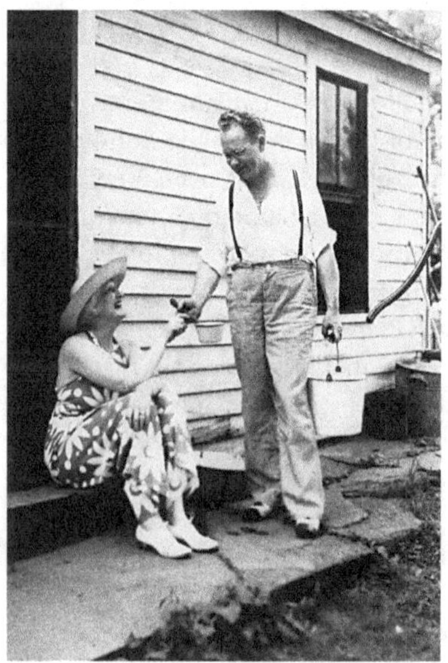

Fig. A.1. Grant Wood and Sara Sherman Wood, Waubeek, Iowa, 1935.

One wonders why Johnson would initially have approached Sherman about the book rather than approaching Wood himself. Did Sherman perhaps overstate her role in these affairs? My personal suspicion is that Sigmund inspired the original plan. Through him, Wood met writer Christopher Morley (1890–1957), whose long-standing connections with Doubleday positioned him well to advocate for the project. Johnson and Morley were on friendly terms. (Together, for example, they were among the founding members in January 1934 of the Baker Street Irregulars, the New York-based society established in the wake of Doubleday's 1930 publication of *The Complete Sherlock Holmes*.) Morley praised Wood's work repeatedly in his regular column, "The Bowling Green," in *The Saturday Review of Literature* and hosted a cocktail party for the artist in New York in 1934. Wood subsequently helped bring the writer to Iowa City to lecture at Frank Luther Mott's Times Club, entertained him royally at the newly founded Society for the Prevention of Cruelty to Speakers, and took him around Cedar Rapids to show off the Veterans Memorial Window and his painting *Young Corn* hanging at Woodrow Wilson High School.[5] An important figure in Wood's social and professional network during this period, Morley may be the missing link in Sherman's account of how "Return from Bohemia" came to be.

Rinard, moreover, seems already to have been in Wood's employ by the time she proposed that he assist Wood with the manuscript. The two men had met in 1933 when Rinard was working as a purchasing agent at Collins Radio Company in Cedar Rapids.[6] Like Wood, he had grown up in Iowa and, though a generation younger, would have had a similar sense of the region and its culture. His collaboration with Wood on "Return from Bohemia" was such that he felt confident enough to submit it with only very minor revisions as his master's thesis at the State University of Iowa in August 1939. Thus, scholars' opinions on the authorship of this text understandably vary. Wanda Corn, who met Rinard personally, states unequivocally that he wrote the biography, in consultation with the artist.[7] R. Tripp Evans treats the document as an autobiography, explaining that "the words may be Rinard's, but the memories and impressions are clearly Wood's."[8] Rinard's daughter, Judith Ellen Rinard, stated to me that "Wood told it to him and he wrote it down."[9] The many factual details peppering the account testify to this, with specific people and places recalled—such as childhood neighbors Abbott, Byerly (misspelled "Byerley" in the text, Appendix, p. 217), and Flynn, whose real names are unchanged, the Cottonwood Country School in Jackson Township, or Strawberry Hill Presbyterian Church in Anamosa, where Wood's paternal grandfather had been a founding trustee.[10]

Thoughtfully inconclusive about the authorship problem, Wood scholar Lea Rosson DeLong offers this nuanced assessment:

> It has been widely assumed that Wood played a small role in actually writing *Return from Bohemia*. However, if the writing style is compared with that found in Wood's letters and other documents (such as the foreword to *Young Sam Clemens*), there are enough similarities to warrant some reconsideration of this position. In addition, correspondence indicates that he was spending a good deal of time on this autobiography and that he did, at least at first, regard the writing of it as his obligation. The exact conditions of his contract with Doubleday Doran are not now known nor are the arrangements made with Rinard. *On the other hand, if it were primarily the work of Wood, the essay would not have been accepted as Rinard's Master's thesis.* It is probably not possible to know how to precisely attribute authorship.[11]

The italics above are mine, emphasizing how scholars understandably place unquestioning faith in the university's endorsement of "Return from Bohemia" as a duly supervised, self-generated student exercise. My own sense, however, is that Rinard's use of the manuscript as his thesis should not diminish for us Wood's primary role in its creation, given the artful dodges in which these men regularly engaged. In January 1936, Wood told a reporter from the *New York Herald Tribune* that "the better part of a year's vacation from painting" had gone into his writing of the book;[12] yet by 1939, it appeared that "Return from Bohemia" would not be completed. It may then have been Wood's idea for his assistant to submit their aborted project to the university's English department—where Wood's friend Mott was on the faculty—as his own original work. Perhaps the artist turned the text over to his young friend in a spirit of support and generosity, just as he made him numerous presents of works of art.[13]

One of these gifts, the humorous self-portrait lithograph *Honorary Degree* (1938, Fig. A.2), hints at their collusion. A tongue-in-cheek commemoration of Wood's hooding at Lawrence College in Appleton, Wisconsin, in 1938, the image shows the otherwise academically uncredentialed artist ceremoniously validated by two cronies, Drs. Carl Seashore and Norman Foerster, as a Doctor of Fine Arts. As he bestowed an impression of the print on his young friend, Wood dedicated it "To Park Rinard (Fellow Academician)." If my intuition is correct, then this congratulatory inscription implies how both of them had successfully gamed the system. Wood was never intimidated by university protocol and could work around it. When, for example, he was hospitalized late in 1941, leaving his master's student Willis Guthrie without a thesis adviser, he asked George Stoddard, Dean of the Graduate College, to "move the papers around" so that Guthrie could graduate without impediment.[14] And Wood did not seem to care much about authorial authenticity as a value in itself, at times allowing his illustrious name to appear on others' work—as writer of the pamphlet *Revolt against the City* (1935), in which Mott had the major hand,[15] or as co-author of Jewell Bothwell Tull's playlet *They That Mourn* (1936), to which Wood contributed no more than an idea casually shared in conversation. Explaining his minimal role in co-authoring the drama to his New York dealer Maynard Walker, the artist wrote: "I'm not surprised though that you are all mixed up again. Anyone would be if he tried to keep track of all the things I get in on one way or another."[16]

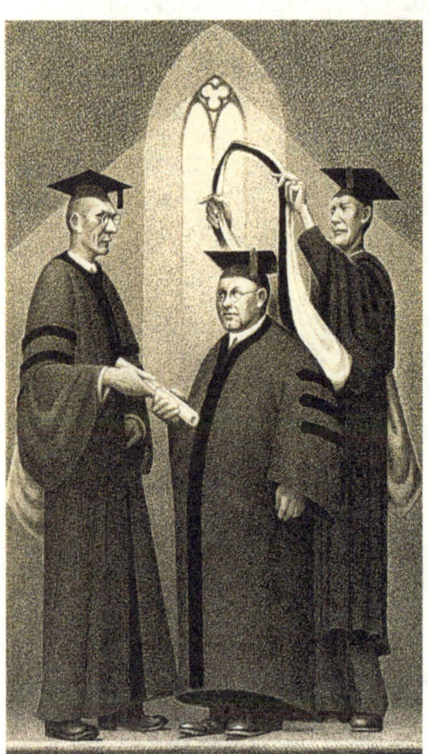

Fig. A.2. Grant Wood, *Honorary Degree*, 1938.

Wood's self-authored published work exemplifies his eloquence and erudition. He thought deeply about painting and writing as creative activities, their similarities and differences, submitting his reflections on the subject in 1935 to the literary journal *American Prefaces*.[17] In an article on "Rural

Influence in Contemporary American Art," published the following year, he celebrated self-reliant artists across the U.S. no longer imitating European tendencies but drawing on their immediate, firsthand experiences, including even rural themes. He offered Benton, Burchfield, Curry, and himself as painters working effectively with native materials, and was cautiously optimistic about the level of taste and appreciation for art among "country people."[18] Also by Wood are the appreciative six-page introduction mentioned above by DeLong to a book about Mark Twain, in which the artist recalled how enchanted he had been as a boy by *Tom Sawyer* and *Huckleberry Finn*, and an article on "Art in the Daily Life of the Child."[19] The latter was based on a talk he gave in 1936, from the perspective of an artist-educator, to the Iowa Conference on Child Development and Parent Education at the University of Iowa. In it, Wood presented an impassioned defense of the child's imaginative life, of the role of art in everyday life, and of the importance of art education in public schools. Importantly, these last two essays have in common with "Return from Bohemia" a focus on childhood experience. Judging from these examples and from his letters, Sherman was wrong to dismiss her husband's writerly capabilities—unless she meant that Wood could not write because he had instead to paint—for he had a perfectly fine way with language.[20] He was a man of ideas capable of communicating them engagingly in verbal *and* visual form.

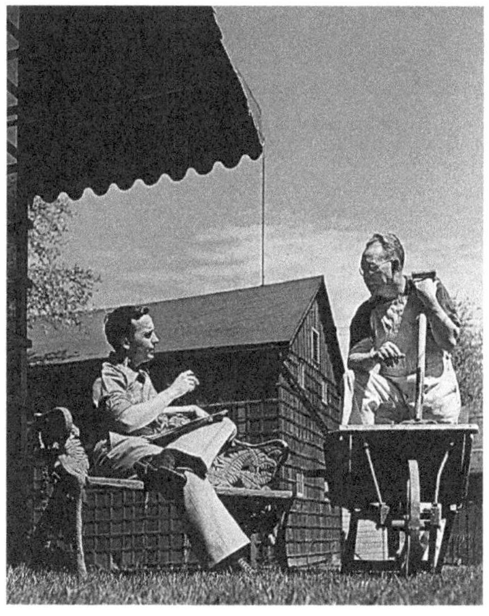
Fig. A.3. Grant Wood dictating a letter to Park Rinard at 1142 East Court Street, Iowa City, late 1930s.

Although Rinard has been hailed as the James Boswell to Wood's Samuel Johnson,[21] this was not the case, for—significantly for my argument—he proved entirely unable to advance Wood's biography on his own after the artist's death in 1942. In trying to assess whether in "Return to Bohemia" he was Wood's typist, amanuensis, interviewer, co-author, or a kind of Gertrude Stein penning an *Autobiography of Alice B. Toklas*, I think it is also crucial to remember that Rinard was only twenty-three at this time, an aspiring English student, while Wood was forty-four, a university professor, worldly, and famous (Fig. A.3). Their friendship would deepen over the next seven years as they worked and traveled together, but in 1935 they were not a team of equals. The familiar model for Wood was that of a studio assistant; he had habitually employed young men as helpers—Edgar Britton, for instance, on the mural decorations at the Eppley Hotels (1926–27), Arnold

Pyle on the Cedar Rapids Veterans' Memorial Window (1928), and later the aforementioned Guthrie as all-around handyman, gardener, and frame builder. Indeed, when Rinard later described his role as Wood's personal secretary, he did so in modest terms, as "a 'schlepper,' a helper, a 'general utility man,'"[22] not as a ghostwriter.

On the occasion of Corn's 1983–84 Wood retrospective, Rinard remembered "the real Grant Wood" for the *Des Moines Sunday Register*, stressing among other things the artist's profoundly emotional attachment to the Iowa landscape. To demonstrate the depth of this love for "the naked earth in rounded, massive contours," Rinard quoted at length from the first few pages of "Return from Bohemia," never mentioning his master's thesis but identifying the euphoric passage as Wood's. At the same time, he could not reasonably disabuse a distinguished academic like Corn of the sacrosanct notion of a solo-authored graduate thesis, with its university imprimatur. Even at that late date, he still spoke of writing a biography of his beloved friend, though the prospective publisher had of course long given up on "Return from Bohemia," donating the 128-page fragment, signed by Wood on its title page, to the Archives of American Art in December 1958. Rinard's name does not appear on that document, which is the one I have transcribed and presented here.

Richly imagistic and engaging, the text provides a flavor of rural American life lived by an impressionable child in Anamosa, Iowa, in the 1890s. From details of that experience, a series of phantasmatic scenes coalesce in the narrative and give rise to an authorial subjectivity that I have treated as Wood's throughout this book. The childish and often dramatic episodes related in "Return from Bohemia" are so vividly described as to possess the haunting effect of screen memories. As such, whether actual or imagined, they open onto a psychic realm of anxieties and desires similarly rehearsed in the many compelling works of visual art discussed in the preceding chapters.

Return from Bohemia: A Painter's Story

GRANT WOOD

PART I
THE GROUND ITSELF

CHAPTER 1
SPEAK TO THE EARTH

In Iowa, the pageantry of growing things is forever before the eye. In early April, as soon as the frost is out of the ground, the farmer seeds his oats. In May, the oatfields are covered with a rich silky green as he turns up the black loam in the adjoining sodfields. He discs and harrows the ground, then plants his corn.

By June, the green shoots of maize have appeared, running in even rows over the rolling countryside, while the winds shimmer in lush waves through the oatfields. Another month of sunshine and rain and the husbandman's old fight with the stubborn children of the prairie—the quack grass, the wild morning glory, and the button-weed, and the corn is knee-high, turning full leaves to the wind. This is the time of the first haying, when the fragrance of clover is in the air.

Late July is harvest time for the oats. Blonde and sun-ripened, they swell the rolling prairie with their abundance. By early August, the grain shocks stand sun-yellow on fields striped green and gold. Soon after comes threshing with the shriek of the machines and the swirling clouds of chaff. The shocks disappear and straw-stacks repeat the shapes of the hills.

Under the blazing suns of August, the cornfields are seas of majestic green, flashing dark, burnished leaves. In another month, the leaves begin to yellow and the stalks bear spidery tassels bone-white against the deep blue of September sky. The approach of the equinox is the signal for the farmer to cut his fodder-corn, and soon the brown pyramids stand evenly spaced on the bare stubble rows. In October, the uncut corn is ready to pick, and over the countryside on frosty mornings can be heard the crack, crack of the hard ears, pitched against the bangboard of the farmer's wagon. After the husking, cattle move noisily among the brittle stalks, feeding on what the huskers have left. And winds charged with the first snows mourn through the desolate fields, rustling the dead leaves and the empty shucks.

Before the winter frost sets in, as his last tillage of the year, the farmer prepares for the next spring with fall plowing.

Such is the drama of the seasons in Iowa, the cycle of the growth of crops. But dominating the pageantry—the golden sweep of oatfields in midsummer, the majesty of tasseled corn in September, the sere remains of the harvest in the bleak months of winter—dominating all this is the infinite solidity and permanence of the ground itself. The naked earth in rounded, massive contours, asserts itself through everything that is laid upon it.

From glacial times the ground has enforced its sovereignty, thrusting away all that would obscure its surface. When first seen by white men, this Midwest prairie was like no other region known to them—a vast, open sea of soil. It was free of the forest and undergrowth common to other American regions, its surface was not roughened by stone and rubble as were the hills of New England. Even the prairie grass was kept in check by great fires that swept each spring and fall from river to river. The deep loam itself was the surface. Rich and illimitable, it awaited the plow.

Three generations of cultivation have brought buildings, trees, fencing, and broad acreages of thriving crops. But all these, by contrast to the land, are but flimsy, transient things. They have not altered the primal character of the region; rather, they have accentuated the structural solidity of the ground and the assertiveness of the raw soil.

How strongly a people can reflect the individuality of the region in which they live. It was thus with the immigrants who came from the east to build upon this prairie. Finding no woodlands or deep valleys to shelter them and help them take root, they had to learn a special intimacy with the soil. They had to adapt themselves to the vast openness of the prairie and the ubiquitous light of an unbroken sky. And they and their children developed a character distinctive from that of other frontier peoples, a nature akin to that land itself. One could see it reflected in their eyes. I saw it in the eyes of my father and mother—a quality bleak, far-away, timeless—the severe but generous vision of the Midwest pioneer.

More than thirty years have passed since I was a boy on an Iowa farm, yet these early scenes and experiences remain clearer than any I have known since. The rhythms of the low hills, the patterns of crops upon them, the mystery of the seasons, and above all, a feeling for the integrity of the ground itself—these are my deep-rooted heritage.

I want to set down here the record of these most vivid years. I want to tell the story of my father and mother. In a sense, the ground is the principal character in the narrative and the lives chronicled but minor figures in its timeless history . . . patterns that come and go while the ground itself remains unchanged.

I

It was mid-day in early June of the year 1898.

I sat on an island of sod beneath an enormous cottonwood tree that split in the middle of the road in front of our farm: a small boy in faded blue overalls—fat, pug-nosed, with a round pinkish face and small blue eyes. Shadows from spruce, catalpa, and cottonwood trees bent over the level farmyard and the patch of road in front of it, making a pool of deep shade.

To my six-year old mind at that particular moment, no problem in heaven or earth existed other than the mysteries of a garter-snake that lay writhing and spitting on the fresh earth of a molehill. I sat cross-legged and watched solemnly and intently, prepared to reach out quickly if the snake began to glide away.

The scene is as clear to me as a passage out of a singularly vivid dream: the brilliant stripes of the garter snake against the black soil, the coolness of the leafy shade, the lazy quiet of the country at noon.

Outside the oasis of the farmyard, the sun was glaring down on the rolling cornfields, baking the soil to dull pink clods between the rows of young corn. The sky was thin blue, flecked with a few pale shreds of cloud. No sound could be heard except the lazy sawing of crickets and an occasional rich bird-note. The countryside was fixed for an intense, breathless moment in the sleeping lull of noon.

Presently I heard the rattle of the harness and father's "Whoa!" as he drove the horses into the farmyard to feed in the shade during the noon meal. I heard my mother calling my older brother, who had been out in the fields with father.

"Frank! Go find Grant. Dinner is almost ready. And fetch a pail of water, please."

Then came two piercing whistles and the broad blurred sound of one calling between cupped hands: "Gra-ant! Dinner's ready."

Leaving the snake reluctantly, I got up and walked along the drive into the farmyard. I picked my way with care to avoid the sharp places in the rutted road. Father was washing at the bench on the back stoop. He seemed very tall and gaunt as he bent over the wash pan. His broad, blue-shirted back was dark with sweat from the morning's work in the fields.

Over by the rain-barrel, Dave Peters, the hired man, was showing my brother Frank some kind of a chain puzzle carved out of wood.

"Hurry up and get washed, son," said father, scrubbing his face dry with a flour-sacking towel.

I stepped into the hot kitchen. It was filled with the aroma of coffee and the yeasty smell of freshly baked bread. Mother was standing before the big wood-range, dishing food out of the steaming kettles: hams, greens, and potatoes boiled in their jackets.

The table was set for six places. Jack, the baby, was already in his high chair.

"Dinner's all ready, son."

"I'll hurry, ma." I drew a pan of cistern water at the sink; then took it outside to the wooden wash bench on the back stoop where I hastily doused my hands, arms, and head, scrubbing my neck and ears vigorously.

By the time I arrived at the table, the others were already seated. Father sat at the head of the table, solemn and quiet. Mother sat at the other end with the baby beside her. Frank, a ten-year-old, round-faced and chunky like me, but darker of complexion, was next to me at one side of the table. Opposite us, the hired man hunched over his place like a great beaky bird. Dishes heaped with steaming food were on the table and the ironstone plate at each place lay bottom up. Before father served, he bowed his head and repeated his usual words of grace:

"Heavenly Father. Bless this, our food, that it may help us in our daily work to do Thy will. We ask it in Jesus' name, amen."

Printed on the backs of the heavy dinner plates was a fascinating trademark, the battle of a lion and a unicorn. When I bowed my head, I could not resist opening my eyes wide enough to peek at this strange spectacle. Mother had tried to explain to me what a unicorn was, but I had been unable to understand. Once I had heard Frank say that if the lion were as hungry as he was, he would make short work of that unicorn.

For several minutes, we ate in silence except for the baby who blubbered to himself and drummed on his plate until mother gently scolded him.

"I see that the brindle cow has broken through the fence again," said father, at last, as he helped himself to more sugar for his coffee. "she's over in Abbott's pasture. I want you to go over after dinner and bring her back, Frank."

Frank was visibly pleased with this important assignment.

"And Dave, as soon as you get a little time, will you fix a yoke for her? This is the third time she's broken fence and I'm tired of it. I saw a forked branch down with the cordwood that you can use."

Dave Peters grunted affirmatively without looking up from his food.

"Pity's sakes," said my mother to the baby. "Will you quit playing with your food and eat something?" She wiped his face and put a spoonful of potato into his mouth.

When the last morsel of apple-pie had disappeared from the plates, the menfolk left the table with a heavy scraping of chairs.

"It will take us until tomorrow noon to finish plowing the corn, Hattie," said father as he went out of the door. "I'll build your wash bench for you tomorrow afternoon."

Mother disappeared into the bedroom to put the baby to bed and I followed the men out the back door.

Outside, the unshaded part of the farmyard was like a griddle under the mid-day sun. The hot dirt burned my bare feet as I hurried across into the tepid shadow of the barn. Frank started down the hill to round up the brindle cow, with Shep, the big tan-and-white collie, bounding along beside him. Father and Dave Peters took the feed bags off the horses and set about hitching the two teams to the plows.

I stood watching Dave Peters harness the dappled horses, fascinated by the way he grumbled to them as he pulled the straps tight. Everything about the hired man was tinged with mystery. His hawk-like face, long reddish beard, and angular figure did not seem to belong to this world. Even the way he walked was queer—striding along, hunched over and scowling at the ground, as if bound on some secret mission. I never saw him laugh or smile, and sometimes he wouldn't say a dozen words in the course of a whole day.

When he finished hitching up the horses, he climbed on the sulky and drove slowly out of the farmyard to the west. I watched him disappear over the hill.

"U-u-uh-a-Roor!" A cock crowed a few feet behind me, rousing me from my daydream.

Remembering a gopher hole I had located that morning in the meadow, south of the farmyard, I started out toward it, dragging my feet in the soft dust along the edge of the barn. I stopped a minute at the hog pen. It was dinner time there. A huge sow was stretched out on her side and six little pigs were sucking at her teats. The other Poland Chinas, barrel-shaped fellows with loose, spotted skins that didn't fit, rooted noisily in the litter.

I went on past the windmill and into the meadow. Sheep were grazing round the place where my gopher hole was. Our sheep were Shropshire Downs—white, with dark faces and ankles. They were stupid creatures that bleated nervously from morning till night. As usual, they went plunging away in great fright when they saw me coming.

I had no more than located the gopher hole when I caught a jolt in the backsides that sent me sprawling on my face in a patch of dirt. The big ram went galloping past; then wheeled and started back belligerently. I scrambled to my feet and ran as fast as I could back into the farmyard.

Tearfully, I limped toward the house. Father had just driven out around the barn into the fields; I was alone with my wounded pride and bruised buttocks.

Deep in self-pity, I was suddenly interrupted by a proud cackling as a fussy hen and her brood of yellow chicks trooped across the farmyard in front of me. I forgot my troubles immediately. Of all the creatures on the farm, I liked the Plymouth Rock chickens the best. Our white turkeys were shy and aloof. And the guinea fowl, so smooth they looked actually metallic, were too cynical to appeal to a child. But the Plymouth Rocks were friendly, human and just the right size. Often when I sat on the back step with a cookie, the chickens came up and shared it with me, clucking appreciatively as they pecked between my fingers.

"Gra-ant, come in now. It's time for your nap."

"Aw, ma, I dwanna take a nap," I whined sleepily as I shuffled across the farmyard, digging my eyes with dirty hands.

II

Supper was over and the men were in the barn doing the evening milking. Mother had finished washing the dishes and was out watering her flowers along the side of the house. I was alone in the kitchen. My feet were washed and I had on my nightgown, ready for bed. A wide shaft of light from the setting sun lay across the scrubbed, softwood floor and illuminated my place of seclusion under the dining table. I was drawing on a cardboard sheet saved from a box of crackers father had bought in Anamosa.

Like most children, I liked to draw and scribble. Mother had found that I would amuse myself for hours at a time if I were given a pencil or crayon and something on which to draw. She encouraged me, thankful for so easy a way to keep me out of mischief.

I felt drowsy and contented. This spot under the dining table was my favorite retreat. The red checked cloth hung with nice arched openings, allowing both privacy and light. Just now, however, the sun was descending and dusk was coming on, as soft and fragrant as woodsmoke. No longer able to see under the table, I moved next to the screen door to continue my drawing. I could hear the deep buzz of the men's voices and the clank of the milk pails out in the barn. Frank was in the woodshed, splitting kindling for the next morning's fire.

Mother came in. "You should be in bed, child," she said to me as she took up the broom to whisk a few last crumbs from the kitchen floor. "All right, ma," I mumbled sleepily, still scribbling on the cardboard.

Dave Peters came in, strode through the house without looking to right or left, and clumped upstairs. I knew that he would read in his room for a while now, muttering to himself as he hunched over his Bible under the lamplight.

I could hear father's heavy steps approaching from the barn. He stopped at the woodshed for a moment to speak to Frank. "Better hurry up with your chores, son. Time to go to bed." Then he came in the door, carrying a pail of foamy milk. He did not see me at first. When he went by, I caught the fragrance of the warm milk, a hay odor with a faintly yeasty tinge reminiscent of newly baked bread.

"Here's the milk, Hattie," he said, setting the pail in the kitchen sink. Mother took it over to the pantry and poured it into a crock. In the morning she would skim the cream off for breakfast.

Father took a lamp from the shelf and fumbled for a few moments in the half-darkness. When he had it lighted, he put it in the center of the kitchen table, adjusting the wick carefully. As the light flickered into the dusky corners of the room, he noticed me.

"Say, young man, don't you know that you should be in bed?"

I got to my feet hurriedly. Father meant business when he gave a command.

"What are you doing?" he asked, not unkindly.

I held out the cardboard to him.

"Hmm," he said, peering solemnly at the rude scrawl. "Why, mother! Look at this. I believe it's a setting hen."

Mother came over from the pantry.

"Mercy's sakes," she said. "Of course it's a hen. A Plymouth Rock too. See the bars?"

"That's a lot of eggs for one hen to lay," said father. Mother laughed. "I wish we could get our hens to lay that many," she said.

I stood over in the corner, a little frightened that I had not gone to bed when I was first told, but pleased at the attention my drawing was receiving.

A sterner note came into father's voice.

"You don't think this will put mischief into the youngster's head, Hattie?"

"No, I don't think so, Maryville. He amuses himself for hours that way. Frank used to like to draw when he was that age too."

She took my hand. "Come, son, let's go to bed."

"That reminds me, Hattie," father called from the kitchen as mother and I were starting upstairs. "Do we still have that book Jenny Abbott brought over for the children?

"The Grimm's Fairy Tales? Yes."

Then I could hear father talking to Frank.

"In the morning after you finish your chores, I want you to take this book back to the Abbotts."

"Oh, gee, pa! We've only started it."

"It was very kind of Mrs. Abbott to loan the book to you. Thank her very much but tell her: *We Quakers can read only true things.*"

III

How strange and wise my father is, I thought, as I watched him guide the plane across the pine board that was to be the top of mother's washbench. Other persons like Frank and Dave Peters could do many things, but the way father did them was the right way—the model by which all other performances were approved or condemned. He sent the plane singing across the wood with long careful strokes and the fragrant pine shavings whispered to the barn floor. If it had been a yoke for a cow, or a fence to be mended, Dave Peters could have done the job. But this was to be a bench for mother; there was no question of having Dave Peters do *this*. Father would build the bench himself and soon it would stand, smooth and firm, in the summer kitchen for mother.

There was a certain mystery and loneliness about father that I sensed even as a child—a strange quality of detachment which no-one would ever be able to understand. Perhaps it revealed itself in the furrows of his long, severe forehead; perhaps in his austere eyes, or in the attitudes to which his lean frame lent itself. Whatever his task might be, *he himself* remained untouched by it. As he leaned over the saw-horse now, sweat dripped from his face and the veins stood out on his arms. He worked hard and expertly and not without pleasure in his task. Yet he was aloof from his work. He did not become entangled in its details and stained by its materials as Dave Peters would have become. This detachment was especially noticeable when he was out in the fields plowing, leaning slightly forward as the horses drew the blade through the loam. One sensed that he understood the soil and was subtly related to it. Yet, there was in him always that stern, haunting loneliness that would never surrender—even to the earth.

This quality stood between Maryville Wood and his family. We loved him and revered him; yet knew that he was not of us.

To me, he was the most dignified and majestic of persons. His low, carefully spoken words were law. I never questioned the infallibility of his judgments or even resented being punished by him. But he was more a god than a father to me.

Only on rare occasions did he reveal the simple affection that was in his heart. The morning I wandered into the north pasture where the bull was grazing had been such an instance. As father scooped me into his arms and carried me to safety, I had seen in his drawn face and his eyes drained thin with fear something very deep and human—an infinite tenderness, powerless to express itself. Later, he had whipped me. But I did not forget what had passed across his face in that one tense moment.

From his Quaker parents, father had inherited a sober dignity, a revulsion against violence, and the love of simplicity and truth that prejudiced him against graven and pictorial representation and fiction. He was better educated than most farmers and looked forward to the day when he would be able to send his children to college. In his living room he kept sets of Macaulay's and Hume's histories of England, well-worn from many evenings spent in reading after the children had gone to bed and his wife was sewing in the lamplight. His library also included a two-volume biography of Abraham Lincoln and a life of William Penn. Some of the neighbors thought him sinfully extravagant with periodical literature since he subscribed not only to the Anamosa *Eureka*, but to *Harpers Magazine* and *Wallace's Farmer* as well. When anyone mentioned this to father, he only smiled quietly and went about his work. Whether he was reading Macaulay, plowing, or doing carpenter work, he kept the same stern aloofness.

Father had finished the top of the bench and was notching one of the solid ends when I noticed a glow of sunlight creeping into the dusky corner of the barn. I looked up and saw mother standing in the doorway, the intense sunshine glancing from the white surface of her apron. The sun made a blurred gold outline around her brown hair. She was smiling and had a tall glass of milk in on hand and two molasses cookies in the other.

"Well, don't sit there like a Stoughten-bottle," she said to me, laughing. "I've brought you some cookies."

Father looked up from his work. "Hello, Hattie, I didn't see you there."

"I came to see how my bench is coming," she said. "Here's a glass of buttermilk for you, Maryville."

While father drank the buttermilk and I munched the cookies, mother admired her bench. "It seems too good to put wash tubs on," she said, feeling its smooth surface.

She sat down beside me on the old sorghum barrel and we watched father work. Her apron smelled clean and crinkly as a cool morning smells in early summer. It was pleasant sitting there in the big, dark barn with her beside me and no sound except the singing of father's plane and the smart rap of his hammer.

If father seemed stern and remote to me, mother, by contrast, was very human and close. Not that she was demonstrative or volatile. One the contrary, she was almost as reserved as father. But her restraint was earth-born; it was penetrable, understandable, and one felt her warm humanness all the more because it was subdued.

I thought she must be the most beautiful lady in all the world. She was small and willowy and people always remarked that she seemed too delicate for farm-work. Mother was very sensitive on this point and quick to refute it by her actions. She did not like to have others wait upon her, and kept her household going with a steady, indomitable efficiency. Her body was a slender wire, tempered far beyond its logical strength by her will, and she had the Yankee knack of getting things done.

In the musty half-light of the barn, I watched her face intent on father's actions. From her expression, one might guess that he could do nothing that was not perfect in her eyes.

Her face had some of the cherubic roundness characteristic of her father's family, the Weavers, although it was more angular and serious than mine. The nose was small, even, and chastely turn-up—a suggestion of the Puritan there. Her chin was firm, indicating Dutch stubbornness underlying her gentle ways. At base, hers was the canny, practical nature of the New Englander, contrasting with father's southern deliberateness.

One of the first flowers I learned to recognize was the Sweet William and it always seemed to me that mother's eyes were that same prairie-sky blue. They had a far-away remembering light in them—not sad, like the unfathomable loneliness that haunted father's, but merry and practical.

Her voice was small and well-modulated and rang with a faintly abstract twang bearing the slightest suggestion of prophecy. Some nights she read to me before I went to sleep—usually a moral tale published in the Sunday School paper. When I was too sleepy to follow the story (which was always the same anyway), I loved to hear the unstrained cadence of her voice, easing me into spacious, leafy sleep.

* * * * * * * *

How natural, how inevitable it seemed that we three should be together in the generous twilight of the great barn. In retrospect, the scene remains as simple and clear as the impression of a rain that fell this morning. I can still smell the fragrance of the pine shavings, hear the whistling of my father's plane, feel the presence of my mother at my side. It was as if we three had been drawn together in that place and moment to create an image that would be remembered in after time.

These early years were composed of many such images. The world we lived in was like a green meadow against which things and people and events stood out with startling clearness. All took place upon that meadow in an ordered flow, attuned in some mystic way to the great central rhythm which determines the growth of crops and the coming and going of the seasons. I accepted our little world as complete and self-explained; I did not ask how it came to be, or what ground lay outside.

Today I look back and wonder . . . what were the paths my parents traveled, and their people before them,—the paths that led to the meadow? What strange convergence of destinies brought together my father and mother, those two so different in background and personality?

The paths fade quickly with the years, yet segments of them may still be seen, stretching back over the hills of the past. There are the lanes, clear for a way; now obscured by foliage, now clear again; they drop below hillsides, emerge like gray tapes from far valleys, and finally lose themselves forever in the distance.

Like all other paths of human life, they varied with countless factors of race and time and place. But always one force was dominant in fixing their direction. This was the power of the soil.

It was not gold or lust for adventure that drew the Weavers from Rhode Island to Connecticut to Up-State New York and thence to Iowa. And the Woods from Pennsylvania to Virginia, then half-way across the continent. And caused the North and South, the Puritan and Quaker, to meet on strange ground and fuse there into a new type—the Midwestern.

The magnet was the soil. In the soil was written the history of these people for generations; they were builders in the earth. Drawn by the power of the ground itself, the parents of my father and mother had come west to build up the new country. To Iowa they had come: beyond the great river, midway between oceans, into the very heart of America.

IV

The story goes that the grandfather of De Volsen Weaver was a revolutionary soldier who entered the war as a lad of twelve or fourteen to take the place of his father, killed in battle. Like Cincinattus, he left his plow to fight for the land he tilled. Or did he? Time can glaze over many indecorums in family history. Perhaps this grandfather of De Volsen Weaver was not a revolutionary patriot—perhaps he was a Tory sympathizer or even a spy for the British.

In either case you may think of him as a hero—a stout loyalist, faithful to the mother country, or a young revolutionary fired with the love of freedom. It depends on the way you look at it.

Whatever fiery blood may have flowed in the veins of this grandfather, there was nothing spectacular about De Volsen Weaver himself. He was a chubby Anglo-Saxon with a brown Henry VIII beard and merry blue eyes, who operated a farm in Upper State New York. He was a good farmer and had a shrewd Yankee head for business. As he went through the routine of plowing, cultivating and harvesting, he dreamed of a new land, broader and more fertile than the rocky acres of his father.

One day, he packed his possessions and turned west. A thousand miles and more he traveled and arrived in central Iowa about the time the "forty-niners" were rushing across the country to the California gold-fields.

"Oh, Susanna," Weaver would hum (as who didn't in those days?), "Don't you cry for me. For I'm off to Californuah with my wash pan on my knee!" But he was satisfied to remain in Iowa where the gold was the friable deep loam of the prairies.

Instead of starting to farm at once, he took a job managing the hotel at Fairview, a village in Jones county, four miles southwest of Anamosa. He stayed in Fairview for several years and was married there to his boyhood sweetheart, Nancy Smith, who had come with her people from Chenango county, New York, to the little town of Barclay, Iowa. In 1858, the year the Lincoln-Douglas debates were being held in the neighboring state of Illinois, the Weavers' first child, Hattie, was born.

By this time, De Volsen Weaver was thoroughly tired of the hotel business. A farmer at heart, with the heritage of an agrarian people in his blood, he wanted to try his fortune at this rich Iowa land. So two years later, he at last gave up the Fairview hotel and moved to a farm a few miles west of town.

That fall, Abraham Lincoln was elected president.

"No telling what will happen now," declared De Volsen Weaver, who was a Democrat from the thick soles of his boots to the crown of his ample-brimmed hat.

Nor was there. In April of the next year, after Fort Sumter had been fired on, the Anamosa *Eureka* changed its masthead to: "We Compromise under No Menace: No Surrender of Principles; No Concessions to Traitors."

De Volsen Weaver did not go to war. He was moderately patriotic, but he had a sick brother, his mother, and his own wife and children to support. So he stayed on the farm, harvested his grain, and gave what money he could spare to the Union cause.

One October day, the sorghum mill on the Weaver farm set fire to the crisp grass in a side pasture, and in a few hours every building on the farm was burned to the ground.

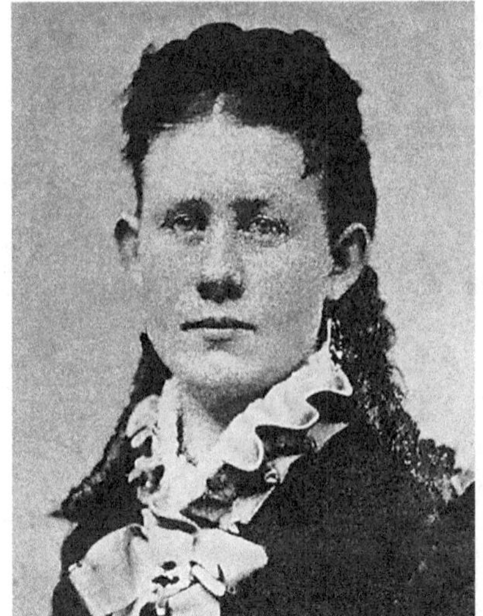

Fig. A.4. Hattie Weaver, c. 1874.

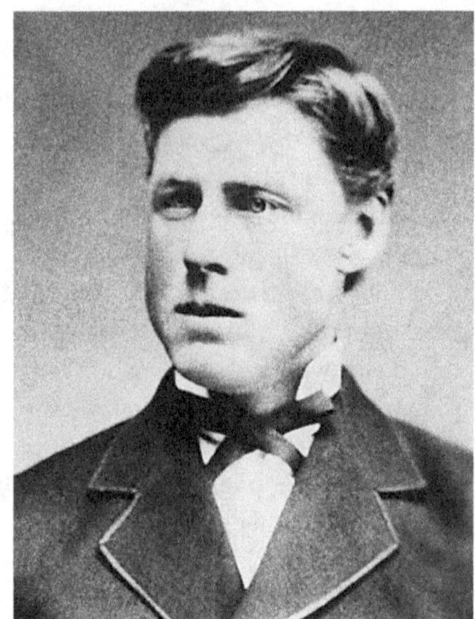

Fig. A.5. Francis Maryville Wood, 1875.

The family moved back to Fairview, taking a house just south of the town limits. Indians, passing through the town, often stopped at the door to beg food and trinkets. Hattie's maiden Aunt Tillie, who lived with the Weavers, was deathly afraid of them. Once when Hattie's father and mother were gone, a stolid-faced brave came to the house. Frantic, Aunt Tillie hid Hattie under an enormous iron soap kettle and took refuge herself under a bed in the loft.

Hattie was seven years old and first being introduced to the mysteries of McGuffey's readers when Lee surrendered to Grant. Three years later when she was a chubby youngster with two pleated braids down her back, the Weavers moved to Anamosa where De Volsen Weaver became deputy sheriff of Jones county. There Hattie grew to womanhood and although she became a slender girl, as fragile as fine glass, she soon showed amazing energy and determination. She taught the Anamosa children their ABC's in the little plain brick schoolhouse on Strawberry Hill and was an untiring, capable mistress of the arts of housekeeping and cooking. She sang to her own accompaniment on the melodean and took her place as a popular belle in the social life of the community. Sundays, she taught Sabbath school at the Strawberry Hill Presbyterian church.

The superintendent of the Sunday School was a tall, bony young farmer with solemn blue eyes and a stern, angular face. His voice was low, and he formed his speech deliberately as if he were measuring each word by some larger vision. His name was Francis Maryville Wood. He lived with his widowed mother on a farm three miles southeast of Anamosa. His people were Quakers, descended from the colony of English Friends who had settled in Pennsylvania with William Penn. Out here in Iowa, however, the family attended the Presbyterian church in Anamosa, since the nearest Quaker meeting house was in Whittier, ten miles away.

Maryville Wood had been a mere boy when his parents, Joseph and Rebecca Wood, had left Winchester, Virginia, to build a new home in the midwest. Thrifty and hard-working, his people had soon rooted themselves in the new soil. By the time Maryville had reached manhood, there had been many fruitful harvests and the family had prospered in a moderate way.

From his early years, Maryville Wood had been lonely and detached, separated from the other members of his family by a strange, unbridgable chasm. Although his first interest was in the things of the soil, he was a student by nature. In his early twenties, he had left the farm for a few years to attend Lennox Collegiate Institute, a tiny denominational college at Hopkinton, Iowa; then had returned home with his learning, satisfied to resume his labor in the fields.

Having reached the maturity of thirty, he still worked long hard hours on his mother's farm and saved what money he could. In the evenings, he occasionally drove into Anamosa and called on the little school-marm who taught his Sunday school. The couple sat stiffly in the carpeted Victorian parlor and talked about the weather and what the crazy railroads were going to do next. Week-nights, she sang sentimental ballads (her favorite was "I'll Take You Home Again Kathleen") and on Sunday nights, the family group gathered around the parlor organ to sing hymns.

One evening when they were alone in that parlor, Maryville asked Hattie if she would be his wife.

He borrowed money and bought the farm next to his mother's place. On it he built a new white frame house, a fine big barn, and renovated the various other outbuildings.

By winter of 1885, the farm was ready to be occupied, and on the sixth day of the following January, the couple were married. The event was faithfully recorded in the Anamosa *Eureka*.

"MARRIED, In Strawberry Hill, January 6th, 1886, by Reverend D. Russell: Francis M. Wood and Miss Hattie D. Weaver.

"This wedding was one of the happiest social events of the season. A very large company—about fifty invited guests—witnessed the ceremony and most heartily congratulated the happy pair upon the auspicious circumstances under which they commence the voyage of matrimonial life. The bridesmaid was Miss Mishler of Maquoketa, a most accomplished young lady. The groomsman was Mr. Frank Weaver, who came home from Ann Arbor, Michigan, where he is attending the university. His cultured and manly bearing added much to the interest of the occasion. The father and mother of the bride seemed very happy in bestowing their daughter upon a young man whom everyone esteems and honors. Nor were the family of the groom less pleased with the alliance. The bride was superbly arrayed in dark green silk, with plush trimmings, and made a most queenly appearance. Of the bridegroom it is not too much to say that he is the manliest of men, and one of the most energetic and prosperous of our young farmers. Through working hard on the farm in his early youth, he has had opportunities of education, which he has well improved, and by a well selected library and the choicest periodical literature, he has kept himself well informed of the progress of events and will take his place among the thoughtful, intelligent and progressive men of our time. A few years ago the writer of this had the joy of receiving both these young people into the church of which he is pastor and where they have remained as worthy members. In their new and beautiful home, the Man who came so often and so lovingly to the home at Bethany, will be a welcome and abiding guest. —D. R."

Among the "auspicious circumstances" under which the young couple commenced the "voyage of matrimonial life" may be listed the weather which dropped to twenty degrees below zero with apparently no disposition to abate. The cold was too bitter and the roads too nearly impassable with towering drifts to permit the bride to move out to the farm. Three weeks later the weather moderated somewhat and Maryville Wood and his young wife loaded their belongings in a lumber wagon and made their way over the rutted, drifted roads to their new home.

* * * * * * * *

To reach the farm, you took the main road south of Anamosa about three miles until you were well beyond the steep Cheshire hill. Then you turned to the east on a narrow side road, following it a half-mile to the crest of a broad, gently sloping rise. There was the farm, a rectangular little colony of buildings, sheltered on three sides by spruce, catalpa and hard maple trees. In all directions the smooth hills rolled away, open to the sky, except for a few lonely trees on the hillsides and the clustered shapes of two or three neighbor farms in the distance.

In the years that followed, the interest and vitality of Hattie and Maryville Wood were closely confined to this patch of Iowa farmland. There were long periods when they were almost as completely shut away from the outside world as if they had been on an island in the ocean. The telephone had not yet come into general use and they had to drive three miles to Anamosa for mail and supplies. Often, when the roads were swollen with snowdrifts or covered with deep mud from the spring thaws, the Cheshire hill became an unconquerable barrier, and it was impossible to get to town in a wagon.

The couple knew poverty as well as loneliness. Maryville Wood had borrowed heavily to buy his farm and was forced to lag behind in his payments. He worked hard in the fields and his wife managed frugally. But always, it seemed, when they were getting a little ahead, some misfortune came—a devastating storm, a drought or a plague of insects—to put them back where they were. Still, they were not unhappy. They survived the lean years and built hopes for the future.

In 1888, when the country was beginning to talk about Benjamin Harrison as a candidate for President, Hattie Wood, on a day as bitterly cold as that on which she had been married, gave birth to a boy whom she called Francis or Frank after his father.

In February, four years later, the Woods were expecting a second child. During the long winter nights of waiting, Maryville Wood sat in the living room, keeping very quiet so as to hear the slightest call of his wife from the adjoining bedroom. He thrust spongy cottonwood logs into the fire until the stove grew rosy and the dry boards of the floor around it crackled.

Would the child who would come into the world in the next few days be boy or girl, he wondered, as he sat in his hickory rocker under the lamplight. He wanted another boy; he had prayed for strong sons to farm this Iowa land. There would be time for girls later.

Always in the back of his thoughts was a lump of cold fear. His frail wife . . . the agony of another childbirth . . .

He picked up the newspaper and scanned it listlessly. He saw an official statement by James G. Blaine, announcing "I am not a candidate for the presidency," and read it several times before it registered in his mind. An account of the Fireman's Grand Ball at Holt's Opera House in Anamosa flickered dully into his consciousness. There was a rustle and a slight moan from the bedroom; he laid the paper aside and tiptoed to the door to see that all was well.

* * * * * * * *

On February 13, a boy was born. What should it be named? One neighbor whose given name was Daniel offered Maryville Wood a handsome pair of rubber boots if he would name the baby after the prophet of the lion's den. Name and boots were declined.

"Let's call him 'Grant,'" said Hattie Wood. A cousin in Waterloo had been thus christened after the great general.

"Grant," repeated Maryville Wood. "Grant Wood has a good firm swing to it. Grant it shall be." For a middle name, they chose De Volsen after the infant's maternal grandfather.

The honor therby [*sic*] conferred on cousin and grandfather was questionable. The new arrival had such squawling [*sic*] fits it seemed that evil spirits must be in him. "Pity's sakes," said Hattie Wood, "I wonder what ails this young one. He's good as pie one day and the next day he's meaner than poison. . . . Can't be under-nourishment. He's so fat I can hardly lift him around."

"It's good to have him chunky," said Maryville Wood philosophically. "He'll make a good farmer."

CHAPTER 2
AND IT SHALL TEACH THEE

[1]

The morning coolness was wilting into the dank heat of an early September day. My brother Frank walked briskly down the road to school, swinging his lunch pail beside him. I padded along behind, like a fat puppy. We kept to the middle, for the road-edge was sharp, while the ruts were full of warm feathery dust, comforting to bare feet.

Green giants of corn loomed on either side of us, nodding their bleached tassels in the sharp sunlight. It was as if we were traveling through a lane hewed out of dense forest.

Every few steps, I stopped to inspect tumble bugs and Daddy Long Legs in the road or to capture a big grasshopper who had hopped out of the roadside weeds to crouch glassy-eyed in a hot rut.

Frank waited at the narrow wooden bridge for me to catch up. The little creek was almost dry now; much of its bed was baked hard, and broken in great cracks. It was choked with thick patches of smartweed and arrow-head lilies.

"There's a snapper," Frank said, pointing to a tiny black periscope sticking out of the murky water below the bridge.

A little farther down the road, I stopped to pick some lavender horsemint out of the thick vegetation along the roadside.

"What are you going to do with that?" scoffed Frank. "Take it to teacher?"

We could hear the first bell ringing.

"Hurry up, slow-poke, or we'll be late to school."

As we neared the school, we saw other children coming along the road, the sun gleaming on their lunch-pails, and heard the shouts of boys and girls playing in the schoolyard.

Cottonwood school, so named for the trees forming a semi-circle in front of it, appeared abruptly out of the cornfields as you came down the road. The simple white frame schoolbuilding and the two outhouses were startling in their bare simplicity against the rich textures of the landscape. Scraggly lilac, snowball and siringa bushes, planted by the children on the preceding Arbor Day, struggled to relieve the bleakness of the yard.

The final bell rang; the children who had been playing Run Sheep Run lined up with the rest of us in front of the door, and we marched in, depositing lunch buckets on the shelves just inside the door.

The teacher was standing at the back of the schoolroom where we came in, taking care that no dogs or cats should be brought in to disturb the peace. As I passed her to go to my desk, I handed her the bouquet of horsemint. She smiled her broad, sunny smile and dimpled prettily.

Miss Linden was a husky farmgirl with reddish hair tied in an efficient knot on the back of her head and a complexion the color of strawberries. She was good-natured, patient, and practical. She was not easily provoked, but when she did become angry, she could bring a twelve-year old boy out of his desk with one powerful jerk.

When we had all taken our places, Miss Linden walked up to her desk that stood on a raised platform in the front of the room. She blew a melancholy blast on her mouth-organ and we all stood to sing the first verse of "America." School had begun.

I liked being in the warm, chalky-smelling room with the buzzing excitement of all the children. It was fun having a desk of my own, and a slate on which I could draw to my heart's content. The novelty of school had not yet worn off. Only two weeks before, mother had said: "I'll have to use the big lard pail now. With two lunches to pack, the little one won't do any more." And I had come with Frank to school for the first time.

I felt very important about it, too—or at least, I should have, had it not been for Lily May. She was an impudent eight-year-old who had an annoying way of turning up her nose and tossing her mouse-colored pigtail to express her disdain. I was too young to be going to school, she sniffed, and although she sat across the aisle from me, she made it a point to pay very little attention to anything I did.

I was the only one in the beginning class at the time and my recitation came first thing in the morning. While the other children, ranging in age from six to fourteen were supposed to study, I went up to the bench in front of Miss Linden's desk to recite. I rattled off my ABC's like a child prodigy, thanks to mother's careful home-training, and returned to my own desk, glowing with the teacher's approval.

For a certain length of time, after this, I contented myself by scribbling on my slate and listening to the other children recite. Then I began to get restless and fidgety. Since I could be counted on to start squirming about this time every morning, it was Miss Linden's custom to send me outside for an extra recess. Sometimes she devised some kind of "busy work" for these periods to keep me out of mischief.

This morning, my bringing her the horsemint gave her an idea for my busy work. Eager to encourage this interest in flowers, she sent me out in the yard to get her a sample of every kind of plant I could find.

I was delighted. Here was my chance to show off before Lily May and to please the teacher in the bargain. So I trotted outside and spent a busy and painstaking two hours breaking off or pulling up generous specimens of every plant I could find.

Just before noon,—tired, dirty, but triumphant, I plodded back into the schoolroom, dragging a great load of branches.

Immediately a great wail went up from all the children.

"Teacher, teacher, look!" shrieked Lily May. "That dirty little stinker has pulled up everything we planted on Arbor Day!"

[11]

One November morning when I awakened, the air had a new tang: a quality fresh and tingling that I had not noticed before. When I looked out of the window, I saw the reason. Tiny grains of snow were swarming down slantwise from the northwest; a cupful of glistening powder had sifted in under the sash. It was the first snowfall of the year.

As Frank and I climbed into our clothes down in front of the sitting room stove, we could hardly contain our excitement. The very feel of the air was enough to make one want to get out and race into the teeth of the wind.

After breakfast, however, our jubilant spirits received a set-back. Mother had heard that one of the Byerly boys had the measles. So before we bundled up for school, she tied little square bags of asafetida gum around our necks.

"Aw gee, ma," said Frank, making an agonized face. "This stuff makes us stink like skunks."

"Hush, child," said mother. "Do you want to get the measles."

Father and Dave Peters were just starting out of the farmyard in the wagon as we came out of the back door.

"Come on, boys," father called to us. "We're going to pick corn over by the northwest fence. We'll give you a ride part way to school." Frank and I needed no second invitation.

Standing up in the box as the wagon creaked and bumped out over the pasture hill, we caught the sting of the new snow in our faces. The sky was a sodden gray out of which at some indefinable point the tiny white granules took form. The windmill, barn, and other familiar objects were wrapped in a ghostly pallor. The snow sifted through the brown grass and whirled in eddies down the gullies.

Frank and I stopped for a few minutes to watch the men pick corn. They filled the air with echoes as they moved through the brittle forest of stalks, snapping off the ears of corn, tearing away the shucks, and tossing the glazed, bare ears into the wagon. Hard at work, father did not see at first that we had stayed to watch. When he did notice, he spoke to us sternly. At that same moment, we heard the frosty tinkle of the school-bell. We climbed hurriedly over the fence and ran top-speed down the road—two young polecats, intoxicated by the first snow of the year.

The first snowfall turned out to be only a slight dusting of powder over the crusty surface of the earth. We did not get a genuine blizzard until mid-January. When it came, however, it was a stem-winder. Two days and a night the skies poured down snow, burying the country waist-deep and cutting off transportation altogether. On the third day the snow stopped, but the mercury fell to thirty below and the gale swooped across the open fields, whipping up swirls of loose snow and beating them into great drifts.

It was terrible getting up that morning. Everything in the kitchen was frozen and the farmyard was drifted so high the men had difficulty getting from the house to the barn to care for the livestock. When father finally did get out to the stock, he found that two pigs had frozen to death during the night.

All day the house moaned in the wind, and screeched as the houseboards contracted in the cold and pulled their nails agonizingly. I was outside for only a few minutes that morning, but long enough to lose heart before the slash of that wind. It cut my face like sand blown out of a shotgun. About noon, a sudden onslaught cracked one of the cherry trees in our yard and toppled it into the snow.

In the morning, Mother and Frank and I were busy getting things thawed out in the house, while the men worked outside as much as they could. But after dinner, we didn't have much to do but to sit inside and listen to the wind howl.

The events of that afternoon are clearly etched in my mind. Frank and I were stretched out on the dining room floor on our stomachs, absorbed in the pages of the Montgomery-Ward mail order catalog. Mother was standing at the window trying to see out through the heavy coating of frost.

"I believe this is the worst blizzard I ever saw," she said absently. "I was afraid all my plants would freeze last night."

Dave Peters sat over at the other side of the room, braiding a bull-whip. Crabbedly, near-sightedly, he hunched over his work, grunting with disgust when a braid went wrong but otherwise keeping his bitter, twisted silence.

A great blast of wind shook the house to its foundation, rattling the window-panes and sucking through the cracks with melancholy organ notes.

"Gosh, listen to the wind howl," said Frank, emerging from the spell of Montgomery-Ward for a moment. "Bet it'll be three weeks before we can go to school again."

"What is Mr. Wood doing outside?" mother asked the hired man as she turned to go back into the kitchen.

"Puttin' wood in the tank heater."

"He seems pretty upset about those pigs getting frozen last night."

"Three [*sic*, corrected in Rinard's version to "Two"] little pigs ain't much to lose in a bad freeze," snarled Peters contemptuously. "One place I worked, they lost thirty hogs and fifty head of cattle. Warn't such a bad blizzard neither."

"Look at that bicycle," said Frank, admiring a shiny "Speed King" pictured in the catalog. "Bet a fellow could ride as fast as a horse can run if he had that."

[Vigorously scratched out but still legible in the original typescript is the following paragraph:] For Frank and me, the Montgomery-Ward catalog held the complete stock of Aladdin's genie, and no tale of mystery or adventure could have engrossed us more completely. In fact, the whole family considered it an event of major importance when father brought the new edition home from Anamosa with the mail. From the catalog, mother got the styles in house-furnishing and clothing, and father got information on harness [*sic*] and new labor-saving devices for the farm. In a few months, the pages of the volume were soft and dog-eared and it was relegated, upon the arrival of its successor, to the outhouse. There, it served two purposes, one of which was to provide reading matter. [End of deleted passage.]

Father came stamping into the kitchen from outside, bundled in his sheepskin coat. A gust of cold wind whistled through the house.

"Think I have the barn banked so that nothing will freeze tonight," he said as he laid off his coat. He picked up the newspaper and sat down in the kitchen to read.

The days were very short now; it was pitch dark by supper time. That evening, after mother had rubbed our chapped hands with mutton tallow, Frank and I went in by the sitting room stove to toast ourselves a while before we went to bed. Mother and father were cleaning lamps out in the kitchen, but Dave Peters was finishing the last braids on his bull-whip in front of the fire.

"Tell us a story, will you Dave?" we coaxed.

The hired man did not answer for a while. He sat there in the lamplight, chewing tobacco glumly. At long intervals, he opened the glowing door of the stove and spat discreetly into the fire.

Frank and I waited breathlessly for his answer. If we could pry him out of his silence, we knew we would be rewarded. The hired man's past was a dark, mysterious bag out of which he could produce any number of blood-curdling stories. Sometimes he told us about his early experiences as a bargeman on the Mississippi; at other times, he talked about the far West where he had been a sheepherder. Most of all, he liked to tell about Indians. He never actually said so, but we knew from his stories that he must have been an Indian fighter at one time himself.

"Did I ever tell you about the Spirit Lake massacre?" he growled, at length, looking up craftily to make sure that mother was busy out in the kitchen.

Open-mouthed, we sat at his feet to listen.

"It was a long time ago . . . I was only a brat about the same size as you . . ." He told the story in a hoarse, ominous whisper, making sudden curving gestures with his talon-like hands. How in the raw morning of March eighth, 1857, *Inkpaduta* or "Scarlet Point," the Sioux, and his warriors, had stolen upon the settlers of the Spirit and Okiboji lakes region in northeastern Iowa, and murdered them family by family. How by the chill sunset of March ninth, the tomahawks of the braves had been red with the blood of all of the 32 settlers, save three women and one 14-year-old girl who were carried away. How, out of these four, only one of the women and the girl had survived to return to their people.

The hired man gouged out the bloody details so vividly that Frank and I were fairly popeyed.

"An' little kids about your size are what the Indians liked best," he concluded. "They'd kill you with a tomahawk and scalp you like this—"

He grabbed me suddenly by the hair and made a motion as if to scalp me. I squealed in terror.

That night in bed, under heaping comforters, with a hot soapstone wrapped in cloths at my feet, I thought about *Inkpaduta*, the murderous Sioux, shivered with fright, and snuggled closer to my brother.

III

In the winter, our world became very small and gray. The snow covered the varied pageantry of the land and the bitter cold drew the family indoors by the fire. At first the change was pleasant. No image lies more warmly in my mind than that of a winter evening when the family was gathered around the sitting room stove. At such times, I think we felt most strongly the clumsy, inarticulate affection that bound us together as a family.

But as the winter dragged on, we began to chafe under the monotony. It was the time of sickness and discomfort. Chores were hard and the constant fight against the cold wore us down. Crowded into the house so much of the time, our dispositions began to grate against one another. I think father suffered most from the confinement. His temperament needed the nourishment of solitude and the soil; he was happiest when he spent his days out in the fields alone. For all of us, February was the dreariest month of the year.

By March, however, the backbone of the winter was broken; the world began to open up and become spacious again. Gradually the ground emerged from under the snow; the meadow-slopes and gullies began to turn green and the highlands olive drab. March was a robust, noisy month with harsh days of snow and sleet, varied by gorgeous, open days when the wind cracked merrily and the clouds bellied like white sheets in a cobalt sky. In the latter part of the month, flocks of wild ducks and geese passed overhead, flying northward in great V's. Every morning we were awakened at dawn by the tremendous booming sounds the wild prairie chickens made in the marshy spots of the region.

At first, April stung with sarcastic, sensual winds, and unexpected flurries of snow sent the early robins hopping about in fat pain. Then came fragrant showers, sunshine, and the full bloom of spring. Grass-flowers and Sweet Williams appeared in the meadows and April melted into warm, luxuriant May.

Everyone was light-hearted these days. The season of the planting was the most joyful time of the year. Dave Peters strutted around like an old game-cock and mother sang as she hung out the washing. Even father seemed unusually buoyant and cheerful as if he had suddenly regained his youth. And is this not the great blessing of the farmer—that in the spring when he plants his seed and visualizes the cycle of growth and harvest, he is born again himself, and through his husbandry, recaptures the spirit of his lost youth?

Before this spring, my physical horizons had been confined to the immediate vicinity of the farmyard. But now I ran footloose over the hills like a young colt. After school in the afternoons, or on Saturdays, I often went out to watch the men work in the fields. Frank was old enough to work with them now; I envied him his increased importance.

I liked to stand on the crest of a hill and watch father or Dave Peters plowing in a field below. They guided the plow parallel to the sides of the rectangular field and progressed concentrically inward, cutting great square patterns with light stubble centers. Gradually the stubble disappeared under the plow until only a sea of black furrows remained. Later when the tender shoots of corn peeked out of the dark earth, I thought the fields looked like black calico comforters tied with green yarn.

I explored the surrounding prairie with unending interest. Often I took a roundabout route home from school and searched the hills southeast of the farm for wildflowers and birds' nests. One such afternoon I remember especially well.

I came in from the fields laden with the souvenirs of my travels—a great bouquet of wildflowers, together with prairie weeds of many varieties. Mother, who had been out looking at her garden, met me at the edge of the farmyard. Her face lighted up when she saw the flowers.

"My, but those are pretty," she said. "Let me get something to put them in." She disappeared into the kitchen door and returned in a few seconds with a large earthenware jar.

The two of us sat down on the back stoop and she set about trimming the bouquet, removing part of the foliage and separating the flowers from the weeds.

"Do you know what these are, son?" she asked, holding out two delicate blossoms, one pink and the other powdery blue.

"Sweet Williams," I said triumphantly.

"Yes. And this?"

She held out a fuzzy scarlet blossom. I didn't know its name.

"That's a fireball," she said. "And this other one of about the same color is a paintbrush. She how the blossom is green to start with and then suddenly turns bright red as if it had been dipped in paint?"

As we sat there, she told me the names of all the flowers I had brought—buttercups, marsh marigolds and cowslips; lavender wild geraniums; prairie pointers; wild strawberries; blue flags; red-orange meadow lilies; and one great plume of Solomon's Seal.

She held out a prairie pointer for me to see its exquisite, spirited form. It was like a tiny wild horse. Its stem was long and slim, arching gracefully at the top and ending in a slender, pointed head.

As she added the flowers and leaves, the bouquet became like a patch of green foliage on which a vari-colored rain was falling. The cowslips and marigolds made great blobs of waxy yellow, while the more delicate blossoms sprinkled the foliage with tiny drops of white and pink and blue.

She made me recite after her the flowers that had bloomed earlier in the spring and those that would come in summer and early fall. The names ran through my mind like music . . . Johnny-jump-ups, shooting stars, Black-eyed Susans, jewel weed, milkweed blossoms, Bouncing Betts, gentians, asters, golden rod . . .

Mother spoke these names fondly, for to her, each flower was a personality, frail, exquisite, almost human. It was inevitable that I, sitting there beside her and observing the great love she had for everything that grew, should share some of this feeling—for her sake, if not for the sake of the flowers themselves. Later on, she was greatly pleased when I drew pictures of many of these flowers with a set of colored crayons father brought me from Anamosa.

Our session with the flowers was interrupted by Frank who came running in from the fields east of the farmyard.

"I know where there's a meadow lark's nest with three baby birds in it," he said.

"Show it to me," I cried, jumping up eagerly.

"Don't stay long, boys," mother called after us as we scampered away. "Remember, Frank, it's almost time for you to start your chores."

We found the nest, hidden in the edge of an oatfield. While we inspected the three tiny birds, the mother lark put up a great clatter a short distance away, trying to lure us away from the nest. But we didn't harm her babies. Instead, we put up a stake in front of the nest so that the men wouldn't destroy it when they cut the oats.

My education concerning the birds of the region was furthered greatly by the Arm and Hammer baking soda company who ran a series of cards in color illustrating American birds. The neighbors were kind enough to save their soda box inserts for me and in the course of time I had a large collection. I knew by sight the common prairie birds: robins, meadowlarks, bluejays, Baltimore orioles, cardinals, bobolinks, crows, blackbirds, song-sparrows, cowbirds and the others.

Although Frank was chiefly interested in mechanical things, he did share my enthusiasm for birds. It was he who discovered that what we called the rain crow, a bird which made the first announcement of coming rainstorms by a queer, throbbing noise like the sound of rocks being rubbed together beneath water, was formally known as a "black-billed cuckoo."

We watched the dramas of the birds as they built their homes, raised their young, and struggled for existence against the elements and larger predatory birds. With partisan excitement, we saw tiny kingbirds drive large crows and owls from the vicinity of their nests. We marveled to see a group of cowbirds light on one of the family cows and exterminate the flies and ticks on the premises. The lack of maternal instinct in the female cowbirds who laid their eggs in other birds' nests utterly mystified us. And we were shocked at the tragedies of smaller birds impaled on thorns and barbed wire by the butcher birds.

When we returned to the farmyard from out trip to see the baby larks, the sun was blazing forth in the west, lighting up long, salmon-colored clouds.

Father and Dave Peters had just come in from the fields where they had been giving the corn its first cultivation of the year. Shep, the big collie[,] was chewing a bone under the cherry trees.

"Here, Shep," called Frank. "Let's go get the cows."

IV

"I see by the *Eureka*," said father as he dished the supper food, "that they had a big cyclone down in the southern part of the state. A real twister. Nobody killed, but it took the roofs off houses and barns and killed some livestock."

"The Lord giveth and the Lord taketh away," said Dave Peters sonorously.

"Goodness," said mother, shuddering. "I'm glad we have a storm cellar."

Dave Peters snorted. "People nowadays don't know nothing about cyclones," he growled, without looking up from his plate. "Back in 1860, when I was kid, a cyclone blowed the whole town of Comanche acrost the river into Illinois."

"Cyclone!" cried Baby Jack, drumming with his spoon on the shelf of his high-chair.

"I guess they did have some awful storms in the old days," father said, "but the ones they have nowadays are bad enough for me. We want to be especially on the lookout for them the next few weeks.

"Do you boys know how to tell when a cyclone is coming?" he asked Frank and me.

"A funnel-shaped cloud," said Frank.

"That's right. Now I want you to always keep an eye out for a cloud like that. It doesn't take long for a twister to come once it's started."

All this talk about cyclones ran wild in my imagination. Several nights before, mother had read Frank and me *The Midnight Ride of Paul Revere*. The poem had made quite an impression on me at the time and still remained fresh in my mind. Slowly and unconsciously now, my fancy began to recreate the story to a new pattern. In this version, I was Paul Revere; the lantern in the Old North Church was a funnel-shaped cloud; and the approaching disaster was a dreaded "cyclone." I saw myself warning the countryside in the nick of time and being handsomely praised when the storm was over and everyone had been saved.

Next morning, I was pleasantly day-dreaming about all this as I lay on my back in the shady part of the schoolyard, enjoying my customary special recess from school. This time, the teacher had been unable to think of any "busy work" for me to do. So I reclined in the shade lazily and thought of my imaginary acts of heroism. Through the branches of a cottonwood tree, I could see the radiant sky, clear blue except for a few white flakes of cloud, shaped like the utensil mother used when pouring vinegar into a jug. Here was the funnel-shaped cloud against which I had been warned!

Into the schoolhouse I ran, yelling "Teacher! Teacher! There's a cyclone coming!"

The younger children began to cry and scream. I caught a glimpse of Miss Linden's broad face suddenly transfigured by fear.

She took charge of the situation admirably.

"Be quiet, children," she commanded. "We'll run to Byerleys [*sic*] and get into their cyclone cellar."

Out of the schoolhouse rushed the terrified children and down the road towards the Byerley [*sic*] farm. So great was the excitement and haste that the group was half-way to the farmer's house before Miss Linden got control of herself enough to realize that it was a bright, shiny day with no threatening clouds in sight.

"Stop," she cried to her hysterical flock. "There's no cyclone coming. The sky is as clear as it can be. Turn around and come back."

In the meantime, my little cloud had either melted away or taken another shape. I began to feel uneasy. I did not like the grim look that had set upon the teacher's face. After she had herded the children back into the schoolhouse and quieted them as best she could, she took me firmly by the nape of the neck and dragged me around behind the schoolhouse.

She was a strong woman and she didn't stop spanking me until she was exhausted. I bawled and screamed my innocence but my cries were drowned in the silence of the prairie.

V

I was wrenched out of warm sleep into chaos. A light flashed into my face. Half-conscious, I opened my eyes to see father standing over the bed, in his nightshirt, holding a kerosene lamp. A strong wind was blowing across the room making the yellow flame of the lamp sputter low until it almost went out.

"Get up, sons. Hurry!" he said. "Bring your clothes. Don't wait to put them on."

A shattering crash of thunder shocked me wide awake. The air was chill and ominous with storm-feeling. Father strode across the room and slammed the window shut. My brother slipped out of bed and I did likewise. As I snatched up my clothes, lightning flashed and I saw the cherry tree outside the window outlined very clearly against the dark sky. Then came another great sprawling volley of thunder. I could feel the house sway in the quickening torrent of the wind.

Father got the window closed and hurried downstairs, guarding the flickering lamp as he went. Frank and I stumbled along behind him. I could hear the baby crying. In the kitchen, mother, with a wrapper thrown over her nightgown and her hair in braids down her back, was hurriedly stuffing food into a basket. The baby was on the floor bawling lustily. Dave Peters in a long striped nightshirt was throwing open the trap door to the cellar.

"That's enough food, Hattie," shouted father over the roar of the storm. ["]Come on now."

The hired man, with his Bible in one hand and a lamp in the other, descended into the dark cellar first. Frank and I followed him; then came mother with the baby in her arms. Father came last, bringing the basket of food and a bundle of clothing hastily gathered up.

As we went down the steps, the damp chill struck us like the icy water of a well. The lamp-light searched out eerie shapes in the dark corners. I was glad that Dave Peters was in front of me. A musty, earthy smell hung in the still air, mingled with the sour stench of last season's cabbages. Dave Peters stopped a moment to see that everyone was safely down. Then cautiously he led the way on through the darkness.

Instead of a special cyclone cave, father had built an enclosure in the main cellar with a double roof of heavy planks, supported by tree trunks. Now we all crowded into this compartment, feeling our way around by the pale, sickly glow of the kerosene lamp. Father found a barrel for mother to sit on and the rest of us huddled about her wretchedly.

"What time is it, Maryville?" mother whispered, her teeth chattering with the cold.

"About half-past twelve," said father. "Here, Hattie, put this blanket around you."

Mother took the blanket and wrapped it around the baby who was still whimpering in her arms.

The fury of the storm was muffled down here but deeper and more ominous. Pale blue flashes of lightning went flickering through the darkness. Familiar objects like the hams hanging from a rafter and the barrels in the corner were transformed into strange, menacing shapes in the ghostly light.

Sick with exhaustion, shuddering from the fluid cold, we crouched in the darkness and wondered miserably what fate the storm would bring us. Frank, who had not said a word since we had been roused out of bed, now whispered to me: "Gee, I'll be this is a real cyclone. Are you scared?" "N-no," I chattered.

"Listen to that thunder," said mother, "I'm glad we have this place to come to."

"You should not be afraid," said Dave Peters, peering at her by the lampglow. "The Lord will protect us. I have no fear of this storm."

"Well, I must say," said mother drily, "You did get downstairs in a hurry just the same."

It began to rain heavily now; we could hear the angry pattering of the drops against the cellar windows.

"Pa, is this a real cyclone?" asked Frank.

"No, I guess it's turning out to be just a bad thunderstorm. We'd better stay down here a while though. It's still lightening [*sic*] pretty bad."

"I seen thirty head of cattle killed once by lightenin' [*sic*] that struck a wire fence," said Dave Peters, almost cheerfully.

"Let's pray that it doesn't hail," father said. At his very words, there was a sharp rap at a cellar window, followed by a fierce sustained tapping that threatened to break the glass.

After a long while the hail stopped and the storm settled down to a steady rain. We dragged ourselves wearily upstairs. The rain was drumming monotonously on the roof when I climbed into bed and fell instantly asleep.

Next morning, everyone was up at the usual time. The sky was clear blue and the sun was shining brightly as if there had never been a storm. But when I stepped out into the farmyard, the evidence was everywhere to be seen.

Branches were broken off the trees and turned so you could see the silvery underside of the leaves. The new little cabbage plants in the garden were pounded into the mud. Deep grass along the fences was all blown in one direction and looked as if it had been combed. Under the cherry tree I found three broken robin's eggs that had been blown out of a nest. Water was standing in the hollow places in the farmyard and the horse-tank was running over. Chickens, ruffling their dam feathers in the sunlight, came out of the chicken-house and walked through the wet grass with tall steps.

Father came around the edge of the barn with Dave Peters.

"Just had a look at the corn over east," I heard him tell the hired man. "It's all in shreds too."

He stooped a moment to pick up a big cottonwood branch.

"Well, anyway," he said, "the windmill is still standing."

VI

In deep summer, the country dozed in the stifling heat. The sky was a concave blue mirror, diffusing hard sunlight over the treeless fields and the air was choked with the musty fragrance of grain and weed and drying grass. The landscape became a glory of patch-work color; the bleached yellow of the small grain contrasting with the deep-forest green of the corn and the lighter greens of pasture and meadow.

Each field was separated from the others by sharp, geometric lines. Yet, the whole landscape was unified by the underlying solidity of the land and by the unceasing repetition of corn and oats and clover in the patchwork effect. And the gentle topographical roll gave to all the country a deep-seated sense of movement like the sea, movement that was repeated on the surface when the wind rippled through the cornfields and the banks of ripening grain.

A field of half-grown corn, the corrugations of each leaf throwing reflections from the blue sky, is a sight that cannot be described. About July first, the men "laid the corn by" or discontinued its cultivation, and in the dry heat of July and August, it shot up like Jack's beanstalk. On hot summer nights, I could actually hear it grow—making a slight popping sound of the joints.

Summer was a wonderful time for farm boys. Free from the cares of school, we went out with the men in the fields, roamed the prairie or played in the farmyard.

From morning till night there was always something exciting to do. Frank had a good many chores these days, but my duties about the farm were still light. My principal task was to look after my younger brother, Jack, who was big enough now to rove about the place by himself. If left alone, he had a habit of wandering into some out of the way place and falling asleep. When he was missed, all work on the farm had to be stopped until he could be located. After a frantic search, we were sure to find him asleep in some unpredictable place—in an old, abandoned buggy; out along the fence-row; or even in the outhouse.

Most of my time, however, I had to myself, and I divided it between the farm itself and the surrounding prairie. I spent long happy hours tagging about after the men as they worked in the fields, and doing little odd jobs to help them. This was most fun during haying season, and many pleasant images connected with that summer's haying remain in my mind. One is especially vivid.

It was a hot July morning and I was standing out in the hay field southwest of the farm watching Dave Peters pitch the great, sweet-smelling forkloads onto the rack. He did not like this work and grumbled bitterly all the while.

"Why don't you like to load hay, Dave?" I asked him.

"Well, if ye must know," he said peevishly, "*It takes too much pitch.*"

When the hay was loaded high up on the rack, the hired man got up on the seat and picked up the reins. Wasn't he going to take me along? Tears of disappointment came to my eyes.

Impatiently, he scowled at me. "Well, I suppose you'd like to ride in on the hay!" Would I! He boosted me to the top of the towering load.

Alexander, Caesar, Napoleon: you all had your great moments, but you never tasted the supreme triumph; you were never a farm boy, riding in from the fields on a bulging rack of new-mown hay.

* * * * * * * *

June was marred by one major tragedy. One day, Shep, the big collie, disappeared from the farm. Father searched the vicinity for him and put notices in the Anamosa *Eureka*, but we never saw the old dog or heard of him again.

Several weeks later, when the family grief had somewhat healed, father returned from a trip to Anamosa one evening with a mysterious looking gunny-sack.

"I brought you something," he said to me, as he dismounted from the lumber wagon. He took the sack out of the wagon and set it down on the ground at my feet. Jumpy with curiosity, I untied the top and very carefully emptied the contents of the sack onto a patch of sod. Out tumbled a soft, fuzzy, tan-and-white puppy, looking even more surprised than I was.

There was no argument over what to name the new arrival. Every farm in the vicinity had at least one pet named after the hero of Manilla Bay. By tacit, unanimous consent of the family our new collie pup became known as "Dewey."

Shep, although he had always been a good friend of mine, had really been Frank's dog. But Dewey was mine from the first. I supervised his puppyhood like a jealous mother, and when he was big enough to run in the fields, he accompanied me on my long jaunts over the countryside.

Another new personality was added to the farm that summer when father bought a horse he had been needing for some time. The new horse was a small, black fellow with white markings on his face. He was uncommonly well-behaved and served both before the plow and as a riding horse. "Pat," as we named him, soon became a favorite of the entire family.

* * * * * * * *

Father buried my overalls out beyond the cowshed.

"You'll know a skunk next time you see one, won't you, son?"

I would, indeed. My education in the wild life of the prairie was progressing.

There were few wolves and foxes in the region, but minks, weasels, and skunks were plentiful. I despised these animals, for my pets, the Plymouth Rocks, were never safe from their attacks. The minks and weasels seemed especially vicious; they killed the chickens and sucked their blood, but did not eat them.

The largest animals of the prairie with which I was familiar, and the most bothersome to the farmers, were the woodchucks. They made pests of themselves by throwing up great mounds of earth when tunneling their holes in fields or pastures. The farmers of the region did everything they could to exterminate them, but the chucks were far too cunning to be easily trapped or shot.

To us, they were the arch-villains of the prairie—the most revolting and insolent of animals. They were fat, oily rascals of a brindle color, with long yellow front teeth and fleshy tails. Nothing could be so exasperating as to see one sticking out of his burrow, motionless as a stump, making a derisive whistling noise through his hideous teeth. At the first sign of danger, he would uncannily rise up, turn, and disappear into the ground as if the whole process were done on mechanical springs.

It was just a year after the United States fought her war with Spain that my brother and I delivered our ultimatum to the woodchucks of Jones county.

On an afternoon when a warm summer rain was pattering on the roof, we sat in the summer kitchen and held a council of war. Frank had heard that gunpowder was made from potash, sulphur and charcoal, and the plan he proposed to the general staff was that we manufacture a private stock for the destruction of woodchucks.

The general staff clapped his hands and squealed with delight. I saw visions of our producing the great explosions that would send the woodchucks hurtling out of their burrows into the air.

When the rain stopped, we crept into the kitchen to get the ingredients. In the kitchen cupboard were crystals of chlorate of potash, kept to make gargles for sore throat in the winter time, and a bottle of yellow sulphur that was mixed with molasses for dosing in the spring. I got these bottles without arousing mother's attention, and in the meantime, Frank obtained a quantity of charcoal from the stove and some matches.

Fully equipped, the artillery withdrew behind the bar for field practice. Trembling with fear and excitement, we powdered the charcoal finely on a smooth stone and mixed it with the sulphur and potash crystals. Frank threw a match into the mixture.

Phoo—it went! A mild, fizzing, but unmistakable explosion. Our exultation was complete.

For several days after that, our favorite diversion was to lie near the burrow of the enemy, attempting to "bomb" him from the earth. The process was highly satisfactory in our eyes. As a matter of military record, however, it is doubtful if the puny explosions ever proved more than a faint annoyance to the wily chucks.

* * * * * * * *

During the summer, father made frequent trips away from the farm—into Anamosa or over to the grist mill on Buffalo Creek. Occasionally he took me with him and I developed such a passion for travel that one day when he chose to leave me at home, I trudged along behind the lumber wagon anyway. Some distance down the road, discovering that I was in pursuit, he turned around grimly and took me back home. There he administered a "tanning" with a razor strop that made my cheeks glow. But even this was not enough to curb my stubborn travel-lust. A few days later, I duplicated my performance, and this time he put me down in the dark cellar to repent my ways. For a while, I contented myself down there scribbling on the stone walls, inspecting the shelves of preserves and jellies, and sticking my finger down in the molasses barrel to sample the sugary syrup. But soon the novelty of this enforced cave-dwelling wore off. Thereafter, I waited for father's consent before going with him on his trips away from the farm.

Saturday afternoons in good weather, the entire family went in to Anamosa to take in produce and buy supplies. This was an event of great excitement to my brothers and me. As we breasted the final hill before coming into Anamosa, Frank always cried with a perennial enthusiasm of discovery: "I smell town!"

Anamosa, an ordinary midwestern village of 2,000 inhabitants, seemed to us a great metropolis. We admired its elegant false fronts, especially those of Holt's Opera House, the Niles Hotel, and (Lord forgive us) the gilded saloons. We were sure that no sight could be so impressive as the main street of Anamosa on Saturday night when it was lit up with gas lights and crowded with wagons and buggies.

In the lull between haying and harvesting, after the corn was laid by, we made a couple of Sunday excursions over into the Wapsipinicon valley near Stone City. This was a magnificent region of towering tree-dotted hills,

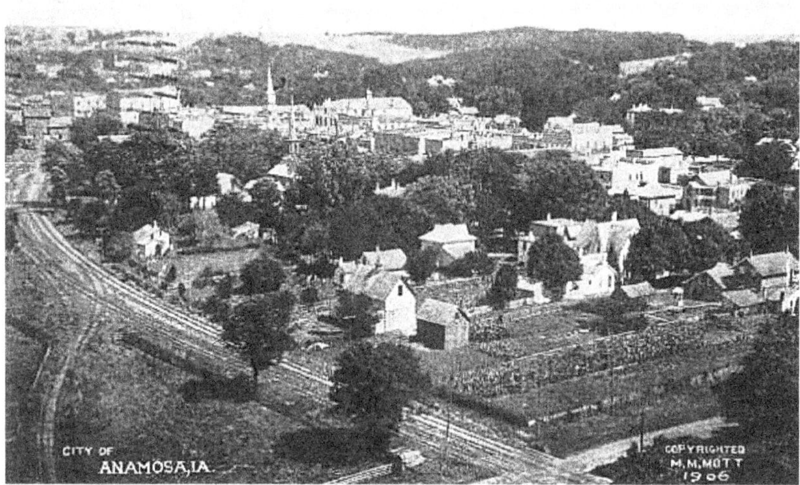

Fig. A.6. Anamosa, Iowa, 1906.

breaking off into sheer limestone cliffs. The heavy woods along the river seemed to us fabulously rich treasure troves after the cool sparseness of the prairie. In this canopied wonderland, ferns grew higher than our heads, velvety moss-beds lay at the trunks of trees, columbine grew profusely, and yellow ladyslippers peered out of the leaf-mould. The river also fascinated us. Along its edge, Frank and I picked up petrified snails and clamshells—precious souvenirs we would save to gloat over on winter nights when snowbound on the lonely farm.

After such a trip, I was content to stay close to the farm for several weeks. I felt like Marco Polo home from his travels. In my own private world, Anamosa was as important as Europe was to Columbus, and the Wapsie valley, a half dozen miles from our farm, had all the glamor that the Orient had for Magellan and Vespucci.

There was only one haunting reminder of a great world outside, a fabulous world that exi[s]ted only in legend, geography books, and Dave Peters' strange stories. To the north of the farm and out of sight over the hills, ran the main line of the Milwaukee. At sunset on a clear summer evening, I could see a feather of smoke balanced on the horizon, and if the wind was right, could hear the weird, mournful whistle of the locomotive, wailing across the fields.

VII

After the fourth of July, all the family's thought and conversation pointed to the banner event of the farm year—threshing.

Threshing, in our part of the country, as in most rural districts, was done as a neighborhood affair in threshing "rings." A farmer in the vicinity a bit more adventurous than the others—it was Slim O'Donnell in our region—owned the threshing equipment. Each summer, in the latter part of July, he assembled a crew to handle the machinery and started out on a threshing run that included all the farms for a dozen miles around.

When the machine stopped at a farm, all the men in the neighborhood convened to help that particular farmer with his threshing. In the meantime, the women of the household prepared a mighty dinner for the threshers and the young belles of the neighborhood came in to help serve it. For young and old, threshing was the most important social event of the year, as well as the climax of the season's work.

By the middle of July, our oats were ripening into a gold wave and we were assured of an abundant yield. I knew that in a few days, father and Dave Peters would harvest the grain, cutting it down to a close stubble and arraying the low hills with the tawny sheaves. A week or two later, the big machine would arrive and all the farmers of the neighborhood would congregate at our farm.

Then, as luck would have it, an accident happened that wrecked all my plans. On afternoon when I was playing behind the barn, I ran a rusty nail into my foot. Infection set in and I was sent to bed with a fever. During all the reminder of July and a week of August, I was laid up, flat on my back. To my bitter disappointment, I missed all of the harvesting and threshing—the most exciting time of the farm year.

* * * * * * * * *

When I was finally able to walk again, it seemed so good to get out in the open that I spent more time than ever in the fields south of the farm. With only Dewey for company, I limped about happily, looking for snakes or ground-squirrels, or just lying on the side of a hill, daydreaming.

I think it was at this time I first began to experience a feeling that was strong in me ever after: namely, that these low hills were *haunted*—haunted by ghostly herds and by the tribes of a phantom race.

The events of one afternoon had a great deal to do with shaping this illusion in my mind.

We had just finished dinner and I was standing by the back stoop when Dave Peters came out of the kitchen door. As he passed, he slipped a small, hard object into my hand.

"What is it, Dave?" I called after him. He did not answer, but strode on toward the barn with his peculiar, stumbling gait, scowling at the ground.

I inspected the object he had given me. It was a flat, pointed stone, scarred with innumerable tiny planes. I was puzzling over it when father came out of the barn, leading the black horse, Pat.

"Look, pa," I cried, running up to him. "Look at the rock Dave Peters gave me!" Father took it and examined it gravely.

"That's not a rock, son. That's an Indian arrowhead and a fine one too. Dave must have picked it up in the field this morning."

The word "Indian" gave me a delicious, creepy feeling.

"What's an arrowhead?" I asked.

Patiently, he explained how the flint head was fastened to the shaft of the arrow and then shot with the bow.

"Did they kill buffaloes with them?"

"Why yes, they did. What do you know about buffalo, son? Did your teacher tell you about them at school?"

"Yes," I replied excitedly, "and Dave Peters told us about them, too."

Father stood stroking his chin for a moment.

"I'm going over to the east pasture to look at some fence," he said. "You come along with me and I'll show you something."

He got on Pat and lifted me up in front of him. We rode slowly out around the windmill and across the pasture over towards the north fence. We stopped in the northeast corner of the pasture beside a circular depression that looked like the imprint of a great dishpan in the green pasture. It was 50 or 60 feet across, flat, hard-packed and bare except for a few scraggly tufts of grass.

"This place," father said, "used to be a buffalo wallow. See how hard it's packed down? The herds used to stand in a circle here with their heads in. When a buffalo swished his tail, it shooed flies not only from his own back but from the flanks of his neighbors on both sides. They all stamped their feet and switched their tails to keep off the flies. That's why this place is packed down so hard."

I was profoundly impressed. I already had an exaggerated image of the buffalo in my mind, gained from some terrifying pictures in a book at school, and particularly from the buffalo robes father brought out in cold weather when the family drove to town in lumber wagon or sleigh. These were great coarse hides, unlined and untrimmed, with legs, neck and part of the tail left. Their rank, savage smell was enough to summon up all the terrors of primitive beasts. I remember that the horses used to snort with fear when we piled the robes into the wagon.

The thought of having a herd of these shaggy monsters in our west pasture was genuinely alarming.

"No telling how many hundreds of years they came," father went on. "They stamped this place down so hard the plow won't break it. If I plant this field to corn as I plan to next year, I'll have to blast this buffalo wallow out with dynamite."

As we rode back to the farmyard in silence, I felt a queer, unearthly sensation, the kind of feeling one might have if he suddenly discovered that the place in which he had been carelessly walking was a graveyard.

The fields were never empty for me after that. In my imagination, the great herds of bison still ruled the prairie, and over the low hills sped the brown feet of the restless tribes: the Sioux, the Ioways, the Sauks, Foxes and Mascoutins.

Walking along the road to school in the fall, when the corn was fully grown, tasseled, and turning brown in anticipation of frost, I imagined the stalks were a body of Indian warriors drawn up for a charge. And in October when the corn was shocked, Indian villages sprang up in the fields; their brown wigwams dotted the hills. In the aching silence of the country night, I could hear the beat of the war drums and smell the smoke of council fires.

CHAPTER 3
WHOM THE LORD LOVETH HE CHASTENETH

I

On an afternoon in late August, I stood on the back stoop, slowly chugging up and down the dasher of the wooden churn. It was one of those rich, languid days of the late summer that melt all the ambition in your body. Dewey was snoozing on the stoop nearby, one paw hanging over the edge. Occasionally he woke up long enough to snap at a fly. Mother was making jelly in the kitchen, singing softly as she worked. "*Oh! don't you remember sweet Alice, Ben Bolt?*"

Frank and Dave Peters had riven over to Grandmother Wood's place to haul some lumber, and father was out in the fields mending fence. I could see him through the spruce trees to the west, a tiny speck down in the lowland, moving slowly along the edge of the pasture.

Mother stepped out of the kitchen door to see how the butter was coming. She was still humming to herself as she looked inside the churn. "*Sweet Alice, whose hair was so brown.*" Only a few yellow points floated on top of the cream.

"Goodness, child," she said, "You'll have to churn harder than that or we won't even have butter for Christmas dinner."

Ashamed, I worked the dasher up and down for several minutes like the piston of a steam engine. When mother came to look in the churn again, the cream was covered with fat, yellow flecks and the butter was ready to be taken out. She brought out the big wooden crock and the paddle and dipped the flaky, yellow butter out of the churn into the crock.

After she had finished squeezing out the water and working in the salt, she cut a slab of home-made bread for me and spread it with fresh butter and jelly. Then she fixed a sandwich and filled a pint mason jar with buttermilk for father and gave them to me to deliver.

Happily I scampered over the pasture hill, with Dewey loping along beside me. I was used to this task, for often during the summer, mother sent me out in the middle of the afternoon with food and drink for the men in the fields: buttermilk and a sandwich, or cookies and a jug of water flavored with molasses. I liked especially to take father's lunch to him. When he saw me coming, he would dismount slowly from cultivator or mower, and stand there in the field, with legs firmly apart, while he took his lunch. He ate in silence, chewing his food thoughtfully, drinking with strong, deliberate gulps. And always he was looking away, looking off into the gray distance where the land met the thin blue of the prairie sky. There was a dignity to his silence like that of the fields themselves. It gave me a feeling of space and tranquility to be out there alone with him.

This afternoon, I found him in the corner of the west pasture, putting in a brace for a fence post. He swung the maul with loose, powerful strokes, driving the stake easily into the brown turf. When he saw me, he stopped work and stood beside the fence while he ate.

"Fence is bad here," he said when he had finished. "This fall when we market the hogs, I think I'll put in new fence all around."

Then he paused from his work a few minutes longer to tell me about the effect of the dry August on the crops—how the corn was ripening early and that he expected a poor yield from our little patch of sugar cane. I stood opposite him, my feet planted solidly apart like his, and listened attentively.

(And why shouldn't I discuss such matters with father? Wasn't I old enough now to handle my share of the farm work? Didn't I feed the chickens sometimes and climb the thatched roof of the cowshed to get the eggs the hens had laid there?)

In a few days now, father was saying, it would be time to strip the sugar cane. I nodded my head knowingly and my forehead tried to wrinkle up like his.

(And why shouldn't I feel my responsibility? Didn't I distribute the hay in the mangers every evening now? Hadn't I helped with the milking three different times already?)

After father had said all there was for him to say, he resumed his work and I stood and watched him for a while.

* * * * * * * *

As I grew old enough to take an interest in the serious aspects of farm life, I began to understand my father's solitary temperament a little. True, his silence and detachment were due in part to a strange, mystic quality peculiar to him alone, a quality which no-one would ever comprehend. But in many respects, his was a nature common to all farmers, all men whose moods are shaped by unceasing conflict with droughts, storms, plagues, and other violent and unpredictable forces.

The farmer knows no security; at the time his fortunes look the best, his investment and a season's labor may be wiped out by a hailstorm or a plague of insects. This year, everything seemed to be coming well for us: the loft of the barn was filled with hay; the oat bins were overflowing; and the corn was bursting to good harvest. But still, uncertainty brooded in father's eyes. Newspapers carried ominous accounts of hog cholera in other parts of the state; frost might nip the corn before it was hardened; a sudden panic in the market might topple the price of pork before we sent our hogs to market. And the burden of the indebtedness on the farm hovered over father like a vulture.

I do not remember that he or mother ever spoke of this indebtedness before the children; yet we all knew about it. We could tell when financial matters were especially troubling him, because he would sit in the living room after supper with a lost, frustrated look in his face and no taste for the book in his lap. He would sit that way for a while; then he would twist himself nervously out of his chair to give a lamp attention it did not need, or to stalk out of the front door into the darkness.

Father was a poor hand in a business deal; he had no patience with money matters and was easily duped. Unfortunately, this was a sphere in which mother could give him little help. For all her shrewdness in various practical ways, she was lost at the mention of figures. The two of them feared the indebtedness, and its interest and compound interest, with the hysterical fear of those who do not understand the force which threatens them. They were incapable of seeing the situation in its totality; their own solution was to work hard and to save with a care that sometimes bordered on fanaticism.

Frugality was not preached as a virtue in the household; it was practiced as a necessity. One incident, occurring that September, is typical of this fact and remains in my mind very clearly.

From a neighbor, we heard that a newspaper in the town of Cedar Rapids, 25 miles away, was advertising a drawing contest for children. When father consented to let me enter the contest, my excitement knew no bounds. India ink was required by the rules, and father said he would get me some in Anamosa the next day. For two days, I worked and planned in a fury of preparation and when father returned from town late the following afternoon, I was out in the yard to meet him.

He got down from the lumber-wagon slowly; I could see in his face that something was wrong.

"Did you remember—?" I asked tremulously.

He put his hand on my shoulder for a moment.

"I'm sorry, son. The smallest bottle of India ink they had was 25 cents. We simply can't afford it." That was all; and I was left with my disappointment and the wonder that a bottle of ink could cost that incredible sum.

Our poverty was not the kind that existed in the slums of the great cities where thousands lacked food, clothing and shelter. Except for a few staple items such as salt and coffee, the farm produced the food we needed. Mother made a great part of our clothing, and we cut and hauled our own fuel-wood.

Still, we were money-poor, and cursed with the insecurity which that implies. The possibility that we might lose the farm and everything we possessed was never remote from our lives. And because that fear hung over us always, the loss of a herd of hogs by cholera, or the demolition of a cornfield by hail was a tragic event of the first order.

II

My brother and I had been stripping sugar cane all day, walking between the tall green rows with long wooden paddles and chopping the leaves from the stalks. I was dead-tired from the unaccustomed labor in the broiling September sun, and after I climbed into bed, I lay awake for a few minutes while my blood seemed to pulse sluggishly to the rhythm of the crickets, locusts and frogs that squeaked like batteries of rusty grindstone wheels in the darkness. I was just dropping off to sleep when I hear someone rush into the back door of the house, slamming the screen sharply. Dave Peters was talking down there in a high-pitched, excited voice; I caught a few of his words—". . . fire . . . cholera . . . hogs . . . Byerly farm . . ." In a few moments, the door slammed again and father and the hired man were out in the yard, mingling their voices with the insects' drone in low, blurred conversation. I tried to stay awake, vaguely wondering what was wrong, but my drugged senses were slipping, slipping and soon I was lost in oceans of sleep.

Next morning, my mind was clear of all this until I sat down at the breakfast table. There, the atmosphere of deep gloom I at once sensed brought back vividly the things I had heard the preceding evening. Mother was more distracted that I had ever known her to be; she poured coffee on the tablecloth and almost forgot to get our lunches ready to take to school. Through the window, I could see father and Dave Peters standing beside the hog lot, talking, and I could tell from their very attitudes that something was seriously amiss.

"Father wants to see you before you go to school," mother said, as she put the last sandwich in our lunch pail.

Father was harnessing the dappled horses to the lumber wagon when we came outside. He stopped a few moments to talk to us, looking away to the south through the open space between the windmill and barn, as he spoke.

"There's hog cholera in the neighborhood," he said. "I've been expecting it for some time. Will Byerly told me Sunday that some of his young pigs had been acting sick. Last night, we saw the fire in Byerly's pasture where they were burning their first dead hogs. You can see the smoke over there now, and if the wind was right, you could smell it."

Frank and I followed his gaze to the south where a wisp of smoke was curving into the sky.

"The plague is likely to hit our herd no matter what we do. But we'll have to take every care. We'll keep Dewey tied up, and if you see any strange dogs or cats coming into the farmyard, scare them away. There are a good many ways cholera can spread."

A few days later, a half-dozen of our young pigs began to show signs of infection. They lost their appetites, became dumpish and watery-eyed, and separated themselves from the rest of the herd. Every time I saw them, they were either lying dopily in the corner of the pen, or else they were huddled together, trying to hide their heads under the litter. As the days passed, they became emaciated, and tottered on their legs pathetically as they moved about the lot.

When we got up the following Sunday morning, two of our young pigs were stiff upon the ground. After that, the disease spread, taking from one to three hogs a day. Playful young pigs, fat porkers almost ready for market, enormous brood sows, and even the big boar, the terror of the barnyard, became listless, ceased eating, and quietly died. Father did little these days except to putter about the hog pen, clearing debris from outside the fence, repairing a board here and there, or just standing and watching the hogs. There was nothing he could do for them, and at the last, he shot some that were hopelessly stricken. By the end of the month, only two young sows survived from the entire herd.

It was too much labor to bury the dead hogs, and if they were buried, there was the risk for a considerable length of time, that rodents might spread the infection to the neighbors' hogs. So, according to custom, the men carted the dead animals out to a far corner of the farm, well away from buildings, and made a huge funeral pyre. The stiff, grotesque bodies were soaked with kerosene and ignited. There, the pyre burned for weeks, filling the air for miles around with the pungent scent of burning flesh.

I shall never forget that fire. At night, I could see it from my bedroom window, an ominous beacon, flashing its warning to neighboring farms not yet reached by the plague.

III

There was no cheer in our household during the weeks that the cholera wiped out our herd of hogs. Everyone tried to act as if nothing unusual had happened, but the efforts to break the gloom were obvious and only made matters worse. Unfortunately, we were having one of the hottest and driest early autumns in the history of the region and the weather added to our listlessness and depression.

The swine plague, my first really serious experience with death, had a profound effect on me. The hogs had always seemed to me the most solid and hardy of animals. To see the entire herd, including the huge boar and the great brood sows, reduced to skeletal monstrosities, tottering about the pen, and finally to stiff, ghastly carcasses; [*sic*] was a tragedy that sank deeply into my mind. Furthermore, the experience had greater force now that I was old enough to grasp at least vaguely the significance of this loss to father.

My response, however, was chiefly of horror rather than sorrow. The hogs, except for the very small pigs[,] seemed inhuman, somewhat mechanical beasts to me; they were not poets like the cows and chickens. If our Plymouth Rocks had been exterminated, I should have been inconsolable.

In fact, I think I felt more grief one afternoon when I came home from school and found one of our fine cockerels lying motionless in the yard than I had been at any time during the swine plague.

"Is he asleep?" asked my little brother, Jack.

I felt of [*sic*] the chicken's wings and his breast. The body was cold.

"I believe he's . . . dead."

Death was a word we had heard many times during the past month. When the hogs were dead, father took them away to burn and that was an end of it. But I could not accept the fact that this chicken's life was destroyed as the hogs' had been. Before the stricken pigs had died, they had changed pathetically, had become skinny and weak. But this chicken lying on the ground, looked the same as in life; so far as I could see, there wasn't a mark on him.

It seemed to me that I had to do something about this. The Plymouth Rocks were not only my favorite pets; now that I had the chore of feeding them and gathering their eggs, they were also my responsibility. I had watched them hatch and grow up, and when they had been in the featherless, adolescent stage, I had even gone so far as to rub mutton tallow on their wings to relieve sun-burn. I could not let them die.

"He looks all right," said Jack, stooping down to pet the chicken's wing. "Won't he wake up?"

An inspiration popped into my mid.

"I know!" I cried. "You wait here, Jack, and watch the chicken. I'll be right back."

A story I had heard Dave Peters tell was humming in my mind as I ran into the house—something he had read in the newspapers or heard in the general store in Anamosa. Tugging at his whiskers portentously, the hired man had recounted how Mrs. McKinley, the president's wife, had "died" and then been brought back to life by *an injection of salt in the arm*. The details were vague, but that was the gist of it.

Luckily, mother was down [in the] cellar when I came into the kitchen. I got a fistful of salt from the jar over the stove and took father's carving knife out of the china cupboard drawer. When I returned to the scene of the tragedy, Jack was shaking the chicken's head, trying to get him to open his eyes.

We took the body around to the side of the house where no-one would be likely to see us. Then I cut a long slit in the flesh of the cockerel's wing and rubbed the salt into the wound.

"What will that do?" asked Jack wonderingly.

"Bring him back to life," I said with complete confidence.

Knowing that a dog or stray cat might carry the body away if we left it lying in the yard, we built a little compartment out of loose bricks to put it in. Although the walls of our makeshift hospital were only a foot high and very unstable, it seemed a satisfactory shelter to us.

I had the idea that the salt treatment was a sort of magic that would work better if we didn't watch it, so we forced ourselves to stay away all that evening.

But the next morning, the first thing we did was to rush out to see how the chicken was. I arrived at the scene first. The brick shelter was thrown apart and empty!

"He's gone!" I cried. Jack and Frank came running to see. "Gone!" they echoed. We all danced about, hysterical with delight.

"Chicky woke up! Chicky woke up!" chanted Jack over and over again.

When our first excitement had somewhat subsided, we searched the flock for the revivified bird—just to be positive. Sure enough, there was one cockerel with a scratch on his wing. That erased all possible doubts.

As usual, Dave Peters didn't say a thing when we told him about it. He only grunted and scowled at the stick he was whittling.

IV

The minister had a nasal, bargaining voice with which he said prayers and started his sermons. He also had a terrible thunder-voice for frightening the sin out of his flock, but that would come later. "Our text this Sabbath," he was saying, "is the wrath of the Lord and the destruction of Sodom and Gomorrah, Genesis Twenty-Nine . . ."

Scrubbed and starched into godliness, the congregation of the Strawberry Hill Presbyterian church settled themselves stiffly on the hard oak pews and prepared to deliver judgment on the two wicked cities—and upon their own neighbors.

I sat in the grim Calvanistic twilight like a wooden image, walled in by my parents. My starched Eaton [*sic*] collar cut into my neck and my throat was crumbling for the need of a drink of water. Out of the corner of my eye, I could see father sitting very straight and solemn beside me, his arms folded and his eyes fastened gravely upon the minister. On my other side was mother, with her hands in her lap in an attitude of sweet composure, gently accepting every word that came from the preacher's lips. Beyond her, I could see Dave Peters, his long torso crooked forward, his eyes smouldering.

As soon as the sermon was under way and the minister's voice was coiling and uncoiling in a monotonous flow, I relaxed a little and rubbed my nose—it had been itching for what seemed like hours. Outside, the sun had emerged from the clouds, flooding bright sunlight through the stained glass windows in the east side of the church. The light from the biggest window came down on the pew in front of us like a gorgeous rainbow. My heart leaped up to see Widow Schmidt's jowls become green and Deacon Jones' whiskers blossom into an exquisite lavender.

While the congregation grappled with problems of original sin and eternal damnation, my mind reverted to the topic that was of greatest importance to me at the time—namely, joint snakes. For several days, I had been able to think of little else. It had all started one evening the week before when Dave Peters had told my brothers and me about an actual experience he had once with a joint snake. As the minister's voice writhed on, I seemed to hear the hired man telling the story, paring his fingernails with his jackknife as he talked.

"I was walkin' along the fence in the east pasture when I come on him. Prettiest sight I ever seen—long and clear with the sun shinin' through him and showin' all his joints. Here was my chance to catch the snake and git the reward that P. T. Barnum offered. I knowed that if I hit him with a stick, he'd break up and git away, so I took off my coat and sneaked up to throw the coat over him and catch him whole. Well, I got up to him all right but when I lifted up my coat to throw it over him, that snake busted up into a thousand pieces. I was so surprised, I dropped my coat. Then what happened while I stood there? Ask me—just what happened? Why, quick as lightenin' [*sic*], all the parts of the snake run themselves together, and away he glided as fast as a blue racer!"

As these words came back to me, I was no longer in church. I was out in a pasture capturing a joint snake; I was taking it to Barnum and collecting the reward; I was accepting a job as a snake charmer in the circus.

Father's hand came down firmly on my arm and brought me back into the atmosphere of the church. No wriggling allowed here. I braced up and paid attention to the preacher. His voice was coiling now, ready to strike out in the climax of his sermon. The Lord, he was saying, was terrible in His wrath, and would deal with all those who sinned today even as He had dealt with Sodom and Gomorrah. I began to feel qualms. Why hadn't I paid attention instead of thinking about joint-snakes. The minister pointed an accusing finger into the congregation. My heart went cold. He was pointing directly at me!

"*Then the Lord rained upon Sodom and upon Gomorrah brimstone and fire from the Lord out of heaven.*"

I no longer needed father's hand to keep me still. I was scared stiff. Surely the Lord's punishment was aimed at me for dreaming about joint snakes in church. I didn't know what brimstone was, but the picture of fire raining down from heaven was far too vivid for comfort. Oh, why had I been so foolish as to offend the Lord? I listened breathlessly to the rest of the sermon.

It was a relief when the fireworks were at last over and I was still intact. The choir began to sing "How Gentle God's Commands" and I relaxed.

Hymn singing these Sundays was not the sober, prosaic business it had once been. Something revolutionary had happened in the choir. Several of the younger members were now putting great passion and vibrato into their singing; they competed to see who could obtain the most coloratura effects. The competition was close this Sunday, but Nell Abbott was the prima donna; her soprano fluttered in shrill triumph over all the others.

Everyone agreed that the corruption of the choir had resulted from a visit of Jenny Sales to Anamosa. Jenny Sales was a local girl who had gone away to Europe, launched on a spectacular musical career, and eventually emerged as "Madame de Seales."

When the Madame had returned to Anamosa on a visit, she had created a sensation, and the young ladies of the town, admiring her magnificent trills, had undertaken to render the church hymns in what they considered an operatic manner.

The older ladies of the congregation were horrified at this blasphemy, and even the more liberal members of the church were shocked to hear *Lead Kindly Light* sung as if it had been the *Misere* [*sic*] from *Il Trovatore*.

When the services were over that Sunday, and we were slowly milling out of the church, I got separated from my parents in the aisle and wedged in between two elderly ladies who were engaged in a lively whispering conversation.

"Wasn't it awful today?" said one lady, making a grimace as if she had tasted alum.

"Shameful!" hissed the other. "I can't answer for *some* folks, but as for me, *I* don't approve of all this qua-averin' in a person's voice when they are singin' 'Lord Dismiss Us with Thy Blessing'—"

V

Weeks upon weeks, the rains had held off. The pastures were bleached to hay-color and the corn leaves became yellow as old parchment. Leaves were dropping early; the trees and fence-rows were already sparse and sere.

From time to time, we sighted blue smudges of smoke on the horizon. Knowing that it was too early for the hazes of Indian summer, we concluded that there were grass fires in the vicinity. These fires were usually started by the sparks from railroad locomotives, and when the landscape was as dry as it was this year, they could do a great deal of damage. We felt reasonably safe from them, however, since we were a good two miles from the Milwaukee line.

One afternoon after school, I was sitting in the shade at the east side of the house, carving my name in a piece of wood with an old jackknife. Dewey lay nearby, panting from the exertion of his run across the fields to escort us home from school. These October days were still hot, although the nights and early mornings were sharp. Frank was digging potatoes in the garden.

"Hey, you!" he called to me. "Come over here and help. You can pick up while I dig."

I reluctantly laid aside my knife and wood and started back to the garden. I could hear a loud pounding from the barn. Father and Dave Peters were up in the loft making some repairs. I stopped a moment at the back stoop to get a drink from the water bucket. As I lifted the dipper to my mouth, I happened to look out over the sun-crisped hills to the west. Something caught my eye. I gazed intently for a minute until I was sure. It was smoke, blue clouds of it, rolling up from the hills.

"Mother, Frank!" I yelled, "there's a fire coming this way."

Frank dropped his spading fork and ran across the garden. Mother hurried out the back door. They looked into the west where I was pointing.

"Grass fire!" cried mother. "Run and tell the men. Hurry!"

Father and Dave Peters came out of the barn at a dead run. Father took one long look at the clouds of smoke and gave orders.

"I'll plow a strip across the west pasture down as far as the fence. Won't have time to cut through the fence. Dave, you'll have to start a back-fire below the fence to protect the barn. Frank can help you—no, Frank, you run the stock into the farmyard. Grant, you help Dave."

Father hurried to throw the harness on his fastest team. I followed the hired man. He rushed into the barn and snatched up a bunch of gunny sacks from a corner. I hastily picked up the sacks he missed and ran outside after him.

"Watch out for that backfire," called father. "Let one spark get away and the barn will go!"

Dave and I dashed around behind the barn and plunged the gunny sacks into the horse tank. Mother came running from the house with a box of matches for us.

As the hired man and I hurried down the grassy slope south of the farm, loaded with dripping gunny sacks, father drove the plow around into the west pasture. To the east I could hear Frank shouting at the cows as he started rounding them up.

"I'll start the fire along here," shouted Dave Peters, indicating an imaginary line. "We'll beat it out with the sacks when it gets even with this here bare patch."

We did not have time to look to the west to see how swiftly the big fire was approaching, but we could smell the smoke plainly now.

Dave Peters lit the grass in several places and soon we had a little blaze crackling. The wind carried it back to the line in no time and we began beating it out with the wet sacks. Mother ran out with more wet cloths and helped us smother the flame. The hot breath of the backfire spit into our faces; our throats were choked with smoke.

As we worked, I caught an occasional glimpse of father, plowing across the pasture at as near a gallop as he dared. Frank was returning with the stock; the cattle came past our backfire, lowing and balking with fright.

By the time we finished beating out the near side of the backfire, father had plowed a strip a dozen feet wide across the pasture. This was joined by the gap made by our backfire.

The big fire was drawing very near now; dense clouds of stinging smoke were rolling over us. Father drove back into the farmyard and tied his sweat-lathered, frightened horses in the shade. We all stood along the south and west edges of the farmyard, ready to slap the wet gunny sacks on any sparks that might leap across the gaps made by backfire and plow. Two hay stacks and a straw sack stood beside the barn, and the cowshed was thatched with wild hay, dry as tinder. Any of these would burn in short order if ignited, and once fire was started in the farmyard, the barn and other buildings would be swept away too.

The grass fire was a billowing irregular wall of smoke at the bottom of which orange flames reached out like snake-tongues as it moved forward. Urged by a good wind, the fire ran easily down and up the hills; we could hear its subdued crackling. As it swept down into the marshy spots of the west pasture, it struck the patches of waist-deep wild hay and the flames sprang high, hurling sparks into the air.

Up the west pasture hill straight toward us raced the wall of smoke. It reached the firebreaks and the tongues of flame leaped out onto the bare strips.

"Look out, Peters!" shouted father. "Sparks in the grass by the cowshed there."

The hired man turned quickly and beat out a patch of fire that had flamed up without warning.

At the gaps, the fire seemed to pause a moment, like a spirited horse. Then the wall parted into two sections and swept past the ends of the firebreaks. One section reached the trees north and west of our house and stopped. The other traveled south of the farmyard, left a wide space untouched to the east; then extended into a long crooked wall again, as it traveled on across the hills.

For more than an hour, we walked around the farmyard with wet cloths, taking no chances that some bit of fire might remain to destroy our buildings. Father climbed high up on the windmill to look around. "Our place looks like a green island in a black lake, from up there," he said when he came down. Darkness had fallen by the time he and Dave were satisfied that we were completely out of danger.

At supper that night, everyone was in good spirits except Jack. He was peeved because he had been taking a nap and nobody had wakened him to see the excitement. As for me, I felt very proud to have helped stop the fire. A slight burn I had on my hand made me feel like a battle-scarred hero.

"Thank heavens, it didn't turn out any worse than it did," mother said as she set the gravy on the table. "Lucky you men were here this afternoon."

Dave Peters had singed his whiskers in the backfire and looked fiercer than ever with the patch of gray frizzle on his reddish beard.

"That warn't no prairie fire," he growled. "Just a low grass fire—nothin' like what they uster have. Not enough to get excited about."

Mother started to say something but held it back.

"Yes," said father, "in the old days when the tall buffalo grass grew on the prairie, we could have never stopped it the way we did. But this fire might have done enough damage."

There was one matter troubling me when I went to bed that night. When mother came to tuck Jack and me into bed, I asked her about it.

"Ma, did God punish us with that fire like the minister said in church?"

"I don't know, son," mother said. "Perhaps he did. If so, we must not have been too wicked because he didn't let the fire get into our farmyard."

Apparently this idea of the Lord punishing us with the fire made even more of an impression on my little brother than it had on me. For he lay there in the darkness for a long time, murmuring to himself: "God punched us. God punched us."

VI

All that fall and winter, ill luck dogged us. The loss of our hogs from the cholera made us poorer than ever before, and all manner of other evils flocked in upon us. I heard mother say years later that this was the most troubled period she and father had ever known.

On top of other misfortunes, Jack and I caught the measles in early December. We had scarcely recovered from this annoying disease when mother took sick with a severe cold. The cold grew steadily worse, finally developing into pneumonia. She was in bed two months.

It was a shock for us to see mother, whose energy seemed so inexhaustible, collapse. She lay there, white as the pillow on which she rested, the spirit drained completely from her. We all hovered about rather helplessly, suddenly realizing how much we depended upon her.

The house was a bleak, gloomy place without her moving about in it. Childishly, I resented the unseen force that had stricken her. I remember my vague, wondering grief when I saw her arms and hands resting limp above the covers. They lay at her sides like wilted flowers, the blue veins traced against the white flesh.

Her mother came out to take care of her during the worst part of the illness. Grandmother Weaver was a good person to have around at such a time. A tiny, white-haired old lady, with finely arched wrinkles over her eyebrows, she was like her daughter in many ways. She was cheerful and energetic, and had a competent, if rather nervous way of getting things done. She did a good job of nursing, cooked our meals, and sometimes in the evenings told Louisa Alcott stories to my brothers and me. We were all very fond of her.

Frequently, Grandfather Weaver stopped for a meal at the farm when he came from Anamosa to bring grandmother out, or to take her back to town. It seems to me that I never saw Grandpa Weaver in those days when he wasn't clinching a point with some time-worn homily. "Penny wise, pound foolish—that's McKinley," he would say, wagging a stumpy forefinger. He was round-faced and bearded, always full of gruff talk about business and politics. Jolly enough when conversing with adults, he seemed a little stern and exacting in his attitude towards children.

We did not see much of father's people during this period in spite of the fact that they lived only a quarter of a mile away. The feeling between our household and theirs was far from cordial. Grandmother Wood, a lean, gray-haired old lady with something rather helpless and pathetic in her face and manner, had not approved of father's marriage. Nor had father's unmarried sister and two brothers who lived at home. Uncle Clarence, an ingrown, sullen individual, and Uncle Eugene, the blustery, overbearing member of the family, were especially cool to mother. The only one of the Wood family who came to see us often was Aunt Sarah, father's older sister.

She was a tall, gaunt old maid, a strange mixture of Quaker austerity and Victorian romanticism. Like the weather, her actions were decisive but unaccountable. With the best of intentions, she sometimes volunteered to help about the house, but her eccentric manner of doing things invariably upset the household and gave mother a nervous relapse. Aunt Sarah considered father's children a special duty of hers like membership in the Ladies Aid, and she worked diligently at amusing and instructing us. It pleased her to have us call her Aunt Sally.

Part of the time during mother's sickness, we had no-one in to take care of her, and one of the things I remember most vividly from this whole unhappy period was the way in which father took over mother's responsibilities in the household at these times. He had been brought up to accept as immutable the distinction between the duties of man and woman in the family, and I doubt if it had ever occurred to him before that a man could do housework if necessary. But when Grandmother Weaver had to go back to Anamosa, he took over the offices of housewife and nurse as if he had always expected to assume them some day. Awkward and frequently bewildered, he washed dishes, scrubbed, tended to mother's needs, and even tried to bake graham muffins. He took care of us children as best he could; I remember especially how he saw Jack and me to bed every night and stood there, grave and slightly embarrassed, while we said our prayers.

Another thing remarkable about this period was the change in Dave Peters' attitude towards mother. There had always been a certain hostility between mother and the hired man. She had no patience with his tall stories and bragging and Dave had frequently ruffled under the sting of her tongue.

But when mother fell sick, something happened to Dave. He was like a faithful old dog whose mistress was ill. He pounced on the slightest opportunities to do things for mother and thought nothing of driving to Anamosa on the most bitter day of winter to get her medicine. When he was in the house, he kept his sharp, condor-eyes fastened upon her door. Let any of us make the tiniest noise, and he made us feel as if we had committed a crime more serious than murder. Once when father dropped a piece of firewood on the sitting room floor, Dave upbraided him so fiercely that I was horrified. Apparently father didn't mind, though, because when I went out in the kitchen a few minutes later, I found him chuckling to himself as he peeled the potatoes. This was one of the few times I ever heard father laugh.

* * * * * * * *

So the winter dragged on, and in adversity we became acquainted with many sides of one another that might otherwise have remained hidden. When spring broke through the next year, the bad luck that had been following us seemed to depart and everyone felt new confidence and vitality. Then, that summer an important event occured [*sic*] that I like to think of as officially terminating our long period of misfortune.

Mother was unwell again, and father had brought Mrs. Zimmers, a fat, good-natured German woman, from Anamosa to help with the housework. I knew that the illness was not so serious as that of the preceding winter because no-one seemed to be greatly alarmed about it. Besides, mother did not look ghastly this time, and even after she had gone to bed, she was able to talk to me the same as always. But there was a secretiveness about it all that puzzled and disturbed me. When I asked father or Frank or Mrs. Zimmers about mother's sickness, they only shook their heads mysteriously and went on with their work. This, of course, made me all the more curious, but some intuitive sense of delicacy forbade my speaking to mother herself about it.

One afternoon, Jack and I were standing in the farmyard, watching Frank tinker with the mowing machine, when Mrs. Zimmers came running out of the kitchen, very much excited. She called Frank to her, said something to him, and hurried back into the house. Frank turned and ran like a shot through the farmyard and out towards the field where father was cultivating corn. A few minutes [later] father came running into the yard, having left Frank to bring in the horses. He disappeared into the farmhouse, and Jack and I stood beside the back stoop, waiting for the unknown to happen. Presently Mrs. Zimmers came to the door and handed me a note.

"Your father wants you boys to take this over to your Aunt Sally right away," she said.

Jack and I, thinking that we had been entrusted with an important mission, ran nearly all the way over to Grandmother Wood's. When we had delivered the note, we wanted to return home immediately to see what was happening there. But after Aunt Sarah had read the message, she flatly insisted on keeping us with her. She made us sit in the living room for hours while she read aloud from a tedious book called "Pilgrim's Progress."

It was nearly supper time before she let us go, and when we reached home, there was evidence of great excitement awaiting us. As we came down the road, we saw Dr. Perkins of Anamosa just turning out of our drive in his buggy; and Grandfather Weaver's buggy and the Abbotts' rig were standing in the farmyard.

The house was buzzing with low talk and laughter when we came in the kitchen door. Grandpa Weaver, father and Mrs. Abbott were having a mysterious adult conversation in the kitchen, and the other people were standing about in the living room. Nobody paid any attention to Jack and me. We stood forlornly in the corner of the kitchen, wondering what it was all about. Finally, father saw us, smiled, and motioned for us to come into the living room. Grandmother Weaver, Mrs. Zimmers and the others were gathered around in the middle of the living room, peering down at something, and whispering. As we came closer, I could see that they were standing around the cradle in which my brothers and I had slept as babies. I followed father up to it and peeked in.

There was a tiny, red, puckered-up new babe, sound asleep.

"What do you think of her?" whispered father, proudly. "That's your new sister."

* * * * * * * *

They christened the newcomer Nancy after her Grandmother Weaver, and Rebecca after her Grandmother Wood. But we all called her Nan. She had a round face, pale hair, and blue eyes, and looked exactly the same as mother had when she was a baby, so Grandmother Weaver said. With the arithmetic I learned at Cottonwood school, I figured precisely how much older I was than my new sister, and the results were highly satisfactory to my pride.

For the most part, Nan was a good baby, but she did have her bad points. For one thing, she was very wayward about being put to sleep. This was frequently my task, and I found that if I rocked her with the utmost care for a half hour, she would appear to be sound asleep. But the moment I started to tip-toe out of the room, "*Yaaaa!*" she would squawl, and I would have to come back to the cradle and do the whole process all over again. This was rather annoying to a fellow who was eight years old going on nine.

CHAPTER 4
THE KINDLY FRUITS OF THE EARTH

[1]

The grain harvest was something to describe to one's grandchildren. The yield had been fairly abundant the year before but father said he had never seen anything like the oats crop this summer. The straw was rich yellow, almost a butter color, and the grain heads were fat and perfectly formed. In mid-July, the fields were fairly choked with the banks of thick oats, ripe for the harvest.

By July 20th, we had cut and shocked our grain, and once more the family was tingling with the excitement that always preceded threshing. Each morning, we heard the shrill whistle of the threshing machine at some farm in the vicinity, calling in all the neighbors in the threshing run. Father and

Dave Peters left with hayrack and team at dawn these days and didn't return until dusk. Supper every evening was enlivened by exciting talk about the day's threshing. Father and Dave became almost loquacious as they discussed the adventures and mishaps of the day's work in the fields. My brothers and I listened to this talk avidly and tried to content ourselves with the thought that our own big day would be at hand very soon. Mother was forever asking questions about the other farm women's dinners and fretting as to whether she would be able to get so good a meal when we had our threshing.

Morning after morning, the whistle of the machine was heard closer to our farm. Father and Dave Peters spent any spare minutes they could find, checking our wagon box and hayracks to see that they were in good repair, and trimming the trees in the front yard so that the threshing machine could get through our drive.

"That's a pretty rickety bridge over the crick," Dave Peters said, brightening up at the prospect of calamity. "Do ye suppose the machine can get over it all right?"

"They'll get over it all right," said father, drily. "Slim O'Donnell carries a half-dozen big oak planks on his machine. With those he can get across any bridge around here."

Mother was working furiously now preparing for the great dinner she would have to serve the threshers. She cleaned the house from top to bottom until it fairly glistened. From the cellar she brought up quantities of jellies, preserves, and pickles and lined them up on the pantry shelves. She gathered all manner of garden vegetables and put them in baskets out in the summer kitchen. She sent Frank into Anamosa to buy crash toweling for roller towels and to borrow extra silverware from Grandmother Weaver. And as time grew short, a thousand smaller jobs occupied her, such as getting the table leaves out, taking inventory of chairs, and sorting out the best china.

The last two days, she did a baking such as I had never seen. Golden loaves of bread, pies, cakes, doughnuts, and big crocks of baked beans appeared in the pantry. She prepared chickens for frying and baked two great hams.

With a nursing babe on her hands, mother was still none too strong. All the extra work and excitement made her so tired she became a little lightheaded. Luckily, father had insisted that Mrs. Zimmers should come out to help with the dinner. And when that good, dependable lady arrived at noon on the day before out threshing, I think mother could have kissed her for joy.

Frank and I had plenty to do in the way of preparation too. We cut the weeds in the yard and picked up all the untidy odds and ends around the place. We cleaned the kitchen chimney and brought in wood and corncobs for the range. We swatted flies for hours at a time, and got a place ready on the back stoop where the men could wash. One fussy job I had was to take the combs from the comb-box on the kitchen wall and clean them all out with a pin. As our last measure of preparation, Frank and Jack and I had baths and shampoos in a wooden washtub by the kitchen stove. Painfully clean, and with our best overalls laid out for the next day, we were ready for the big event of the year.

That night, the threshing machine arrived at our place, and the excitement of its coming is something I shall never forget. Darkness had settled, except for a few silver splinters in the west, when we sighted the great hulk lumbering up the narrow side road to our farm. It looked for all the world like some immense fire-dragon. Sparks flew from it; lanterns which the crew carried to guide the way, swung like roving eyes in the darkness; the stillness was shattered for miles around by the ungodly rumble and clatter. When it finally turned into our drive, it looked as if it would crowd the trees and buildings out of the farmyard with its towering bulk. And the bedlam it created was such as you never heard, with the engine puffing, the gears and other apparatus rattling, and the crew shouting in the darkness like mariners bringing in a ship.

I had a hard time getting to sleep that night, for when I went to bed, every nerve in my body was tingling with excitement. A thousand hopes and fears and anxieties were jostling about in my mind. I lay there sharp-awake in the hot bedroom for what seemed like hours, staring at the pool of silver moonlight on the floor and listening to the countless languid voices of the night. Somewhere out of the darkness drifted a wistful voice . . . *Whip-poor-will . . . whip-poor-will . . .* [*sic*].

Glad excitement sang in my blood when I got out of bed the next morning. Day had dawned still and clear, with no sign of a cloud in the pale sky. The sun was pouring a dazzling flood on the stubbled, sweet-smelling fields where the shocks of grain stood ready for the threshers. The day was tailor-made for our threshing.

I raced through breakfast and my morning chores in record time. And when the threshing crew arrived to start the machinery, I was on hand to watch.

For the center of operations, they selected a level spot in the pasture just west of the farmyard. I was completely awed by the stupendous size and complexity of the threshing equipment. The steam engine which ran the other machinery and pulled it seemed to me as big as a railroad locomotive, and the huge body of the separator with its auxiliary mechanisms, had so many bolts and wheels and arms that I wondered how the crew could remember what they were all for.

The three men who ran the equipment were in a jolly humor this morning. They laughed and spat and swore lustily while they got their dragon ready for a preliminary tryout. I watched them turn the engine around and hook up the big belt that ran from the engine to the separator, governing all the innumerable gears of the machinery. Then suddenly, the throttle was thrown open, the main belt moved, and the separator started with a loud, shuffling roar. The vibrations shook the earth under me.

The man who seemed to me to be the hero of the affair was Slim O'Donnell, the dashing devil-may-care young farmer who operated the engine. He was known in the vicinity as a plunger and dare-devil who cared more about baseball and horse-racing than he did about tending to his farm. With a broad smile on his face and an old white cap set jauntily on his head, he sat under the canopy of the engine, handling the levers in such a grand manner that one could not help admiring him. When he blew a tremendous blast on the whistle to remind the neighbors that this was our threshing day, he did it as unconcernedly as if he were striking a dinner gong.

Now the hayracks were beginning to stream through our farmyard, and we could see the men starting to load the shocks down in the lowland. They looked like ants, moving about on the bright fields.

Seeing that his machinery was all in order, Slim stopped the great belt to wait for the men to bring in the first load of hay from the fields. He vaulted down from his perch and leaned carelessly against one of the big back wheels of the engine, joking with the other members of the crew, and spitting great gobs of tobacco juice. Finally his merry glance lit on me.

"Hello there[,] son," he drawled. "What's your name?"

"Grant," I piped, the blood running to my face.

"Grant what?"

"Grant Wood."

"Your hair's kind of red ain't it?"

"Y-yessir."

"Well then, I guess I'll call you Redwood."

The threshing crew guffawed appreciatively, and I stared at the ground, speechless and pleased.

Presently, the first hayrack arrived from the fields, loaded with shocks; the machinery started up again, and the threshing was begun. The man on the rack pitched the bundles of oats onto a pronged belt that carried them into the body of the separator. By this time, father had backed up a wagon to the side of the separator. The grain, divided from the straw in the separator and sifted of chaff by a blower arrangement, poured into father's wagon box. Meantime, the straw was carried up a steep incline by means of a wide, canvas belt, and discharged upon the ground. Dave Peters was stationed where the straw came from the machine to build it into a compact, well-shaped stack.

All morning, the hayracks came in an unending stream, bringing the shocks of oats; while father and the other two men driving high boxed wagons, formed another continuous chain hauling the grain to the barn. When I had tired of watching the threshing machine, I climbed up on the seat with father and rode with him on several trips to and from the oat bins. Then, for variety, I rode out in the fields with Mr. Abbott on his hay rack [*sic*]. It was thrilling to see the hayracks spread out over the hills and the swarms of men loading the yellow straw. But being out there was too hot to be fun for long. The hard sunlight glared on the bleached grainfields [*sic*] so brightly that it made your head ache and the dry heat nearly stifled you.

Perhaps the most fun of the morning was going with Jim Flynn, the "water monkey" of the threshing crew, while he filled the water-wagon. The water-wagon, out of which the boiler of the threshing engine was replenished, was a wooden tank on wheels, equipped with a large hand pump. Since there was not enough breeze to drive our windmill this morning, Jim did not fill the wagon from the horse-tank, but instead, drove down to the open well in the marshy part of our east pasture.

By the time we had returned from this trip, it was noon. All operations suddenly stopped and the ravenous men swarmed in from the fields for dinner. When all the teams pulled into our farmyard, you would have thought we were having a fair at our house. Some men left their horses hitched and used nose bags for feeding. The more careful ones removed the harness and rubbed the animals down with big handfuls of grass.

Mother and Mrs. Zimmers had been at work all morning getting the meal ready. They had set three tables end-to-end in the sitting room, covering them with neatly overlapped cloths so that they looked like one. All available chairs, including the piano stool, and even boxes and kegs, were placed around the table.

For the great event, the ironstone china of everyday use had been set aside in favor of mother's prized moss rose Haviland set. And since there was not enough of this to go around, mother supplemented it with a set of brown willow-ware that Grandmother Wood had brought long ago from Virginia. Some of the knives and forks on the table had red strings tied around them—this was the borrowed silver identified from our own.

When the men had taken care of their horses, they took turns at the wash basins on the wooden bench outside the kitchen. They soused their heads in the cold wellwater and scrubbed their hands and arms to get rid of the sweat and fine chaff. Then, after combing their wet hair so that their heads were sleek and glistening, they all went in to dinner.

Meantime, the long table had been loaded with food for regiments: mountainous dishes of mashed potatoes, great platters of fried chicken, garden vegetables of all kinds, preserves and jellies and pickles in fabulous profusion.

All the crowd could not be seated at once, and the hired man and my brothers and I had to wait for second table. I went around to the front door and watched the men at the first table put away the dinner. Never had I seen food disappear so rapidly; it seemed to me their [*sic*] must be no bottoms to their appetites. A half-dozen belles of the neighborhood had come in to serve for mother, and they fluttered about the table, replenishing serving dishes and carrying on shy flirtations over bowls of potatoes and platters of chicken.

At last, the hungry men satisfied their appetites, rounding off the enormous meal with huge slabs of apple pie and chocolate cake. Then we had our chance at the second table, and I did my best to duplicate the performance of the threshers. But long before I got to the apple pie, I was so stuffed I couldn't eat another bite.

All afternoon the threshing machine puffed and roared in our west pasture and sounded its shrill whistle when the racks were slow in hauling the shocks from the fields. And the procession of wagons continued between the machine and the barn, heaping our bins with the clean bright oats. At dusk, the last half-load of shocks was brought in. Then all hands stood by while the last of our grain dribbled from the separator.

Slim O'Donnell closed the throttle and stopped the great belt.

"Hey, there, Redwood," he shouted merrily. "How would you like to blow the whistle?"

Would I? I clambered up to the seat beside the operator so fast that I skinned my shin. The engine was still hot and sweating from its long day's labor and the air was pungent with the smell of hot oil. I could not reach the whang which blew the whistle, even from the beam over the driver's seat, so O'Donnell lifted me up. I grasped the leather thong firmly and tugged.

"*Schleep!*" screamed the whistle, loudly enough to shake down the straw-stack. I let go in fright.

"That'll never do," said O'Donnell, roaring with mirth. "Give her a real yank!"

This time, I pulled as if my life depended on it, and held on. And what a terrific blast it was that I sent screaming over the dusky countryside!

Neighbor women, hearing it, knew that the Woods' threshing was over, and that tired and hungry husbands would soon be home for supper.

II

Aunt Sarah Wood's voice droned on, stern and unbending like all things about her. Its monotony made every sentence she read sound like the minutes of the Presbyterian Ladies' Aid society.

I was perched on a big straight-backed chair, facing her, my legs dangling an uncomfortable half-way to the floor. The course of the story had long since escaped me. I watched the antics of a fly, looked out of the window, or studied Aunt Sarah's countenance.

At the moment, I was wondering how she could close her eyes at night—so tightly was her hair combed to her head. Her hair was dead-black and she wore it parted austerely in the middle so that it framed the long, pale oval of her face with mourning. Her expression was stiff and humorless, with long nose and chin and thin lips.

"*Dick turned his face to Torpenhow,*" she read, "*and raised his hand to set his helmet straight, but, miscalculating the distance, knocked it off. Torpenhow saw that his hair was gray on his temples, and that his face was the face of an old man . . .*"

I could hear a yellowhammer making his nervous, whirring song in a tree outside and wished that I was over in Grandfather Wood's orchard, the edge of which I could see under the drawn window blind. I was far too young to appreciate literature dealing with love or tragedy, or even adventure of any subtelty [*sic*]. Mr. Kipling's "The Light that [*sic*] Failed" was lost on me.

"*His luck,*" Aunt Sarah read on, "*had held to the last, even to the crowning mercy of a kindly bullet through his head.*

"*Torpenhow knelt under the lee of the camel with Dick's body in his arms.*"

She sighed a deep sigh and closed the book primly.

"If I had known it was going to end so sad," she said, pecking at her cold eyes with a handkerchief, "I'd never have bought the book!"

As far as I was concerned, any ending was a good one.

"May I go out and play now, Aunt Sally?" I asked eagerly. She nodded and within the minute, I was outside in the sunlight running towards the orchard.

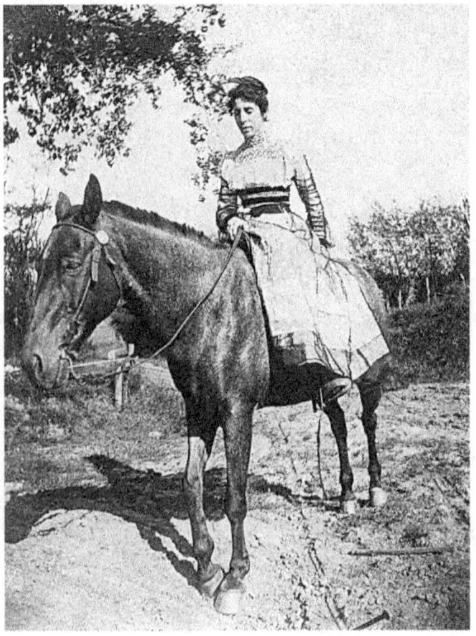

Fig. A.7. Sarah Wood, c. 1900.

The fact that I was too young to understand what she read to me did not seem to discourage Aunt Sarah[,] for despite her Quaker upbringing she was a determinedly literary woman. No book of Laura Jean Libbey or Gene Stratton Porter escaped her, and she had even tried her own hand at writing. In fact, the heart-heavy romances and poems she contributed to farm papers had gained her quite a reputation among the women of the neighborhood. When I went over to Grandfather Wood's to play in the orchard or the big hay-mow, there was always the danger that she might call me in for a reading session in the airless living room. Fortunately, this was not too often, for Aunt Sarah was a busy person. She had many social cares, such as being an officer in the Presbyterian Ladies' Aid, a worker in the Foreign Mission group and a Daughter of the American Revolution. Her membership in the last-named organization shows her tenacity of purpose, for it must have been no small task to single a revolutionary fighter out of her Quaker ancestry.

Now that I was old enough to participate in the various social events of the neighborhood, it seemed to me that Aunt Sarah dominated nearly all of them. The two most important festivals of the year: [*sic*] the threshing and the county fair, were somewhat out of her jurisdiction. But over the strawberry festivals, church socials, and patriotic gatherings, the shadow of her grimly-corseted figure fell like that of a patron saint. That August, she herself held a church social that I remember as being one of the most impressive affairs I ever attended.

For the occasion, she had transformed Grandmother Wood's front yard into an exotic bower, with Japanese lanterns strung between the great pines and chairs and tables spread over the lawn. The tinted glow of the lanterns lit up the flower garden with its neat rows of zinnias, petunias and verbenas. And the lights were skil[l]fully arranged to show off Aunt Sarah's two most highly prized garden ornaments: one, an arbor vitae tree, trimmed to resemble a huge rooster; and the other—this was the masterpiece of the neighborhood—a man-high cottonwood stump, completely covered with clam-shells nailed inside out so as to give the irridescence [*sic*] of mother-of-pearl.

Our family arrived at the affair early, since mother was to help with the final preparations. Already, various members of the "committee" were there, efficient ladies in starchy, ball-sleeved dresses with sweeping skirts. Daintily-aproned, they glided about the yard, arranging cakes and other delicacies and supervising the boys who were winding the handles of ice cream freezers.

Self-conscious in my Sunday clothes, and shy of all the strange people, I lurked in the shadows and waited for the guests to come. Soon, the buggies began to arrive, bringing the good Presbyterians from Anamosa and vicinity. Matrons hurried about, putting their babies to sleep and delivering baskets of food. Star-eyed belles walked in the garden, full of shy glances and soft laughter. Gangling girls in pigtails took care of the very small children. Bashful adolescent boys and jolly older men, all uncomfortable in store-clothes, gathered in little groups, joshing among themselves. Always the country people were a little shy of those who had come from town.

Aunt Sarah's moment of supreme triumph came when the minister arrived.

"Why, the Lord bless you, Sister Wood," he said as he shook her hand. "This is *beautiful*. Your church social is the greatest event since Dewey took Manilla!"

After a while, the guests seated themselves on the folding chairs facing the front porch and Aunt Sarah gave the signal for the program to begin. A flustered young lady stood up on the porch, opened her mouth, and out rolled "How They Brought the Good News from Ghent to Aix," accompanied by vigorous stabbing gestures. When this recitation was over (in what may have been record time), the audience applauded heavily and was rewarded with an encore in the form of "Horatius at the Bridge." Then came music. The walnut parlor organ had been dragged outside, and to its accompaniment, various members of the church choir sang and an elbowy young man performed on the violin.

I was just beginning to get over my self-consciousness and to have some fun, playing with the town kids, when Aunt Sarah drafted me into the hateful task of selling little bouquets of garden flowers. From then on, the evening was misery for me. My sales procedure, never very successful, was to advance within a few feet of the prospective customer and whisper in a wee, trembling falsetto: "You don't want to buy some flowers, do you?"

* * * * * * * *

Ordinarily, Aunt Sarah would have been horrified at the thought of going to the theatre [*sic*] herself, let alone taking Frank and me with her. But this play was different.

"It's something every Christian ought to see, Maryville," she had said, and in the end, father had agreed.

Thus it was that on a hot August evening, she and Frank and I sat in the opera house in Anamosa, waiting for a performance of "Uncle Tom's Cabin" to begin.

The peculiar animation of the theatre [*sic*] crowd, the rococo interior of the opera house, the orchestra tuning up—all this stirred up in me a strange excitement I had never before experienced. But most of all, I was fascinated by the stage; once I had set eyes on it, I could not look elsewhere. In front, two velvet curtains parted to reveal a large picture, lovely beyond description. It was a Venetian boating scene: moonlight played upon the water, gondolas were silhouetted against the sky, lovely ladies swooned in glamorous balconies. It was framed in gilt, and around the outside was a border of signs such as "Buy Your Groceries at Shaw and Duttons" and "Eat Herrick's Pills." All in all, it was the most gorgeous thing I had ever seen.

And behind this curtain . . . behind, was the enchanted world of make-believe, a world I little knew, but longed for with immeasurable yearning.

Lights out, the play begins. Frank and I forget the strange surroundings, the strange people; we are swept away in the great human torrent of the melodrama.

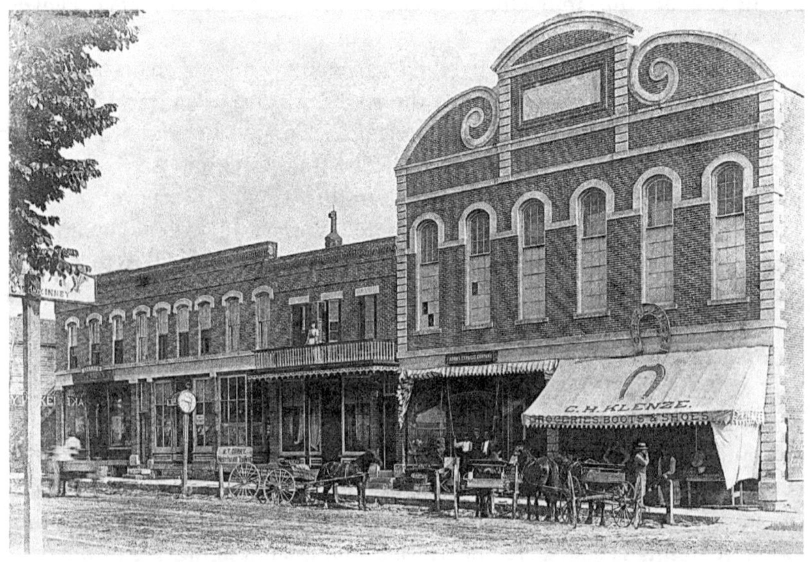

Fig. A.8. Holt's Opera House (at right), Anamosa, Iowa, 1891.

With her son in her arms, Eliza is fleeing . . . the bloodhounds are baying at her heels . . . she is at the river's edge . . . jump, girl, or be torn to pieces! . . . one last look back . . . she leaps! . . . teeters perilously on an ice cake . . . gains her balance . . . slowly drifts across . . . Saved!

Frank and I whoop as loudly as anyone in the house.

And so the play goes on in thrills, laughter and tears until at last, loveable [*sic*] old Uncle Tom falls in the clutches of the fell Legree.

Twirling his moustache and laughing his devil's laugh, the fiend snaps the great blacksnake over the poor slave's back. Uncle Tom very obviously has a board in the seat of his pants, but that makes no difference to me; each cut of the whip is a cut in my soul.

Now, snarls Legree, he is going to *kill* Uncle Tom unless he tells . . . But Uncle Tom will never tell . . . he is not afraid to die . . . with a curse in his throat, Legree raises the great whip . . . he strikes . . . with the *butt* of the whip! . . . this is more than I can stand—

I jump up.

"You stop that!" I scream. "Stop it this minute, I say!"

Aunt Sarah jerks me down in the seat so hard my teeth rattle. A few in the audience guffaw. Most of the people scarcely notice. The players go on as if nothing had happened. In spite of me, Uncle Tom dies.

Now comes a wonderful scene. The space above the stage is suddenly flooded with gorgeous pink clouds. In the midst of them is Little Eva . . . she is soaring upward . . . my mouth and eyes stretch wide open . . . I have always wondered about heaven—at last I am able to see it—

But suddenly, Aunt Sarah bends over and hisses in my ear: "Come now, we must go." She grabs Frank and me each by the arm, and bundles us out of our seats and up the aisle.

"Waaaa!" I bellow into the grief-hushed darkness of the opera house. "I want to see heaven! Waaaa!"

Aunt Sarah never explained why she jerked us away from the gates of paradise. As I have already mentioned, her actions, like the weather, were decisive but unaccountable.

III

We left mother and Baby Nan at the "art hall" where the cookery and needlework exhibitions were being held, and went out to make a tour of the fairgrounds. Father led the way, with Jack clinging to one hand and me to the other. Frank and Dave Peters brought up the rear. Although it was early morning, the crowds were already swarming among the stands and sideshow tents, and the sun was steaming down without mercy through clouds of hot dust. The fair was bedlam spread out over four acres. A merry-go-round piped and thumped gaily; hawkers were shouting their wares: "*Canes*[,] *balloons, fancy whips! Take home a soo-veneer!*" Barkers were howling the wonders of sideshows, peanut roasters were chugging. The good-natured crowd rippled with loud talk and laughter. And above all other sounds, the morning was punctured by the strident ba-a-a-a's of balloon squawkers, inflated from the lungs of hundreds of Jones county children.

Jack and I bobbed around at the ends of father's arms like game-fish on lines. We passed a shooting gallery; a machine whipping pink webs of cotton candy; a fortune teller's tent. We paused a moment before a big peanut and drink stand, waiting for Dave and Frank to catch up with us. Great scoopfuls of peanuts were turning in the roaster and the air was rich with the exotic smell of their roasting. I looked yearningly at the sacks of snowy popcorn in the glass case of the machine, then at the round bowls of pink lemonade and the tall glasses standing wetly on the counter, surrounded by clouds of flies. Father had given each of us two nickels, and in the face of temptation, I put my hand in my pocket and clutched my wealth tightly.

Progress was slow because every few steps father had to stop to talk to some neighbor. It seemed as if everyone we knew was there. We had already seen the Abbotts, the Welches and the Flynns, and here was old Adolph Schmidt waddling up to father now and wanting to know: "Vood, how iss tings by you?"

We brushed past a man who had a great bouquet of colored balloons and squawkers, passed a pea and walnut shell game, and paused in front of a stand where a tall, evil-looking man in a checkered suit and derby hat was exhorting a handful of spectators to try his gaming device.

"Right this way, folks," he whined, flashing his gold teeth in a lecherous grin. "Only ten cents, a dime. A child could do it. A child could win. Tee-ry your luck on the Golden Wheel."

The crowd around the stand was slowly increasing, but as yet, no-one would venture to play the wheel. They stood about, listening to the barker's talk with good-humored skepticism. We were in front and were pressed more and more tightly to the counter as the crowd grew.

"Tell you what I'm going to do, folks. To show you that this game as [*sic*] absolutely fair and that any of you may be the winnah, I am going to let one of you play the Golden Wheel *free*!"

The crowd moved in closer.

"Now, Governor," said Gold-Teeth, pointing a nicotined finger at father. "I want you to have a play on me. Just pick your lucky number. What'll you take?"

All eyes turned to father, tall and dignified in his dark Sunday clothes.

"Thirteen," he said, somewhat sheepishly.

"Thirteen is the gentleman's number!" howled the barker. "Now, ladies and gentlemen, keep your eyes on the Golden Wheel."

Around it spun in a whirl of gaudy colors, then slowed down, clicking the paddles deliberately: 9, 10, 11, 12—13!

The crowd gasped.

"A winnah! A winnah!" cried Gold-Teeth. "Good for five dollars. Hear that folks? Five dollars! My friend, I congratulate you. There, you see how easy it is! One spin of the wheel and the gent wins five dollars."

He grinned evilly, then affected a broken heart as he stacked five silver dollars on the counter in front of father.

"There you are, Governor. I sure hate to do this but you won it fair and square. Five silver dollars. All with one spin of the Golden Wheel! And it didn't cost you a cent."

Father smiled with slow, good-natured contempt and pushed the silver dollars back.

"I don't want your money," he said quietly. With this, he turned away and herded Jack and me out through the bystanders. The last I saw of Gold-Teeth, he was standing motionless in front of his wheel, his evil mouth hanging wide open. As we went on down the midway, we could hear the surprised murmur of the crowd. Tears came to my eyes as I thought of that neat pile of silver dollars, but I did not dare question father's decision.

We passed the gilt whirl of the merry-go-round and stopped in front of a cluster of side-shows [*sic*]. I was greatly impressed by the big, gaudy paintings strung up outside the tents to advertise the freak attractions. Emma Huge was shown, peering out squint-eyed from her 500 pounds of fat; Professor Bilbo, the sword-swallower, was caught in the act of eating his steely breakfast; Juanita, the world's most famous snake-charmer, was pictured, wreathed in her Sunday serpents.

As we were admiring these lurid effigies, Dave Peters edged over to father, scowling mysteriously. "I got to see a feller," he muttered. "Business. May take a long time; then agin it may not."

"All right, Dave," said father. "You know where our table is at the picnic grounds. You can meet us there at noon, or if you're still busy, we'll see you at the wagon after the main show's over this afternoon."

The hired man turned and hurried back through the crowd with that crazy, stumbling gait that was half walk and half run. I stared after him. It seemed to me that he was headed back to the Golden Wheel, but I couldn't be sure.

With incredible patience, father conducted us over every part of the fairgrounds. After we had looked over all the stands and sideshows and invested in a sack of peanuts apiece, he took us over to the livestock pavilion. There, prize-winning Poland China hogs were being exhibited, Holstein cattle and Shorthorns, enormous Percheron stallions, and finely bread Hampshire sheep. Father gravely inspected each exhibit, asking question from time to time of the owners. Meanwhile my brothers and I hung about restlessly. So far as we were concerned, this championship livestock was not a bit better than our farm animals at home. We craved the glamor of sword-swallowers and the music of balloon squawkers.

At noon, we went back to the art hall to get mother and the baby. I remember how mother hurried down the aisle between the exhibits to meet us. She was carrying Nan, and looked very young and pretty in her Sunday hat.

"I thought you'd never come," she said to father, her eyes shining. "You can't guess what I have to show you."

"Why, Hattie," father said. "I knew your grape jelly would win the blue ribbon."

"And the fanciwork, too," said mother, blushing.

* * * * * * * *

In the grandstand that afternoon, sat a majority of the able-bodied population of Jones county, perspiring, fanning themselves, and trying to calm restless children. A steady breeze was blowing in from the west, but it was like the breath from a blacksmith's forge and provided no relief for the sweltering audience.

Father and my brothers and I had arrived at the beginning of the program, and we had watched as attentively as the heat permitted, the trotting races, the livestock parade, and the various clown and tight-rope acts. All of these had been interesting, but they were only preliminary attractions. Now we were to see the main feature of the afternoon, the most thrilling single event of the entire fair—the balloon ascension.

Down in the grassy oval inside the race track, a crew of men were at work preparing for the inflation of the balloon. The great bag lay inert on the ground—an enormous gray-black mass of cloth. Near it, was a long metal ridge with a smokestack at one end. And over the stack were placed two very long poles, braced together in the form of an inverted "V."

It was hard to see what the men were doing because of the crowd of spectators who had climbed the fences and were standing in a circle, watching the preparations close at hand. Frank and Jack and I kept up a continual stream of questions, and father did his best to answer them all.

A long trench had been dug, he told us, and this had been filled with firewood and covered with iron roofing. The roofing was the long metallic ridge we saw. At one end of this trench, an iron flue about the size of a small barrel had been installed, and the other end had been left open.

Now we could see for ourselves the purpose of the tall, inverted "V." The men were hoisting the limp balloon by means of pulleys to the top of the poles. When it was up, it hung there, flopping in the breeze like an enormous peaked tent. A crew of six or eight held onto the folds of the cloth, keeping them away from the fire trench, and one man pressed the mouth of the great bag over the flue.

At the same time, we could see flames leap up at the other end of the trench where a fire had been started. All eyes were fixed intently on the balloon now. For some time, nothing seemed to happen; then the cloth began to swell out slowly, and as it did, the men who were holding the bag fed it gradually upward. Bigger and bigger grew the balloon and harder to manage in the breeze. Now and then we could see a glow lighten through the dark silk of the bag from the interior when the fire leaped up from the flue. Finally, the balloon pushed off from the long poles, and the men who had been holding the folds of cloth now took hold of the guy ropes. Officials were busy forcing the crowd out of danger.

"Pa, where's the balloon man?" asked Frank.

"I don't know, son, unless that's the man over to the right of the balloon." Father pointed to a man in overalls who had been directing the preparations for the ascension. He was busy now straightening out the various ropes of the parachute and trapeze rigging that were stretched out on the ground to the right of the trench.

No, that couldn't be the performer. Surely, so great a personage as a balloon jumper wouldn't wear common overalls!

Even as we were assuring ourselves of this, the mystery was solved. The man withdrew to the edge of the crowd and quickly peeled off his outer garments. And there he stood—a slim, athletic daredevil in black tights and a red waist glittering with silver spangles. The grandstand cheered him wildly.

The balloon was a huge black gourd over the arena now, tugging so hard with the wind that the men holding the guy ropes could hardly control it. The balloonist strutted out in front of the crowd to make his last bow. To the gentlemen he waved his hand gaily, to the ladies he blew a kiss. It was the adieu of a brave man who departs carelessly on a journey from which he knows he will never return.

Suddenly, the men let go of the ropes and the great bag angled upward to the east. The crowd in the arena parted before its swoop like scared sheep. Horses hitched at the edge of the fairgrounds began to whinny and jerk their heads upward in terror. The ascensionist, running swiftly to keep from being dragged, was finally lifted into the air. He held onto the trapeze with one hand and waved the other gallantly at the audience. "Goodbye [*sic*]," he seemed to say, "I'm off to the moon."

The balloon steadied and floated out to the southeast towards the Cheshire hill. Boys outside the fences scurried like ants in the direction of the flight. Higher and higher sailed the balloon. Now it was a dark bubble in the clear sky and the man a tiny drop hanging from it.

In the stands a great cry: *"He's jumping!"*

The black speck shot down through space, the parachute rigging streaming after him. Then the miracle. The parachute blossomed out like a white flower in the sky. It rocked a little, then steadied, and the daredevil wafted slowly downward.

The balloon, released of its passenger, now turned on its side. In another minute, it had turned completely over and was slipping down, leaving a trail of smoke in its wake. It deflated rapidly as it fell and finally became a mass of heavy cloth, dropping into some farmer's cornfield.

* * * * * * * *

As we were coming out of the grandstand gates, we passed an Indian medicine show. On the back of the wagon, a squat, dingy-faced Indian woman was beating a tom-tom. A dark little man in a plug hat stood beside her, holding up a bottle for the crowd to see. Apparently, he was about to make a speech.

"Look, Pa," said Frank excitedly. "There's Dave Peters."

We all looked just in time to see the hired man climb up on the back of the wagon. He brushed off his trousers, then stood up stiffly, his hat pressed against his bosom, his sharp eyes looking proudly out over the crowd.

"Ladies and Gentlemen," the little medicine man shouted, with a foreign accent difficult to understand. "It is with the greatest pleasure that I introduce to you the gentleman who will be your local agent for Dr. Alverdi's Famous Pain-Killer. He will have a supply of this celebrated elixir for you at all times and you can obtain it from him at the same reasonable price of fifty cents. Ladies and Gentlemen, I introduce to you—Mr. David Zephaniah Peters!"

IV

October days were like symphonies in my blood: symphonies of sound and smell and dripping color. The days were full of bird song again after the long heat-silence of August and September, and the nights were hushed with the mystery of falling leaves. On every hand lay the ripe fruits of the harvest; the clear air was flavored with their fragrance. The sky deepened into a ripe blue that seemed darker than the grass on the bleached prairie. Patches of scarlet sumac flamed along the roadside, and the woodlands glowed with purples, violets, reds, oranges, salmons, yellows—flowing through the month from dark to bright like the colors in the morning sky. All the pigments of the landscape were blended in the last great display of the year. October was the long sunrise of Indian summer.

* * * * * * * *

Far away, a voice. Then again and closer—not a voice out of dreams, but mother calling Jack and me: "Get up, sleepy heads, do you want to be late for school?"

Bright sunlight streamed into my face. As I lay in the warm bed, rubbing my eyes, I could hear the pigeons thrashing about on the roof, then subsiding with low, sobbing coos. A bluejay was scolding in the plum tree outside the window, and when he stopped, I could hear the small-talk of the robins, as cheery and contented as the voices of children at play.

The white yellow edge of the sun was emerging from a ruddy glow in the east when I slipped out of bed. From the farmyard came the muffled thunder of hooves and a dog's barking, and I knew that Dave Peters was driving the cows out to pasture. These October mornings were sharp; goose pimples appeared quickly on my arms and legs.

Jack was curled up with his arms over his face, snuggled in the warm luxury of sleep. It seemed a shame to wake him. I leaned across the bed and shook him by the shoulder and he turned over, mumbling incoherent, childish protest, and finally blinking his eyes.

I could smell the aromas of coffee and frying mush as I hurried downstairs to dress by the warmth of the living room stove. When I stepped into the kitchen, mother was at the range and Frank was getting up from the table to leave. He went to high school in Anamosa now, and early each morning rode into town on horseback. Baby Nan was cooing to herself in her cradle over by the kitchen window.

"Will you get a pail of water, please, before you sit down?" mother asked.

Sunlight was filtering through the trees, making yellow pools in the farmyard, when I went outside. The sting of the wet, frosty grass on my warm feet made me step gingerly. Father was out beside the barn, hitching up a team to the wagon. As I returned from the pump, I breathed deeply the wine-fragrance of the ripe grapes in the arbor along the west fence. Jack was at the table when I returned with the water, and the two of us ate hungrily of savory fried mush and thick molasses, eggs, and graham gems covered with sugar and cream.

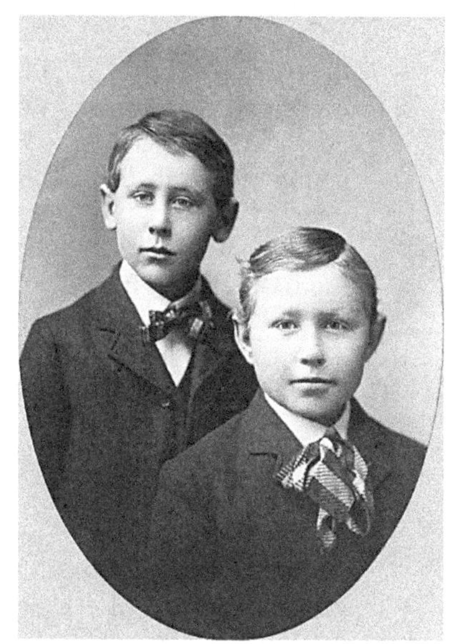

Fig. A.9. John "Jack" Wood and Grant Wood, c. 1900.

A few minutes later, we were swinging down the road to Cottonwood school. The Indians had pitched their villages again; cornfields on either side of the road were dotted with the brown wigwams of fodder. The air was perfumed with the fruity odor of wild crabapples and plums, ripening in the copses along the fence row. No sign of a cloud cluttered the ultramarine sky, but a blue atmospheric haze lay over the horizon and gave the illusion of distant, mist-enveloped mountain ranges. Long, filmy streamers of cobweb hung in the air and the milkweed pods had burst, sending their seed parachutes floating over the meadows.

Jack was loitering behind. I turned just in time.

"Here, spit those out—poison!" I cried sharply. He had picked a cluster of the maroon sumac berries and was stuffing them greedily into his mouth.

We arrived at school as the last bell was ringing, and left the brown fields and sunshine to enter the severe little room with its smell of chalk, books and soured slate rags. Geography and arithmetic were tiresome these mellow days. Most of the while, I sat covering my slate and book-margins with pictures, or just day-dreaming. The only time I fully awakened was when the teacher let me borrow the copy of Wood's *Natural History* from the little library shelf behind her desk. In this book were fascinating pictures of zebras, lions, and hippopotamuses that I tried to copy on my slate.

At noon, Jack and I had our lunch out of the lard pail I had carried to school that morning: sandwiches of home-made bread with fillings of raspberry jam which oozed through the bread and made it a brilliant magenta; hard-boiled eggs soon spotted with prints of dirty fingers, and a piece of apple pie. We ate hurriedly; then joined the other children in strenuous games of Pom Pom Pullaway and Ante High Over.

This taste of the outdoors during the noon hour completed my ruin for the rest of the school day. I drowsed during the long, hot afternoon, longing impatiently for dismissal time. Through the open windows, I watched the purple grackles flock into the schoolyard in black waves, awakening the countryside with their loud clacking. I wondered vaguely whence came these white-eyed, jewel-feathered birds that stopped for a few hours each autumn and spring and then disappeared. Lazily I hoped that a gray field mouse, seeking winter quarters, might venture into the room and send the teacher and little girls climbing to the tops of their desks. My mind wandered away to a nearby cornfields [*sic*] where crows were cawing raucously, and I was startled momentarily out of my daydreams by the loud riveting of a woodpecker on the roof.

Finally, the teacher jingled the desk bell for dismissal. Free! Joyously I ran outdoors and up the road, shouting back to my brother to hurry. From the meadows, I could hear the clear tinkle of the baby meadowlarks, trying to imitate the notes of their parents. I kept my eyes on a landmark straight ahead as I ran, a maple tree in our farmyard whose leaves had turned a bright yellow. The afternoon sun had kindled this tree into a globular flame, like a haystack burning amid the dark evergreens.

A field length away from the farmhouse in the lee of the hill, Jack and I could smell the spicy odors of pickling. The fragrance became sweeter with each step until we reached its source in our kitchen.

When we came in the back door, canning was done for the day and mother was putting the spices back in the cupboard. Jars of vari-colored fruits and preserves were cooling, tops-down on the table.

Mother looked tired and her face was streaked with perspiration.

"You[']r[e] just in time, Grant," she said, smiling. "Will you please carry these jars down [to the] cellar?"

Of course, I would! She knew this was a job I liked. I begged some cloves and stick cinnamon for Jack and myself; then went about my task. Filling a basket with jars, I carefully descended the steep cellar stairs.

The outside cellar door was open, and the slanting rays of the afternoon sun were falling directly through the opening. One side of the moist cellar was flooded with bright sunshine. Now for my favorite ceremony. In the jars of preserves, glowing with warm light, were colors infinite in variety and richness. I arranged them on the shelves with care.

The blue green of stuffed, bull-nosed peppers; light greenish yellow of gooseberries and currants; pale yellow of pears; warmer yellow of apple jelly (each glass with a leaf of rose geranium on the top to give it flavor); the richer yellow of spiced Siberian crab-apples; brownish yellow apple butter and ground cherry preserves; yellow plums with a slight orange tint; great two-quart jars of orange-tinted peaches; the red orange of wild plums; the flecked vermillion of tomatoes; the crimson of strawberries and raspberries; the deeper red of blackberries; red violet of loganberries and pickled beets; the blues and purples of tame plums, given variety and depth with grapes; the varied greens of cucumber pickles, water melon pickles, picallilly [*sic*], green tomato pickles, chow-chow, bread-and-butter pickles; and moss-green dills covered with grape leaves.

When I had finished, I turned from this outlay of gorgeous, liquid colors to the raw fruits and vegetables that were heaped in bins adjoining the fruit shelves. There were heaps of bright orange carrots; white turnips with purple at the stems; purple beets; tan parsnips, soil-colored Irish potatoes; heavy, green cabbages; brownish red onions; and massive, dark-green Hubbard squashes, covered with knobs and armored like rhinosceroses [*sic*].

Near the cyclone compartment lay a glowing heap of pumpkins and beyond that, barrels of apples; brown russets; greenish Baldwins splashed with red; yellow Pipins; deep maroon Jonathans; Greenings; dark red Ganos and Ben Davises; scarlet wealthies; and yellowish, crimson-cheeked Iowa blushes. Two barrels, one of molasses and the other of cider, stood in the corner, guarding the fruit like somber sentinels.

The cellar air was crowded with the ripe odors of the various fruits and vegetables, mingled with the good, firm smell of sun-washed earth.

* * * * * * * *

By the time the early farm supper was ready, my appetite was keen. I ate swiftly with a healthy, animal appreciation for every taste—potatoes, fried brown and crisp[;] roast pork that crumbled beneath the carving knife[;] garden vegetables[;] and thick slices of moist, yeasty bread coated with yellow butter. While we were eating, the kitchen was lighted up by the glory of the sunset. The autumn haze had become an irridescent [*sic*] veil in the west, and the sun was a huge ball of fire, slipping down slowly into a sea of gold and amber. Then it was gone and only a patch of borrowed flame remained in the sky.

When we had finished supper, the farmyard was misty with twilight. The rhythmic see-saw of the windmill dipped into the air already vibrant with the sad, thinned-out fiddling of the insects. Walking out to the barn to tend to my evening chores, I could hear the tinkle of the cowbells out in the pastures. Frank and Dave Peters had already gone to drive the herd in.

The dusk of the big barn was alive with a strange mixture of odors: the ammonia smell of the stables; the linseed odor of cottonseed oil meal; and the mealy scent of shorts and middlings and millet. I paused an uneasy moment before going up the ladder into the haymow. In the loft lurked enormous yellow and black spiders brought in with the hay and not yet killed by the frosts. Thistles were also mixed with the hay and could cause painful wounds to bare feet.

I was aroused by the low thunder of hooves, the sudden loud clank of cowbells, and deep mooing, as the cows came into the farmyard. As usual, I was dawdling over my chores. I started quickly up the ladder to the mow. Up through the loft floor I climbed and through the long, choking-dark tunnel in the hay. Heads of timothy hung out and dropped down my neck. As I sprang from the ladder to the sloping top of the hay, I felt a stab of fear lest I slip and fall headlong through the dark opening. Hurriedly, I pitched down enough hay for the horses. I descended cautiously to the loft level, then jumped away from the ladder and plunged down, down to light with a cushioned impact on the heap of hay I had thrown to the floor. I stretched out for a moment on the sweet-selling bed, and a feeling of ineffable contentment and drowsiness flowed over me. A medley of sounds lulled my thickened senses: the regular chunching [*sic*] of the horses and the occasional thump of a hoof on the wooden floor; the soft mooing of the cows outside, waiting to be milked; the complaining grunts and squeals from the nearby hog-pen; and the barking of a dog in the distance.

Sleepily I got up and went about my task of filling the mangers with hay. When I had finished, I went outside to help with the milking. The cool night air cleared my head. As I put a pail of feed down in front of one of the cows, preparatory to milking her, I could smell her warm, grain-milk breath. I balanced myself on the stool, clamping the big milk-pail between my knees with difficulty. The teats of the cow were warm and comforting to the touch in the chill evening, and it was pleasant to hear the whine of the milk stream as it struck the bottom of the empty pail.

The harvest moon, a jumbo, pumpkin-colored disc, was appearing over the purple skyline to the east as I plodded into the farmhouse, every sense numb with delicious exhaustion. If I could only go to bed now! But from the living room, my mother was calling: "Be sure to wash your feet, son."

The water heated on the kitchen range for dishwashing had long since cooled. Sleepily, I went to the sink and pumped the wash-basin full of leafy-smelling water from the cold cistern. I dipped my warm feet into the icy water for a cruel instant. Then I wiped them, passing tenderly over the stone-bruises and especially the raw little cracks between the toes, caused by sharp granules of sand.

In front of the living room stove, I slipped out of my clothes and into my outing flan[n]el night dress. Then, with mother's kiss on my cheek, I shuffled wearily upstairs to bed. In the bedroom, hard, blue moonlight was streaming through the east window; the little wooden rocking chair in front of my bed made a soft shadow on the rag rug. The air was brittle-cold and tense with the unmistakable premonition of winter. Jack was already in bed, breathing evenly in sound sleep.

I knelt, shivering at the be[d]side.

"Our Father Who art in Heaven . . . " the prayer started in a sing-song and gradually wandered into a sleepy whine like a gramaphone [*sic*] running down. ". . . thekingdomandthepowerandthegloryforeverAmen."

I climbed between the cool sheets and lay there for a moment, thinking no thought, stirring no muscle. I was completely resolved in a great rhythm in which there was no yesterday or tomorrow, only one mysterious flow. The sheets had a clean, grassy smell from having been recently washed and dried on the sod, and the touch of the blankets was rough and firm beneath my chin. Outside, the wind stirred in the spruce trees.

CHAPTER 5
YOU CAN HELP WITH THE PLOWING

I

Once a week, except in the most extreme weather, father drove to Anamosa to get the mail. His return from these trips always caused a little flurry of excitement in the household, although the mail seldom consisted of more than the Anamosa *Eureka* and perhaps one of the magazines to which father subscribed. Once in a while mother heard from Uncle Frank Weaver of Omaha, or father received a solemn epistle from his Quaker cousins in Virginia, but these occasions were very rare. And so far as I know, Dave Peters had never received a bit of mail since he had been working for us—that is, until the mysterious letter arrived.

It was in late October that he received this letter; I remember very well the evening it came. Father drove in at dusk, and Dave and I hurried out in the yard to help him unhitch the horses.

"Guess I'm a little late tonight," father said as he climbed down. "Here, Dave, here's something for you."

He handed the hired man a long bulky envelope.

Dave took it hesitantly and stood blinking at it for a few moments in mute unbelief. Then all at once, he turned and went like a streak across the farmyard and into the house.

He was not at the table when father and I came in to supper. He had gone straight up to his cold bedroom without eating. When I went to bed that night, his door was ajar, and I could see him hunched over his dresser, a column of fog rising from his whiskered lips as he spelled out the words of the letter.

The next evening, I was drawing in my favorite place under the table in the kitchen, and mother was preparing supper, when father came in the back door and said:

"What do you think, mother—Dave Peters is leaving us!"

I stopped my drawing in vague alarm.

"What's that?" said mother in a shocked voice. "Why, has anything happened—was that letter some bad news?"

"No, I don't think so. He didn't say what the letter was about. But whatever it was, it made him decide to do something he's been figuring on for a long time. He says he's going back to Cairo, Illinois[,] to get a job on the river."

"Oh pshaw!" said mother, somewhat relieved. "He's always talking about going somewhere. Remember how he went on about going to the Klondike that time? But he never made a move to go."

Father sat down beside the stove.

"This time, I'm pretty sure he means it."

Mother shook her head slowly.

"I'd about as soon believe you were leaving yourself. Did he say when he is planning to go?"

"After corn-picking."

* * * * * * * *

Dave Peters leaving?

My brothers and I talked it over and decided that it was impossible.

Who would cut willow whistles for us in the spring, if the hired man went away? Who was to make us toy windmills, and paddle boats to sail in the horse-tank? And figure-four box traps for catching wild rabbits? Ever since we could remember, the hired man had been doing that sort of thing for us. He would make us almost anything he wanted, and when he had finished, he would go striding away, muttering to himself, as if offended by our efforts to thank him.

If Dave Peters went, who would tell us stories about Indians, buffalo hunting, and dark adventure on the great river?

The hired man was part of our lives. He couldn't go away. You might as well say the sun wasn't going to rise the next morning.

Still, father seemed to be convinced that Dave was going to leave.

"I do hate to see him go," I heard him tell mother. "In spite of his grumbling and tall stories, I don't think I could find a better man anywhere. Besides, he seems to belong here."

"He's always been real good about doing things for me, too," mother said. "Even though he sometimes gets me so riled I could choke him. But I don't think he's really going. I'll believe it when I see it."

This conjecture was carried on strictly within the family. As usual, the hired man was non-committal and mysterious about his plans and father warned my brothers and me not to bother him with questions. Only once did I disobey this order.

One afternoon when I came home from school, I found Dave Peters sitting on the back stoop, his long, grotesque figure outlined against the thick-glowing colors of the fall sunset. He was carving husking pegs—small pointed sticks the men strapped to their palms in corn-picking for ripping the husks open.

I sat down beside him for a while and watched.

"Dave," I asked suddenly, "Are you going away?"

He blinked at me in mild surprise.

"Why, I reckon," he said gruffly.

"When are you coming back?"

He didn't answer this, but only went on with his work, scowling in silence at his nimble blade.

* * * * * * * *

But Dave Peters did not go when he had planned.

For right in the midst of corn husking, father was taken sick with a severe attack of asthma. He had been subject to the disease for years, but this was the worst attack he had ever had. I heard mother telling Grandmother Weaver about it later—how he awoke after midnight, gasping for breath, sprang out of bed and ran to the open window. All through the night he struggled for air, his face as pale as a ghost's and the veins of his forehead standing out in purple cords.

On top of the asthma, father contracted a bad case of the grippe and this combination laid him up for three weeks or more. During that time, Dave Peters took charge of the farmwork and said nothing more about leaving. He finished the husking, got the corn stored for the winter, and did what fall plowing father wanted done.

Frank and I helped as much as we could and I remember that during these weeks, Dave Peters taught me a great deal about farm processes. Most jobs around a farm, one learns gradually and cannot definitely say just when he did start doing them. But apparently Dave decided I was old enough to handle a man's share of the chores now. He showed me how to do many new things and took great pains to see that every move I made was exactly right. When I was milking a cow, or pitching manure, he watched me like a hawk.

"Ye can't pitch right, just usin' your arms!" he would snarl. "Use all your weight. You can lift twice as much and it ain't only half the work."

He instructed me how to hitch up a team, although I was too small to get the heavy harness on the horses alone. When I asked him why you had to warm the bit by blowing on it before putting it in the horse's mouth, he was eloquent in his disgust.

"Don't ye remember how it felt that winter when ye got your tongue stuck to the window pane?" he growled.

* * * * * * * *

At last father was able to be about again, and the hired man spoke once more about leaving.

"We've been hoping you would change your mind about going," father told him. "But we want you to do what seems best to you. When you're ready to go, I'll drive you into Anamosa."

Having declared for a second time his intention of leaving, Dave seemed a little lost and wistful about it. Nonetheless, he began getting ready for the departure in earnest. Evenings he spent in the frosty privacy of his room, packing his clothes and sorting out the odds and ends that he had treasured in the pine chest in his closet. He finished a hardwood teething ring he had been carving for Nan, and divided among my brothers and me some arrowheads and pieces of buffalo horn he had picked up over a period of years. But for all his mysterious preparations, he didn't leave, and as the days passed, we began to wonder if he hadn't changed his mind.

Sunday morning came and all the family got ready to go to church. But when father called Dave, the hired man replied that he wasn't going this morning.

"Goodness," said mother, "I wonder what's come over that man. This is the first time he hasn't gone to church with us since he's been here."

That noon, when we returned from Anamosa, we discovered the reason why. *Dave Peters had left!*

"Walked all the way into town in this cold wind!" father said, shaking his head, perplexedly.

"—with that heavy suitcase too!"

"Look," said Frank, "he left something here on the table."

On the dining table in the kitchen lay a package, wrapped in old newspaper. "Mrs. Wood" was written on the outside in the hired man's clumsy scrawl.

Mother unwrapped the package and inside she found a small book, bound in worn, brown plush.

"Why," she said, her eyes moist, "it's the Bible he read every night . . . he ought not to have done this."

Jack and I cried, and everyone else was solemn and depressed. Dinner was a gloomy affair, with scarcely a word spoken. We missed the hired man's crabbed, eccentric silence; the atmosphere of the house lacked savor without it.

"Well," said mother, trying to cheer us up. "Perhaps Dave Peters will come back in the spring."

But we all knew in our hearts that he wouldn't.

II

We prepared for the holidays with a special enthusiasm that year for it was to be Baby Nan's first Christmas. "We'll need an extra good tree," father said, and in spite of the fact that he was not well, he made a long trip to the Wapsie valley where he cut a young cedar to set up in our living room. When he was not occupied with farm chores, he could be found in the barn, doing carpenter work about which he kept a strict secrecy. Mother began to get good things together for the holiday dinner, and in every spare moment, she sewed like a woman possessed. During the two days before Christmas, we all had a hand in decorating the tree with candles, popcorn, cranberries, and cotton batten.

It looked as if we were in for a drab Christmas as far as the weather was concerned. The 24th was cold and cheerless, with the sun a pale smear in the sky and the land partially covered by a layer of drab, greyish snow. But Christmas eve, it became much warmer, and in the dusk, the snow began to fall. Swiftly and silently, the cotton flakes came down like a pale army in the night, changing the world completely.

After supper, the family gathered in the living room where we turned down the lamps and lit the candles on the tree. It was even more beautiful than we had dared hope—a tall, snowy pyramid, glittering with candles and ornaments and crowned by a silver star. We all felt a warm glow of pride in our handiwork. Mother brought the baby out to see the tree, and Nan gurgled in what we took to be approval. Frank and Jack and I were so excited that we spent most of the evening putting on our wraps and running outdoors to see how the tree looked from the yard. Outside, the sight was unforgettable; the newly fallen snow caught the brilliance of the candles and sparkled like drifts of diamond dust.

We would not be able to go to church in the morning, so after our first thrill over the Christmas tree had somewhat calmed, father read to us from Saint Luke.

"And the angel said unto them, Fear not: for, behold, I bring you good tidings of great joy which shall be to all people."

Father read the chapter slowly and gravely, as one in whom reverence is a deep, intuitive thing, and faith is the dignity of life itself. We children sat at his feet to listen and the silence of the country night became alive for us with the mystery of the first Christmas.

When we were ready for bed, my brothers and I hung our stockings above the stove, and mother put up a tiny one for the baby. As I went to sleep, I was wondering uneasily if Santa Claus would have trouble getting down the chimney through our stove.

Next thing I knew, it was morning. I was awakened by Jack who pulled my hair and screamed "Merry Christmas" in my ear. I jumped out of bed and ran downstairs after my brothers to see what Santa had brought us.

He had been there, all right. In each of our stockings was a pink mosquito netting bag full of striped hard candy, a wooden toy, and—most exotic and exciting of all—an orange! My toy was a small battleship with the word "Maine" painted on the bow. In the baby's little sock was a rattle, and a silver spoon with "Nancy" engraved in the bowl.

In addition to the gifts in the stockings, there was a home-made sled for Jack, a box of colored pencils for me, and a new pair of boots for Frank. Each of us had a few items of clothing too—shirts that mother had made, and the red mittens Grandmother Weaver knitted for us every year.

After breakfast, Frank and I hurried through the chores and cracked nuts for dinner. Then we went outside and played the rest of the morning in the new snow.

The climax of the day came at noon. For dinner, mother had roasted one of our big white turkeys and with it she served sage dressing, cranberry sauce, and all manner of delicious trimmings. Only one thing kept it from being a perfect Christmas. As we sat down at the table, I think we were all wishing that Dave Peters was there with us.

Christmas had been the hired man's favorite day. He would always have presents for the entire family—slingshots for my brothers and me, and some little items bought in Anamosa for mother and father. He would enjoy with great relish the Christmas tree, the big dinner, and the glow of family affection that was warmest on this day. And after dinner, he would invariably go into the parlor, removing his felt boots reverently before entering. There he would spend the afternoon, looking contentedly at the tintypes in the plush album and the colored engravings in the big family Bible.

Father elaborated on his usual grace a little, asking the Lord, among other things, to "bless Dave Peters wherever he was and make him happy this Christmas." That made us all feel better.

Dessert was thick mince pie. Then, to round off the big dinner, mother brought out the bowl of nuts Frank and I had cracked that morning. There were black walnuts, butternuts, and hickory nuts, gathered in the woods the preceding fall, and, as a special treat for the occasion, a few English walnuts father had bought in Anamosa.

Grandfather and Grandmother Weaver had planned to drive out, but we knew they would not come, for the roads were too snowy for a wagon and not packed enough for a sleigh. In the afternoon, however, Aunt Sarah came wading over in Uncle Eugene's boots. My brothers and I staged a program for the grown-ups. Under Frank's direction, we sang a mournful ditty about how grandfather went to heaven and had no end of trouble because no-one was there to find his spectacles for him. Then Jack, with the benefit of considerable prompting from mother and Aunt Sarah, recited "The Night Before Christmas." As the final number on the program, we gave an original melodrama in which Frank was General Custer, and Jack and I were redskins. My most important duty in this play, I remember, was to end Custer's last stand by popping a paper sack.

Father especially seemed to get a deep pleasure out of all this. Throughout the afternoon, he sat contentedly by the stove, moving only when the fire needed wood. When the baby woke up from her nap and was brought out in the sitting room, he took her up and she went back to sleep in his arms.

But in the evening when the family was sitting around the fire eating popcorn, father began to get restless.

"I feel a little stuffy, mother," he said. "Guess I'll go outdoors for a while."

He stayed outside for a long time, walking slowly back and forth in the snow. When mother kissed me goodnight, I saw there was a worried look in her eyes.

III

During the winter, father was kept indoors more and more frequently with attacks of asthma. Finally mother persuaded him to go to a doctor in Anamosa for a physical examination. Dr. Perkins said something about heart trouble, gave him some medicine, and cautioned him severely about overwork.

"Why don't you take a two weeks' rest, Maryville," mother urged. "Jim Flynn will come over to help the boys with the chores if they need it, and by the end of two weeks, you'll feel a sight better."

Father said he would think it over, and looked at her as if to say: "Hattie, you're a good little wife, but this is one of those things you don't understand very well." He went on working as he had always worked.

People remarked how haggard he was looking. With the bluntness of country folk, they seemed eager to tell him so. Mother became furious at Aunt Sarah because her manner of greeting father these days was invariably: "Well, I declare, Maryville, you look more poorly every time I see you." Father only smiled at such remarks and said he guessed he felt about the same as ever.

Mother was very worried about him. Often when he was outside longer than she expected him to be, she sent me to see what he was doing. This seemed strange because she had always accepted everything father did without question. Even now, she did not nag at him. But as she went about her work, she quietly watched his every move, husbanding her comment until she could stand it no longer. Then she would scold him—all the more severely because she was a little frightened about doing it. Father was amused at these outbursts that seemed so out of character for mother. He listened patiently but never took them seriously.

Where mother failed in persuading him to let up with his work, however, the sickness succeeded. The attacks of asthma came suddenly, cutting short his breath and exerting an enormous pressure on his heart. Then he was laid up for days at a time, helpless and in agony.

As the attacks recurred with greater frequency, we could see a change in him. One of my most vivid memories of former winters was of father's impatience at being confined to the house by the bad weather. But this winter, he got so that he didn't chafe at staying in. Something within him had given way. He didn't worry about Frank and me doing the chores, either, as he had at first.

During the periods when he was well enough to be out of bed but too weak to go outside, he spent most of his time in his hickory rocker, looking out of the window to the west. He took an unending delight in the baby, and would sit for hours, watching her play, or gently rocking her cradle. He seldom touched his Macaulay or Lincoln biography any more. Some days he seemed fairly contented, but on others—especially when money matters were troubling him—he had spells of extreme depression.

Occasionally after a gloomy day during which his eyes had been dull with despair and he had spoken scarcely a word, his spirits revived in the evening. Sitting by the living room stove after a good supper, he relaxed and appeared to enjoy the family and the comforts of home more thoroughly than ever before. He talked some too. As he leaned back and closed his eyes, all the seasons of his life seemed to pass before his mind in a measured flow. A warm light played on his memory, illuminating corners and niches he had not disturbed in years. He remembered the Quaker meeting house he had attended as a boy in Virginia, the sight of tobacco fields in early morning, and the mists of the Blue Ridge mountains blending into the sky. He spoke of the first years after his family had settled in Iowa, and recalled how his father had tanned him once when he had tried to hitch a yearling steer to the good buggy. Most of all, he remembered things about the weather and the soil; the storms, the droughts, the bumper harvests: these had been vividly traced in his mind. He told of a tornado he had once seen, and of the great drought of a few years before when all the creeks and springs in the vicinity had dried up. He had been forced to haul water for the stock in great hogsheads from the Wapsie River. I dimly remembered going with him on one of these trips although I couldn't have been more than three at the time. When he talked about things like this, his speech was rich with allusion to impressions first experienced in his boyhood and deepened by repetition in the succeeding years. Such as the smell of corn pollen in August, or the good feel of a plow beneath the hands in the spring turning when the soil is still moist from the recent thaws.

Father had ever been one to reminisce, and in the few evenings that winter when he opened up his memory, we probably came closer to really knowing him than at any other time. Yet, in another sense, such brief flashes only emphasized all the more strongly the solitary, mystic qualities that formed his inner personality. These had not changed. One had but to watch him as he sat at the window looking out, to realize he was still a stranger in his own house and always would be.

IV

It seemed to us we had never had such a lovely spring. The winter had been especially long and depressing with father sick so much of the time. We had thought February would never end. Then, when we were almost worn out with the monotony of the bleak months, spring suddenly arrived. It seemed to come all at once. One day we had been hemmed in by drab, snow-grey hills and blotched fields where drooped the slattern remnants of last year's cornstalks. And the next day—as if by magic—the meadows had changed to a deep emerald; the plowed fields lay neat and chocolate-hued in the mellow sunlight; and the slate-colored sky had opened into a fresh blue torrent across which big clouds swept like rafts of clean snow.

With the coming of spring, father began to feel much better. There were no more sick and dizzy spells. He worked from dawn to darkness as he had always done, and in the evening he read his books. He looked so much better that even mother stopped fretting about him.

"Going to get the crops in early this year," he said cheerfully.

He was as good as his word. He had his oats in before the first of April and a few days later, he began to plow the sodfields for the corn. Afternoons when I got home from school, I liked to go out to watch him lay open the rich furrows.

"Next year," he told me, "you can help with the plowing."

The entire family was happy these days. Seedtime, the most joyful season of the year, had returned and father was well again. We were all busy outside. After school, Frank worked with father in the fields, and Jack and I helped mother prepare her flower and vegetable garden. Father had built a little pen for the baby so that she could play outside on the back stoop while mother was in the garden. It was a joy to see how mother's cheeks brightened after she had been working in the earth. She promised Jack and me that some Sunday before long, she and father would take us over in the woods along the Wapsie to gather wild ferns, may apples, and Jack-in-the-pulpits. It was as if we had plowed under the past with the old cornstalks and were concerned now with only the good future.

Then, one gray morning when Jack and I came down to dress in front of the sitting room stove, we knew that something was wrong again. Breakfast had not been started. Mother was nowhere to be seen. Her bedroom door was closed; I went to it and listened. Apparently, she was inside, for I could hear someone moving about.

I was just starting out to find Frank when he came in the kitchen door, looking worried.

"Father's having another spell," he said. "A real bad one, I guess."

We hung around for a while in the kitchen, feeling helpless and uneasy. After a while, the bedroom door opened abruptly and mother came running out. Her face was drawn and there was a scared look in her eyes.

"Grant," she said—her voice trembled—"you must run over to Grandmother Wood's just as fast as you can. Tell them to drive into town for a doctor. I want Frank to stay here. Tell them, for the love of heaven, to hurry!"

Scared, half-crying, I ran out of the back door. The moist wind slapped my face as I raced down the road to the east. I scrambled over a fence and cut across plowed fields. My throat went dry; tears smarted in my eyes. My feet bogged down in the wet loam. *Hurry, hurry* throbbed in my ears, but each step was like lead. At the edge of Grandmother Wood's farm, I ran into a great tangle of willow brush cut down and left on the ground. I climbed over the logs, fought myself free of branches, plunged through the twisted foliage into the farmyard.

Uncle Eugene was in front of the barn, hitching up a team. No change came over his rigid face when I gasped the message to him. He turned quickly and started toward the house.

A few minutes later, Uncle Gene, Aunt Sarah and I were in the one-seated rig, driving down the road as fast as the horses could pull through the mud. Aunt Sarah asked me questions about father's attack until she saw that I knew none of the details. Then she and Uncle Gene began to talk about how sick father had been and how they wouldn't be surprised at anything that might happen. This made me want to cry, but I managed not to.

When we stopped at our place, Frank came running out to the buggy.

"You won't have to go to town, Uncle Gene," he said. "Jim Flynn was just by and he's started in for the doctor on his fast bay."

Aunt Sarah and Uncle Gene got out and went with Frank to the house. I followed them, awed by their grim, ominous expressions. All was still in the house; our footsteps echoed unnaturally as we walked through the kitchen to the sitting room. Jack was by the sitting room window, rocking the baby's cradle, his eyes wide with fear and wonder. The bedroom door was closed. Aunt Sarah opened it quietly and she and Uncle Gene and Frank tiptoed in. They did not let me come too, but I caught a glimpse of the inside of the bedroom. I could see the lower end of the bed and the long still mound of covers under which father's figure lay. Mother was standing at the window, looking into space. Her body sagged forward as if she were very tired. Tears streamed down her face. When the others came in, she did not seem to notice.

V

They had services for him at the Strawberry Hill Presbyterian church. I sat in one of the front pews between mother and Aunt Sarah. It seemed to me we waited for hours in the chill, hanging silence. Everything was heavy and oppressive about the place: the massive gray coffin, the sickening fragrance of the roses, the stiff black of the mourners. An occasional cough or sob grated harshly on nerves worn raw. It seemed that something must happen to ease the tension; yet nothing could happen. I felt Aunt Sarah's thin body quivering with sobs. Mother's eyes were red and swollen, but she was not crying now. She sat motionless, looking straight ahead. Once she reached over and took my hand. But that was small comfort; her hand was cold and lifeless.

At last the minister arose to give the funeral sermon.

"The departed . . . loving father and husband . . . upright citizen . . . devout Christian . . ."

I listened but could not realize he was talking about my father in that hollow voice. He was talking about someone far away whom I had never known, someone who had died. ". . . whom Thou hast seen fit to cut off in the prime of life . . ." Presently I was crying, but it was because I was tired and frightened, not because I realized my father was dead and that I should mourn. They had told me what had happened all right; that father had been called to heaven and would not come back in this life. I had heard the words and repeated them. I was very brave about it, they said. But inwardly I had not understood. Nor did I know.

"*For this corruptible must put on incorruption . . .*" What did these words mean? And the family, assembled here in their heavy grief; the friends looking down at us long-faced from the distant hills of their sympathy—why were they here?

Perhaps if I had understood a little better, I should have wondered how those who had been unable to understand father in life, appeared to understand him so well in death; grieving so confidently and so confidently consigning him to the hereafter. There was something businesslike about their grief. It was as if they were making a final entry in a ledger: *Maryville Wood, born 1845, died 1901.* "There, that account is balanced; let us turn to another page."

* * * * * * * *

They buried him in the green, wooded cemetery southwest of Anamosa. This was the same rich soil, the same firm, rolling hill-land he had farmed from boyhood.

Even when they lowered the casket into the grave, I did not realize that father was gone. For these rites were alien, unintelligible to me, while in my mind was stamped another and clearer image of a tall figure, plowing; a gaunt figure, leaning slightly forward, who seems a man of the earth and the plow, yet in whose attitude is a mystic aloofness that will never surrender—even to the ground.

VI

The wagon jolted slowly along the hot road, rousing up clouds of powdery dust in which winged grasshoppers played. There was scarcely a sound other than the *plop plop* of the horses' hooves and the rumble of the milk cans in the back of the wagon . . . and occasionally a sudden loud trumpeting as one of the horses cleared his nose.

Frank and I rode in silence, yielding our weights lazily to the swaying of the wagon. Once in a while, Frank stirred himself to brush a fly from the back of one of the horses with his whip.

The crawling progress of our wagon seemed the only movement on the countryside this morning. Windmills stood without turning, cattle grazed motionless on the hills, and the fields of corn and ripe oats lay asleep in the metallic sunshine. Yet everywhere the landscape breathed the mystery of hidden forces at work in the earth; the silence pulsed with the slow rhythm of growing crops.

It was unpleasant riding, especially through the airless lanes where the road was shut in on both sides by corn, and the dust hung in thick, static clouds. But Frank and I didn't mind. We were on our way to Anamosa and were thoroughly enjoying the luxury of going somewhere. Other days of the week, we took our milk to the crossroads and put it on a platform for the Flynns to haul with theirs. But this was Saturday morning when we went to Anamosa ourselves, hauling the milk to the creamery and getting our mail at the postoffice [*sic*]. The weekly trip to town was about the only diversion Frank and I got now. Twenty cows to milk morning and night; stables to keep clean; sheep, hogs and poultry to tend; and various other chores to look after—all this did not leave much time for recreation.

So it was with the satisfaction of a respite well-earned that we rode along on this July morning, unmindful of heat and dust and the discomfort of the hard wagon-seat.

As we came out of the side road up to the highway, we could see a man working on the fence at the edge of the pasture across the road.

"Hello, Mr. Abbott," shouted Frank. His words had an unusual resonance in the bright morning air.

John Abbott stopped his fence-mending long enough to give us a friendly wave.

"Hello there," he called back jovially[.] "How are you Wood boys getting along running the farm?"

"Just fine!" replied Frank with a trace of pride in his voice.

Riding was a little smoother on the main road. Frank began to whistle cheerfully.

"Look here," he said suddenly, pointing to a patch of dusty grass by the roadside. "That's where I pulled out to the side of the road when that horseless carriage came by last week."

"Gee," I said, admiringly, "I wisht I'd been with you."

"Honest, you never heard such a racket in your life. If I hadn't got out and held the horses' heads, they'd have run away sure. Maybe you'd have been scared if you'd been along—"

"I would not!"

When we got to the top of the Cheshire hill, we could see a big cloud of dust far down the road. A horse and rig were coming towards us, traveling at a good speed. The marking of the horse was plain from quite a distance. It was black with a white chest.

"Must be a stranger," said Frank. "Nobody around here has a horse like that."

When the approaching driver got within hailing distance of us, he reined over to the side of the road and stopped.

"Must want to ask directions," said Frank.

We could see now that he was an elderly man with a gray beard—

"Why it's Grandfather Weaver!" Frank and I both cried at once.

It was grandfather, all right, sitting straight and austere with a light linen duster over his lap.

"Hello, boys," he said when we drew up beside him. "I recognized you back there a way, so I thought I'd stop and wait for you."

Frank and I wanted to ask a dozen questions all at once.

"Where's grandma?—"

"—and where did you get the horse and buggy?"

"Well," said Grandfather Weaver, smiling at our curiosity, "grandmother had to stay in Cedar Rapids this time. So I came over to see you and your mother by myself. I came from Cedar Rapids to Anamosa on the train. Then I rented the horse and rig from the livery stable in Anamosa. Ain't she a dandy?"

"Gosh, yes!" We admired the young mare, whose flanks shone shiny black under the coating of dust.

"Well, I suppose you boys will be back to the farm in time for dinner. I'll see you then. Be careful with the team."

Grandfather clucked at the fine mare, who perked up her ears and started smartly up the road again.

As we resumed our way toward town, Frank and I could hardly hold our excitement. A visit from Grandfather Weaver was a real event now that he and grandmother lived in Cedar Rapids.

"Won't mother be surprised?" said Frank. "Say—do you suppose grandpa brought us anything from the city?"

* * * * * * * *

When we returned to the farm that noon, we found, as we had hoped that grandfather had brought each of us a package of candy from Cedar Rapids.

But that was nothing, compared to the news he had for us!

After we had finished our dinner and Frank and I were about to go out to work again, mother said: "Wait a few minutes, boys. I want you to come into the sitting room for a little while before you go out. Grandfather has something to say to you."

"Me too?" piped Jack, fearful of being left out.

"Yes, you too."

In the sitting room, we three boys stood around uncomfortably, wondering what this was all about. Grandfather Weaver sat down in the rocker we had always called father's chair and rocked in silence for a few moments, tugging at his beard thoughtfully. In a few moments, mother came in with the baby in her arms and grandpa was ready to begin.

"Well, boys," he said, clearing his throat solemnly, "I've been talking to your mother about something this morning and now I'm going to talk it over with you.

"Your mother tells me you have been doing a good job of taking care of the farm—better than could be expected. That's fine. We're proud of you. And the work won't hurt you none, either—do you good, in fact.

"But pretty soon now, school will be starting, and you won't be able to do all the chores and go to school too. And your mother says that whatever happens, she's going to see that you go on with your studies. That means we'll have to figure out some new way for you to get along.

"Now, you could stay here on the farm and try to get on the best you can. But even letting the crop-land out on shares, you would have to have a hired man. The trouble there is that a good hired man is hard to get and besides you can't afford one. As you boys may know, there's a good deal of money owed on this farm. If you had to pay a hired man, it don't look like you'd be able to keep up the payments. So that has to be considered too.

"This morning, we were talking all these things over and we finally hit upon a plan that seemed to me about the best of any. Your mother thought so too, but she said she wanted to see how you boys felt about it before she made up her mind. So now it's up to you.

"How would you like to move to Cedar Rapids?"

VII

Within a week after mother had inserted ads in the Anamosa paper, offering our farm for sale, several prospective buyers turned up. In the middle of August—sooner than we had expected—we sold the farm on what Grandfather Weaver called "very satisfactory terms" and the prospect of our moving to Cedar Rapids became a certainty.

My brothers and I were walking on air. When we woke in the morning, our first thoughts were about Cedar Rapids; we chattered about it during our meals; and at night, mother had to scold us for lying awake in bed, talking.

Frank was as pleased about moving to the city as Jack and I were, but he tried to appear matter of fact about it since he was older and better traveled than we were. Anamosa was the biggest town Jack and I had ever seen, but Frank had been to Cedar Rapids itself. He had made the trip that spring shortly after Grandfather and Grandmother Weaver had moved there, and had returned to the farm with glowing accounts of urban wonders. His description of a modern bathroom had been especially vivid.

"Instead of privies, you just do it right in the house. You pull a chain and there is a tremendous gurgling sound . . . "

Now that we were actually going to move to the city, Jack and I had to hear everything about it over and over again.

"Is Cedar Rapids really bigger than *Anamosa*?" we asked with persistent incredulity.

"Anamosa!" Frank would snort contemptuously. "Why Cedar Rapids' *little finger* is bigger than Anamosa!"

As usual, mother fitted inconspicuously into the background of our excitement. If she was hurt by our childish and somewhat callous eagerness to leave the farm, she never showed it. And we, in our turn, were too enthusiastic about going to wonder what the uprooting might mean to her.

I realize now that this was perhaps the hardest time of her life. Not that she was reluctant to leave the farm for its own sake. She had never been fully suited to farm life—had never had the same zest for it father had. Yet, after all, the farm had a strong hold upon her. It had seen the early years of her marriage, full of hardships and bright hopes for the future; the births of the four children; the sudden overwhelming tragedy of father's death. When she left it, she would prematurely bury that part of her life lived in its own right. The future she would live for her children.

Uncertainty clouded that future, too. From the sale of the farm and from father's insurance, mother hoped to get enough money to buy us a small house and get us started in the city. But after that, we would have to shift for ourselves, and as Grandfather Weaver had admitted, it would be no "bed of roses."

All of these things must have been in mother's mind during the weeks that we were getting ready to move. Most of all, I think, in the memories awakened by our preparations, she was living over again the horror of father's death. She didn't show this much; hers was too reserved a nature to reveal profound feeling. To outsiders she seemed as cheerful and serene as ever. But I remember there were a few little changes in her manner. She didn't sing at her work any more, for example, and she had little spells of absent-mindedness when she would stop in the midst of some task and look off into space as if trying to remember something dear and long forgotten.

And on one occasion I got a real glimpse of the unhealed grief she was keeping to herself. The shock—the mingled surprise and tenderness and childish humiliation—I felt at discovering the secret depth of her sorrow, remains with me yet.

It was late one night, long after my brothers had gone to sleep, and I was tossing in bed in unaccustomed wakefulness. Frank and I had been talking about Cedar Rapids and the excitement burned in my mind like a fever, driving sleep away. Finally, I crept out of bed to go downstairs for a drink.

I padded down in my bare feet, a little frightened by the darkness and a little ashamed of my fright. There was no sound in the house but the ticking of the clock. I was relieved to see there was a light in the sitting room. Mother, I thought, had forgotten to blow out the light before she went to bed. Now, when I got to the bottom of the stairs, I saw her, lying on the caterpillar couch behind the stove, her head buried in her arms. She was in her nightgown, with her wrapper about her and her hair down over her shoulders. At first, I thought she was asleep; then I saw that her body was shaking. She was crying—not as a grown woman, a mother,—but as a little girl who was lost and afraid.

She started with fright when I went over and put my arm on her shoulder, but when she saw who it was I knew she was glad that I had come.

* * * * * * * *

The people who were buying the farm wanted us to vacate by the first of September. We couldn't get away that soon, mother told them, but we would try to be out by the end of the first week in September. Even that was cutting time short, considering all that was to be done. Our household goods we planned to ship to Cedar Rapids, but we would have to dispose of our livestock and implements before we left the farm.

That meant an auction. There was more excitement for you! I had always wanted to go to an auction—now, one was coming to us.

Grandfather Weaver made another trip out to the farm to help us make arrangements for the sale and for moving our household goods to Cedar Rapids. He had dodgers printed for us in Anamosa, and a few days later, the cross-roads blossomed out with bright yellow, blue and red bills advertising the sale of our livestock and implements. These were illustrated with pictures of huge horses and pop-eyed hogs which, to my distress, resembled none of our own farm animals.

Curiously enough, in looking forward to the auction, it did not for some time occur to me that this would mean parting with all my farm pets. When the fact finally did dawn on me, I took the matter up with mother in alarm.

"Ma, will *all* the cows be sold at the auction?"

"Yes, son. We couldn't take them with us."

"And the—chickens?"

"Yes."

"And even *Pat*?"

"Yes, I'm afraid so—even Pat."

This was putting a different slant on things. I no longer looked forward to our departure with feelings of unmixed joy. And when I learned that Dewey was to be left behind, I very nearly rebelled. But the lure of the city was strong, even pitted against my attachment for the farm animals. Besides, we were too busy with preparations for leaving to have much time for regrets. So, if I wasn't able to quell my misgivings, I at least put them aside for a time.

Early September brought its usual hard, soaking rains and we were afraid that the roads would be so bad that we wouldn't have anybody at our sale.

When the morning of the auction day itself came—cold, misty and with a heavily overcast sky,—we simply gave up hopes for a good attendance. But as it turned out, we needn't have worried at all. For even before we finished our chores that morning, wagons plastered to the boxes with mud began to pull into our farmyard, bringing prospective buyers to inspect the stock and implements at their leisure before the bidding started. By mid-morning, a big crowd of farmers, heavily-booted and burly from thick clothing under their overalls, were milling about our barn and farmyard.

The auctioneer was to be fat, kindly "Dad" Walters, who had known father and mother for twenty years or more. He was a ruddy, stub-legged little man with a droopy, tobacco-stained moustache and an inexhaustible fund of optimism. I don't remember that we ever saw Dad when he didn't have time to stop and talk indefinitely and to fish some dingy peanuts for us boys out of his pockets. He was so rotund that when Jack climbed up on his lap to play with his massive gold watch fob, the stomach left scarcely enough ledge for the boy to sit on.

Dad arrived about half-past nine, wearing his broad-brimmed black "campaign hat" and driving his ancient strawberry roan. Jack and I ran out to meet him.

"Well look at this, would you," he bayed at the dried-up little clerk-of-the-sale who was riding with him, "Durned if here ain't a welcome committee."

I helped Dad unhitch his decrepit old nag and put it out to pasture. The horse was a familiar object of jest in the vicinity. Wherever the auctioneer went, some farmer would shout at him: "Well, Dad, when are you gonna auction off that old crowbait of yours?" And Dad would defend his nag good-naturedly. "Why, that's the best horse in Jones county. Only two things wrong with him—he's hard to catch in the pasture and he ain't no good when you catch him!"

Jack and I tagged proudly along after the auctioneer as he walked through the crowd of farmers. Everybody in the county, it seemed, knew him and he could call them all by name. "'Lo, Herm . . . H'are ya, Rufus . . . What are *you* doin' here, 'Dolph Schmidt? This is an auction—ain't givin' away nothin' free here! . . ."

Dad Walters didn't stop outside but marched on into the kitchen where mother was busy preparing the lunch she would have to serve that noon.

"Just thought I'd gossip with you a few minutes before the sale begins, Hattie," he shouted genially, sitting down by the kitchen table.

Mother was trying to appear calm this morning, but I could tell she was having a hard time to keep the tears back. Before Dad went out to start the auction, however, he had got her to chuckling in spite of herself over the latest story about Ed Struble, the region's most hen-pecked husband. The tale was that Struble had escaped from his shrewish wife for a day, had gone to the county fair (via the Anamosa saloons), and had returned home that night with the image of an undraped lady tattooed on his forearm.

For all Dad's easy-going ways, he knew how to handle a sale better than any other auctioneer in the county. People counted on him to put on a good show and he never disappointed them. He kept up a constant stream of banter and when the buying slowed up, he would single out some farmer in the crowd and josh him into bidding.

He was in fine form this morning. Once the sale was underway, he kept things moving so fast I couldn't keep track of what was happening. In two hours, he disposed of our farm implements and all of our hogs.

Then it was time for lunch. Mrs. Abbott, fat and explosively good-natured, had come over to help mother. The two women served the hungry crowd great stacks of hogshead cheese sandwiches and gallons of steaming coffee. After lunch, the sale was resumed.

It was not pleasant to stand by and watch our sheep, cows, turkeys, and my old friends, the Plymouth Rocks, auctioned off as if they had been so many vegetables. But I managed to keep up a stout front during the afternoon except for one time. That was when I had to lead our favorite horse, Pat, up and down a lane of prospective buyers.

VIII

I opened my eyes with that vague, half-suppressed anxiety with which one wakes on the momentous days of his life. Bare walls and a naked expanse of pine floor . . . I remembered—the sitting room. We had gone to bed on mattresses laid out on the floor. Our furniture had been hauled away the day before. And this morning, we ourselves were leaving for Cedar Rapids!

The excitement came back with a sickening rush and forced me wide awake. I sat up and looked around.

The room was grey with the chill of early morning. Light from the east was beginning to sift through the curtainless windows, thinning the shadows. Jack was curled up beside me, sound asleep. Frank was sleeping on a mattress next to ours and beyond him were mother and the baby. I heard mother's regular breathing.

A soft thumping sound made me turn quickly. Dewey was lying at the head of my mattress, watching me with affectionate interest, his tail gently twacking the floor. For once—on this last night—he had been given the privilege of sleeping in the house. I felt a sudden twinge, remembering that we were going to leave him today.

I could stay in bed no longer. Anxious to escape the cold gloom of the house, I got up, slipped into my clothes and tiptoed out through the dusky kitchen. Dewey followed, yawning, and wagging his tail gratefully.

Outside, the dawn was beginning to spread, firm and clear, out of white mists in the east, suffusing the barnyard with restrained, lucid light. This was going to be one of those perfect, abundant days of late summer.

I jumped off the back stoop into the dew-chilled grass and started towards the barn. I took a few steps, then stopped dead-still. An uncanny feeling came over me.

Day was stirring, but the farm was not awakening with it. The whole place lay silent and deserted, like a country churchyard.

No rooster crowed. No cows grazed in the yard, ready to be milked. The wagon that had stood between house and barn was gone. No pigs were squealing for their food from the nearby hog-pen; no white turkeys hung about, waiting for their morning feed.

All that could be heard in the silence was the steady whistling of the windmill and the rapid click click of the pumpshaft.

All at once, the farm had become a foreign, unfamiliar place. Dewey noticed the change too; his tail drooped and he stayed close by me.

I heard a thrashing and guttural cooing in the barn eaves and looked up eagerly. A white dove took noisy wing and flapped off into the wind. The pigeons, ignored when the barnyard was full of animals and fowl, now assumed a role of friendly importance. They were the only familiar sign of life.

* * * * * * * *

We ate breakfast on a packing box in the kitchen that morning in an atmosphere of mixed excitement and gloom. None of us had much to say. When we did talk, we kept our voices down to half-whispers because ordinary tones stirred up loud echoes in the empty house. My brothers and I, up to this time so overjoyed about leaving, were now curiously subdued. Even Jack was quiet and sober-faced.

"We'll have to hurry like everything," mother said nervously. "We don't want to keep John waiting." John Flynn, our kindly Irish neighbor, had volunteered to haul us to Anamosa in his lumber wagon.

After breakfast, we made haste to pack the cooking things and to roll up the mattresses and bed clothing in neat bundles. We had everything ready a full hour before John was to come.

"Now," said mother, as she was getting the baby's things together, "I want all of you to look through the house for one last time to see that you haven't left anything."

Small chance of that, we thought, the way mother had scrubbed the place out for the new tenants.

I slipped upstairs first. The hired man's room was clean and bare as a bone. I looked carefully to see if there was any remembrance of Dave Peters left—a religious motto on the wall or an Indian relic in the window-sill. But the room was empty, with only the stern silence to remind me that Dave Peters had once occupied it.

In our bedroom, broad sunlight lighted up the big-flowered wallpaper at which I had stared so many mornings. There was the china matting on the floor, and the black-japanned stove pipe register down which Jack and I had often dropped marbles. But all the other familiar things were gone.

The parlor was the most changed room in the house. It had always been aloof from the other rooms, shut away with its billowy carpet and plush furniture for such occasions at [i.e., as] the semi-annual visits of the preacher. Now, stripped of its finery, it was suddenly pulled down to the level of the other rooms. There was something cheap and pathetic about its bareness. I noticed particularly a shelf above where the parlor organ had been. Formerly, mother had kept this covered with an elegant satin cover, embroidered with red roses. But now, the cover was gone, and the shelf was revealed as an ugly, unfinished pine board.

The sitting room—next to the kitchen, the most used room in the house—was full of memories. Over the high shelf on the east wall was a startling, ragged-edged silhouette where the walnut clock had stood. It was as if the clock had gone and left its ghost behind. Other ghosts were stamped on the wall too. Behind the stove were the memories of many calendars, one imprinted on the other. Above these, a clean oblong betrayed the place where "Thunder and Lightning" had hung, that memorable picture of the black horse and the white horse, frightened by a terrific storm.

When I went out in the kitchen again, Mrs. Abbott was there, saying goodbye. She had brought over a bulging shoe box of chicken sandwiches for us to eat on the train, and a present for mother of several crocheted table mats.

"Of course, we'll come in to see you," she was telling mother[.] "That is, provided I can ever budge that husband of mine from the farm."

I wandered outdoors again, feeling once more the ghostly silence of the farmyard. Dewey tagged along with me, nuzzling my side. I felt a curious empty and let-down sensation. Could it be that there were no chores to do—no milking, no stock to feed, no cattle to drive down the lane to the pasture?

All at once, the delicious anticipation of going to the city was smothered by the sadness and infinite disquiet of departure. I had a vague, calamitous feeling the world would never be the same again.

I sat down on the back stoop beside the neat bundles of bedding and the little red grocery cupboard in which mother had packed her cooking things. I was glad we were taking this cupboard along. It was one that father had made—a simple pine box coated with red barn paint and equipped with a cast iron latch. I had always liked it; it had seemed like a little house to me. And always it had been haunted by the good smells of spices mother kept in it.

Frank was down in the basement, poking about to see that nothing was left down there. Jack came around the corner of the barn with a great armload of cedar darts, toy windmills, and other home-made contrivances—most of them the handiwork of Dave Peters. He deposited them in an untidy pile by the back stoop.

"There," he said, emphatically[.] "We'll need those when we get to Cedar Rapids.

* * * * * * * * *

A whirl of last minute confusion. John Flynn's friendly, confident laughter as he helped us load our things. One last look about the place, and we were gone.

I remember noticing the garden as we pulled out of the farmyard and being startled by its unkempt appearance. Weeds were growing high among the flowers; radishes and onions had gone to seed; lettuce was flowering out with spikes of yellow blossoms.

Mother rode on the wagon seat beside John Flynn, the baby in her arms. As we turned to go west on the little side road, she did not look back, back to where the house stood, bleak and curtainless like a man without any eyelids.

Jack and I and Dewey were tucked in the front of the wagon box. Frank rode behind to see that nothing fell off.

I was tired from all the excitement; the slow, regular bumping of the wagon made me drowsy. The warm sun cast a dreamy haze over the countryside. This was the period of over-lushness; summer had reached its peak and was coasting along on its seedy abundance. Vegetation was thick everywhere and the air was rich with its pollen. Golden rod gilded great stretches of pasture land; horse-mint nodded among the weeds at the roadside; and black-eyed susans winked from the fence row. The countryside was alive with the insects that screeched and sawed their crescendo until the whole landscape seemed to sway lazily to their rhythm.

The early September rains had brought out the emerald in the pastures again; patches of tufty green grass had appeared in the brown stubble-fields. The corn was ripening; I heard the coarse leaves whispering drily in the breeze. Once more the tasseled giants were drawn up along the fence row, like Indian warriors ready for a charge. From the bottom of a hill, looking up, the rows of stalks, silhouetted against the sky, were as neat and regular as the teeth of a comb.

We jolted slowly over the little wooden bridge. Droopy smart-weeds, studded with coral blossoms, were blooming in the creekbed where water was trickling once more. Out of the willow brush down the creek rose a cloud of noisy grackles. Other birds that had been in couples during the hot months could be seen in flocks in the meadows.

At the crossroads, John Flynn's mother and wife were waiting to say goodbye to us. They had packages, too.

"Just thought you'd maybe like some apple pie to eat on the train," Mrs. Flynn said to mother.

We passed Cottonwood schoolhouse and I had a disturbed feeling that I should be there. No, this was Saturday; the building was closed. A lone figure was in the yard, splitting wood. I recognized him as one of the Byerly boys. He waved and stopped to watch us go by.

When the wagon started up the Cheshire hill, I began to feel panicky. Now came the hardest part of all—we were to leave Dewey at the Cheshires. They had lost their dog recently and had said they would be glad to have our collie.

"Don't look like anybody's home," said John Flynn as he stopped in front of the farm.

Dejectedly, I climbed out of the wagon and hurried up the drive. Dewey bounded along beside me.

The barnyard was empty.

"Hello," I shouted. No answer. The house was locked up and the lumber wagon was gone.

I unhooked a door of the big barn and looked inside. It was quiet and dark in there. Dewey went on in, trustfully. I banged the door shut and ran blindly back to the wagon.

The road was shaded in front of the farm and the mud was still bad there. John Flynn's team had to pull hard to make the remaining few yards to the top of the steep hill.

"At least," said mother, trying to break the gloom, "We won't have to struggle up and down this hill any more."

At that, I had a terrible feeling that we were never coming back again . . . never.

At the top of the Cheshire hill, we all looked back for a last view of the farm. I saw our place and Grandmother Wood's very plainly. They looked like green islands in the tacky patchwork of the landscape.

Suddenly John Flynn cried out: "Look ahead! Look at this fellow coming up the hill!"

We jerked our heads forward.

A big white horse was galloping up the road, top-speed, the rider bending low over its neck.

"A stranger. Lord but he's riding! Wonder what's wrong."

The horse was fast bearing upon us, plowing up mud furiously. We heard the splatter of hooves on the moist roadbed. We saw the horse's broad laboring chest, its distended nostrils, the muscles straining in its neck.

For a moment, it seemed as if horse and rider were going to plunge by us. Then, just in front of us, the stranger pulled his mount short. The big horse wheeled on its hind legs with a storm of hooves, splattering mud in all directions.

The rider turned in his saddle and shouted:

"President McKinley has been assassinated!"

❖ CHRONOLOGY ❖

1891—Born Grant DeVolsen Wood on February 13 on a farm near Anamosa, Iowa, the second son of Francis Maryville Wood and Hattie Weaver Wood. Brother Francis, Jr. ("Frank"), born 1886.

1893—Birth of brother John Clifford ("Jack").

1897–1901—Attends Antioch School, Anamosa.

1899—Birth of sister Nancy Rebecca ("Nan").

1901—Death of father Francis Maryville on March 17. Family moves to Cedar Rapids, Iowa. Grant attends Polk Elementary School.

1902—Mother Hattie buys a house at 318 14th Street N.E. in Cedar Rapids.

1910—Graduates from Washington High School, Cedar Rapids.

1910–11—Attends Minneapolis School of Design, Handicraft, and Normal Art for two summer semesters to study with renowned Arts and Crafts Movement proponent Ernest Batchelder.

1911–12—Teaches at Rosedale Country School, Cedar Rapids. Commutes from Cedar Rapids to attend evening life drawing classes at the University of Iowa (then State University of Iowa), Iowa City, under Charles Cumming.

1913—Employed at Kalo Silversmiths Shop, Chicago, residing at 3550 S. Ellis Avenue. In October, begins evening figure drawing classes at the School of the Art Institute of Chicago, continuing through January 1915.

1914—With his friend Kristoffer Haga, opens the Volund Crafts Shop, specializing in jewelry and other fine metalwork, in Park Ridge, Illinois.

1916—Enrolls in European-trained Chicago artist-educator Antonin Sterba's two-week life drawing class at the Art Institute, receiving an honorable mention.

1917—Following the failure of the crafts shop and foreclosure of his mother's house in Cedar Rapids, builds a bungalow at 3178 Grove Court S.E. in Cedar Rapids for himself, his mother, and his sister. Paints a mural at Harrison School, *Democracy Leading the World to Victory*.

1918—Enters United States Army at Marion, Iowa, on September 5. Paints artillery camouflage at Camp Leach near Washington, D.C. Discharged at Camp Dodge, Herrold, Iowa, on December 20.

1919—Begins teaching at Jackson Junior High School, Cedar Rapids. Exhibits paintings with Marvin Cone at Killian's department store.

1920—Travels to Europe with Cone. Stopping in London, spends summer painting in Paris. Exhibits with Cone at Cedar Rapids Art Association gallery in the Carnegie Public Library.

1921—Joins Masons in Mt. Hermon Lodge No. 263, Cedar Rapids. Receives commission for *First Three Degrees of Free Masonry*.

1922—Commissioned to paint *Adoration of the Home* for realtor Henry Ely. Begins teaching at McKinley Junior High School, Cedar Rapids.

1923–24—Travels to Europe with Cone, studying at the Académie Julian in Paris, wintering in Sorrento, Italy, where he exhibits paintings at the Hotel Coccumello. Visits Rome and Sicily.

1924—Returns to Cedar Rapids in August after traveling from Paris through the French provinces. Remodels carriage house loft offered by funeral home director David Turner as a studio and home for himself and his mother, No. 5 Turner Alley.

1925—Leaves teaching to offer his artistic skills on a freelance basis. Commissioned to paint workers at J. G. Cherry Company, a dairy equipment manufacturing plant in Cedar Rapids.

1926—Summers in Europe; exhibits at Galerie Carmine, Paris. Exhibits at Cedar Rapids Art Association gallery in the Carnegie Public Library.

1926–27—Paints dining room murals in Eugene Eppley hotels in Cedar Rapids, Council Bluffs, and Sioux City, Iowa.

1927—Commissioned to design stained-glass memorial window for Cedar Rapids's Veterans Memorial Coliseum.

1928—Travels to Munich for four months to supervise manufacture of memorial window; exposed to Northern Renaissance and New Objectivity painting.

1929—Installs memorial window. Exhibits at Little Gallery, Cedar Rapids. *Woman with Plants* included in 42nd Annual Exhibition of American Paintings and Sculpture at the Art Institute of Chicago.

1930—Wins the Norman Wait Harris bronze medal and $300 purchase award for *American Gothic* in the 43rd Annual Exhibition of American Paintings and Sculpture at the Art Institute of Chicago, and the landscape prize for *Stone City* at the Iowa State Fair.

1931—Exhibits *Appraisal* and *Woman with Plants* at the 126th Annual Exhibition at the Pennsylvania Academy of Fine Arts, Philadelphia, and *Midnight Ride of Paul Revere* at the 44th Annual Exhibition of American Paintings and Sculpture at the Art Institute of Chicago.

1932—Establishes Stone City Art Colony with Edward Rowan and Adrian Dornbush. *Arbor Day* and *Victorian Survival* included in Exhibition of Modern American Painting at the Carnegie Institute, Pittsburgh, and *Daughters of Revolution* included in the First Biennial Exhibition of Contemporary American Painting at the Whitney Museum of American Art, New York.

1933—*Daughters of Revolution* shown at the Carnegie International Exhibition in Pittsburgh. Second and final summer of Stone City Art Colony. Completes five panels on the History of Penmanship for the A. N. Palmer Method Company at the Century of Progress Exposition in Chicago. Exhibits at Increase Robinson Gallery, Chicago. Appointed Iowa head of the Federal Public Works of Art Project (FPWAP).

1934—Supervises painting of library murals for Iowa State University (then Iowa State College of Agriculture and Mechanic Arts), Ames. When this project is absorbed into the curriculum of the University of Iowa, Wood becomes a faculty member in the university's Department of Graphic and Plastic Arts. *Dinner for Threshers* voted third most popular at the Carnegie International Exhibition of Paintings in Pittsburgh.

1935—Marries Sara Sherman Maxon on March 2 in Minneapolis. Acquires and restores house at 1142 E. Court Street, Iowa City. Exhibits at Lakeside Press Galleries, Chicago, and Ferargil Galleries, New York. Elected to the National Academy of Design. Signs book contract with Doubleday Doran, employs Park Rinard to assist. Hires New York agent Lee Keedick for lecture engagements. Publishes *Revolt against the City*, ghostwritten by Frank Luther Mott. Death of his mother on October 11 and of his brother Jack on December 20.

1936—Receives honorary doctorate from University of Wisconsin-Madison. Exhibits at Maynard Walker Galleries, New York. Illustrates children's book *Farm on the Hill* by Madeline Darrough Horn. *Spring Turning* exhibited at the Carnegie International Exhibition of Paintings, Pittsburgh

1937—Illustrates *Main Street* by Sinclair Lewis for Limited Editions Club. Begins creating lithographs for Associated American Artists. Installs final mural at Iowa State.

1938—Exhibits *Woman with Plants* in Carnegie International Exhibition of Paintings, Pittsburgh. Receives honorary doctorate from Lawrence University (then Lawrence College), Appleton, Wisconsin. Separates from Sherman.

1939—Divorces Sherman.

1940—Exhibits *Parson Weems' Fable* in the Annual Exhibition of Contemporary American Art at the Whitney Museum, New York. Paints *Sentimental Ballad* at Hollywood studio filming *The Long Voyage Home*. *Portrait of Henry Wallace* appears on the cover of *Time*. Named Artist Laureate by Delta Phi Delta, an honorary art fraternity. Vexed by departmental politics, takes leave of absence from University of Iowa.

1941—Appointed Professor of Fine Arts at University of Iowa. Receives honorary degrees from Wesleyan University, Middletown, Connecticut, and Northwestern University, Evanston, Illinois. With Rinard, summers in Clear Lake, Iowa. Falls ill, admitted to hospital for surgery in December.

1942—Dies of pancreatic cancer on February 12. Wood Memorial Exhibition held at the Art Institute of Chicago.

❖ ENDNOTES ❖

INTRODUCTION

1 Grant Wood, quoted in Nan Wood Graham, with John Zug and Julie Jensen McDonald, *My Brother, Grant Wood* (Iowa City: State Historical Society of Iowa, 1993), 164.
2 Paul Engle, quoted in Joan Liffring-Zug, comp., *This Is Grant Wood Country* (Davenport, IA: Davenport Municipal Art Gallery, 1977), 17.
3 Hazel E. Brown, *Grant Wood and Marvin Cone: Artists of an Era* (Ames: Iowa State University Press, 1972); Darrell Garwood, *Artist in Iowa: A Life of Grant Wood* (New York: W. W. Norton, 1944).
4 James Dennis, *Grant Wood: A Study in American Art and Culture* (New York: Viking Press, 1975; Columbia: University of Missouri, 1986).
5 In correspondence with her friend Ed Green, Graham complained of Dennis as "a very nervy cuss," but explained, "If the cuss agrees to my conditions, I will go ahead with him, I'm that anxious to get the book written. . . . By retaining editorial rights, I can control what is said and that it is not a pack of lies," letters dated April 25 and March 28, 1971, respectively, Figge Art Museum Archive, Davenport, IA.
6 Wanda Corn, *Grant Wood: The Regionalist Vision* (New Haven, CT: Yale University Press, 1983).
7 Joseph Czestochowski published the Cedar Rapids Museum of Art collections in *Marvin D. Cone and Grant Wood: An American Tradition* (Cedar Rapids, IA: Cedar Rapids Museum of Art, 1989), for example, and Brady Roberts organized an exhibition with an accompanying catalogue, *Grant Wood: An American Master Revealed*, for the Davenport Museum of Art (San Francisco: Pomegranate Artbooks, 1995).
8 Graham, *My Brother, Grant Wood*; Liffring-Zug, comp., *This Is Grant Wood Country*.
9 Christopher Hommerding, "As Gay as Any Gypsy Caravan: Grant Wood and the Queer Pastoral at the Stone City Art Colony," *Annals of Iowa* 74:4 (Fall 2015): 378–415.
10 Alan Wallach, "Grant Wood: The Insider as Outsider" (Seminar on Homosexuality and Modernism, Institute for the Humanities, New York University, May 21, 1990); Henry Adams, "The Truth about Grant Wood" (Annual College Art Association Conference, New York, February 24, 2000); John E. Seery, "Grant Wood's Political Gothic," in *America Goes to College: Political Theory for the Liberal Arts* (Albany: State University of New York Press, 2002), 117–38, 223–31.
11 Lea Rosson DeLong, *Grant Wood's Main Street: Art, Literature, and the American Midwest* (Ames: Brunnier Art Museum, University Museums, Iowa State University, 2004); DeLong, *When Tillage Begins, Other Arts Follow: Grant Wood and Christian Petersen Murals* (Ames: Brunnier Art Museum, University Museums, Iowa State University, 2006).

12 Jane C. Milosch, "Grant Wood's Studio: A Decorative Adventure," in Milosch, ed., *Grant Wood's Studio: Birthplace of* American Gothic (New York: Prestel, 2005), 79–109, 132–35.

13 Joni L. Kinsey, "Cultivating Iowa: An Introduction to Grant Wood," in Milosch, ed., *Grant Wood's Studio*, 11–33, 130–32; Paul C. Juhl, *Grant Wood: Abandoned Plans* (Iowa City, IA: Brushy Creek Publishing, 2012); and Juhl, *Grant Wood's Clear Lake Summer* (Iowa City, IA: Brushy Creek Publishing, 2007).

14 Luciano Cheles, "The Italian Renaissance in *American Gothic*: Grant Wood and Piero della Francesca," *American Art* 30:1 (Spring 2016): 106–24; Travis Nygard, *Seeds of Agribusiness: Grant Wood and the Visual Culture of Grain Farming, 1862–1957* (Ann Arbor, MI: University Microfilms, 2009).

15 R. Tripp Evans, *Grant Wood: A Life* (New York: Alfred A. Knopf, 2010). The impact of Evans's account is strongly felt in Barbara Haskell's recent exhibition and accompanying catalogue, *Grant Wood:* American Gothic *and Other Fables* (New York: Whitney Museum of American Art, 2018). Although published too late to draw upon for the present study, Haskell's project constitutes a milestone in Wood scholarship and will be invaluable for future studies of American art in general.

16 Grant Wood, "The Writer and the Painter," *American Prefaces: A Journal of Critical and Imaginative Writing* 1:1 (October 1935): 3.

CHAPTER 1: A FAMILY AFFAIR

1 Rudolph Ingerle, quoted in Wendy Greenhouse, "Rudolph Ingerle," in Elizabeth Kennedy, ed., *Chicago Modern 1893–1945: Pursuit of the New* (Chicago: Terra Museum of American Art and Terra Foundation for the Arts, 2004), 123.

2 James M. Dennis, *Renegade Regionalists: The Modern Independence of Grant Wood, Thomas Hart Benton, and John Steuart Curry* (Madison: University of Wisconsin Press, 1998), 193. Dennis is quoting here from Leo Stein's *A-B-C of Aesthetics* (New York: Boni and Liveright, 1927), 169.

3 Nan Wood Graham, with John Zug and Julie Jensen McDonald, *My Brother, Grant Wood* (Iowa City: State Historical Society of Iowa, 1993), 75.

4 John E. Seery, "Grant Wood's Political Gothic," in *America Goes to College: Political Theory for the Liberal Arts* (Albany: State University of New York Press, 2002), 126.

5 Herbert Asbury, quoted in Clarence Andrews, *A Literary History of Iowa* (Iowa City: University of Iowa Press, 1972), 86.

6 Grant Wood, quoted in "Could Be Good Farmer! Grant Wood Denies Reputation as Glamour Boy of Painters," *Los Angeles Times*, February 19, 1940.

7 Graham, *My Brother, Grant Wood*, 74. In one of the many conflicting reports Wood himself gave about *American Gothic*, "An Iowa Secret," *Art Digest* 8:1 (October 1933), he said that he "sent to a Chicago mail order house for the prim, colonial print apron," 6. Perhaps Graham simply added the trim.

8 Sigmund Freud, *The Interpretation of Dreams* (1900), *The Standard Edition of the Complete Psychological Works of Sigmund Freud*, vol. 5, trans. James Strachey (London: Hogarth Press and the Institute of Psycho-analysis, 1953), 488–511, esp. 490. Subsequent references to the *Standard Edition* are abbreviated "*SE*."

9 Freud used this now familiar term throughout his writings to describe what he believed was one of three sources of dreams: physical sensations (such as digestive disturbances) experienced during sleep, childhood memories, and ordinary recent events or "day residue," that is, "the [dreamer's] experiences of the previous day," *The Interpretation of Dreams* (1900), *SE*, vol. 4 (1953), 165.

10 R. Tripp Evans, *Grant Wood: A Life* (New York: Alfred A. Knopf, 2010), 65, gives priority to *Portrait of John B. Turner, Pioneer* (1928/30) as the first painting in Wood's mature style, begun before the Munich trip and reworked after.

11 Grant Wood with Park Rinard, "Return from Bohemia, A Painter's Story," for which see the Appendix in this volume. This particular quote appears on page 221. Subsequent citations will be given in the text, with page references to the appendix in parentheses.

12 Wood, quoted in Graham, *My Brother, Grant Wood*, 83.

13 Hattie's brooch resides in the collection of the Figge Art Museum, Davenport, IA. Evans, in *Grant Wood: A Life*, 86–88, 100, has perceptively identified the figure on the brooch as Persephone, with her flowing hair and crown of pomegranates, and further suggests that in this private allusion, Wood associated the classical figure with his sister and Persephone's mournful mother, Demeter, with Hattie.

14 Wanda Corn, *Grant Wood: The Regionalist Vision* (New Haven, CT: Yale University Press, 1983), 133.

15 Donald Kuspit, "Representing the Mother: Representing the Unrepresentable?" in Barbara Collier, ed., *The Artist's Mother: Portraits and Homages* (Huntington, NY: Heckscher Museum and Washington, DC: National Portrait Gallery, Smithsonian Institution, 1987), 26.

16 Wood, quoted in Joan Liffring-Zug, comp., *This Is Grant Wood Country* (Davenport, IA: Davenport Municipal Art Gallery, 1977), 7.

17 Evans, *Grant Wood: A Life*, 82.

18 Freud, *Leonardo Da Vinci and a Memory of His Childhood* (1910), *SE* 11 (1957), 59–138.

19 I am indebted to Dr. Gerald Fogel for these insights about the special tragedy of Wood's loss of his father at the age of ten, personal communication with the author, March 27, 2012.

20 Darrell Garwood, *Artist in Iowa: A Life of Grant Wood* (New York: W. W. Norton, 1944), 20.

21 Sara McClain Sherman, 1959 reminiscence on Grant Wood's art, Donna Clausen cat. no. 4, n.p. [3], Sherman Papers, Marysville, WA.

22 Wood, quoted in Garwood, *Artist in Iowa: A Life of Grant Wood*, 119, where the artist's "long treatments for pyorrhea" (now called "periodontal disease"), due to lack of early dental care, is also noted.

23 See Freud, *The Interpretation of Dreams* (1901), *SE* 5 (1953), 387, where the loss of a tooth in a dream, like haircutting or decapitation, signals castration anxiety, and *Introductory Lectures on Psycho-Analysis* (1916–17), *SE* 15 (1963), 156–57, where Freud observed that "the *falling out of a tooth* or the *pulling out of a tooth* is a particularly notable dream-symbol. Its first meaning is undoubtedly castration as a punishment for masturbating" (emphases in the original).

24 Garwood, *Artist in Iowa: A Life of Grant Wood*, 120.

25 Evans, *Grant Wood: A Life*, 96, reminds us that among Maryville's personal effects, his eyeglasses were the only item Wood kept, investing them "with an almost totemic power." The glasses are now in the collection of the Figge Art Museum.

26 Ibid., 99–101; Matthew Baigell, "Grant Wood Revisited," *Art Journal* 26:2 (1966–67): 117.

27 Freud, "The Devil as a Father-Substitute" (1923), *SE* 19 (1961), 86.

28 Sherman, 1959 reminiscence, n.p. [2], Sherman Papers.

29 Robert Hughes, "Scooting Back to Anamosa: Grant Wood at the Whitney: A Fresh Look at an American Icon," *Time*, June 27, 1983, 69; Norman Mailer, quoted in

Doris Guy Jerdee, "The Iconography of Grant Wood's *American Gothic*" (MA thesis, Arizona State University, 1969), 64.

30 Walter Prichard Eaton, "American Gothic," *Boston Herald*, November 14, 1930.

31 Graham, *My Brother, Grant Wood*, 5. For Wood's grandfather Joseph's role in establishing the First Presbyterian Church of Anamosa at Strawberry Hill, see *The History of Jones County, Iowa* (Chicago: Western Historical Co., 1879), 443.

32 The joint snake turns up in a playlet performed at the Stone City Art Colony in 1932 or 1933, in which a professional storyteller reports: "I was about twelve years old. My mother and me was goin' out after raspberries. All at once we come along by an osage hedge. . . . Our dog rushed in under the hedge and came up with a long black snake. He shook the snake and shook him until the snake come unjointed and the pieces flew every way. Well, we went on and picked berries. And when we come back, the snake had got together and crawled away. That I see [*sic*] myself, and anybody can believe it or not just as they please." The short drama, *Folk Stuff*, was written by Jay Sigmund, for which see Zachary Michael Jack, ed., *The Plowman Sings: The Essential Fiction, Poetry, and Drama of America's Forgotten Regionalist Jay G. Sigmund* (New York: University Press of America, 2008), 114.

33 Melanie Klein, "Mourning and Its Relation to Manic-Depressive States" (1940), *Love, Guilt and Reparation and Other Works 1921–1945* (New York: Delacorte Press/ Seymour Lawrence, 1975), 349.

34 Joanna Field [pseud. Marion Milner], *On Not Being Able to Paint* (New York: Jeremy P. Tarcher/Putnam, 1957), 66.

35 Ibid., 67.

36 Biographical information on Frank and John Wood from Garwood, *Artist in Iowa: A Life of Grant Wood*, 47, and from Nan Wood Graham's scrapbooks and personal correspondence file, Grant Wood Archive, Figge Art Museum. John Wood's lawsuit was reported by Joan Liffring-Zug Bourret, in "The Life of Nan Wood Graham, Model for *American Gothic*" (Symposium on Grant Wood Today, University of Iowa, Iowa City, April 14, 2012).

37 Graham, interviewed in Dean Rathje, *Poetry of Place: Iowa's Regionalist Artists between the World Wars* (Ely, IA: New Leaf Interactive Media, 2008), DVD.

38 Corn, *Grant Wood: The Regionalist Vision*, 102.

39 Hazel E. Brown, *Grant Wood and Marvin Cone: Artists of an Era* (Ames: Iowa State University Press, 1972), 85.

40 Field, *On Not Being Able to Paint*, 87.

41 Baigell, "Grant Wood Revisited," 121.

42 Steven Biel, *American Gothic: A Life of America's Most Famous Painting* (New York: W. W. Norton, 2005), 44.

43 Jonathan Weinberg, *Ambition and Love in Modern American Art* (New Haven, CT: Yale University Press, 2001), 3.

44 Seery, "Grant Wood's Political Gothic," 130.

45 Brady Roberts, "The European Roots of Regionalism: Grant Wood's Stylistic Synthesis," in *Grant Wood: An American Master Revealed* (San Francisco: Pomegranate Artbooks, 1995), 24.

46 Ibid.

47 Wood, quoted in "Iowa Secret," 6.

48 Graham, *My Brother, Grant Wood*, 74.

49 Ibid., 128. Brown, *Grant Wood and Marvin Cone*, 85, reports that Hattie survived only two weeks after her move to Iowa City.

50 Garwood, *Artist in Iowa: A Life of Grant Wood*, 198.

51 Ibid.
52 Joan Liffring-Zug interview with Nan Wood Graham, c. 1983, transcript p. 7, State Historical Society of Iowa, Iowa City.
53 Nan Wood Graham (1899–1990) is also buried in the Weaver section. The two plots adjacent to Maryville's grave were eventually given by Graham to her cousin Althea (Graham to Edwin Green, August 5, 1973, Grant Wood Archive, Figge Art Museum, Davenport, IA). Thus, in a row next to the Wood family monument rest the artist's paternal uncles and aunt, Clarence (1856–1937), Sarah (1846–1927), and Eugene (1870–1914); his paternal grandparents Rebecca (1820–1908) and Joseph (1822–1884); his father (1855–1901); and Althea Pope Hines (1907–1967) and her husband, Edward Hines (1905–1988).
54 Garwood, *Artist in Iowa: A Life of Grant Wood*, 40.
55 Evans, *Grant Wood: A Life*, 58.
56 Wood, quoted in Garwood, *Artist in Iowa: A Life of Grant Wood*, 73. Maternal toward Wood and always supportive, Prescott herself enjoyed what was then referred to as a "Boston marriage" with Dr. Florence Johnston, a gynecologist and anesthesiologist in Cedar Rapids. They belonged to one of the several generations of newly educated women in the 1870s and 1880s who refused conventional marriage in favor of professional careers and who maintained passionate relationships with other women; see John D'Emilio and Estelle B. Freedman, *Intimate Matters: A History of Sexuality in America* (New York: Harper & Row, 1988), 190–91. (Johnston's nephew, Ernest Johnston Dieterich, described her to me as Prescott's roommate when we met in Cedar Rapids on September 9, 2005.)
57 Wood, quoted in Graham, *My Brother, Grant Wood*, 128.
58 According to the 1900 U.S. Census, Sara McClain Sherman was born on December 12, 1883 in Monticello, IA. In an eighty-four-page genealogy (Clausen cat. no. 26, Sherman Papers) created by her older sister, Edith Sherman Averill, in 1936, Sara Sherman altered the year of her birth to read 1890. With the recent exception of Evans in *Grant Wood: A Life*, writers on Wood, including myself, have accepted the misinformation Sherman provided about her age, claiming that she was older than her second husband by only a few months, rather than seven years.
59 Klein, "Mourning," 354.
60 Graham, *My Brother, Grant Wood*, 128.
61 James M. Dennis, *Grant Wood: A Study in American Art and Culture*, (New York: Viking Press, 1975; Columbia: University of Missouri Press, 1986), 229, explains that "*Revolt Against the City* appeared as the first of four pamphlets edited and independently published in Iowa City in 1935 by Frank Luther Mott, a renowned journalism professor and historian of the press." Dennis reprints the manifesto in its entirety, 229–35.
62 Corn, "Grant Wood (1892 [*sic*]–1942), *Death on the Ridge Road*, 1935," in Nancy Mowll Mathews, ed., *American Dreams: American Art to 1950 in the Williams College Museum of Art* (New York: Hudson Hills Press, 2001), 158–61, and Corn, *Grant Wood: The Regionalist Vision*, 82; Anedith Nash, "Death on the Highway: The Automobile Wreck in American Culture, 1920–40" (PhD diss., University of Minnesota, 1983), esp. chapter IV, "Death on the Ridge Road," and *idem.*, "*Death on the Ridge Road*: Grant Wood and Modernization in the Midwest," *Prospects* 8 (1983): 281–301.
63 Edward Pierce Ferreter, "Grant Wood Meets Jay G. Sigmund: From Word to Image; From Image to Word" (MA thesis, University of Iowa, 1985), 20.
64 Zachary Michael Jack, "America's Forgotten Regionalist: Jay G. Sigmund," in Jack, ed., *The Plowman Sings*, 7.

65 Ferreter, "Wood Meets Sigmund," 20.
66 Garwood, *Artist in Iowa: A Life of Grant Wood*, 176. Nash, as explained in "*Death on the Ridge Road*," 300n42, discovered the report of Pyle's accident in the *Cedar Rapids Gazette* of July 14, 1934.
67 Jay G. Sigmund, "Death Rides a Rubber-Shod Horse," *American Poetry Magazine* 16:6 (October 1934): 2. See also Ferreter, "Wood Meets Sigmund," 58. Wood had already begun his drawing when, as he reported to his dealer at Ferargil Galleries in late December, he had skidded off the icy road en route from Cedar Rapids to Iowa City, his car "practically standing on its radiator when it ended up in a snow bank"; quoted in Nash, "Death on the Highway," 106.
68 Corn, "Grant Wood (1892 [*sic*]-1942)," 158; Evans, *Grant Wood: A Life*, 196.
69 Corn, *Grant Wood: The Regionalist Vision*, 112, where Wood's comment to the *Cedar Rapids Gazette* is also quoted.
70 Ibid.
71 Evans, *Grant Wood: A Life*, 70–71.
72 "Iowa Cows Give Grant Wood His Best Thoughts," *New York Herald Tribune*, January 23, 1936.
73 Corn, *Grant Wood: The Regionalist Vision*, 11; Evans, *Grant Wood: A Life*, 75. Dennis, *Grant Wood*, 152, first identified the figure immediately behind the artist in the drawing as David Turner. Ferreter, however, in "Wood Meets Sigmund," 22, indicates that Wood used Jay Sigmund as the model, and photographs of the poet suggest that this might be a possibility.
74 Klein, "Mourning," 354.
75 Corn, *Grant Wood: The Regionalist Vision*, 112.
76 Janette Stevenson Murray and Frederick Gray Murray, *The Story of Cedar Rapids* (New York: Stratford House, 1950), 217, reported that "all of Wood's records and correspondence were given to Rinard with the idea that he was to write the official biography," but it did not appear. Wood's sister, who detested Garwood's book, hoped that Rinard would complete the work, and for a while this seemed a possibility. In a letter to Graham dated June 24, 1947 (Grant Wood Archive, Figge Art Museum), Rinard wrote from Clear Lake, IA, on the progress of his research, listing the individuals he planned to interview, but in subsequent correspondence he would seek to distract Graham from the subject with friendly news of his family. As late as 1984, he claimed still to be working "sporadically on the 'authorized' biography," which he considered "an important mission"; see "A 'Schlepper,'" unattributed sidebar accompanying Park Rinard, "The Real Grant Wood," *Des Moines Sunday Register*, January 15, 1984. Despite Rinard's intentions, the completed *Return from Bohemia* remained a pipe dream.
77 Garwood, *Artist in Iowa: A Life of Grant Wood*, 207, 206.
78 Ibid., 181, and, on the shortened title of "Return to Bohemia," 207.
79 Donald Kuspit, "Grant Wood: Pathos of the Plain," *Art in America* 72:3 (March 1984): 142–43.
80 Ibid., 143.
81 Corn, *Grant Wood: The Regionalist Vision*, 3.
82 Field, *On Not Being Able to Paint*, 67.
83 Inez Keck, Washtaw, IA, "Snatches from the Mail," *Des Moines Register*, December 14, 1930.
84 The reaction Wood reported here is entirely characteristic of preadolescent children who lose a parent. The lack of affect signals a denial of the reality that would otherwise evoke terrible tears. In her study of how children respond to the death of a parent, Martha Wolfenstein posits adolescence itself as a precondition for the normal reality-

testing and gradual decathecting of a lost love object that constitutes mourning. Before that period, the child cannot mourn a parent but hypercathects the object and continues unconsciously to anticipate his/her return. See Wolfenstein, "How Is Mourning Possible," *The Psychoanalytic Study of the Child* 21 (1966): 93–123.

85 Garwood, *Artist in Iowa: A Life of Grant Wood*, 156.

CHAPTER 2: FEAR AND DESIRE

1 Alan Wallach, "Grant Wood: The Insider as Outsider" (Seminar on Homosexuality and Modernism, Institute for the Humanities, New York University, May 21, 1990). I am grateful to Professor Wallach for sharing the typescript of this paper with me.

2 Robert Hughes, *American Visions: The Epic History of American Art* (New York: Alfred A. Knopf, 1997), 439.

3 John E. Seery, "Grant Wood's Political Gothic," in *America Goes to College: Political Theory for the Liberal Arts* (Albany: State University of New York Press, 2002), 117–38, 223–31.

4 Henry Adams, "The Truth about Grant Wood" (Annual College Art Association Conference, New York, February 2000). I am greatly indebted to Professor Adams for sending me the typescript of his presentation. See also Joni L. Kinsey, "Cultivating Iowa: An Introduction to Grant Wood" in Jane C. Milosch, ed., *Grant Wood's Studio: Birthplace of* American Gothic (New York: Prestel, 2005), 27–32, for a discussion of the attacks on Wood in the art department in 1940 and 1941.

5 Sara McClain Sherman, 1959 reminiscence, Donna Clausen cat. no. 4, n.p. [2], Sherman Papers, Marysville, WA.

6 Adams, "The Truth about Grant Wood," 14.

7 See Eve Kosofsky Sedgwick's critique in *Epistemology of the Closet* (Berkeley: University of California Press, 1990) of what she describes as the "don't ask/you shouldn't know" approach, 52–53. Norma Broude has argued eloquently for the importance to art history of addressing artists' sexuality and lived experiences in "Outing Impressionism: Homosexuality and Homosocial Bonding in the Work of Caillebotte and Bazille," in Broude, ed., *Gustave Caillebotte and the Fashioning of Identity in Impressionist Paris* (New Brunswick, NJ: Rutgers University Press, 2002): "No matter how imperfectly those experiences may now be reconstructed, they cannot, in my view, be responsibly ignored. For to discuss these images solely as cultural artifacts that can be divorced from the sexuality of their makers would be to collude in the effacement of gay history and identity, an effacement that is itself symptomatic of that still lingering condition of 'homosexual panic,' whose pivotal role in modern patriarchal culture and social organization Sedgwick has so cogently analyzed," 121.

8 MacKinlay Kantor, *I Love You, Irene* (New York: Doubleday and Company, 1972), 139–40.

9 R. Tripp Evans, *Grant Wood: A Life* (New York: Alfred A. Knopf, 2010), 107–8.

10 Ibid., 52.

11 Luciano Cheles, "The Italian Renaissance in *American Gothic*: Grant Wood and Piero della Francesca," *American Art* 30:1 (Spring 2016): 108.

12 Marie O'Connell DeVries, "Cedar Rapidians Contributed to Wood's Work," *Cedar Rapids Gazette*, August 21, 1983, lists all the locals who posed for *Adoration of the Home*, starting with the central figure of Cedar Rapids, "Mr. Wood's cousin, Mrs. R. C. Conybeare. The others . . . were S. W. Neville, who was the model for two of the figures, the carpenter as representative of the building trades, and the farmer, representing animal husbandry; William Funcke, the man with the shovel and wheel-

barrow representing labor; George Holmes as the miller; C. L. Charles as the foundry man; and Nan Wood, the artist's sister, who posed as the figure of agriculture. Francis Neville appears as the winged spirit of commerce; Paul C. Hanson as the civil engineer; Mrs. Hanson as religion, and their little son, Donald, as education."

13 Moreover, according to Jane C. Milosch, "Grant Wood's Studio: A Decorative Adventure," in Milosch, ed., *Grant Wood's Studio*, 102, Wood's twenty-four-by-twenty-foot project is recorded as the largest stained-glass window in the United States.

14 Nan Wood Graham, "Catalog of the Works of Grant Wood," in scrapbook 10, "Copyright Information," Grant Wood Archive, Figge Art Museum, Davenport, IA. Graham identifies the female figure as Peace and notes seven pen-and-ink drawings for the window, providing the first names of six male models. In her personal annotated copy of Darrell Garwood's, *Artist in Iowa: A Life of Grant Wood* (New York: W. W. Norton, 1944), in the State Historical Society of Iowa, Iowa City, Graham writes on page 93 that the young men were former students of Wood's. She added the name of Harry Robinson, another one-time pupil, in Nan Wood Graham, with John Zug and Julie Jensen McDonald, *My Brother, Grant Wood* (Iowa City: State Historical Society of Iowa, 1993), 62.

15 Evans, *Grant Wood: A Life*, 362.

16 Jane C. Milosch, "*American Gothic*'s Munich Connection: A Window into Grant Wood's Regionalism," in Christian Fuhrmeister, Hubertus Kohle, and Veerle Thielemans, eds., *American Artists in Munich: Artistic Migration and Cultural Exchange Processes* (Berlin: Deutscher Kunstverlag, 2009), 251.

17 Ibid.

18 The National Archives and Records Administration indicates that Wood served in the U.S. Army from September 5 through December 20, 1918. He entered at Marion, IA, was assigned to the 97th Regiment of Engineers, Company B, and separated at Camp Dodge, Herrold, IA. Information provided by the National Personnel Records Center, St. Louis, October 17, 2005.

19 Graham, *My Brother, Grant Wood, Grant Wood*, 29.

20 Jennifer Wingate, "Over the Top: The Doughboy in World War I Memorials and Visual Culture," *American Art* 19:2 (Summer 2005): 2–47.

21 I owe this comparison to Cheles, "The Italian Renaissance in *American Gothic*," 108, who invokes the *Madonna Misericordia* (1444–65) of Piero della Francesca as a prototype for Wood's figure of Peace.

22 The drawing was still among his effects when he died; it passed to his sister, who included it with the cache of Wood material she sold to the Davenport Municipal Art Gallery in 1965, now the Figge Museum, where it resides today.

23 Graham, *My Brother, Grant Wood*, 108. The drawing in question, the charcoal and pastel *Study for Self-Portrait* (1932, see Introduction, opposite p. 1 in this volume), was at some point acquired by Wood's patron Wellwood Nesbit, passed to his heirs, and subsequently sold to the Cedar Rapids Museum of Art, acc. no. 93.11.

24 Evans, *Grant Wood: A Life*, makes this same observation, 113.

25 Corn, *Grant Wood: The Regionalist Vision*, 68.

26 Grant Wood, "The Writer and the Painter," *American Prefaces: A Journal of Critical and Imaginative Writing* 1:1 (October 1935): 3.

27 Park Rinard, letter to Nan Wood Graham, July 31, 1962, Grant Wood Archive, Figge Art Museum, Davenport, IA.

28 Graham, *My Brother, Grant Wood*, 93.

29 Naomi Doebel, "Artists Have Neglected One of Iowa's Great Assets," *Cedar Rapids Gazette*, August 20, 1933.

30 "Beaux-Arts Ball: Life Goes to a Party," *Life Magazine*, March 21, 1938, 62. The telling nature of this photograph vis-à-vis Wood's awkward position within "the stridently heterosexual image" of Regionalism also struck Evans, who reproduces the group shot in *Grant Wood: A Life*, 238–39.

31 Leata Rowan to Edward Rowan, January 11, 1934, Edward B. Rowan Papers, Archives of American Art, D141.

32 Sherman, autobiography, Clausen cat. no. 1, 95, Sherman papers.

33 Winnifred Cone, quoted in Julie Jensen McDonald with Joan Liffring-Zug Bourret, *Grant Wood and Little Sister Nan: Essays and Remembrances* (Iowa City, IA: Penfield Press, 2000), 17.

34 Sherman, autobiography, 116.

35 Garwood, *Artist in Iowa: A Life of Grant Wood*, 219.

36 James M. Dennis, "Grant Wood's Matriarchate," in *Renegade Regionalists: The Modern Independence of Grant Wood, Thomas Hart Benton, and John Steuart Curry* (Madison: University of Wisconsin Press, 1998), 94.

37 Jay G. Sigmund, *Frescoes* (Boston: B. J. Brimmer Co., 1922), 40–42.

38 Wanda M. Corn, "Grant Wood: Uneasy Modern," in Milosch, ed., *Grant Wood's Studio*, 111.

39 Evans, *Grant Wood: A Life*, 119.

40 Corn, "Grant Wood: Uneasy Modern," 115.

41 Gerald Fogel, "Interiority and Inner Genital Space in Men: What Else Can Be Lost in Castration," *Psychoanalytic Quarterly* 67 (1998): 663–64.

42 Nan Wood Graham, undated interview by Joan Liffring-Zug, c. 1983, transcript p. 21, State Historical Society of Iowa, Iowa City.

43 Corn, "Grant Wood: Uneasy Modern," 114.

44 Despina Kakoudaki, "Pinup: The American Secret Weapon in World War II," in Linda Williams, ed., *Porn Studies* (Durham, NC: Duke University Press, 2004), 351.

45 "Grant Wood Spurns Modern Girl, Paints Lillian Russell Type," *Cedar Rapids Gazette*, April 9, 1940, quoted in Paul C. Juhl, *Grant Wood: Abandoned Plans* (Iowa City, IA: Brushy Creek Publishing, 2012), 35. Wood never delivered on his peculiar plan to paint an image of his supposed ideal, a full-figured woman.

46 Benton's inscription reads: "Ideals / The full scale but nothing said / [illegible] / Political Philosophy."

47 I am grateful to Wellwood Nesbit's granddaughter Mary T. Varda of Madison, WI, for allowing me to have the panels photographed and for sharing a typescript, dated August 25, 1983, of her great aunt Blanche's account of the evening they were decorated. (One discrepancy: Blanche recorded the date of the evening as September 18, 1938, though Curry signed his panel 1937.)

48 Philip E. Slater, *The Glory of Hera: Greek Mythology and the Greek Family* (Boston: Beacon Press, 1968), 88–89.

49 Garwood, *Artist in Iowa: A Life of Grant Wood*, 48.

50 Sterling North, *Plowing on Sunday* (New York: Macmillan, 1934), 117.

51 Anedith Nash, "*Death on the Ridge Road*: Grant Wood and Modernization in the Midwest," *Prospects* 8 (1983): 299n20.

52 On this subject, see Broude, "Outing Impressionism," fig. 56 and pl. 11.

53 Inscriptions on *académies* sometimes identified the models by name and profession, for example "Mr. Anderson, the miner" or "William Bewlay, Police Sergeant, aged 26." In his essay "Life Class," Edward Lucie-Smith further explained how "handsome, well-built working-class men appeared to have been happy to pose in the nude for a small fee. Many of the models seem to have been off-duty soldiers; others were young

Italians, who made modelling their profession, both in Paris and in London," in Stephen Boyd, ed., *Life Class: The Academic Male Nude 1820–1920* (London: The Gay Men Press, 1898), 8, 10.

54 Garwood, *Artist in Iowa: A Life of Grant Wood*, 75. James M. Dennis notes that *The Spotted Man* and *Portrait of Nan* were the only paintings in Wood's possession at the time of his death, in *Grant Wood: A Study in American Art and Culture* (1975; Columbia: University of Missouri, 1986), 237n8.

55 Evans, *Grant Wood: A Life*, 73. Dennis, *Grant Wood*, reports that Wood reworked the painting in 1934, "so that the figure lost most of its spots," 237n8.

56 During his third trip to France in 1926, Wood spoke to his friend William Shirer from Cedar Rapids about the examples of Cézanne, Monet, and Renoir, and declared Picasso a genius; Wood had struggled to find his artistic place and decided that it wasn't among them, but back in Iowa. William L. Shirer, *20th Century Journey: A Memoir of the Life and Times of William L. Shirer* (New York: Simon and Schuster, 1976), 274.

57 "A Notable Gift" brochure, Edwin Green Papers, Special Collections Department, University of Iowa Libraries, Iowa City. The painting was bought from Schoonover by one Otto Schatz and donated to the lodge in 1944.

58 Wood produced an independent painting of Rodin's sculpture during his first trip to France in 1920 that is currently in a private collection in Cedar Rapids. Among other images of Parisian landmarks and environs, *The Thinker* is listed in Wood exhibitions at the Cedar Rapids Public Library in 1920 and 1923; Joseph Czestochowski, *Marvin D. Cone and Grant Wood: An American Tradition* (Cedar Rapids, IA: Cedar Rapids Museum of Art, 1989), 195.

59 Evans, *Grant Wood: A Life*, 252.

60 Mabel Lang sorts out contrasting respective reports by Thucydides, Aristotle, and Herodotus in "The Murder of Hipparchus," *Historia: Zeitschrift für alte Gescichte* 3:4 (1955): 395–407.

61 Evans, *Grant Wood: A Life*, 252.

62 Wood had his own past practice in mind when, after his conversion to Regionalism, he celebrated its "reversal of the vogues of only a few years ago seeking the picturesque abroad, taking refuge in the classics or looking at our own country through borrowed hazes," "Rural Influence in Contemporary Art," *Rural America* 14:2 (1936): 41.

63 Alex Potts, *Flesh and the Ideal: Winckelmann and the Origins of Art History* (New Haven, CT: Yale University Press, 1994), 182.

64 Garwood, *Artist in Iowa: A Life of Grant Wood*, 78.

65 Byrne Fone, "This Other Eden: Arcadia and the Homosexual Imagination," *Journal of Homosexuality* 8:3/4 (1983): 13. The phrase quoted in the following sentence is from ibid.

66 Garwood, *Artist in Iowa: A Life of Grant Wood*, 48, mentions an apparently lost drawing of "a group of boys around a swimming hole" done when Wood was in his mid-twenties, that is, around 1916.

67 In 1983, Funcke reported to DeVries in "Cedar Rapidians Contributed to Wood's Work" how Wood had asked him to model for a picture "of a boy in the nude getting ready to plunge into his favorite swimming hole." DeVries's article includes a reproduction of the painting's central panel and a photo of Funcke at age seventy-nine in front of his Cedar Rapids home. Wood's painting apparently still had the power to arouse an anxiety that had to be assuaged: the one-time artist's model is shown with his arm around his wife, and the article further constructs him as reassuringly manly and heterosexual, highlighting his career as a policeman and his marriage, which produced two sons.

68 Michael Camille, "The Abject Gaze and the Homosexual Body: Flandrin's *Figure d'étude*," in Whitney Davis, ed., *Gay and Lesbian Studies in Art History* (Birmingham, NY: Haworth Press, 1994), 162.

69 Signund Freud, "On Narcissism: An Introduction" (1914), *The Standard Edition of the Complete Psychological Works of Sigmund Freud*, vol. 14, trans. James Strachey (London: Hogarth Press and the Institute of Psycho-analysis, 1957), 90.

70 The date of this lithograph is often given as 1937, but according to Sylvan Cole, Jr., *Grant Wood: The Lithographs, A Catalogue Raisonné*, ed. Susan Teller (New York: Associated American Artists, 1984), 4–5, 18, the artist wrote to Reeves Lewenthal at Associated American Artists (AAA) on September 11 that year indicating that he needed more time to complete the stone matrices he had been given three years earlier. *Sultry Night*, the sixth print Wood produced with AAA, was finished in 1938 and published in 1939.

71 Ibid., 6.

72 Wood to John O'Connor (misspelled "O'Conner"), July 8, 1938. The original letter is in the possession of Mary T. Varda, Madison, WI.

73 Garwood, *Artist in Iowa: A Life of Grant Wood*, 210.

74 Wood cites Resor's purchase option in his letter to O'Connor, July 8, 1938.

75 David McCosh in an undated letter (summer 1933) to his then fiancée, Anne Kutka, University of Oregon Foundation McCosh Memorial Endowment Archive, Jordan Schnitzer Museum of Art, Eugene, OR.

76 This information and all the quotes following in this paragraph are drawn from Ruth Weller's recollections in an audiotaped interview with Mary Bennett, Special Collections Coordinator, State Historical Society of Iowa; Fred Kent's daughter Barbara Kent Buckley; and Don Roberts, head of the University of Iowa's photo services, September 1, 1993. The cassette recording is in the collection of the State Historical Society of Iowa, Iowa City.

77 Lea Rosson DeLong, *When Tillage Begins, Other Arts Follow: Grant Wood and Christian Petersen Murals* (Ames: Brunnier Art Museum, University Museums, Iowa State University, 2006), 259, 265.

78 Mary Bennett interview as cited in note 76. Weller reported how, for *Seedtime and Harvest* and *Arbor Day*, for example, she would drive Wood out to the site he had selected, set up her four-by-five-inch camera, and follow Wood's instructions on how to arrange the composition.

79 Henry Adams made this same comparison in "The Truth about Grant Wood." In the typescript Adams generously shared with me, this observation appears on page 12.

80 "Wood has a regular system for landscape painting," wrote McCosh to Kutka from Stone City in the summer of 1932, "which makes a swell formulae [*sic*] to teach beginners," University of Oregon Foundation McCosh Memorial Endowment Archive, Jordan Schnitzer Museum of Art, Eugene, OR.

81 Photographs of such troughs in the 1930s show them typically made of corrugated metal, as in *Saturday Night Bath* (1937 or 1939); Wood likely substituted the pocked surface here to avoid distracting attention from the farmhand by what would have been a series of repeated verticals across the foreground of his picture.

82 Diana Fuss, quoted in William J. Spurlin, "Remapping Same-Sex Desire: Queer Writing and Culture in the American Heartland," in Richard Phillips, Diane Watt, and David Shuttleton, eds., *De-Centring* [*sic*] *Sexualities: Politics and Representation Beyond the Metropolis* (New York: Routledge, 2000), 184.

83 John Selby, "Grant Wood Paints Iowa Because He Knows It Best," *Washington Post*, May 1, 1938. "So Wood made a lithograph," Selby wrote, "of a farmer bathing

himself—front view. It is about as pornographic as a statue of Apollo, but he has temporarily withdrawn it rather than to make a 'cause célèbre' of it."

84 Graham, *My Brother, Grant Wood*, 141.

85 Wood, quoted in ibid.

86 Recalling Wood's destruction of *Sultry Night*, Graham reported how "more than half the painting remained—oddly shaped because the painting had been arched on top. Grant had an odd-shaped mat made for it and framed it, selling it to Dr. Wellwood Nesbit of Madison, Wisconsin," ibid., 141–42 (see Fig. 2.31). One of Nesbit's four daughters, Martha Nesbit Frankwicz, "relayed this bit of hearsay" about *Sultry Night* to her niece Mary T. Varda, who relayed it to me (email communication with the author, April 30, 2012): Visiting his friend's studio, Nesbit noticed the landscape portion of the destroyed painting on the floor, "apparently discarded, and wanted it." It was at Nesbit's instigation that the fragment was retrieved. According to Wood's onetime student Willis Guthrie, the artist's assistant at that time, the special wooden frame for *Sultry Night* was handmade by him at Wood's request (personal communication with the author, April 14, 2012).

The fragment was shown along with an impression of the lithograph in 1986–87 at the Madison Art Center in the exhibition "Another Country," as noted in "Grant Wood 'Cut-Out' on Display," *New Art Examiner* 14 (January 1987): 72. The property of Martha Frankwicz and her family, the painting is on long-term loan to the Chazen Museum of Art, University of Wisconsin, Madison. I am indebted to the Nesbit descendants for sharing the history of their family's friendship with Wood.

87 As far as I can determine, *Saturday Night Bath* first appeared in the literature in 1972, undated, in an exhibition of drawings at the Cedar Rapids Art Center recorded by Czestochowski in *Marvin D. Cone and Grant Wood*, 198. Dennis was apparently the first to reproduce the image, in his 1975 monograph *Grant Wood* (2nd edition, 1986); he dates it to 1937 (on what grounds he does not say), juxtaposing it without discussion with the lithograph *Sultry Night*, which he also dates to 1937. The latter date is inaccurate: see notes 70 and 83 above and Bruce E. Johnson, *Grant Wood: The 19 Lithographs, A Catalogue Raisonné* (Fletcher, NC: Arts and Crafts Research Fund, 2016), 147.

88 Cheles, "The Italian Renaissance in *American Gothic*," 113–14. Adams also invoked Piero's *Baptism* in his discussion of *Sultry Night* and *Saturday Night Bath* in "The Truth about Grant Wood," 10.

89 Graham, quoted in McDonald, *Grant Wood and Little Sister Nan*, 28.

90 Other actual names are unchanged in "Return from Bohemia," but I have not been able to verify that of David Zephaniah Peters, either through the Social Security Death Index or in the annals of the Alexander County Clerk. It is possible that Peters's birth (if that was his name) predated birth records there, which commenced in 1878, or that he was born in a different county from the one in which Cairo is located.

91 Again Wood's full statement reads: "Psychologists tell us that we're conditioned in the first 12 years of our lives and that everything we experience later is tied up with those first 12 years," quoted in Graham, *My Brother, Grant Wood*, 164.

92 See, for example, Will Fellows, ed., *Farm Boys: Lives of Gay Men from the Rural Midwest* (Madison: University of Wisconsin Press, 1996), for the memoir of Cornelius Utz (b. 1909), who grew up on a farm in northwestern Missouri and lived to come out as a gay man in the 1980s. In addition to prepubescent sex play with six of his seven brothers, Utz reports how the hired man on his family farm had engaged him in mutual masturbation when he was about five years old, 37–38.

93 Dennis, *Grant Wood*, 220.

CHAPTER 3: QUEER HABITS OF DISSEMBLING

1 Wanda M. Corn, "Grant Wood: Uneasy Modern," in Jane C. Milosch, ed., *Grant Wood's Studio: Birthplace of* American Gothic (New York: Prestel, 2005), 112.

2 Letter preserved among the Grant Wood materials in the archives of the Cedar Rapids Museum of Art.

3 Thomas Craven, "Grant Wood," *Scribner's Magazine* 101:6 (June 1937): 17. Despite Wood's repudiation of Charles Cumming's instruction to Craven, he had recorded one year of art study at the University of Iowa on his official registration card at the School of the Art Institute of Chicago in 1916.

4 William A. Kittredge, "I Went to School with Him," Grant Wood Memorial Issue, *Demcourier* 12:3 (May 1942): 21; Nan Wood Graham, with John Zug and Julie Jensen McDonald, *My Brother, Grant Wood* (Iowa City: State Historical Society of Iowa, 1993), 121.

5 MacKinlay Kantor, *I Love You, Irene* (New York: Doubleday and Company, 1972), 141–42.

6 Barbara Kent Buckley remembered the artist's insistence on secrecy vis-à-vis his photographic *aides-mémoire*: "Grant Wood did *not* want people to know that he worked from photographs. And he said [to her photographer father, Fred Kent], 'You must not show these to anybody.' . . . Because it was a no-no at that time." Audiotaped interview with Mary Bennett, Special Collections Coordinator, State Historical Society of Iowa; photographer Ruth Weller; and Don Roberts, head of the University of Iowa's photo services, September 1, 1993, cassette recording in the collection of the State Historical Society of Iowa, Iowa City.

7 Section 1 of the *Laws of the Thirty-Fifth General Assembly*, enacted April 19, 1913, quoted in George Painter, *The Sensibilities of Our Forefathers: The History of Sodomy Laws in the United States*, http://www.glapn.org/sodomylaws/sensibilities/iowa.htm, accessed July 4, 2012. Statistics in this paragraph are all drawn from Painter's research.

8 My thanks to Dr. Randall Lengeling of Dubuque, IA, for explaining how, without drugs to effect chemical castration, male sterilization at the time would have consisted of surgical orchiectomy. Personal telephone communication with the author, October 10, 2005.

9 The Wood-Longman conflict has been examined by Henry Adams, "The Truth about Grant Wood" (Annual College Art Association Conference, New York, February 24, 2000); Graham, *My Brother, Grant Wood*, 168–71; Paul C. Juhl, *Grant Wood's Clear Lake Summer* (Iowa City, IA: Brushy Creek Publishing, 2007), 11–13; Joni L. Kinsey, "Cultivating Iowa: An Introduction to Grant Wood," in Milosch, ed., *Grant Wood's Studio*, 27–32; and R. Tripp Evans, *Grant Wood: A Life* (New York: Alfred A. Knopf, 2010), 282–84. Evans also points to Longman's prejudices, citing the testimony of Elizabeth Catlett, the first African American to receive an MFA from the University of Iowa, 283. Longman's anti-Semitism is unvarnished in his official correspondence. As he tries to belittle Wood's accomplishments, for example, he suggests that the artist's success is the result of a "high powered publicity campaign through a local agent who lives in his house, as well as in conjunction with the leading (Jewish) art sales promoter [i.e., Reeves Lewenthal] in New York," Lester Longman to Dean George F. Kay, December 9, 1940, Edwin Green Papers, Grant Wood file, Special Collections Department, University of Iowa Libraries, Iowa City (hereafter cited as "Green Papers").

10 Undated, handwritten summary in the university president's confidential file on the Wood-Longman controversy, Virgil M. Hancher Papers, Special Collections Department, University of Iowa Libraries, Iowa City (hereafter cited as "Hancher Papers").

11 Grant Wood to President Virgil Hancher, June 18, 1941, Hancher Papers.

12 Lester Longman, "Statement Made to *Time Magazine* upon Request," November 18, 1940 (copied to president Virgil Hancher and deans George Kay, Earl Harper, and George Stoddard), Hancher Papers.

13 Virgil Hancher, memorandum on his "Conference with Mr. John C. Reid, re. Art Department," May 12, 1941, Hancher Papers.

14 Juhl, *Grant Wood's Clear Lake Summer*, provides details of Wood's summer activities, the guests he and Rinard entertained, and the warm embrace Wood received from the local community in Clear Lake.

15 Hancher, "Telephone Conversation with Professor Grant Wood on April 21, 1941," April 26, 1941, Hancher Papers. The depths to which the anti-Wood campaign sank were truly ugly. When Welch met with Longman, art historian Horst W. Janson, Martin, and painter Charles Okerbloom, one of them suggested that to obtain proof of Wood's reliance on photographs it might "be necessary to bribe one of Fred Kent's employees to deliver the pictures," according to Hancher's seven-page summary of a "Conference with Mr. Park Rinard and Mr. Dan Dutcher Held May 7, 1941," May 8, 1941, Green Papers. Wood, moreover, apparently considered responding in kind to Longman's ad hominem attacks. A page of penciled notes among the Hancher Papers in what looks to be Wood's handwriting (perhaps preparing Rinard and Dutcher for the above-mentioned conference) is titled "Vindication" at the top and divides into two columns, one proposing Wood himself as "Head [of] Creative Art Dept." and noting "Grant's Character Perfect," and the other column proposing "Demote Longman." In the Longman column is a list of complaints against him: "Hired Stew bums / Hired Bohemian / Neurotically vicious / Sex Trouble Ahead / Coeds and perverts." A note after the name "Ganso" (that is, painter-printmaker Emil Ganso, then on a one-year appointment in the art department) claims his "interest in fornication." The mention of Ganso indicates a date prior to April 18, 1941, when he died suddenly from a heart attack.

16 Scott Tucker, "Key West, Florida," in John Preston, ed., *Hometowns: Gay Men Write about Where They Belong* (New York: Dutton, 1991), 291.

17 The poet Frederick Nicklaus (1936–1993), Williams's traveling companion in the 1960s, conveyed this information ("Grant Wood was gay and frequented Key West bars") to Francis V. O'Connor on June 16, 1984, who shared it with me in New York on March 5, 2005. O'Connor further mentioned Wood's alleged sexual involvement with one Kelly Greenwell at the Stone City Art Colony; Greenwell was also Dornbush's lover at that time. My efforts to learn more about Greenwell have yielded only his life dates (b. June 25, 1900 in Joplin, MO, d. March 29, 1982 in Sedgwick, KS) and his employment by the Federal Theater Project in New York during the later 1930s. When he applied for a Social Security card in 1939, Greenwell was living at 15 West 51st Street in Manhattan and working in the theater district. In his brief obituary, the *Wichita Eagle* listed his profession as "retired draftsman."

18 Tennessee Williams, *Memoirs* (Garden City, NY: Doubleday, 1972), 64. Williams also notes the presence in Key West during that time of artists Arnold Blanch and Doris Lee; Elizabeth Bishop to Frani Blough Muser, March 11, 1941, *One Art: Letters, Selected and Edited by Robert Giroux* (New York: Farrar, Straus, Giroux, 1994), 99. I am grateful to Susan Gladstone for the latter citation.

19 Hancher, "Confidential Memorandum," May 2, 1941, citing Ned Bruce, "principal person in charge of the Federal Arts Projects for some time," who obtained his information from Wood's onetime colleague in Cedar Rapids, Ed Rowan. Hancher Papers.

20 Adams, "The Truth about Grant Wood."

21 The cache of six undated pencil drawings to which these sketches belong (Grant Wood Archive, Figge Art Museum, Davenport, IA) includes a portrait head by Wood inscribed "Chamberlain," i.e., Neville Chamberlain, negotiator of the infamous 1938 Munich Agreement. In this transaction, in which a portion of Czechoslovakia was surrendered to Hitler, Chamberlain of course became a veritable symbol of betrayal. James Dennis interprets the sketches as "caricatures of Hitler as the snarling wolf and Prime Minister Neville Chamberlain as a weak-kneed lamb," *Renegade Regionalists: The Modern Independence of Grant Wood, Thomas Hart Benton, and John Steuart Curry* (Madison: University of Wisconsin Press, 1998), 85. Dennis does not comment on the possible political significance of the other drawings in this group of the fox and the lion, to be discussed below.

22 Wood had also employed this formula to charming effect in his illustrations for Madeleine Darrough Horn's children's book *Farm on the Hill* (New York: Scribner, 1936).

23 Hancher Papers, as in note 15 above.

24 Earl E. Harper, "Notes on the Art Department Crisis," November 27, 1940, Green Papers.

25 Lincoln Kirstein, "An Iowa Memling," *Art Front* 1:6 (1935): 6.

26 Hilton Kramer, "The Return of the Nativist," *The New Criterion* 2:2 (October 1983): 61.

27 Frederic Newlin Price, "The Making of an Artist," *New York Herald Tribune*, January 20, 1935.

28 Robert Proost, typescript of an audiotaped recollection on the occasion of an annual Grant Wood Art Festival, c. 1980–90, Grant Wood Art Gallery, Anamosa, IA.

29 Bruce McKay, quoted in Hazel E. Brown, *Grant Wood and Marvin Cone: Artists of an Era* (Ames: Iowa State University Press, 1972), 67. The story is also repeated in Julie Jensen McDonald with Joan Liffring-Zug Bourret, *Grant Wood and Little Sister Nan: Essays and Remembrances* (Iowa City, IA: Penfield Press, 2000), 29.

30 Evans, *Grant Wood: A Life*, 107–8.

31 Graham, *My Brother, Grant Wood*, 110.

32 Graham spelled the name "Whittlesly" or "Whettesley." A search of the Social Security Death Index and of cemetery records in Margaret's supposed home state of Connecticut yielded no results for either of these surnames. I did discover, however, two Margarets of Wood's generation named "Whittlesey." One was born in 1890, expiring in 1966 in Washington state; the other, Margaret Whittlesey Perkins, was born in 1892, married one Mortimer H. Camp, and died in 1982.

33 Graham, *My Brother, Grant Wood*, 46.

34 Mark Simpson, *Male Impersonators: Men Performing Masculinity* (New York: Routledge, 1994), 101.

35 There had reportedly been a short-lived, long-distance flirtation with a girl in Chicago, brought to an end by Wood's army service in 1918, though that lasted only four months. The peculiar imagery Wood used to frame his report of the "Chicago girl" suggests a sexual encounter: along with "glowing accounts of the girl's apartment," he described to Graham "a thick, syrupy after-dinner drink they enjoyed but which was unfamiliar to him," *My Brother, Grant Wood*, 29. Unlike this unnamed girlfriend, and unlike the hopeful love interest Dawn Hatter, sister-in-law of Wood's friend Paul Hanson in Cedar Rapids, the mysterious Margaret Whittlesly as good girl fiancée had the advantage of being very far away and, finally, fatally inaccessible.

36 Ibid., 46.

37 William L. Shirer, *20th Century Journey: A Memoir of the Life and Times of William L. Shirer* (New York: Simon and Schuster, 1976), 186–89, 273–79. "Alas, I cannot help you about Margaret Whittlesly," Shirer responded to Graham's inquiry in a letter of January 31, 1977. "As you know, Grant was very shy about telling others about his private life. And though he opened up to me in Paris about his future and his determination to go back to Iowa and paint what he knew and felt, he never mentioned the romance with Whittlesly." Grant Wood Archive, Figge Art Museum.

38 Graham vented her frustration with the nephew in a letter to Ed Green on September 30, 1977, while complaining of the fact-checking insisted upon by one of her co-authors on *My Brother, Grant Wood*: "I guess John Zug was so used to verifying everything that he can not take anyone's word for anything, especially so since Margaret's nephew (who probably wasn't even born then) said it was a product of my imagination, etc. The whole thing was nasty business, Ed, and some day when I see you in person, I'll tell you. It's real ugly.

"You would think anyone would be proud to have their aunt as the one real love of Grant's life, and a well kept secret that no one knew about but Lee Jefferies (who introduced the girl to Grant, in Paris), mother and me, and then Park, whom he told on his death bed. . . .

"There is something behind this nephew not wanting his aunt's name connected with Grant's, and I don't know how to handle it. I am going to tell John Zug to just call the girl Margaret and not mention anything about her father being so and so, etc., or where she is from. I think it is wretched of her relatives to deny her place in history. (Don't mention this to the Zugs. Any of it.)

"I wonder what motive the nephew thinks I have in choosing his aunt if he doesn't believe my story. The girl was an unknown." Nan Wood Graham correspondence, folder 2, Grant Wood Archive, Figge Art Museum (spelling errors corrected). Graham never anticipated that this letter would some day come to light for scholars. Her correspondence with Green was donated in 1998 to the then Davenport Art Museum by Green's niece Jeannine Enwright.

39 Park Rinard, quoted in Graham, *My Brother, Grant Wood*, 46. Rinard then attempted to placate Nan with the possibility that Wood had destroyed Whittlesly's letters to him after her death.

40 Nan Wood Graham correspondence, folder 5, Grant Wood Archive, Figge Art Museum.

41 Graham's personal copy of Garwood's *Artist in Iowa: A Life of Grant Wood* is preserved in the State Historical Society of Iowa, Iowa City.

42 Evans, *Grant Wood: A Life*, 109. Struck by the similarity of the names "Margaret" and "Marcel," Evans speculates that they may represent the same individual.

43 Frederick Rufenacht Walters and Richard Douglas Powell, *Sanatoria for Consumptives in Various Parts of the World* (London: S. Sonnenschein and Co., 1905), 293–95.

44 Graham Scrapbook 3, "Early Postcards and Letters of Grant Wood," Grant Wood Archive, Figge Art Museum. (If Margaret Whittlesly wrote this postcard, however, she was not Marcel, because the card's author refers to Bordet in the third person.)

45 Robert Hughes, *American Visions: The Epic History of American Art* (New York: Alfred A. Knopf, 1997), 439, 442.

46 John Howard, *Men Like That: A Southern Queer History* (Chicago: University of Chicago Press, 1999), xiv.

47 Ibid., 261.

48 Evans, *Grant Wood: A Life*, 225–27. There are two versions of the *Draft Horse-Race Horse* drawings, dating to 1932 and 1933 respectively, the former in the collection of the

Cedar Rapids Museum of Art (illustrated here), the latter reproduced by Evans (226) in a private collection. See also James Dennis, *Grant Wood: A Study in American Art and Culture* (1975; Columbia: University of Missouri, 1986), 118–19.

49 Evans, *Grant Wood: A Life*, 225.

50 Carson McCullers, "The Jockey" (1941), in 55 *Short Stories from the New Yorker* (New York: Simon and Schuster, 1949), 310–14.

51 The strange outfit, pairing "denims with a starched, long-sleeved white shirt and two-toned shoes," also struck Corn, "Grant Wood: Uneasy Modern," 129.

52 Graham, *My Brother, Grant Wood*, 110. Like many of his contemporaries, Wood himself regularly consumed bootlegged liquor and, according to artist Virgil Matheny (a former resident of Stone City, IA, now living in Rohnert Park, CA), imported supplies of it at the art colony during the summers of 1932 and 1933 on night-flying airplanes landing without lights; personal telephone communication with the author, November 15, 2005. Wood's sense of humor about the so-called "evils of drink" is conveyed in a report by David McCosh, a printmaking teacher at the colony, that Wood named the beer cellar on the colony grounds the Sickle and Sheath, after the ruinous tavern in a maudlin 1931 temperance movie, *Ten Nights in a Barroom*; McCosh, undated letter (summer 1933) to Anne Kutka, University of Oregon Foundation, McCosh Memorial Endowment Archive, Jordan Schnitzer Museum of Art, Eugene, OR.

53 Wood, quoted in Graham, *My Brother, Grant Wood*, 160.

54 Ibid.

55 This entire anecdote is drawn from Lawrence Tenney Stevens, typescript describing a trip, November 1940, Lawrence Tenney Stevens Archives, Superior, AZ. My thanks to John Faubion, Director of the Lawrence Tenney Stevens Trust, who provided me this text in a series of emails, September 16–20, 2012.

56 I am grateful to Lea Rosson DeLong, who first told me about the impersonator and the possible connection to the Lindbergh case in an email communication, April 25, 2010, and to the artist's adoptive granddaughter, Sally Maxon Harris, who confirmed all this in my telephone interview with her, August 24, 2012.

57 As reported in the *Daily Iowan* of September 6, 1935, Reginald Marsh was one of the five artists Wood intended to treat in future chapters of "Return from Bohemia," see Paul C. Juhl, *Grant Wood: Abandoned Plans* (Iowa City, IA: Brushy Creek Publishing, 2012), 33.

58 Phyllis Greenacre, "The Impostor" (1958), in *Emotional Growth: Psychoanalytic Studies of the Gifted and a Great Variety of Other Individuals*, vol. 1 (New York: International Universities Press, 1971), 96.

59 Helene Deutsch, "The Impostor: Contribution to Ego Psychology of a Type of Psychopath," *Psychoanalytic Quarterly* 24 (October 1955): 503.

60 Lionel Finkelstein, "The Impostor: Aspects of His Development," *The Psychoanalytic Quarterly* 43:85 (1974): 87.

61 Greenacre, "The Impostor," 102.

62 Ibid., 104.

63 Kramer, "Return of the Nativist," 62, and in the next sentence, ibid.

64 Greenacre, "The Relation of the Impostor to the Artist" (1958), in *Emotional Growth*, vol. 2, 533.

65 Thomas Hart Benton, *An Artist in America*, 3rd rev. ed. (Columbia: University of Missouri Press, 1968), 320, and in the next sentence, ibid.

66 Jane C. Milosch, "Grant Wood's Studio: A Decorative Adventure," in Milosch, ed., *Grant Wood's Studio*, 95. In this essay, Milosch provides an excellent account of all

Wood's decorations at 5 Turner Alley, including the "faux finishes" he developed for walls, ceilings, and floors.

67 Kantor, *I Love You, Irene*, 140.

68 See Juhl, *Grant Wood's Clear Lake Summer*, 24, where Wood wittily describes himself in this image as a modern-day sea god, "one of Clear Lake's current stellar attractions: Neptune 1941."

69 Greenacre, "The Impostor," 98.

70 Craven, "Grant Wood," 18, and in the next paragraph, 19.

71 Sigmund Freud, *Jokes and Their Relation to the Unconscious* (1905), in *The Standard Edition of the Complete Psychological Works of Sigmund Freud*, , vol. 8, trans. James Strachey (London: Hogarth Press and the Institute of Psycho-analysis, 1960), 133. *The Standard Edition* is hereafter cited as "*SE*."

72 The *Sioux City Tribune* article was cited verbatim in the Eppley Hotels' in-house magazine, *Hospitality*, in a feature then re-presented in "Eppley Hotels Magazine Praises Grant Wood and Edgar Britton for Work," *Cedar Rapids Republican*, October 17, 1926.

73 Hal Fischer, *Gay Semiotics* (San Francisco: NFS Press, 1977), 21.

74 Evans, *Grant Wood: A Life*, 256.

75 Bruce Rodgers, *The Queen's Vernacular: A Gay Lexicon* (San Francisco: Straight Arrow Books, 1972), 27.

76 Wood, quoted in Brown, *Grant Wood and Marvin Cone*, 71.

77 My thanks to artist Wendy Guida of Monkey Island, OK, for bringing the photograph of her grandmother Dorothy Belland's friend Bette Sanbourne to light, and also to curator Sean Ulmer at the Cedar Rapids Museum of Art for sharing information about Sanbourne's education (at Iowa State Teachers College and the Art Institute of Chicago) and employment, in a personal email of June 11, 2012.

78 Graham, *My Brother, Grant Wood*, 83.

79 Wanda M. Corn, *Grant Wood: The Regionalist Vision* (New Haven, CT: Yale University Press, 1983), 80. Figure 114 reproduces a photograph of the painting in its original state.

80 Evans, *Grant Wood: A Life*, 142.

81 Adams, "The Truth about Grant Wood," 12. According to Rodgers, *Queen's Vernacular*, a "chicken" is a fair-faced boy under the age of consent; "chicken dinner" is "sex with a teenager"; "butchered chicken" is a "boy who recently lost his anal virginity"; a "poultry dealer" is a man who pimps boys; and so on, 44–46.

82 Alfred Kinsey, Wardell Pomeroy, and Clyde Martin in *Sexual Behavior in the Human Male* (Philadelphia: W. B. Saunders, 1948) reported that "about 17 per cent of the farm boys have complete sexual relations with other animals [i.e., other than human beings], and perhaps as many more have relations which are not carried through to climax," 459.

83 Park Rinard, "Return from Bohemia: A Painter's Story, Part I" (MA thesis, State University of Iowa, 1939), 11. Wood, however, repeated his description of the chickens verbatim in *Art in the Daily Life of the Child*, University of Iowa Child Welfare Pamphlet no. 73 (May 10, 1939), 5.

84 Darrell Garwood, *Artist in Iowa: A Life of Grant Wood* (New York: W. W. Norton, 1944), 17.

85 Sherwood Anderson, "The Egg," in *The Triumph of the Egg* (New York: B. W. Huebsch, 1921), 47.

86 Ibid., 47–48.

87 Adams, "The Truth about Grant Wood," 12.

88 Freud, "Analysis of a Phobia in a Five-Year-Old Boy" (1909), *SE* 10 (1955), 1–147.

89 Sándor Ferenczi, "A Little Chanticleer" (1913), *Contributions to Psychoanalysis*, trans. Ernest Jones (Boston: Richard G. Badger, 1916), 204–13. The following sentence is from 212.

90 Ibid., 209.

91 Ibid., 211–12.

92 Freud, *Totem and Taboo* (1913), *SE* 13 (1955), 131.

93 Garwood, *Artist in Iowa: A Life of Grant Wood*, 158.

94 McDonald, *Grant Wood and Little Sister Nan*, 64.

95 Graham, *My Brother, Grant Wood*, 28.

96 Sara McClain Sherman, 1959 reminiscence on Grant Wood's art, Donna Clausen cat. no. 4, n.p. [4–5], Sherman Papers, Marysville, WA. The following quotation is from ibid.

97 Horst W. Janson, "The Case of the Naked Chicken," *College Art Journal* 15:2 (Winter 1955): 124–27.

98 Ugo's woodcut retains its exemplary status in Linda C. Hults, *The Print in the Western World: An Introductory History* (Madison: University of Wisconsin Press, 1996), 181, 462.

99 The painted self-portrait is reproduced in August L. Freundlich, *William Gropper: Retrospective* (Los Angeles: Ward Ritchie Press, in conjunction with the Joe and Emily Lowe Art Gallery of the University of Miami, 1968), 79, fig. 56. My thanks to Jane Myers McNamara and Gail Windisch for helping me identify Gropper's images in personal email communications, August 28, 2013.

100 See Cécile Whiting, "American Heroes and Invading Barbarians," chapter 4 in *Anti-fascism in American Art* (New Haven, CT: Yale University Press, 1989), esp. 98–113.

101 Wood's statement of January 2, 1940, quoted in ibid., 100.

102 Corn, "Grant Wood: Uneasy Modern," 116.

103 "Almost before the paint was dry on this picture it started a battle," reported *Life* magazine, continuing that the painting had "raised the dander of literal-minded patriots all over the country [who] bombarded Wood with angry letters," "Grant Wood Paints George Washington & Cherry Tree," February 19, 1940, 33. See also Garwood, *Artist in Iowa: A Life of Grant Wood*, 227.

104 Corn, *Grant Wood: The Regionalist Vision*, 122.

105 Graham, *My Brother, Grant Wood*, 154.

106 "Painting Attempts to 'Debunk' Legend," *New York Times*, December 31, 1939.

107 Evans, *Grant Wood: A Life*, 272.

108 Garwood, *Artist in Iowa: A Life of Grant Wood*, 224.

109 John F. Riggs [Superintendent of Public Instruction], comp., *Flag Day: Iowa Public Schools* (n.p. [IA], Department of Education, 1904), 3.

110 Ibid., 13.

111 Brown, *Grant Wood and Marvin Cone*, 52–54. Garwood, *Artist in Iowa: A Life of Grant Wood*, gives a date of 1929 for the founding of the Community Theater, 112. Juhl, *Abandoned Plans*, 16, also reports that Wood undertook to paint scenery for the Omaha Playhouse in 1931, a project that, for unknown reasons, the artist never completed.

112 "*Show Boat*: A Painting for *Life* by Doris Lee," *Life*, November 27, 1939, 48.

113 Garwood, *Artist in Iowa: A Life of Grant Wood*, 242. The couple socialized with Wood in Key West (see note 18 above) and were among Wood's last guests in the house on Court Street before he was hospitalized in November 1941; see ibid. Shown on Nan Wood Graham's 1984 inventory of a "Collection of Works of Art, Mementoes, and Personal Belongings of the Late Grant Wood, Offered for Sale, as a Unit" to the

Davenport Municipal Art Gallery are lithographs by Blanch (*Victor*) and Lee (*Eagle's Rest*) respectively. Graham identifies them as "exchange gifts, Grant gave them one of his lithographs for one of theirs," Grant Wood Archive, Figge Art Museum.

114 For a remarkable analysis of *Dinner for Threshers*, see Evans, *Grant Wood: A Life*, 169–76. Evans reads this picture as a commemoration of Maryville, whose "last supper" *Dinner for Threshers* evokes.

115 As reported in "Return from Bohemia," 268–69. I have not found any mention in the Anamosa newspapers of the play presented in the town's Holt Opera House during Wood's childhood, but in 1900, when Wood was nine years old, brief notices appeared about a performance of *Uncle Tom's Cabin* on September 13 in Olin, IA, about ten miles southeast of Anamosa: see *The Anamosa Journal*, September 6, 1900; *Anamosa Eureka*, September 20, 1900; and *Cascade Pioneer*, September 21, 1900.

116 Phyllis Greenacre, "The Primal Scene and the Sense of Reality," *Psychoanalytic Quarterly* 42:1 (1973): 12.

117 Garwood, *Artist in Iowa: A Life of Grant Wood*, 61.

118 Freud, "From the History of an Infantile Neurosis" (1918), *SE* 17 (1955), 1–122.

119 Melanie Klein, "A Contribution to the Psychogenesis of Tics" (1925), and "Early Analysis" (1923), both in *Love, Guilt and Reparation and Other Works 1921–1945* (New York: Delacorte Press/Seymour Lawrence, 1975), 115, 102.

120 Klein, "Early Analysis," 99. This common equation is further explained by Bertram Lewin, who writes how "the fear of being devoured, or the wish to be," originates in the earliest memory of the infant at the breast, "when active eating is followed by the passive relaxation which later comes to be conceived as a being swallowed and which ultimately merges into sleep," *The Psychoanalysis of Elation* (New York: The Psychoanalytic Quarterly, Inc., 1950), 117.

121 John Gedo, cited in Mary Mathews Gedo, *Looking at Art from the Inside Out: The Psychoiconographical Approach to Modern Art* (New York: Cambridge University Press, 1994), 285n22.

122 Lewin, *Psychoanalysis of Elation*, 72.

123 Evans, *Grant Wood: A Life*, 277, and for staircase dreams see Freud, *The Interpretation of Dreams* (1900), *SE* 5 (1953), esp. 355n2.

124 Dennis, *Grant Wood*, 113.

125 Ibid.

126 Edna Ferber had been among the notable signatories in the guestbook for Wood's 1935 exhibition at the Ferargil Galleries in New York. Other signatories include poet Stephen Vincent Benét, Edward Hopper, printmaker Martin Lewis, Duncan Phillips, Eleanor Roosevelt, and Wood's friends Thomas Hart Benton, John Steuart Curry, and MacKinlay Kantor. The book is preserved in the Grant Wood Archive, Figge Art Museum.

127 My thanks to James P. Hayes, current owner of the house at 1142 East Court Street, for information about the star medallions, which "are the decorative end points of iron rods . . . placed through the wall for stability"; personal email communication with the author, September 12, 2013. In a history of Hayes's house, Richard Alan King reports how Faye Oakes Kruse, who lived next door to Wood on Court Street, had chatted with him through the window of her second-floor bedroom while he worked on *Parson Weems*. See *1142: The History and Growth of the N. Oakes–Grant Wood–Dr. Pauline Moore–James P. Hayes House* (n.p.: privately published, 2008), 53.

128 Milosch, "Grant Wood's Studio: A Decorative Adventure," 84–85, 97–101.

129 Frank Luther Mott, *Time Enough: Essays in Autobiography* (Chapel Hill: University of North Carolina Press, 1962), 138. Mott notes how African American SPCS guests—

James Weldon Johnson and Countee Cullen were also among them—could not be put up in Iowa City hotels, "and we took them into our own homes," 143.

130 Ibid., 139.

131 Ibid., 139–40.

132 Wood, quoted in ibid., 139.

133 For Wood as ironist, see John E. Seery, "Grant Wood's Political Gothic," in *America Goes to College: Political Theory for the Liberal Arts* (Albany: State University of New York Press, 2002), 133, 137–38, and for the qualities of camp, see Jack Babuscio, "The Cinema of Camp (*aka* Camp and the Gay Sensibility)," in Fabio Cleto, ed., *Camp: Queer Aesthetics and the Performing Subject, A Reader* (Ann Arbor: University of Michigan Press, 1999), 119.

134 Adams, "The Truth about Grant Wood," 13; Susan Sontag, "Notes on Camp" (1964), in Cleto, ed., *Camp*, 56.

135 Babuscio, "The Cinema of Camp," 123.

136 Garwood, *Artist in Iowa: A Life of Grant Wood*, 112.

137 George Bernard Shaw, *The Bodley Head Bernard Shaw, Collected Plays with Their Prefaces*, vol. 4 (London: Bodley Head, 1972), 636.

138 Ibid., 640.

CHAPTER 4: THE GROUND ITSELF

1 The mural was salvaged from the hotel in 1970, donated in 2000 to the Cedar Rapids Community School District by Dr. Milton Heifetz, Westwood, CA, and currently hangs in Washington High School, in Cedar Rapids. See Angela Meng, "A Place of Honor," *Cedar Rapids Gazette*, April 2, 2006.

2 The book Wood consulted was *Route from Liverpool to Great Salt Lake Valley: Illustrated with a Splendid Series of Steel Engravings and Wood Cuts by Frederick Hawkins Piercey*. See Wanda Corn, *Grant Wood: The Regionalist Vision* (New Haven, CT: Yale University Press, 1983), 152n59.

3 Corn, *Grant Wood: The Regionalist Vision*, 26. The twenty-four-foot oil-on-canvas hotel mural is reproduced in ibid., 28–29.

4 All of the influences cited in this paragraph are well documented, beginning as early as 1935 with an essay by two of Wood's protégés and subsequently explored throughout the literature. For the first mention of willowware and Currier and Ives lithographs, see Arnold Pyle and Park Rinard, "The Work of Grant Wood," *Catalogue of the First New York Exhibition of Paintings and Drawings by Grant Wood* (New York: Ferargil Galleries, 1935), 6. See also Corn, who reproduces a Blue Staffordshire platter in *Grant Wood: The Regionalist Vision*, 75, and an antique Linn County map in "Grant Wood: Uneasy Modern," in Jane C. Milosch, ed., *Grant Wood's Studio: Birthplace of* American Gothic (New York: Prestel, 2005), 117, fig. 109. Travis Nygard discusses the importance to Wood of Currier and Ives prints in *Seeds of Agribusiness: Grant Wood and the Visual Culture of Grain Farming, 1862–1957* (Ann Arbor, MI: University Microfilms, 2009), esp. 45–47.

5 Grant Wood and Edward B. Rowan, "Stone City Colony and Art School—Summer of 1932," n.p., from an original example of the brochure in the collection of Dr. Randall Lengeling, Dubuque, IA.

6 My reference is to Robert Louis Stevenson's poem, in which a bedridden child delights in imagining the blanket spread out before him as a landscape through which he moves his toy soldiers: "I was the giant great and still / That sits upon the pillow-hill, / And sees before him, dale and plain, / The pleasant land of counter-

pane," *A Child's Garden of Verses* (New York: Charles Scribner's Sons, 1901), 14. Wood's landscapes to me have a similar charm.

7 Wood, quoted in Irma Rene Koen, "The Art of Grant Wood," *Christian Science Monitor*, March 26, 1932, 6.

8 See, for example, Corn, *Grant Wood: The Regionalist Vision*, 70–71, fig. 108 and pl. 5 respectively.

9 *Kunstausstellung München 1928 Glaspalast* (Munich: Knorr & Hirth, 1928), cat. no. 2592. For the complete exhibition catalogue, see www.arthistoricum.net/en/subjects/sources/catalogues-of-the-art-exhibitions-at-the-glaspalast-in-munich/, accessed July 22, 2014.

10 The figurine, albeit in damaged condition, is preserved in the Grant Wood Archive at the Figge Art Museum, Davenport, IA.

11 Wood, quoted in Koen, "The Art of Grant Wood," 6.

12 Pyle and Rinard, "The Work of Grant Wood," 5.

13 Sigmund Freud, *The Interpretation of Dreams* (1900), *The Standard Edition of the Complete Psychological Works of Sigmund Freud* (hereafter cited as *SE*), trans. James Strachey (London: Hogarth Press and the Institute of Psycho-analysis, 1953), vol. 5, 399.

14 The drawing, *hors catalogue*, was mentioned as number 40 on the exhibition checklist by Joseph S. Czestochowski, *Marvin D. Cone and Grant Wood: An American Tradition* (Cedar Rapids, IA: Clio, 1935), 197.

15 Lincoln Kirstein, "An Iowa Memling," *Art Front* 1:6 (1935): 8. The following quote in this paragraph is from ibid.

16 Grant Wood, with Frank Luther Mott, *Revolt against the City*, Whirling World Series 1 (Iowa City, IA: Clio, 1935), reprinted in James Dennis, *Grant Wood: A Study in American Art and Culture* (New York: Viking Press, 1975; Columbia: University of Missouri, 1986), 233.

17 Dennis, *Grant Wood*, 206, who outlines a brief history of the Farm Holiday Association, organized in 1932 in protest against Midwestern farmers' distressed economic conditions.

18 Rodney D. Karr, "Farmer Rebels in Plymouth County, Iowa, 1932–33," *The Annals of Iowa* 47:7 (Winter 1985): 637.

19 Karal Ann Marling, quoted in Corn, *Grant Wood: The Regionalist Vision*, 90.

20 For the complete series, see Lea Rosson DeLong, *Nature's Forms/Nature's Forces: The Art of Alexandre Hogue* (Norman: University of Oklahoma Press, 1984). Although the date of *Erosion No. 2—Mother Earth Laid Bare* has sometimes been given as 1938, the artist reported a date of 1936 to the Philbrook Museum of Art, per Mark Andrew White, "Alexandre Hogue's Passion: Ecology and Agribusiness in *The Crucified Land*," *Great Plains Quarterly* 26:2 (2006): 81n1.

21 Melanie Klein, "A Contribution to the Psychogenesis of Manic-Depressive States" (1935), in *Love, Guilt and Reparation and Other Works 1921–1945* (New York: Delacorte Press/Seymour Lawrence, 1975), esp. 262 and 292.

22 Phyllis Greenacre, "The Childhood of the Artist," *The Psychoanalytic Study of the Child* 12 (1957): 53.

23 Ibid., 57.

24 Corn, *Grant Wood: The Regionalist Vision*, 90; R. Tripp Evans, *Grant Wood: A Life* (New York: Alfred A. Knopf, 2010), 134.

25 Evans, *Grant Wood: A Life*, 135.

26 Freud employed this term for the wide-ranging non-genital sexual satisfactions experienced in infancy in "Three Essays on the Theory of Sexuality" (1905), *SE* 7 (1953), 191.

27 This awestruck attitude toward pregnancy was mentioned, relative to the worship of the Virgin Mary, by Greenacre, "Experiences of Awe in Childhood," *The Psychoanalytic Study of the Child* 11 (1956): 19.

28 Robert Boston, "Spring 1955," in Clarence A. Andrews, ed. *Growing Up in Iowa: Reminiscences of 14 Iowa Authors* (Ames: Iowa State University Press, 1978), 139. This anthology also contains essays by Wood's friends and contemporaries Frank Luther Mott and Paul Engle.

29 Freud, *Civilization and Its Discontents* (1930), *SE* 21 (1964), 66–67, and in the next sentence, 68.

30 Ibid., 68.

31 Phyllis Greenacre, "The Family Romance of the Artist," in *Emotional Growth: Psychoanalytic Studies of the Gifted and a Great Variety of Other Individuals*, vol. 2 (New York: International Universities Press, 1971), 530.

32 Dennis, *Grant Wood*, 92.

33 The commission resulted in Wood's multi-figure composition *Sentimental Ballad* (1940, New Britain Museum of American Art, CT). See Corn, *Grant Wood: The Regionalist Vision*, 56–57, fig. 100, and Erika Doss, *Benton, Pollock, and the Politics of Modernism* (Chicago: University of Chicago Press, 1991), 241–43.

34 In *Barnstorming the Prairies: Aerial Vision and Modernity in Rural America, 1920–1940* (Minneapolis: University of Minnesota Press, 2015), Jason Weems analyzes Wood's "aerial sensibility" in terms of the visual culture in which he was immersed, and explains how "barnstorming and aerial shows were so ubiquitous across the Midwest (especially Cedar Rapids)" that Wood likely had some real experience with flight in the 1930s, personal email communication with the author, August 26, 2014. From Wood's sister, we learn how the fearless Thomas Hart Benton once chartered a small plane for a speaking gig of his own and asked Wood to accompany him, making an emergency landing in a snowy cornfield. Nan Wood Graham, with John Zug and Julie Jensen McDonald, *My Brother, Grant Wood* (Iowa City: State Historical Society of Iowa, 1993), 123.

35 Nygard, *Seeds of Agribusiness*, 38, explains how the aerial view in *Spring Turning* reveals the small square fields that derived from the 1862 Homestead Act, which platted land "in a gridiron pattern with township roads running north to south and east to west one mile apart from each other."

36 This telling detail seems to me not only to distill the fantasy of a phallic mother but also to reflect the child's confusion between the urinary and ejaculatory functions of the penis, which fascinates him as he tries to puzzle out the mysterious facts of life.

37 Greenacre, "Experiences of Awe in Childhood," 9, 21–22.

38 Ibid., 21.

39 Evans, *Grant Wood: A Life*, 172.

40 Nygard has identified the image as a Currier and Ives print, *Horses in a Thunderstorm* (n.d.), *Seeds of Agribusiness*, 33 and 73, fig. 2.

41 Evans, *Grant Wood: A Life*, 173–76.

42 DeLong, *When Tillage Begins, Other Arts Follow*, 248, and Joni L. Kinsey, *Plain Pictures: Images of the American Prairie* (Washington, DC: Smithsonian Institution Press for the University of Iowa Museum of Art, 1996), 126.

43 Millet's importance for Wood was overdetermined; already in the teens, the French champion of peasant painting was a favorite of American farmers, and his works were reproduced in *The Nonpartisan Leader*, the journal of the progressive Farmers' Nonpartisan League. See Nygard, *Seeds of Agribusiness*, 283, 338, fig. 150.

44 Willa Cather, *My Antonia* (New York: Random House Bantam Classic, 2005), 165.

45 Evans, *Grant Wood: A Life*, 137–38.

46 Otto Fenichel, "The Misapprehended Oracle" (1942), in *The Collected Papers of Otto Fenichel*, Second Series, eds. Hanna Fenichel and David Rapaport (New York: W. W. Norton and Co., Inc., 1954), 235.

47 Henry Adams, "The Truth about Grant Wood" (Annual College Art Association Conference, New York, February 24, 2000), typescript, 12. Bruce Rodgers, in *The Queen's Vernacular: A Gay Lexicon* (San Francisco: Straight Arrow Books, 1972), explained that the term "cornhole," whose first usage he dated to the 1920s, derives from the use of "dried corncobs as ass-wipers in the days of the outhouse," 87.

48 Wood to King Vidor, April 26, 1941, quoted in Dennis, *Grant Wood*, 245n2.

49 Paul C. Juhl, *Grant Wood: Abandoned Plans* (Iowa City, IA: Brushy Creek Publishing, 2012), 52.

50 An undated clipping [*Cedar Rapids Gazette*, February 16, 1969] ascribes Wood's Regionalist conversion (simplistically) to his reading of Sigmund's poem, Nan Wood Graham Scrapbook 12, Grant Wood Archive, Figge Art Museum. The Impressionist-style *Cornshocks* (1927) and *Cornshocks* (1928) are illustrated in Dennis, *Grant Wood*, 32, fig. 19, and 33, fig. 20, respectively.

51 I owe this association between picture and poem to Edward Pierce Ferreter, "Jay Sigmund and Grant Wood," *Books at Iowa* 42:1 (1985): 30–31.

52 According to Juhl, "when Wood began to concentrate on the lithographs, he stated that Sigmund's poems provided inspiration for his ideas," *Grant Wood: Abandoned Plans*, 51–52.

53 Darrell Garwood, *Artist in Iowa: A Life of Grant Wood* (New York: W. W. Norton, 1944), 233.

54 See Paul C. Juhl, *Grant Wood's Clear Lake Summer* (Iowa City, IA: Brushy Creek Publishing, 2007).

55 Wood, quoted in "Grant Wood Sees Artists in Significant Role in Defense," *Iowa Press-Citizen*, May 3, 1941.

56 *Saturday Evening Post*, April 18, 1942, illus. in Barbara Haskell, *The American Century: Art and Culture 1900–1950* (New York: Whitney Museum of American Art in association with W. W. Norton, 1999), 311, fig. 601.

57 Garwood, *Artist in Iowa: A Life of Grant Wood*, 236, identified the model for the gardener, as did Graham, in *My Brother, Grant Wood*, 173.

58 For a photograph of the house in 2007 (taken from the backyard), see Juhl, *Clear Lake Summer*, 48, fig. 42. Joan Liffring-Zug, comp., *This Is Grant Wood Country* (Davenport, IA: Davenport Municipal Art Gallery, 1977), 61, misidentified Oakland Cemetery as "Oaklawn Cemetery."

59 Zachary Michael Jack, "America's Forgotten Regionalist: Jay G. Sigmund," in Jack, ed., *The Plowman Sings: The Essential Fiction, Poetry, and Drama of America's Forgotten Regionalist Jay G. Sigmund*, 7, follows Edward Pierce Ferreter's identification of *Spring in Town* with Sigmund's backyard.

60 Ibid., 6.

61 Garwood, *Artist in Iowa: A Life of Grant Wood*, 237.

62 Klein, "Mourning and Its Relation to Manic-Depressive States" (1940), in *Love, Guilt and Reparation and Other Works 1921–1945*, 358.

63 See DeLong, *When Tillage Begins, Other Arts Follow*, 243, for a complete list of the twenty-four species.

64 Wood, quoted in Graham, *My Brother, Grant Wood*, 174.

65 Klein, "Mourning," 360.

66 Ibid.

APPENDIX: "RETURN FROM BOHEMIA"

1 Sara McClain Sherman, autobiography, Donna Clausen cat. no. 1, 106, Sherman papers, Marysville, WA.

2 Sherman, untitled fragment, Clausen cat. no. 8, n.p. [2–3], Sherman papers.

3 Information drawn from Robin Hawkins's interview of Bennett Cerf in "Notable New Yorkers," Columbia University Libraries Oral History Research Office, http://www.columbia.edu/cu/lweb/digital/collections/nny/cerfb/introduction.html, accessed November 22, 2011. We know, moreover, that Wood maintained cordial or even friendly relations with Johnson, dedicating an impression of *Sultry Night* for him sometime after the lithograph's publication in 1939. The print signed by Wood and inscribed "For Malcolm Johnson" is currently in a private collection in Seattle.

4 See Paul C. Juhl, *Grant Wood: Abandoned Plans* (Iowa City, IA: Brushy Creek Publishing, 2012), 33.

5 For Morley as a speaker at the Times Club, see Frank Luther Mott, *Time Enough: Essays in Autobiography* (Chapel Hill: University of North Carolina Press, 1962), 138. Morley mentions Wood in *The Saturday Review of Literature* throughout the 1930s, and it was probably at his invitation that Wood reviewed Thomas Hart Benton's autobiography, *Artist in America*, for the November 6, 1937 issue of the magazine ("Hard-Hitting Artist," 6).

6 "A 'Schlepper,'" unattributed sidebar accompanying Park Rinard, "The Real Grant Wood," *Des Moines Sunday Register*, January 15, 1984. See also Paul C. Juhl, *Grant Wood's Clear Lake Summer* (Iowa City, IA: Brushy Creek Publishing, 2007), 4.

7 Wanda Corn, *Grant Wood: The Regionalist Vision* (New Haven, CT: Yale University Press, 1983), 151n2.

8 R. Tripp Evans, *Grant Wood: A Life* (New York: Alfred A. Knopf, 2010), 237.

9 Judith Ellen Rinard, personal telephone communication with author, January 9, 2012.

10 Onetime neighbor Alvin Byerly, for example, later president of the Antioch School Board, appears in John Reynolds, "Old Friends Pay Tribute to Grant Wood's Memory," *The* [*Anamosa*] *Gazette*, undated clipping in Nan Wood Graham's scrapbooks, Grant Wood Archive, Figge Art Museum, Davenport, IA. For Joseph Wood and the First Presbyterian Church of Anamosa in Strawberry Hill—he also served as landscape designer when the neo-Gothic structure was erected in 1878—see *The History of Jones County, Iowa* (Chicago: Western Historical Company, 1879), 443.

11 Lea Rosson DeLong, *Grant Wood's Main Street: Art, Literature, and the American Midwest* (Ames: Brunnier Art Museum, University Museums, Iowa State University, 2004), 35n23.

12 "Iowa Cows Give Grant Wood His Best Thoughts," *New York Herald Tribune*, January 23, 1936.

13 Wood's gifts to Rinard numbered more than a dozen prints and drawings, including the original oil sketch *sur le motif* of the *American Gothic* house in Eldon, now preserved in the Smithsonian American Art Museum, Washington, DC.

14 Willis Guthrie, personal interview with the author, Waukesha, WI, June 12, 2012.

15 Nan Wood Graham, with John Zug and Julie Jensen McDonald, *My Brother, Grant Wood* (Iowa City: State Historical Society of Iowa, 1993), 124, reports that Mott inscribed a copy of *Revolt against the City*, "I 'ghost-wrote' this for Grant. Frank Luther Mott." Citing this information, Corn, *Grant Wood: The Regionalist Vision*, 153n85, argues convincingly that the anti-urban aspects of the essay, as well as many of the literary references, likely belong to Mott rather than Wood.

16 Wood to Maynard Walker, March 16, 1936, quoted in DeLong, *Grant Wood's Main Street*, 36n27.

17 Wood, "The Writer and the Painter," *American Prefaces: A Journal of Critical and Imaginative Writing* 1:1 (October 1935): 3–4.

18 Wood, "Rural Influence in Contemporary American Art," *Rural America* 14:2 (February 1936): 43.

19 Wood, introduction to *Young Sam Clemens* by Cyril Clemens (Portland, ME: Leon Tebbetts Editions, 1942), n.p.; and idem, "Art in the Daily Life of the Child," *National Parent-Teacher* 33 (October 1938): 5–7, reprinted as *Art in the Daily Life of the Child*, University of Iowa Child Welfare Pamphlet no. 73 (May 10, 1939).

20 Or, perhaps Sherman conflated writing and typing, for we know that Wood never learned to type. Before Rinard and Sherman began to serve him as typists, he employed Lillian Bukacek; see Lea Rosson DeLong, *When Tillage Begins, Other Arts Follow: Grant Wood and Christian Petersen Murals* (Ames: Brunnier Art Museum, University Museums, Iowa State University, 2006), 48n29. When Bukacek was not available, the artist would sometimes importune Leata Rowan, who reported to her husband on December 26, 1933, "typed a letter for Grant Wood today. Lill sick!" Edward B. Rowan Papers, Archives of American Art, D141.

21 Edward A. Maser, "Foreword," *Grant Wood, 1891–1942* (Lawrence: University of Kansas Museum of Art, 1959), n.p.

22 "A 'Schlepper,'" *Des Moines Sunday Register*, January 15, 1984.

❖ BIBLIOGRAPHY ❖

Adams, Henry. "Grant Wood Revisited." Symposium on Grant Wood's World, University of Iowa, Iowa City, April 24, 2010.

———. "The Truth about Grant Wood." Annual College Art Association Conference, New York, February 24, 2000.

Andrews, Clarence A., ed. *Growing Up in Iowa: Reminiscences of Fourteen Iowa Authors*. Ames: Iowa State University Press, 1978.

Baigell, Matthew. "Grant Wood Revisited." *Art Journal* 26:2 (1966–67): 116–22.

Balken, Debra Bricker. *After Many Springs: Regionalism, Modernism and the Midwest*. Des Moines, IA: Des Moines Art Center, 2009.

Barter, Judith A., ed. *America after the Fall: Painting in the 1930s*. Chicago: Art Institute of Chicago, 2016.

Biel, Steven. *American Gothic: A Life of America's Most Famous Painting*. New York: W. W. Norton, 2005.

Brown, Hazel E. *Grant Wood and Marvin Cone: Artists of an Era*. Ames: Iowa State University Press, 1972.

Chauncey, George, Jr. *Gay New York: Gender, Urban Culture, and the Making of the Gay Male World, 1890–1940*. New York: Basic Books, 1994.

Cheles, Luciano. "The Italian Renaissance in *American Gothic*." Symposium on Grant Wood Today, University of Iowa, Iowa City, April 14, 2012.

———. "The Italian Renaissance in *American Gothic*: Grant Wood and Piero della Francesca." *American Art* 30:1 (Spring 2016): 106–24.

Cole, Sylvan, Jr. *Grant Wood: The Lithographs, A Catalogue Raisonné*. Edited by Susan Teller. New York: Associated American Artists, 1984.

Corn, Wanda. "Grant Wood (1892–1942), Death on the Ridge Road, 1935." In Nancy Mowll Mathews, ed., *American Dreams: American Art to 1950 in the Williams College Museum of Art*, 158–61. New York: Hudson Hills Press, 2001.

———. *Grant Wood: The Regionalist Vision*. New Haven, CT: Yale University Press, 1983.

———. "Grant Wood: Uneasy Modern." In Jane C. Milosch, ed., *Grant Wood's Studio: Birthplace of American Gothic*. 111–29, 135–36. New York: Prestel, 2005.

———. "The Painting That Became a Symbol of a Nation's Spirit." *Smithsonian* 11:8 (1980): 84–97.

Craven, Thomas. "Grant Wood." *Scribner's Magazine* 101:6 (June 1937): 16–22.

Czestochowski, Joseph. *John Steuart Curry and Grant Wood: A Portrait of Rural America*. Columbia: University of Missouri Press with the Cedar Rapids Art Association, 1981.

———. *Marvin D. Cone and Grant Wood: An American Tradition*. Cedar Rapids, IA: Cedar Rapids Museum of Art, 1989.

Davenport Museum of Art. *Grant Wood: An American Master Revealed*. San Francisco: Pomegranate Artbooks, 1995.

DeLong, Lea Rosson. "Drawing and Main Street." Symposium on Grant Wood's World, University of Iowa, Iowa City, April 24, 2010.

———. *Grant Wood's Main Street: Art, Literature, and the American Midwest*. Ames: Brunnier Art Museum, University Museums, Iowa State University, 2004.

———. *When Tillage Begins, Other Arts Follow: Grant Wood and Christian Petersen Murals*. Ames: Brunnier Art Museum, University Museums, Iowa State University, 2006.

Dennis, James M. "Essay into Landscapes: The Art of Grant Wood." *Kansas Quarterly* 4:4 (1972): 1–122.

———. *Grant Wood: A Study in American Art and Culture*. New York: Viking Press, 1975; Columbia: University of Missouri, 1986.

———. *Grant Wood: Still Lifes as Decorative Abstractions*. Madison: Elvehjem Museum of Art, University of Wisconsin-Madison, 1985.

———. "Grant Wood's Works on Paper: Cartooning One Way or the Other." In Jane C. Milosch, ed., *Grant Wood's Studio: Birthplace of American Gothic*, 35–48, 132. New York: Prestel, 2005.

———. *Renegade Regionalists: The Modern Independence of Grant Wood, Thomas Hart Benton, and John Steuart Curry*. Madison: University of Wisconsin Press, 1998.

Duncan, Michael. "American Soul Underground." In Toby Kamp et al., eds., *The Old, Weird America*. Houston: Contemporary Arts Museum, 2008.

Eaton, Walter Prichard. "American Gothic." *Boston Globe*, November 14, 1930.

Evans, R. Tripp. *Grant Wood: A Life*. New York: Alfred A. Knopf, 2010.

———. "Grant Wood's Dinner for Threshers: Last Supper or Nativity Scene?" Symposium on Grant Wood's World, University of Iowa, Iowa City, April 24, 2010.

Ferargil Galleries. *Catalogue of the First New York Exhibition of Paintings and Drawings by Grant Wood with an Evaluation of the Artist by Park Rinard and Arnold Pyle*. New York: Ferargil Galleries, 1935.

Ferreter, Edward Pierce. "Grant Wood Meets Jay G. Sigmund: From Word to Image; From Image to Word." MA thesis, University of Iowa, 1985.

———. "Jay Sigmund and Grant Wood." *Books at Iowa* 42:1 (1985): 26–33.

Fone, Byrne. "This Other Eden: Arcadia and the Homosexual Imagination." *Journal of Homosexuality* 8:3/4 (1983): 13–34.

Freud, Sigmund. *The Standard Edition of the Complete Psychological Works of Sigmund Freud*. Translated by James Strachey. London: Hogarth Press and the Institute of Psycho-analysis, 1956–74.

Garwood, Darrell. *Artist in Iowa: A Life of Grant Wood*. New York: W. W. Norton, 1944.

Goldberg, Kenneth Paul. "The Paintings of Grant Wood." MA thesis, State University of New York at Binghamton, 1972.

Graham, Nan Wood with John Zug and Julie Jensen McDonald. *My Brother, Grant Wood*. Iowa City: State Historical Society of Iowa, 1993.

"Grant Wood Denies Reputation as Glamour Boy of Painters." *Los Angeles Times*, February 19, 1940.

Green, Edwin B. "A Grant Wood Sampler." *The Palimpsest* 53:1 (January 1972).

Greenacre, Phyllis. "The Childhood of the Artist." *The Psychoanalytic Study of the Child* 12 (1957): 47–72.

———. "Experiences of Awe in Childhood." *The Psychoanalytic Study of the Child* 11 (1956): 9–30.

———. *Emotional Growth: Psychoanalytic Studies of the Gifted and a Great Variety of Other Individuals*. New York: International Universities Press, 1971.

———. "The Primal Scene and the Sense of Reality." *Psychoanalytic Quarterly* 42:1 (1973): 10–41.

———. *Trauma, Growth, and Personality*. New York: W. W. Norton, 1952.

Guedon, Mary Schultz. *Regionalist Art, Thomas Hart Benton, John Steuart Curry, and Grant Wood: A Guide to the Literature*. Metuchen, NJ: Scarecrow Press, 1982.

Haskell, Barbara. *Grant Wood:* American Gothic *and Other Fables*. New York: Whitney Museum of American Art, 2018.

Hommerding, Christopher. "As Gay as Any Gypsy Caravan: Grant Wood and the Queer Pastoral at the Stone City Art Colony." *Annals of Iowa* 74:4 (Fall 2015): 378–415.

Howard, John. *Men Like That: A Southern Queer History*. Chicago: University of Chicago Press, 1999.

Hughes, Robert. "Scooting Back to Anamosa: Grant Wood at the Whitney: A Fresh Look at an American Icon." *Time*, June 27, 1983, 68–69.

Janson, H. W. "Benton and Wood: Champions of Regionalism." *The Magazine of Art* 39:5 (May 1946): 184–86, 198–200.

———. "The Case of the Naked Chicken." *College Art Journal* 15 (1955–56): 124–27.

Jerdee, Doris Guy. "The Iconography of Grant Wood's American Gothic." MA thesis, Arizona State University, 1969.

Johnson, Bruce E. *Grant Wood: The 19 Lithographs, A Catalogue Raisonné*. Fletcher, NC: Arts and Crafts Research Fund, 2016.

Juhl, Paul C. *Grant Wood: Abandoned Plans*. Iowa City, IA: Brushy Creek Publishing, 2012.

———. *Grant Wood's Clear Lake Summer*. Iowa City, IA: Brushy Creek Publishing, 2007.

King, Richard Alan. *1142: The History and Growth of the N. Oakes—Grant Wood—Dr. Pauline Moore—James P. Hayes House*. Iowa City, IA: Privately published, 2008.

Kinsey, Alfred, W. Pomeroy, and C. Martin. *Sexual Behavior in the Human Male*. Philadelphia: Saunders, 1948.

Kinsey, Joni L. "Cultivating Iowa: An Introduction to Grant Wood." In Jane C. Milosch, ed., *Grant Wood's Studio: Birthplace of* American Gothic, 11–33, 130–32. New York: Prestel, 2005.

———. *Plain Pictures: Images of the American Prairie*. Washington, DC: Smithsonian Institution Press for the University of Iowa Museum of Art, 1996.

Kirstein, Lincoln. "An Iowa Memling." *Art Front* 1:6 (1935): 6, 8.

Klein, Melanie. *Love, Guilt and Reparation and Other Works 1921–1945*. New York: Delacorte Press/Seymour Lawrence, 1975.

Koen, Irma R. "The Art of Grant Wood." *Christian Science Monitor*, March 26, 1932.

Kramer, Hilton. "The Return of the Nativist." *New Criterion* 2 (October 1983): 58–63.

Kuspit, Donald. "Grant Wood: Pathos of the Plain." *Art in America* 72:3 (March 1984): 138–43.

———. "Representing the Mother: Representing the Unrepresentable?" In Barbara Collier, ed., *The Artist's Mother: Portraits and Homages*. Huntington, NY: Heckscher Museum and National Portrait Gallery, Smithsonian Institution, 1987.

Liffring-Zug Bourret, Joan. "The Life of Nan Wood Graham, Model for American Gothic." Symposium on Grant Wood Today, University of Iowa, Iowa City, April 14, 2012.

———, comp. *This Is Grant Wood Country*. Edited by John Zug with Nan Wood Graham. Davenport, IA: Davenport Municipal Art Gallery, 1977.

Marling, Karal Ann. "Don't Knock Wood." *Artnews* 82 (September 1983): 94–99.

McDonald, Julie Jensen, with Joan Liffring-Zug Bourret. *Grant Wood and Little Sister Nan: Essays and Remembrances*. Iowa City, IA: Penfield Press, 2000.

Meyer, Richard. *Outlaw Representations: Censorship and Homosexuality in Twentieth Century American Art*. New York: Oxford University Press, 2002.

Milosch, Jane C. "American Gothic's Munich Connection: A Window into Grant Wood's Regionalism." In Christian Fuhrmeister, Hubertus Kohle, and Veerle Tielemans, eds., *American Artists in Munich: Artistic Migration and Cultural Exchange Processes*, 247–60. Berlin and Munich: Deutscher Kunstverlag, 2009.

———, ed. *Grant Wood's Studio: Birthplace of* American Gothic. New York: Prestel, 2005.

Myers, Donald. *Grant Wood's Lithographs: A Regionalist Vision Set in Stone*. St. Peter, MN: Hillstrom Museum of Art, 2015.

Nash, Anedith. "Death on the Highway: The Automobile Wreck in American Culture, 1920–40." PhD diss., University of Minnesota, 1983.

———. "Death on the Ridge Road: Grant Wood and Modernization in the Midwest." *Prospects* 8 (1983): 281–301.

Nygard, Travis. *Seeds of Agribusiness: Grant Wood and the Visual Culture of Grain Farming, 1862–1957*. Ann Arbor, MI: University Microfilms, 2009.

———. "Reinterpreting the Life and Art of Grant Wood: A Review Essay." *Annals of Iowa* 70:4 (Fall 2011): 358–67.

Raine, Kristy. "When Tillage Begins: The Stone City Art Colony and School." https://projects.mtmercy.edu/stonecity/colony.html.

Reece-Hughes, Shirley. "Theatrical Productions: Grant Wood's Visions of America." Symposium on Grant Wood Today, University of Iowa, Iowa City, April 14, 2012.

Seery, John E. "Grant Wood's Political Gothic." In Seery, ed., *America Goes to College: Political Theory for the Liberal Arts*, 117–38, 223–31. Albany: State University of New York Press, 2002.

Shirer, William L. *20th Century Journey: A Memoir of the Life and Times of William L. Shirer*. New York: Simon and Schuster, 1976.

Shortridge, James R. *The Middle West: Its Meaning in American Culture*. Lawrence: University of Kansas Press, 1989.

Taylor, Sue. "Grant Wood: A Brilliant Subterfuge." Symposium on Grant Wood's World, University of Iowa, Iowa City, April 24, 2010.

———. "Grant Wood's Family Album." *American Art* 19:2 (Summer 2005): 48–67.

———. "Grant Wood's Inner Life and the Dark Side of *American Gothic*." Conference on the Fate of Interiority in Modern and Postmodern Art, State University of New York at Stony Brook Manhattan, NY, March 5, 2005.

———. "In Springtime: Myth and Memory in Grant Wood's Last Paintings." 2016 Grant Wood Symposium, University of Iowa, October 29, 2016.

———. "Reading *American Gothic*." *Art in America* no. 1 (January 2006): 92.

———. "Unmanning Grant Wood." Review of *Grant Wood: A Life*, by R. Tripp Evans. *ArtUS* 31 (2011): 36–43.

———. "Wood's American Logic." *Art in America* no. 1 (January 2006): 86–93.

Wallach, Alan. "Grant Wood: The Insider as Outsider." Seminar on Homosexuality and Modernism, Institute for the Humanities, New York University, May 21, 1990.

Weems, Jason. *Barnstorming the Prairies: Aerial Vision and Modernity in Rural America, 1920–1940*. Minneapolis: University of Minnesota Press, 2015.

———. "Grant Wood's Regionalist Camouflage." 2016 Grant Wood Symposium, University of Iowa, October 29, 2016.

Weinberg, Jonathan. *Speaking for Vice: Homosexuality in the Art of Charles Demuth, Marsden Hartley, and the First American Avant-Garde*. New Haven, CT: Yale University Press, 1993.

Wood, Grant. "Art in the Daily Life of the Child." *Child Welfare Pamphlets* no. 73 (May 10, 1939): 3–8.

———. "Hard-Hitting Artist." Review of *An Artist in America*, by Thomas Hart Benton. *Saturday Review of Literature* 17:2 (November 6, 1937): 6.

———. Introduction to *Young Sam Clemens* by Cyril Clemens. Portland, ME: Leon Tebbetts Editions, 1942.

———. "John Steuart Curry and the Midwest." *Demcourier* 11:2 (1941): 2–4.

———. "Rural Influence in Contemporary American Art." *Rural America* 14:2 (February 1936): 41–43.

———. "The Writer and the Painter." *American Prefaces: A Journal of Critical and Imaginative Writing* 1:1 (October 1935): 3–4.

———, and Frank Luther Mott. *Revolt against the City*. Iowa City, IA: Whirling World Series Press, 1935.

———, with Park Rinard. "Return from Bohemia, A Painter's Story," 1935. Archives of American Art, Smithsonian Institution, Washington, DC.

❖ INDEX ❖

Note: Italicized page numbers refer to illustrations.

GRANT WOOD'S SECRETS is composed in Metro (1935–49) and Electra (1929–30), both created by William Addison Dwiggins (1880–1956). The design of Metro can be seen as an American response to German typographer Paul Renner's streamlined Futura (1927–30), which was among the first new sans serif typefaces to be introduced in the United States and anticipates such later humanist sans-serifs as Lucida Sans (1991) by Charles Bigelow and Kris Holmes. Dwiggins's book type Electra is a twentieth-century update of the serifed modern-style types of Giambattista Bodoni (1740–1813) and, like Metro, emphasizes legibility over pure geometry.